PEARSON EDEXCEL INTERNATIONAL A LEVEL

BUSINESS

Student Book 2

Rob Jones

Published by Pearson Education Limited, 80 Strand, London, WC2R 0RL.
www.pearsonglobalschools.com
Copies of official specifications for all Edexcel qualifications may be found on the website:
https://qualifications.pearson.com

Text © Pearson Education Limited 2019
Designed by Pearson Education Limited 2019
Typeset by Pearson CSC
Edited by Sarah Wright
Original illustrations © Pearson Education Limited 2019
Cover design by Pearson Education Limited 2019
Picture research by Integra
Cover photo/illustration © Getty Images/Dave G Kelly
Inside front cover photo: Shutterstock, Dmitry Lobanov

The rights of Rob Jones to be identified as author of this work have been asserted by him in
accordance with the Copyright, Designs and Patents Act 1988.
First published 2019
24
10 9 8 7 6

British Library Cataloguing in Publication Data
A catalogue record for this book is available from the British Library
ISBN 978 1 292239 16 3

Printed in Great Britain by Bell and Bain Ltd, Glasgow

Endorsement statement
In order to ensure that this resource offers high-quality support for the associated Pearson
qualification, it has been through a review process by the awarding body. This process confirms
that this resource fully covers the teaching and learning content of the specification or part of a
specification at which it is aimed. It also confirms that it demonstrates an appropriate balance
between the development of subject skills, knowledge and understanding, in addition to
preparation for assessment.
Endorsement does not cover any guidance on assessment activities or processes (e.g. practice
questions or advice on how to answer assessment questions), included in the resource nor does
it prescribe any particular approach to the teaching or delivery of a related course.
While the publishers have made every attempt to ensure that advice on the qualification and its
assessment is accurate, the official specification and associated assessment guidance materials are
the only authoritative source of information and should always be referred to for definitive guidance.
Pearson examiners have not contributed to any sections in this resource relevant to examination
papers for which they have responsibility.
Examiners will not use endorsed resources as a source of material for any assessment set by
Pearson.
Endorsement of a resource does not mean that the resource is required to achieve this Pearson
qualification, nor does it mean that it is the only suitable material available to support the
qualification, and any resource lists produced by the awarding body shall include this and other
appropriate resources.

Acknowledgements
The authors and publisher would like to thank the following individuals and organisations for their
kind permission to reproduce copyright material.
We'd like to thank our teacher reviewers for their contribution to this book: Clive Agent,
Arosha Chandima, Pradeep Gangadharan, Mark Hage, Colin Leith and Harrison Mwangi.

Photographs

(Key: b-bottom; c-centre; l-left; r-right; t-top)

Image Credit(s):
2 Shutterstock: Anucha sirivisansuwan/Shutterstock; **4 Shutterstock**: (cl) Motive56/
Shutterstock; **123RF**: (tr) Joshua Resnick/123RF; **Shutterstock**: (cr) Faraways/Shutterstock;
6 Shutterstock: Metamorworks/Shutterstock; **8 123RF**: Stylephotographs/123RF;
11 Shutterstock: Jeffy11390/Shutterstock; **12 Shutterstock**: Heromen30/Shutterstock;
17 Shutterstock: Brizmaker/Shutterstock; **18 Shutterstock**: Tono Balaguer/Shutterstock;
21 Shutterstock: Mhgstan/Shutterstock; **23 International Centre for Integrated Mountain
Development**: ICIMOD. Mr. Tsering Wangdi Sherpa of Darachu, Bhutan with his beehive and
honey; **33 Shutterstock**: AleksSafronov/Shutterstock; **40 Shutterstock**: Irina Strelnikova/
Shutterstock; **41 Shutterstock**: Red Ivory/Shutterstock; **43 123RF**: Scanrail/123RF;
44 123RF: Shariff Che'Lah/123RF; **46 Shutterstock**: Sanjagrujic/Shutterstock;
50 Shutterstock: TTstudio/Shutterstock; **55 123RF**: Fabio formaggio/123RF; **58 123RF**: Dmitry
Kalinovsky/123RF; **60 Alamy**: Hero Images Inc./Alamy Stock Photo; **61 Shutterstock**: PT-lens/

Shutterstock; **62 123RF**: Adrin Shamsudin/123RF; **63 123RF**: Chayapon Bootboonneam/123RF;
70 Shutterstock: chert28/Shutterstock; **71 Shutterstock**: ImagineStock/Shutterstock;
79 Shutterstock: Ilonde van Hoolwerff/Shutterstock; **80 123RF**: Jose
Marie Hernandez/123RF; **85 Shutterstock**: David Hanlon/Shutterstock; **86 Shutterstock**:
Cozine/Shutterstock; **88 Shutterstock**: Evan Lorne/Shutterstock; **90 123RF**:Hongqi
Zhang/123RF; **98 123RF**: Panama7/123RF; **99 Shutterstock**: Somkiat.H/Shutterstock; **101
Shutterstock**: All About Space/Shutterstock; **103 Shutterstock**: Selin Aydogan/Shutterstock;
104 Shutterstock: Daniel Balakov/Shutterstock; **105 Alamy**: Kristoffer Tripplaar/Alamy Stock
Photo; **109 123RF**: Bacho12345/123RF; **112 Shutterstock**: GaudiLab/Shutterstock; **113
Shutterstock**: Weedezign/Shutterstock; **116 Shutterstock**: Asharkyu/Shutterstock; **121
Shutterstock**: Nasirkhan/Shutterstock; **123 Shutterstock**: Africa Studio/Shutterstock; **129
Shutterstock**: Krzysztof Bargiel/Shutterstock; **131 Shutterstock**: CHEN HSI FU/Shutterstock;
140 Shutterstock: Natali Glado/Shutterstock; **141 Shutterstock**: Gumpanat/Shutterstock;
144 123RF: Johnaapw/123RF; **145 Shutterstock**: Christian Lagerek/Shutterstock; **149 123RF**:
Eonaya/123RF; **151 Pearson Education**: Tsz-shan Kwok/Pearson Education Asia Ltd; **154
123RF**: Albertus Engbers/123RF; **158 123RF**: Chokniti Khongchum/123RF; **160 Shutterstock**:
Avigator Thailand/Shutterstock;
163 123RF: Tobias Arhelger/123RF; **165 123RF**: Satina/123RF; **167 Shutterstock**: VanderWolf
Images/Shutterstock; **169 Shutterstock**: Aisvector/Shutterstock; **170 123RF**:
Stanisic Vladimir/123RF; **174 Shutterstock**: Structuresxx/Shutterstock; **177 Shutterstock**:
WHYFRAME/Shutterstock; **178 Shutterstock**: Specta/Shutterstock; **187 123RF**: Georgii
Dolgykh/123RF; **194 Shutterstock**: (t) Pics721/Shutterstock; **194 Shutterstock**: (b) Yannick
Vidal/Shutterstock; **197 Shutterstock**: Kathmanduphotog/Shutterstock; **199 Shutterstock**:
Rphstock/Shutterstock; **205 123RF**: Ekays/123RF; **206 Shutterstock**: Roibu/Shutterstock; **208
123RF**: Nuttawut Uttamaharad/123RF; **212 Shutterstock**: Stephane Bidouze/Shutterstock;
216 Shutterstock: Chonnanit/Shutterstock; **221 Shutterstock**: Katjen/Shutterstock; **224
Shutterstock**: Richard Thornton/Shutterstock; **236 Alamy**: Ren Long/Xinhua/Alamy Live News/
Alamy Stock Photo; **239 Nestlé: Courtesy of Nestlé Vietnam; 250 Shutterstock**: Petr Akulin/
Shutterstock; **253 Shutterstock**: Fascinadora/Shutterstock; **255 Shutterstock**: IM_photo/
Shutterstock; **260 123RF**: Dmitry Kalinovsky/123RF; **264 Shutterstock**: Sreejith tj/Shutterstock;
266 Shutterstock: Katjen/Shutterstock; **267 Alamy**: Bob Pardue-SC/Alamy Stock Photo; **268
Shutterstock**: Heromen30/Shutterstock; **272 Shutterstock**: Tong_stocker/Shutterstock; **274
Shutterstock**: Africa Studio/Shutterstock; **275 Shutterstock**: Dasha Petrenko/Shutterstock;
277 Shutterstock: HildaWeges Photography/Shutterstock; **278 Pearson Education**: Jules
Selmes/Pearson Education; **281 Shutterstock**: Elena Elisseeva/Shutterstock; **282 Shutterstock**:
Pressmaster/Shutterstock; **283 123RF**: Panpote Soontararak/123RF; **288 Shutterstock**:
Rawpixel.com/Shutterstock; **289 Alamy**: James Thew/Alamy Stock Photo; **290 123RF**: Deyan
Georgiev/123RF; **294 123RF**: Max776/123RF; **297 Shutterstock**: Natalia D./Shutterstock; **299
123RF**: Chris Elwell/123RF; **301 Shutterstock**: Pedrosala/Shutterstock; **303 Shutterstock**:
Haak78/Shutterstock; **305 123RF**: Stepan Popov/123RF; **306 Shutterstock**: Ingus Kruklitis/
Shutterstock; **312 Shutterstock**: Maxisport/Shutterstock;
315 Americans for Tax Fairness: Courtesy of Americans for Tax Fairness

CONTENTS

UNIT 3: BUSINESS DECISIONS AND STRATEGY

UNIT 4: GLOBAL BUSINESS

ABOUT THIS BOOK

This book is written for students following the Pearson Edexcel International Advanced Level (IAL) Business specification. It covers the second year of the International A level qualification.

The book has been carefully structured to match the order of topics in the specification although teaching and learning can take place in any order, both in the classroom and in any independent learning. This book is organised into two units (Unit 3: Business decisions and strategy and Unit 4: Global business), each with several topic areas.

Each topic area is divided into chapters to break the content down into manageable chunks. Each chapter begins by listing the key learning objectives and includes a getting started activity to introduce the concepts. There is a mix of learning points and activities throughout including global case studies to show a range of businesses within real-life contexts. Checkpoint questions at the end of each chapter help assess understanding of the key learning objectives.

The content for Unit 3 is applicable for Paper 3 (Business decisions and strategy) and the content for Unit 4 is applicable for Paper 4 (Global business). Knowing how to apply learning to both of these papers will be critical for exam success. There are exam-style questions at the end of each chapter to provide opportunity for exam practice. Answers are provided in the online teaching resource pack.

Topic openers
Introduce each of the key topics in the specification.

Learning objectives
Each chapter starts with a list of key assessment objectives.

Specification reference
The specification reference is given at the start of each chapter and in the running header.

SPECIFICATION 3.3.1 | 1 CORPORATE OBJECTIVES | 3

BUSINESS DECISIONS AND STRATEGY

This section looks at the goals and aims of corporations and the way that they might present strategy in mission statements. It explores the different theories of corporate strategy, such as Ansoff's Matrix and Porter's Strategic Matrix. It identifies the effects of strategic and tactical (i.e. carefully planned) decisions on the resources of the business. The section also considers the way a corporation might assess the strengths, weaknesses, opportunities and threats that it faces. Finally, it will investigate the impact of external influences on businesses such as political, economic, social, technological, legal and environmental factors.

1 CORPORATE OBJECTIVES

UNIT 3
3.3.1

LEARNING OBJECTIVES

By the end of this chapter you should be able to understand:
- the development of corporate objectives from mission statement/ corporate aims
- the critical appraisal of mission statements.

GETTING STARTED

An objective is something that a business aims to achieve. The nature and purpose of business objectives is discussed in Student Book 1, Chapter 21. This chapter explores the role of corporate aims and corporate objectives influencing the strategy that a business follows.

Look at the following two statements.
- **R&F Fitness Centre corporate aim:** To encourage targeted activity to improve levels of fitness.
- **A&L Entertainment Group corporate objective (one of several):** To establish two new attractions every new season.

The first is an aim and the second an objective. What is the difference between an aim and an objective? How do the two work together?

BUSINESS AIMS

All businesses have **aims**. These are the things the business wants to achieve in the long term – its purpose or reason for being. The aims of a business are less specific than its objectives and can be expressed as a vision. Business aims are discussed in detail in Student Book 1, Chapter 21. A business will often communicate its aim through a **mission statement**.

MISSION STATEMENTS

A mission statement states the business's main purpose. It may also reflect its goals and values. It describes in general terms the company's core activities. It may also reference information such as:
- the markets in which it operates
- what its key commercial objectives are
- in what way it values its stakeholders
- what its ethics involve (i.e. what it believes to be good or correct).

The main elements of a mission statement are as follows.
- **Purpose** – a mission statement should outline why the business exists. It should communicate what the business does, for whom and why.
- **Values** – businesses are likely to state the corporate values that they emotionally invest in. These might include qualities such as integrity, sustainability, innovation and quality. The values held by a corporation are likely to influence its culture.
- **Standards and behaviour** – some mission statements may communicate a business's commitment to high standards. For example, always conducting ethical behaviour (i.e. behaviour that is good or correct).
- **Strategy** – some mission statements may outline how the business will try to achieve its main objective. For example, a car manufacturer may say it is committed to the development of driverless cars to help achieve its aim of making transport as easy and convenient as possible.

A good mission statement should help guide the decision-making of the firm. Running a business can be very complicated. It is very easy to get lost in the small details of business decision-making. A good mission statement makes it clear which direction a business should take by reminding the owners and directors why the business exists. Many people may argue that the only purpose of a business is to generate a profit for its owners. However, most employees would like to believe that they go to work to achieve something more than this. A mission statement makes this point.

There are two reasons why a business may create and share a mission statement. The first is to make a commitment to its customers. A mission statement expresses a promise to customers of what they can expect the business to aim for. Secondly, a mission statement can be used to bring a company's workforce (i.e. all the people who work for a company) together with a shared purpose. Many successful businesses have a mission statement that their employees believe in. This is why a mission statement is important in forming a strong corporate culture (see Chapter 14).

Some mission statements are brief. Others are long and detailed. Some examples of mission statements are given below.
- R&F Fitness Centre: 'We improve levels of fitness by providing individual plans for people of all ages and helping them to achieve their aims.'
- R&B Furniture Maker: 'To help create practical and beautiful homes for our customers.'
- DHC Coffee Shop: 'To offer a comfortable environment and an excellent range of coffee to refresh our customers in body, mind and spirit.'

Getting started
An activity to introduce the key concepts in each chapter. Questions are designed to stimulate discussion and use of prior knowledge. These can be tackled as individuals, pairs, groups or the whole class.

Key subject terms are colour coded within the main text.

Activity
Each chapter includes activities to embed understanding through case studies and questions.

Skills
Relevant exam questions have been assigned key skills, allowing for a strong focus on particular academic qualities. These transferable skills are highly valued in further study and the workplace.

Exam hint
Tips give practical advice and guidance for exam preparation.

Worked Example
Practical worked examples help you apply new methods and formulae.

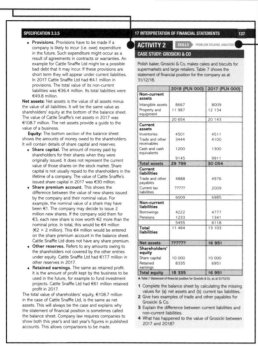

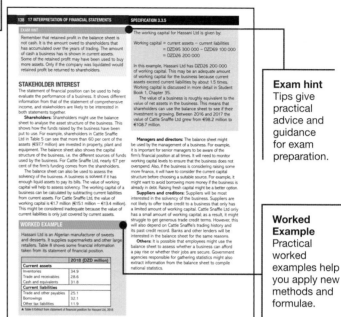

Checkpoint
Questions to check understanding of the key learning points in each chapter. These are NOT exam-style questions.

Exam practice
Exam-style questions are found at the end of each chapter. They are tailored to the Pearson Edexcel specification to allow for practice and development of exam writing technique. They also allow for practice responding to the command words used in the exams.

Thinking bigger
These sections provide opportunity to explore an aspect of business in more detail to deepen understanding.

Subject vocabulary
An alphabetical list of all the subject terms in each chapter with clear definitions for EAL learners. Please note: A collated glossary is available on the ActiveBook.

Links
Suggest ways that topics link to others to build on knowledge and develop synoptic skills.

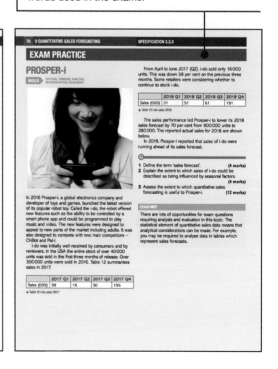

ASSESSMENT OVERVIEW

The following tables give an overview of the assessment for this course. You should study this information closely to help ensure that you are fully prepared for this course and know exactly what to expect in each part of the assessment.

PAPER 3	PERCENTAGE OF IA2	PERCENTAGE OF IAL	MARK	TIME	AVAILABILITY	STRUCTURE
BUSINESS DECISIONS AND STRATEGY Written exam paper Paper code WBS13/01 Externally set and marked by Pearson Edexcel Single tier of entry Calculators can be used	50%	25%	80	2 hours	January, June and October First assessment: January 2020	There will be three sections, A, B and C. Students must answer all questions. Section A: short- and extended-response questions based on sources (40 marks) Section B: one 20-mark essay question, based on one or more sources (20 marks) Section C: one 20-mark essay question, based on one or more sources (20 marks)

PAPER 4	PERCENTAGE	PERCENTAGE OF IAL	MARK	TIME	AVAILABILITY	STRUCTURE
GLOBAL BUSINESS Written exam paper Paper code WBS14/01 Externally set and marked by Pearson Edexcel Single tier of entry	50%	25%	80	2 hours	January, June and October First assessment: June 2020	There will be three sections, A, B and C. Students must answer all questions. Section A: short- and extended-response questions based on sources (40 marks) Section B: one 20-mark essay question, based on one or more sources (20 marks) Section C: one 20-mark essay question, based on one or more sources (20 marks)

ASSESSMENT OBJECTIVES AND WEIGHTINGS

ASSESSMENT OBJECTIVE	DESCRIPTION	% IN IAS	% IN IA2	% IN IAL
A01	Demonstrate knowledge and understanding of terms, concepts, theories, methods and models	27.5	20	23.8
A02	Apply knowledge and understanding to various business contexts to show how individuals and organisations are affected by and respond to issues	25	22.5	23.8
A03	Analyse business issues, showing an understanding of the causes, costs and consequences for individuals and organisations	27.5	30	28.8
A04	Evaluate evidence to make informed judgements and propose evidence-based solutions to business issues	20	27.5	23.8

Note: Totals have been rounded either up or down.

RELATIONSHIP OF ASSESSMENT OBJECTIVES TO UNITS

UNIT NUMBER	ASSESSMENT OBJECTIVE			
	A01	A02	A03	A04
Unit 1	6.9%	6.3%	6.9%	5%
Unit 2	6.9%	6.3%	6.9%	5%
Unit 3	5%	5.6%	7.5%	6.9%
Unit 4	5%	5.6%	7.5%	6.9%
Total for International Advanced Level	23.8%	23.8%	28.8%	23.8%

Note: Totals have been rounded either up or down.

RELATIONSHIP OF ASSESSMENT OBJECTIVES TO COMMAND WORDS

COMMAND WORD	NUMBER OF MARKS	MARK SCHEME	ASSESSMENT OBJECTIVES
Calculate	4	Points based	AO1, AO2, AO3
Construct	4	Points based	AO1, AO2, AO3
Explain	4	Points based	AO1, AO2, AO3
Analyse	6	Points based	AO1, AO2, AO3
Discuss	8	Levels based	AO1, AO2, AO3, AO4
Assess	12	Levels based	AO1, AO2, AO3, AO4
Evaluate	20	Levels based	AO1, AO2, AO3, AO4

BUSINESS DECISIONS AND STRATEGY

This section looks at the goals and aims of corporations and the way that they might present strategy in mission statements. It explores the different theories of corporate strategy, such as Ansoff's Matrix and Porter's Strategic Matrix. It identifies the effects of strategic and tactical (i.e. carefully planned) decisions on the resources of the business. The section also considers the way a corporation might assess the strengths, weaknesses, opportunities and threats that it faces. Finally, it will investigate the impact of external influences on businesses such as political, economic, social, technological, legal and environmental factors.

1 CORPORATE OBJECTIVES

LEARNING OBJECTIVES

By the end of this chapter you should be able to understand:
- the development of corporate objectives from mission statement/ corporate aims
- the critical appraisal of mission statements.

GETTING STARTED

An objective is something that a business aims to achieve. The nature and purpose of business objectives is discussed in Student Book 1, Chapter 21. This chapter explores the role of corporate aims and corporate objectives influencing the strategy that a business follows.

Look at the following two statements.
- **R&F Fitness Centre corporate aim:** To encourage targeted activity to improve levels of fitness.
- **A&L Entertainment Group corporate objective (one of several):** To establish two new attractions every new season.

The first is an aim and the second an objective. What is the difference between an aim and an objective? How do the two work together?

BUSINESS AIMS

All businesses have aims. These are the things the business wants to achieve in the long term – its purpose or reason for being. The aims of a business are less specific than its objectives and can be expressed as a vision. Business aims are discussed in detail in Student Book 1, Chapter 21. A business will often communicate its aim through a mission statement.

MISSION STATEMENTS

A mission statement states the business's main purpose. It may also reflect its goals and values. It describes in general terms the company's core activities. It may also reference information such as:
- the markets in which it operates
- what its key commercial objectives are
- in what way it values its stakeholders
- what its ethics involve (i.e. what it believes to be good or correct).

The main elements of a mission statement are as follows.
- **Purpose** – a mission statement should outline why the business exists. It should communicate what the business does, for whom and why.

- **Values** – businesses are likely to state the corporate values that they emotionally invest in. These might include qualities such as integrity, sustainability, innovation and quality. The values held by a corporation are likely to influence its culture.
- **Standards and behaviour** – some mission statements may communicate a business's commitment to high standards. For example, always conducting ethical behaviour (i.e. behaviour that is good or correct).
- **Strategy** – some mission statements may outline how the business will try to achieve its main objective. For example, a car manufacturer may say it is committed to the development of driverless cars to help achieve its aim of making transport as easy and convenient as possible.

A good mission statement should help guide the decision making of the firm. Running a business can be very complicated. It is very easy to get lost in the small details of business decision making. A good mission statement makes it clear which direction a business should take by reminding the owners and directors why the business exists. Many people may argue that the only purpose of a business is to generate a profit for its owners. However, most employees would like to believe that they go to work to achieve something more than this. A mission statement makes this point.

There are two reasons why a business may create and share a mission statement. The first is to make a commitment to its customers. A mission statement expresses a promise to customers of what they can expect the business to aim for. Secondly, a mission statement can be used to bring a company's workforce (i.e. all the people who work for a company) together with a shared purpose. Many successful businesses have a mission statement that their employees believe in. This is why a mission statement is important in forming a strong corporate culture (see Chapter 14).

Some mission statements are brief. Others are long and detailed. Some examples of mission statements are given below.
- R&F Fitness Centre: 'We improve levels of fitness by providing individual plans for people of all ages and helping them to achieve their aims.'
- R&B Furniture Maker: 'To help create practical and beautiful homes for our customers.'
- DHC Coffee Shop: 'To offer a comfortable environment and an excellent range of coffee to refresh our customers in body, mind and spirit.'

ACTIVITY 1 · SKILLS · CRITICAL THINKING, CREATIVITY

WRITING A MISSION STATEMENT

Choose one of the industries listed below and plan a mission statement for a business in that sector. Use some of the examples for inspiration but try to link your mission statement to the context of the industry. Present your mission statement and explain your thinking. How does it express the vision and aims of the business you have chosen?

1 Airline industry
2 Soft drinks industry
3 Container shipping industry

DEVELOPMENT OF CORPORATE OBJECTIVES

Corporate objectives are objectives set by senior managers and directors for a company. They should be specific to the company, its particular history and vision of the future, and fit well with its mission statement. They should focus mainly on the desired performance and results of the business over time. They may include goals such as market share, profit levels, creation of new products or processes, resource usage and scale economies, management of people and ethical behaviours.

To help a business achieve its aims, corporate objectives must be: Specific, Measurable, Agreed, Realistic and Time specific. These criteria are known as SMART criteria. An example of a SMART objective for a corporation might be to increase global market share from 10 to 13 per cent in the next two years.

- **Specific** means that the objective clearly states what the business is aiming to achieve. It should refer to a particular aspect or function of the business.
- **Measurable** involves evidence to demonstrate whether or not the objectives have actually been

achieved. For this reason, most corporate objectives will have a financial or quantifiable element (i.e. an element that can be expressed by a number). This is because it makes it easier to measure the success of that objective.

- **Agreed** implies that everyone responsible for achieving the objective is happy with the objective and understands what it means for them. Without an objective being agreed by all those involved, there will be no motivation or commitment to achieve it.
- **Realistic** ensures that the objective can be met given the resources available and the current market conditions. If an objective is unrealistic, people may begin to ignore it. This means that the objective will not be achieved. This is likely to have a negative impact on the business.
- **Time specific** gives the stated time frame required to achieve the objectives. All objectives must have a deadline to ensure urgency and a point at which the objective can be assessed.

DEPARTMENTAL AND FUNCTIONAL OBJECTIVES

We now know that general objectives come from the mission statement of a business. Once we have established the general objectives, we can then develop more specific corporate objectives that explain exactly what the business does. These help to inform even more **departmental and functional objectives**. These set the daily goals that may include human resources, finance, operations, logistics and marketing. These all refer back up the **hierarchy** to the corporate objectives and mission statement, so that the goals and activities of the business are consistent. In this way, functional objectives will directly support the corporate objectives. Business functions should be aligned with one another because they are guided by these corporate objectives. For example, if the operations department sets a departmental objective to reduce waste by 25 per cent within the next year, it is likely that this will have to feed into the objectives set by the human resources (HR) department. HR will need to ensure all production workers complete a specific training programme focusing on quality management (see Student Book 1, Chapter 40).

THE OBJECTIVES HIERARCHY

An objective will ultimately flow from the firm's overall aim and be effective if it contributes to achieving the level above.

▲ Figure 1 Objectives hierarchy

THE DIFFERENCE BETWEEN SMALL AND LARGE FIRMS

Chapter 1 in Student Book 1 explores the possible objectives that may motivate a business. Usually, a business aims to make a profit. However, it may have other goals as well, such as:

- maximising sales, sales revenue or market share
- achieving cost efficiencies

- looking after its employees
- ensuring that its customers are satisfied.

A business may even aim to achieve a social purpose. An objective is a desired outcome that allows a business to achieve its stated aims. While some objectives are general, others can be very specific. This includes the quantification (i.e. expressing something as a number) or precise statement of a goal for a department or functional area.

Small businesses may have a wide variety of objectives, such as the following examples:

- to ensure that the company **breaks even** at the end of the tax year (see Student Book 1, Chapter 31)
- to improve the firm's liquidity in the next six months (see Student Book 1, Chapter 35)
- to increase sales by 10 per cent over the next three years (see Student Book 1, Chapter 30)
- to increase pre-tax profits by 5 per cent over the next 12 months (see Student Book 1, Chapter 34)
- to hire five new staff with skills in sales and marketing and build a strong marketing department over the next year
- to reduce energy consumption by 2 per cent and cut the use of non-recyclable packaging over the next three years.

By contrast, the objectives of large firms and multinationals tend to be mostly financial. This is because they have many stakeholders to satisfy (mainly the **shareholders**). Financial objectives are more objective and quantifiable. Therefore, they are easier to communicate to a wide variety of interested parties. For example, a supermarket chain such as Carrefour® might state an objective that covers its entire operation: 'To increase market share by 5 per cent over the next two years.'

ACTIVITY 2   SKILLS   CRITICAL THINKING

CASE STUDY: FORD

Ford® is a USA-based multinational automobile manufacturer. It was founded by Henry Ford in 1903 and is now one of the biggest car makers in the world. In 2016 it employed over 200 000 people across the globe and generated a revenue of $US141.5 billion.

Ford's mission statement emphasises the need for its employees to work together efficiently to achieve automotive and mobility leadership for customers.

Ford is committed to the development of electric vehicles (EVs) and automated vehicles like many automobile companies around the world. In the 2016 annual report and accounts the president and CEO of Ford, Mark Field, outlined some corporate objectives relating to this development. Two of these are summarised below.

- Over the next five years, we'll create 13 electrified vehicles. These will include a fully electric SUV (Sport Utility Vehicle) that will deliver a range of around 300 miles, and hybrids of the F-150 and Mustang.
- We intend to make an SAE level 4 fully autonomous vehicle (i.e. no steering wheel, brake or gas pedal) by 2021.

1 How could the functional objectives of Ford's marketing department support the 2016 corporate objectives stated above?
2 How might the objectives of large firms, such as Ford, and those of small firms differ?

CRITICAL APPRAISAL OF MISSION STATEMENTS AND CORPORATE AIMS

Some argue that mission statements are a little unrealistic and too optimistic. As a result, this may have a negative impact on employees. For example, employees may become demotivated because they know that the mission cannot be achieved. Also, unrealistic mission statements are not useful to anybody. Therefore, they are a waste of management time. They may also be vague and appear insincere, which might cause stakeholders to see the statement as just a marketing tool or a slogan.

This means mission statements must be constantly assessed to ensure they have continued relevance for the business. Sometimes, they are not appropriate.

For example, a company with a mission statement that includes respect and honesty would not be supported if there were reports of fraud in a business.

Many organisations may have a mission statement that is appealing to its customers. However, if it is not believed and followed by employees, then customers may soon lose faith in the business. On any corporate website, you will find objectives relating to corporate social responsibility (CSR), ethical behaviours and sustainable business growth. However, businesses may need to consider the balance of the appeal of some of these objectives to their customers. This is especially true if the organisation is not achieving a profit for **shareholders**.

A critical reassessment (i.e. assessing what is good and bad about something) should involve an appraisal (i.e. a judgement of the value) of the following.

- What is the purpose of the mission statement?
- What audience is it intended for?
- How does the business strategy fit in with its stated mission?
- Are the aims and objectives realistic and achievable?

ACTIVITY 3　SKILLS　CRITICAL THINKING
APPRAISING MISSION STATEMENTS

- **RWDC Technology Company.** 'RWDC innovates and creates cutting-edge mobile technology and software. It is a leader in games and music technology and its focus is on increasing shared experiences and customer fun.'
- **PM Camping, active guides company.** 'PM Camping unites a community of campers, suppliers and advertisers online, in print and on-site, sharing experiences in a spirit of trust and co-operation.'
- **Thomas Therapeutics and Pharmacy.** 'To research, develop, monitor and deliver complementary therapy that eases patients' symptoms and helps to overcome cancer.'

1 What is the purpose of each statement?
2 Who are the intended audiences?

EXAM HINT

When analysing a case study, always try to identify the business's objectives. If a business achieves its objectives, then it is a successful business. Remember that not all objectives are as important as one another. Therefore, by prioritising an objective with a clear justification (i.e. a good reason), you can provide the basis for a recommendation when answering a question. For example, if you can justify that the objective to 'develop leaders at all levels' is the most important, then this helps you justify a decision to invest in a new employee training programme.

Evaluation is about picking out the key issues facing a business. Therefore, if you can argue that a certain course of action will support a business in achieving its objectives, then you have a strong point of evaluation.

THINKING BIGGER

Most large businesses identify various corporate objectives that cover a range of issues and areas of the business. These range from objectives focusing on profitability to corporate social responsibility. For example, see the list of corporate objectives below for LPW car rental company.

- Customer loyalty: We conduct business in an honourable and transparent way that develops customer loyalty and respect.
- Growth: We target new opportunities and ideas to encourage and extend high performance.
- Profit: We deliver high returns for our shareholders through achieving our objectives.
- Market leadership: We provide excellent service and trusted products, continually innovating to lead provision for changing customer needs.
- Commitment to employees: We are committed to open and supportive teamwork, providing honest feedback and rewarding employee achievement.
- Leadership capability: We encourage leadership qualities at all levels, developing career opportunities for those who achieve business results. We enhance individual potential to lead to growth and profitability.
- Sustainability: We research, adopt and promote best working practices that help protect the environment. We contribute to local and global environmental sustainability as part of our charitable giving.

Most large businesses state their corporate objectives on their websites. How SMART are the objectives above? Why might the objectives shown on a company website be more general than those discussed around the boardroom table?

It is common for a business to have a number of objectives that cover a lot of areas. As a result, these objectives may sometimes conflict with each other. So, the achievement of one objective can prevent a business achieving another. For example, providing rewards for staff performance could reduce financial profit. This may be the same for environmental objectives. Although it is attractive to promote a company as an ethical business, the development of technologies and strategies to ensure environmental compliance could lead to the company not achieving its financial objectives.

CHECKPOINT

1 Suggest two corporate objectives that a confectionery manufacturer might set.

2 What is the difference between a functional objective and a corporate objective?

3 Why should objectives be SMART?

4 Why might corporate objectives mainly be expressed as financial objectives?

5 What is the purpose of a mission statement?

6 State three areas of business activity that corporate objectives might refer to.

SUBJECT VOCABULARY

break-even when a business generates just enough revenue to cover its total costs
corporate aim the specific goal a corporation hopes to achieve. For example, to become market leader
corporate objectives the objectives of a medium to large-sized business as a whole
departmental and functional objectives the objectives of a department within a business
hierarchy the order or levels of responsibility in an organisation, from the lowest to the highest
mission statement a brief statement written by the business, describing its purpose and objectives, designed to cover its present operations
objective (or goal) a target of, or outcome for, a business that allows it to achieve its aims
shareholder somebody who owns shares (i.e. one of the parts a company is divided into) in a company or business
SMART acronym for the attributes of a good objective: Specific, Measurable, Agreed, Realistic and Time specific
stakeholder somebody who has invested money in a business or has an important connection with it. They are therefore affected by the success or failure of the business
vision a view of what the corporation wants to be like in the future

EXAM PRACTICE

LEGO® CORPORATE OBJECTIVES

SKILLS ▸ ANALYSIS, INTERPRETATION, REASONING

LEGO® is the world's largest toy manufacturer, making a toy that is highly popular with children. LEGO's mission is 'to inspire and develop the builders of tomorrow'. In Danish, the word 'LEGO' is an abbreviation meaning 'play well'. This unique value is at the centre of what the company does to change the way people understand learning. It focuses on the huge role play has in helping children to learn essential (i.e. extremely important and necessary) skills for life in the twenty-first century.

In 2013, LEGO assessed the needs and attitudes of its stakeholders through an online survey of more than 1500 participants. They interviewed almost 1500 additional participants from their most significant stakeholder groups and industry associates. LEGO found that the following three issues were the most important:

- the safety and quality of their products
- supporting children's right to develop
- communication with children.

In 2014, a letter to the company employees from the Chief Executive Officer, Jørgen Vig Knudstorp, said that LEGO should continue to work very hard to be the best. He said that 2014 was a good year but 'there was also room for improvement'. As part of the LEGO Group Responsibility Report 2014, the company analysed its performance against a set of corporate objectives that were defined in 2009. These were:

- zero product recalls – always
- to be ranked in the Top 10 companies for employee safety by 2015
- to support learning for 101 million children by 2015
- to use 100 per cent renewable energy by 2020
- to adopt a zero-waste mindset.

The LEGO Group believes in transparency. It always tries to provide a very honest assessment of its performance against specific targets. The 2014 report highlighted a number of targets related to its corporate objectives.

LEGO now plans to expand overseas with the opening of offices in Malaysia and China. LEGO still has a relatively small market share of the toy market in Asia compared to Europe and North America. However, as countries such as Malaysia and China become wealthier, so will consumers' willingness and ability to purchase LEGO products.

Objective	Target	Actual
1	Zero product recalls	0
2	Score of +10 for employee satisfaction and motivation	+14
3	101 million children educated	95.4 million
4	+10 per cent improvement in energy efficiency by 2016	+9%
5	90 per cent of waste recycled	91%

▲ Table 1 LEGO Group targets linked to corporate objectives

Q

1 Define the term 'corporate objective'.   **(2 marks)**
2 Explain one reason LEGO might have for setting an objective to achieve 100 per cent renewable energy by 2020.   **(4 marks)**
3 Explain one possible reason why LEGO might have a mission statement.   **(4 marks)**
4 Assess which of the LEGO Group's corporate objectives is the most important for the long-term success of the business.   **(12 marks)**

2 THEORIES OF CORPORATE STRATEGY

LEARNING OBJECTIVES

By the end of this chapter you should be able to understand:

■ the development of corporate strategy – Ansoff's Matrix and Porter's Strategic Matrix
■ the aim of portfolio analysis
■ the effects of strategic and tactical decisions on human, physical and financial resources.

GETTING STARTED

Big Bazaar is controlled by Future Group®. It is a large and growing retail store with 300 branches located in 100 Indian cities. It operates hypermarkets, discount department stores and grocery outlets. Big Bazaar has a wide product range including home furnishings, utensils, sports goods, electronics, toys, footwear, men's and women's clothing, luggage, fruits, vegetables and stationery products.

Big Bazaar employs a low-cost leadership strategy. This means that the retailer sells branded products 10–15 per cent cheaper than its rivals. Big Bazaar is a very large retailer and is able to exploit economies of scale. This helps to lower costs significantly. However, the company is very active in finding new and cheaper suppliers. It is constantly trying to find ways of lowering its operating costs.

The company is also pursuing a growth strategy. In 2017, Big Bazaar announced that it planned to open 100 additional stores over the next 12 months. Manish Agarwal, Business Head (East Zone) of Big Bazaar, said that one of the new stores would open in the P&M hi-tech city centre mall in Bistupur. He said the new store, spread over 32 989 square feet, would be the ideal shopping destination for customers. The new store would have a fresh design and offer a wide range of products.

What is Big Bazaar's competitive advantage? What do you think is meant by a strategy? Describe the strategies used by Big Bazaar. Why might Big Bazaar have to introduce new strategies in the future?

BUSINESS STRATEGY

Businesses have aims that they hope to achieve through their stated objectives. However, this requires a lot of planning. This planning to achieve corporate objectives is known as strategy. The first part of the process involves using analytical tools to understand the current position of the business in the market. The next part of the process involves evaluating where the business wants to be.

A firm might begin this analytical process with a SWOT analysis (see Chapter 3), followed by a Five Forces Analysis (see Chapter 4). The corporate strategy derived from this process is the long-term plan to achieve the aims of the entire business. A successful strategy will give the firm an advantage in the competitive market place. It will help to fulfil stakeholder expectations.

DEVELOPMENT OF CORPORATE STRATEGY

Developing an effective corporate strategy requires a significant amount of time and research. The process of strategic planning involves key members of management looking critically at what the business has done before (i.e. assessing what it has done well and what it has done badly). They look at what the business may need to do in the future in order to achieve its corporate objectives. This is a very big task but there are many tools to help managers during the planning process. Examples include Ansoff's Matrix, Porter's Strategic Matrix and portfolio analysis.

ANSOFF'S MATRIX

Igor Ansoff was an applied mathematician and business strategist. He developed Ansoff's Matrix as a strategic tool to help a business achieve growth. Figure 1 illustrates both existing and new products within existing and new markets. Ansoff's Matrix is a useful decision-making tool because it allows the owners of a business to consider a number of factors that will determine its corporate strategy:

● the level of investment in existing and new products
● the exploitation of different markets
● the growth strategy for the business
● the level of risk the business is willing to accept.

Ansoff's Matrix reveals four possible strategies that a business might adopt. The key issue is that risk becomes greater if a business moves away from its most important existing products and consumers. In other words, the further a business gets from the top left-hand corner of the matrix, the greater the risk.

PRODUCT

		Existing	New
MARKET	**Existing**	Market penetration	Product development
	New	Market development	Diversification

▲ Figure 1 Ansoff's Matrix

Market penetration: As suggested by Ansoff's Matrix, the purpose of **market penetration** is to achieve growth in existing markets with existing products. There are several ways a business can achieve this:

- increase the brand loyalty of customers so that they use substitute brands less frequently. An example might be adopting a loyalty scheme, such as the loyalty card introduced by small restaurant chain Casa Brasil. This card offers points that provides holders with discounts at the restaurants.
- encourage consumers to use the product more regularly. An example might be encouraging people to eat breakfast cereal as a night-time snack.
- encourage consumers to use more of the product. An example might be a crisp manufacturer producing maxi-sized crisp packets rather than standard-sized crisp packets.

A business might adopt a market penetration strategy if it has a successful product and believes that it can make more revenue from it. This is the strategy with the lowest risk because it involves the lowest level of investment. In addition, the business will have a good understanding of the product and how the market might respond.

Product development: Product development is concerned with marketing new or modified (i.e. improved by small changes) products in existing markets. This might be an appropriate strategy to adopt where the product life cycle is traditionally short, or where trends or technology change quickly. This strategy is associated with product innovation and continuous development. The confectionery market is famous for product development. Some businesses have gained a reputation for continuous product development and used this strategy to stay ahead of the competition. Apple® has achieved this through the iPhone®, iPad® and Apple Watch®. A strategy

of product development requires a lot of investment in research and development. There may be a high level of risk in developing new products – it may be that only one in five product launches succeed; for those that do succeed, heavy investment in promotion may be required.

Market development: Market development involves the marketing of existing products in new markets. The most basic form of the strategy is entering geographically new markets. This is not always simple. Tastes and preferences may be different in regions of the same country, let alone between countries. A market development strategy relies heavily on understanding local habits, tastes and needs.

USA-based Enterprise Rent-A-Car is one example of a business that has adopted a very successful strategy of market development. The car-leasing company's model was very successful. However, the business achieved exponential growth (i.e. the rate of growth became faster and faster) when it started to locate its branches at airports. This move opened the company up to an entirely different profile of customers, such as flyers and holidaymakers. By 2018, Enterprise Rent-A-Car had over 7600 branches worldwide with more than 250 in US airports alone.

Even where market development is appropriate and successful, small changes are often made to suit the new market. This might be changing the name to be more acceptable or accessible in a different language or labelling the product differently to meet international laws.

Diversification: Diversification occurs when new products are developed for new markets. It enables a business to move away from depending upon existing markets and products. Therefore, it allows the company to spread risk and increase safety. If one product faces difficulties or fails, a successful product in another market may prevent the overall business facing problems. However, diversification will take a business outside its area of expertise (i.e. the area where the business has special skills or knowledge). For this reason, it is the strategy with the highest risk. This might mean that its performance in new markets is poor compared with more experienced operators.

Examples of this marketing strategy include the move by Mercedes-Benz® into the market for small, high-volume cars, and the diversification by Virgin® into financial services. Diversification is adopted by large corporations and conglomerates that have extensive business networks, considerable capital and strong corporate brands. Virgin is one business where the brand has allowed it to diversify into a range of industries. Remember that that there may be significant barriers to entering a new industry when diversifying (see Porter's Five Forces in Chapter 4).

ACTIVITY 1 SKILLS CRITICAL THINKING

CASE STUDY: ATTA GLOBAL GROUP

In January 2018, newspaper reports stated that Atta Global Group BHD, a Malaysian metal recycling business, was planning to diversify into property. Atta Global is a holding company that owns a number of businesses in the iron and steel industry. The activities of its companies include the processing of steel coil, tubes, strapping, steel furniture, metal roofing, floor decking, perforated metal and the industrial recycling of scrap metal. However, the group said that one of its subsidiaries (i.e. one of the smaller companies it controls), Tetap Gembira Development Sdn Bhd*, planned to start on a development project on land in Barat Daya, Penang in 2018. In addition, other companies under its control, Park Avenue Construction Sdn Bhd and Progerex Sdn Bhd, have bought a number of double-storey bungalows. These two activities are expected to contribute more than 25 per cent of the group's profit in the future.

In March 2018, Atta Group also announced that Park Avenue Construction Sdn Bhd would be purchasing property company, Sungguh Gemilang Development Sdn Bhd for RM12 million. According to a spokesperson for Atta Group, 'The proposed acquisition is a strategic move in view of the company's proposed diversification into property development and would expect to generate synergistic benefits to the group.'

* In Malaysia, 'Sdn Bhd' means that the company has issued shares.

1 Explain how a business might use Ansoff's Matrix.
2 What are the potential benefits of the Atta Group's diversification strategy to the business?

PORTER'S STRATEGIC MATRIX

Porter's Strategic Matrix was developed by Michael Porter, a professor at Harvard Business School, to identify the sources of competitive advantage that a business might achieve in a market. Porter stated that any business that does not adopt one of these three generic strategies is 'stuck in the middle' and unlikely to succeed.

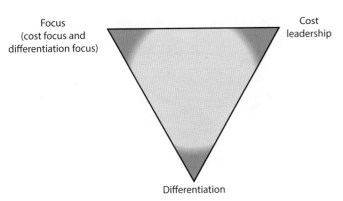

Focus
(cost focus and
differentiation focus)

Cost
leadership

Differentiation

▲ Figure 2 Porter's Strategic Matrix

Cost leadership: This involves striving to be the lowest-cost provider in the market. This does not necessarily mean that the business will offer the lowest price, although this may be an option. Generally, the firm that is able to operate as the lowest-cost provider in a market will compete in two ways:

- increasing profits, while still charging market level prices
- increasing market share, while charging lower prices (still making a profit since costs are reduced).

Cost leadership is generally held by one business in the market as it requires having a significant market share in order to achieve the lowest costs. A firm will achieve the lowest costs by operating on a large scale and therefore exploiting economies of scale. The business will also have a clear focus on reducing costs through negotiation with suppliers, efficiency and streamlining operations (i.e. making them more simple and effective). A cost leader will also offer a basic product in order to minimise costs and limit the options for adding value. The level of service and number of available versions of the product will be minimal and the scale will be associated with mass production. In the 'Getting started' section, Big Bazaar was implementing a cost leadership strategy.

Differentiation: This involves a business operating in a mass market with a unique position instead of the lowest-cost position. Unlike cost leadership, a differentiation strategy may be adopted by any business, provided that it can deliver a way of differentiating itself from the competition. A business adopting differentiation will do so through adding value to their products in a unique way. This might include quality, design, brand identity or customer service.

The advantage of operating under a differentiation strategy is that the business may be able to charge a premium price if customers value their unique selling point. However, it is difficult to guarantee that the rewards of differentiation will justify the additional costs. For example, differentiation will require good research and development as well as effective marketing to highlight the uniqueness to the customer. Differentiation is much easier to copy than cost leadership unless the differentiation is sustainable and defensible. For example, a business may be able to get a patent on a design or register a logo as a trademark so that competitors cannot copy it.

One company that has done well by differentiating its products is Airstream®, the US caravan producer. It produces iconic luxury caravans. The products are very different from the majority of caravans and recreational vehicles (RVs) in the global market.

Focus: This strategy involves targeting a narrow range of customers in one of two ways. A focus strategy is closely aligned to niche marketing (see Chapter 33). It tends to be used by small or very specialist firms. As a business is focusing on a very narrow segment of the market, it is able to gain an advantage by understanding its customers very well. It can deliver products and services that are very specific to their needs. As a result, this can create a high level of customer satisfaction and loyalty. Also, a focus strategy will result in less competition and higher profit margins. However, as the market is very small, a firm adopting this strategy tends to have low bargaining power with suppliers. A focus strategy can take one of two forms.

- **Cost focus** – emphasising cost minimisation within a focused or niche market. The German supermarket chain Aldi® is a good example of this strategy. Although it does not operate as the cost leader in the market, it is able to offer a focused range of products at very low prices.
- **Differentiation focus** – following different strategies within a focused market. Ferrari® is an example of this strategy. Its high-performance cars are targeted at a very small percentage of the population.

ACTIVITY 2   SKILLS ▷ CRITICAL THINKING, REASONING

CASE STUDY: RED BULL

The Red Bull® energy drink is produced by the Austrian company, Red Bull. In 2017, Red Bull was available in over 170 different countries and sold more than 6.3 billion cans. The corporate strategy of Red Bull is to associate the brand with an adventurous lifestyle. The company's marketing slogan implies that the drink gives you so much energy you could fly. The company has a clear product differentiation strategy. Red Bull charges a premium price since the brand is perceived to provide consumers with additional benefits. Consuming Red Bull is believed to help people lead a full and active lifestyle and enhance mental and physical performance.

Red Bull has developed the following competitive advantages:

- **First-mover advantage in developed countries.** Red Bull created a whole new product category when it was launched in 1987. It was the first energy drink of its kind. It was developed from the Thai drink, Krating Daeng.
- **A unique and sweet taste.** The flavouring used in the manufacture of Red Bull is produced in Bangkok and shipped to plants all over the world. It has a unique flavour.
- **An appealing association with extreme sports.** Red Bull owns a number of sports clubs around the world such as RB Leipzig, FC Red

Bull Salzburg, Red Bull Brasil and New York Red Bulls. The brand image is reinforced because it is associated with these clubs.

- **An effective marketing strategy.** Red Bull makes effective use of its Red Bull TV online channel and Red Bulletin online magazine in its marketing strategy. It employs about 150 people in content marketing and media strategy.

1 Explain how Red Bull's corporate strategy relates to Porter's Strategic Matrix.
2 What are the potential consequences for Red Bull of not adopting one of Porter's three generic strategies?

AIM OF PORTFOLIO ANALYSIS

Portfolio analysis is a method of categorising (i.e. grouping according to type) all of the products of a firm (its 'portfolio') in order to decide where each one fits within the strategic plans. The products are then evaluated according to their competitive position and potential growth rates. This involves a two-step process.

- Step 1: Give a full and detailed overview of all of the products in the current business portfolio.
- Step 2: Look at the performance of each of these products and services by examining:
  - current and projected sales
  - current and projected costs
  - competitor activity and future competition
  - risks that may affect performance.

The Boston Consulting Group (BCG) has created an advanced tool for portfolio analysis. First, a business gathers market share and growth rate data on all of its products. Next, the Boston Consulting Group Matrix (or 'Boston Matrix' / Growth Share Matrix) categorises these products into one of four different areas based upon their current and potential market share or market growth.

1 **Stars** are high-growth products that are strong compared to those of competitors. Stars require investment, but the hope is that they will become cash cows.
2 **Cash cows** are low-growth products with high market shares. They generate more cash than they consume, and so can provide a return for investors and fund investment in other areas.
3 **Question marks** are products with low market shares in high-growth markets. They consume a lot of cash but give little return. However, they have the potential to turn into stars. Keeping these lines requires a belief that there is a potential for growth.

4 **Dogs** are products with low market share in low-growth markets. They may break even, but nevertheless take up time and effort with little prospect of future growth. They should be sold or divested.

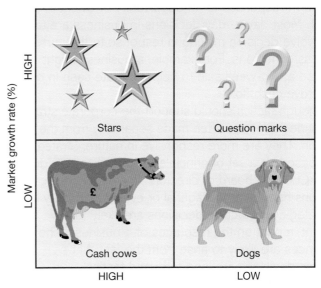

▲ Figure 3 The Boston Matrix

Based on The BCG Portfolio Matrix from the Product Portfolio Matrix, © 1970, The Boston Consulting Group (BCG)

The Boston Matrix may be used to assist a business in identifying which strategy to adopt. For example, if a firm believes that it has a 'Star' it may decide to adopt a market penetration strategy. This is so it can increase sales revenue and maximise market share while the product is competitive. Similarly, a firm may choose to move a product out of a low-growth market and target a market with high-growth prospects. Or, the matrix could be used to identify those 'Dogs' that need to be discontinued. This will help the firm to cut costs and follow its strategy of cost leadership.

ACTIVITY 3   SKILLS   CRITICAL THINKING, ANALYSIS, INTERPRETATION

CASE STUDY: MOTORVITE

Motorvite is a French car manufacturer owned by a Chinese company called MXJ. Since MXJ bought Motorvite in 2014, it has invested heavily in product development, building on Motorvite's reputation for luxury sport and executive saloon cars. Since 2014, Motorvite has launched four new models across these vehicle categories.

Models	Sales – Feb 2016	Sales – Feb 2017	Year-on-year change (%)
P4	2033	2784	36.94
P6	473	337	−28.75
P7	–	79	–
P901	943	1201	27.36

▲ Table 1 Motorvite product range and sales figures

1 Using the information in Table 1 and the Boston Matrix, analyse Motorvite's product portfolio.

EFFECT OF STRATEGIC AND TACTICAL DECISIONS

Strategies set out the long-term direction that a business will take to achieve its objectives. In contrast, tactics are short-term responses to an opportunity or threat in the market. Most day-to-day decisions in business are tactical and involve decision making in response to the current business conditions. For example, a business might organise a two-week sale to help generate cash in order to improve cash flow.

Although tactics should support the corporate strategy, tactical decisions are often made separately from the wider situation. They are more responsive in nature. Strategy is often based on a set of principles or guidelines set down by the CEO and board of directors. In contrast, tactical decisions happen at managerial or even supervisory level.

Strategic and tactical decisions are likely to have a different impact on the resources of a business. The differences are likely to arise from the fact that strategic decisions are long term and tactical decisions are short term.

Human resources: A strategic decision will have a long-lasting effect on the workforce. For example, a new growth strategy might involve increasing the size of the workforce, recruiting different types of labour or moving existing workers to a new location. People may feel the impact of such measures indefinitely. A tactical decision may affect people for a short period of time and only a small proportion of the workforce might be affected. For example, an ice-cream manufacturer may decide to open the factory at weekends to cope with an increase in demand caused by very warm weather. This may only affect some of the workforce, as it is likely that only production workers will be needed. They may be recruited on a voluntary basis (in many countries workers cannot be forced to work overtime). Also, once the warm weather has ended, normal working hours are likely to be resumed.

Physical resources: Physical resources in a business include land, machines, tools, equipment, vehicles, shops, computers, factories and raw materials. A strategic decision could have quite a wide variety of effects on these resources depending on the nature of the decision. For example, if a business decides to permanently outsource its transport and delivery operation, it will need to sell off most of its delivery vehicles. This means only a small proportion of physical resources will be affected. However, if the business decides to develop and launch a new product, a larger proportion of physical resources will be affected, e.g. more research equipment, additional factory space or new types of raw materials may be required. Tactical decisions can also have an impact on physical resources, but they may not be so dramatic. For example, if a catering company agrees to meet an unusually large

order for an event outside of its normal geographical area, it may have to lease some extra kitchen equipment, utensils or dining furniture. But since these additional physical resources are only leased, they will be returned to the hire company after the event. Therefore, they will not affect the company in the long term.

Financial resources: Strategic decisions can have a significant and long-term impact on the financial resources of a business. For example, a company might raise $200 million by issuing some shares to pay for a planned acquisition programme. Once the shares have been issued, the company will have to meet dividend payments on those shares for as long as the company trades. This is a long-term effect on the finances of the business. In contrast, a tactical decision may only have a short-term effect. For example, a business may deliberately go overdrawn at the bank because it is waiting for a delayed payment from a customer. This tactical decision will not have a huge effect on the company's finances as the assumption is that once the customer pays the debt, the overdraft will be cleared.

THINKING BIGGER

There are a range of concepts and theories surrounding the development of corporate strategies and this can sometimes be confusing. The reality is that corporate strategy is not straightforward. What makes one business successful while another fails is not always clear. There are too many variables and external factors for anyone to write a definitive (i.e. one that cannot be improved upon) formula for success. Nevertheless, **theoretical models** can help businesses to simplify reality in order to structure their corporate strategies for the best chance of success.

It is useful to consider how the three main models mentioned in this chapter fit together. Whilst they are separate, they still relate to each other. For example, Ansoff's Matrix is a useful tool for a business to identify its current position and choose an appropriate direction for the company – the 'what and where tool'. In contrast, Porter's Strategic Matrix presents three strategies that a business might use to compete in its market – the 'how tool'. Finally, other theories might help a business decide whether its strategy is sustainable, defensible and has longevity.

Similarly, using the Boston Matrix can help to categorise a firm's products and make informed recommendations on how it should use them for future growth. Business models are not just useful tools for business, they can help to guide your analysis and evaluation in your examinations.

EXAM HINT

In your examination, it is important to understand a range of theoretical models that explain corporate strategy and the issues about each distinguishable strategy. By understanding theories of corporate strategy, you can categorise any business that features in the case study. They can help you to think about points of analysis in your answers. For example, being able to identify a firm as adopting a market penetration strategy will allow you to discuss the following issues and relate them to the firm.

- It is a comparatively low-risk strategy.
- It might require heavy investment in marketing.
- Success relies on building loyal relationships with customers.
- There is a danger of falling behind competitors who innovate.

SUBJECT VOCABULARY

corporate strategy the plans and policies developed to meet a company's objectives. It is concerned with what range of activities the business needs to undertake in order to achieve its goals. It is also concerned with whether the size of the business organisation makes it capable of achieving the objectives set

customer base a group of customers that make continual repeat purchases from a business

diversification developing new products in new markets

market development the marketing of existing products in new markets

market penetration using tactics such as the marketing mix to increase the growth of existing products in an existing market

portfolio analysis a method of categorising all the products of a firm (its portfolio) to decide where each one fits within the strategic plans

product development marketing new or modified products in existing markets

theoretical model a situation that could exist but doesn't really

CHECKPOINT

1. Describe the connection between corporate strategy and business aims.

2. Why is a long-term decision to move into a new market an example of corporate strategy?

3. What are the four strategies outlined by Ansoff's Matrix?

4. Which of Porter's strategies is focused on achieving the lowest costs of production?

5. Describe the aim of portfolio analysis.

6. How might a business use the BCG Matrix to make strategic decisions?

7. What is the difference between a long-term strategy and a tactic?

8. Describe the effect that the construction of a new factory might have on (a) the financial resources and (b) the physical resources of a furniture manufacturer.

EXAM PRACTICE

FLIPKART®

SKILLS CRITICAL THINKING, ANALYSIS, INTERPRETATION, COMMUNICATION

Flipkart is India's leading e-commerce company. It owns the fashion retailers Myntra and Jabong and the PhonePe® payments platform. In addition to its own product range called DigiFlip®, it offers over 30 million products across more than 70 categories including books, media, consumer electronics and lifestyle. Flipkart is one of a few companies that allows its customers to pay cash (or card) on the delivery of goods purchased. Flipkart also offers customers some impressive delivery guarantees. For example, in 60 Indian cities, goods can be delivered within one day of an order being placed (Rs90 per item). In 10 cities it offers a same-day delivery service (Rs140 per item). Flipkart also offers an annual subscription service called Flipkart First. This is the first of its kind in India.

Flipkart employs over 30 000 people and has 75 million registered users. Flipkart's operations allow 8 million shipments per month. In 2017, the company enjoyed revenues of US$3.09 billion. This was a 29 per cent increase on the previous financial year. However, the company's losses increased by 60 per cent to US$1.3 billion.

At the end of 2017, Flipkart made an adjustment to its corporate strategy. It decided to focus more on growing market share rather than reducing its losses. Japanese-based SoftBank® Group (one of Flipkart's key investors) urged Flipkart to grow sales aggressively and build a larger market share. According to a report, SoftBank wanted Flipkart to grow its market share to 60 or 70 per cent over the next few years. Figure 4 shows the current market shares of Flipkart and Amazon® India. Flipkart's market share, including that of its fashion unit, Myntra, slipped to 38.5 per cent in 2016–17 from 40 per cent in 2014–15 in terms of gross sales or gross merchandise value (GMV). At the same time, Amazon India's market share grew from 12 per cent to 29 per cent.

SoftBank said it was willing to invest several billion dollars to help Flipkart increase sales and widen its narrow lead over rapidly growing Amazon. In order to help deliver this strategy, Flipkart has commissioned the consultant Bain & Co to devise a marketing strategy to increase **customer base** and improve customer loyalty. Flipkart is also planning more acquisitions to help boost market share. For example, Flipkart has recently discussed the possibility of investing in food delivery app Swiggy, services firm UrbanClap and furniture retailer UrbanLadder. Flipkart is also looking at some start-ups in insurance and wealth management.

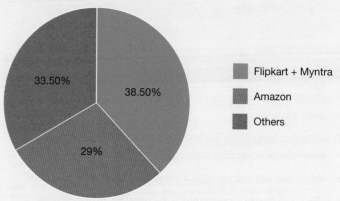

▲ Figure 4 Indian e-commerce market shares, 2016–17

Q

1 Explain what is meant by 'corporate strategy'. **(4 marks)**
2 Explain how a tactical decision may differ from a strategic decision. **(4 marks)**
3 Discuss why Flipkart has adopted a new corporate strategy. **(8 marks)**
4 With reference to Ansoff's Matrix, assess the level of risk associated with Flipkart's new strategy. **(12 marks)**

3 SWOT ANALYSIS

LEARNING OBJECTIVES

By the end of this chapter you should be able to understand:
- SWOT analysis:
  - internal considerations: strengths and weaknesses
  - external considerations: opportunities and threats.

GETTING STARTED

Adamowicz Ltd operates three businesses. One is a roofing specialist, one is a household maintenance business and the other is a solar heating provider. The solar heating business is fairly new and has encountered one or two problems. It has used up a lot of cash resources which has forced the group to borrow a lot of money. However, sales are growing fast and the future looks good. The CEO is worried about overtrading, though.

The roofing business is established and has an excellent reputation for being reliable in the local area. It has high profit margins and currently generates 75 per cent of the group's profits.

The housing maintenance business struggled a little during the recession, but is starting to recover as homeowners increase spending on home improvements. The business offers a 24-hour call-out service, which none of its competitors can match. However, it has had difficulties attracting staff, and existing workers are trying to get a 7 per cent pay increase. This pay increase will affect margins if granted.

Identify the strengths and weaknesses of Adamowicz Ltd. Why might it be important for Adamowicz Ltd to understand the strengths and weaknesses of its operations? Suggest some possible external factors that might threaten the performance of the business in the future.

GATHERING INFORMATION TO HELP DEVELOP A STRATEGY

When making plans or developing a business strategy it is important to gather appropriate information. A business can use a variety of methods to do this.

The internal audit: An internal audit is an analysis of the business itself and how it operates. It attempts to identify the strengths and weaknesses of its operations. It might cover areas such as:
- products and their costs, quality and development
- finance, including profit, assets and cash flow
- production, including capacity, quality, efficiency and stock management
- internal organisation, including divisional and departmental structures
- human resources, including skills, training and recruitment.

In a large business, the internal audit might be conducted by outside management consultants. This could help to produce a more independent-minded analysis of the business's situation.

The external audit: An external audit is an analysis of the environment in which the business operates. The business has little or no control over it. This audit may deal with three key areas: the market, competition and the political, economic, social, technological, legal and environmental issues relevant to the business.

The audit should analyse the market or markets in which the business operates. For example, it should analyse:
- the size and growth potential of the market
- the characteristics of the customers in the market
- the products on offer
- the pricing structure
- how products are distributed
- how products are promoted
- industry practices, such as whether there is a **trade association** or government regulation.

The audit should also analyse the competition in the market. The nature and strength of competitors will be an important influence on the development of a strategy. For example, it should analyse:
- the structure of the industry (including the number and size of competitors)
- the production capacity and marketing methods of competitors
- how likely it is that there will be new entrants to the market
- how likely it is that businesses will leave the industry
- the profits of competitors
- competitors' investments programmes, costs, revenues, cash and assets.

ACTIVITY 1 SKILLS ▸ CRITICAL THINKING, ANALYSIS

CASE STUDY: SALY FISHING TRIPS

Saly is a popular beach resort on the coast of Senegal, Africa. The Gassama family run a small business taking tourists out to sea on fishing trips from Saly. In 2018, Keita Gassama thought it would be a good time to expand the business. However, before making plans, Keita and his family decided to review the current position of the business (i.e. to examine its strengths and weaknesses).

The business had been trading for 19 years and provided good-quality fishing trips for visitors to Saly. There were many businesses offering similar services, but Saly Fishing Trips was probably the market leader. It had a good reputation and had over 200 positive reviews on a tourist website. Saly Fishing Trips did not have a website and did not invest any money in marketing. However, it was profitable and supported the entire family of 12. The business had a positive cash flow and Keita had an excellent local knowledge of fishing in the sea – about 98 per cent of customers caught fish on a four-hour trip.

However, the boat needed some repairs and about 70 per cent of the fishing tackle needed replacing. The boat was also very likely to be affected by poor weather, which meant that trips often had to be cancelled at the last minute.

1 Outline the internal strengths and weaknesses of Saly Fishing Trips.

2 Suggest two possible external threats to Saly Fishing Trips.

3 Suggest two possible opportunities for Saly Fishing Trips.

WHAT IS SWOT ANALYSIS?

It is helpful if the information gathered can then be summarised and presented in a meaningful way. One approach is to use **SWOT analysis**. This involves looking at the internal strengths (S) and weaknesses (W) of a business and the external opportunities (O) and threats (T) that it faces. It is an analytical tool that can help managers with complex decisions.

SWOT analysis might be used by senior managers before drawing up a **strategic plan**. It helps to give an idea of the advantages and disadvantages of a particular decision. It might also help to make the current position of a business easier to understand.

Strengths: These are the positive aspects of a business that may be identified from the internal audit. Strengths are what the business is good at – they are what help make the business a success. Examples might include:

- a respected, intelligent, inspirational and visionary leader
- a highly motivated and loyal workforce
- a product with a unique selling point
- state-of-the-art production facilities

- a loyal customer base (i.e. the people who buy the product)
- an innovative marketing department (i.e. one that uses new methods and ideas).

Weaknesses: These are the negative aspects of a business that may be identified from the internal audit. Weaknesses are what the business lacks or does poorly; for example, in relation to its competitors. They are the characteristics that undermine the performance of a business – perhaps preventing it from growing. They are also areas for improvement. Examples might include:

- a poorly motivated workforce with a high staff turnover (i.e. the rate at which workers leave)
- an organisational structure that has too many layers of management
- a product range that is getting out of date
- poor cash flow and growing debt
- outdated tools and machinery
- a poorly presented and out-of-date website.

Opportunities: The external audit should show up what opportunities are available to the business. These are the options or openings that the business might be able to exploit – resulting in improvements, such as higher revenues or lower costs. Examples might include:

- a new overseas market opening up following a political change
- a fall in the cost of an essential raw material, such as oil
- low interest rates, which provide cheap finance for investment
- a fall in the exchange rate, which will make exports cheaper
- some difficult regulations being abolished
- the failing of a major rival in the market.

Threats: The external audit should show up what threats face the business. Threats are the possible dangers that have the potential to damage the performance of the business. Examples might include:

- a new entrant in the market
- a rival employing a new and highly successful CEO
- a probable recession
- new legislation (i.e. laws) aimed at improving the rights of employees
- increasing pressure from environmentalists
- a change in social attitudes towards the business's key product.

SWOT analysis is often carried out in mind-mapping sessions before being documented (i.e. officially recorded). It can be a powerful way of summarising and building upon the results of internal and external audits. Clearly, it will be a useful tool when developing a corporate strategy, but it may have other uses. For example, it might be used to:

- decide which new product to launch
- design a new marketing strategy
- decide whether to outsource a specific business task or activity, such as IT
- prepare for a completely new business venture
- plan a restructuring of the business.

Finally, by identifying clearly the strengths, weaknesses, opportunities and threats, it may be possible to improve the performance of a business. However, this will depend on the action it takes after carrying out the analysis. For example, performance will only improve if a business acts to remove known weaknesses.

AN EXAMPLE OF A SWOT ANALYSIS

Swedish chocolate maker, Choklad Extas, is an established and well-known confectioner. It has been trading for over 50 years and has around 130 shops located in ideal positions around Sweden and Norway. In 2017, the business made a pre-tax profit of SEK97 million. However, a profit warning in December 2017 suggested that this might be difficult to match. In

the years before 2017, the business had focused on improving profitability. It had closed down marginal stores and tried to increase sales using other outlets. Figure 1 shows a SWOT analysis for Choklad Extas.

STRENGTHS

- Progress is being made developing wholesale and third-party sales
- Market research suggests that the business is increasing its market share
- Online sales have increased significantly – albeit from a low base
- The historic brand is widely recognised

WEAKNESSES

- Profits declining
- Still too much reliance on high street shops (250 in 2014)
- Falling sales, partly caused by operational difficulties at a one of its depots

SWOT ANALYSIS

OPPORTUNITIES

- Overseas markets offer considerable potential for growth – only 3 per cent of sales are currently from exports
- The business is working hard to get its products on the shelves of other retailers
- A number of new products could help lift sales, revenue and market share

THREATS

- Profit margins could suffer as a result of supermarket price wars
- Emerging competition from gift-selling rivals, such as Hotel Chocolat® and Moonpig®
- The cost of raw materials, such as sugar and cocoa, is subject to volatility

▲ Figure 1 SWOT analysis for Choklad Extas

LINKS

A business may use SWOT analysis to help make decisions. Therefore, you could link information in this chapter to any answer where decision making is being discussed. For example, a business might be deciding whether or not to enter an overseas market, which is discussed in Chapter 28. You could explain that a business might carry out a SWOT analysis to help decide whether the move would be desirable given the company's current situation. Other examples of chapters to which SWOT analysis might be linked include Market positioning (Student Book 1, Chapter 3), Pricing strategies (Student Book 1, Chapter 12), Marketing strategy (Student Book 1, Chapter 9), Business choices (Student Book 1, Chapter 22), Corporate objectives (this book, Chapter 1), Inorganic growth (Chapter 7), Investment appraisal (Chapter 10) and Key factors in change (Chapter 20).

EXAM HINT

You need to remember that strengths and weaknesses are internal factors and opportunities and threats are external factors. It is important not to get them mixed up.

CHECKPOINT

1 Give three examples of information that an internal audit might find.

2 Give three examples of information that an external audit might find.

3 Why might SWOT analysis help a business to make decisions?

4 Give three examples of possible uses for SWOT analysis.

5 How might SWOT analysis help to improve the performance of a business?

SUBJECT VOCABULARY

external audit an audit of the external environment in which a business finds itself, such as the market within which it operates or government restrictions (i.e. limits) on its operations

flotation the sale of company shares to the public for the first time. The shares are then traded on the stock market

internal audit an analysis of the business itself and how it operates

strategic planning a process which involves making the vision for the future of a business easier to understand. It also involves identifying the goals that need to be achieved in order to realise that vision

SWOT analysis an analysis of the internal strengths and weaknesses of the business and the opportunities and threats presented by its external environment

trade association an organisation whose members are all involved in the same industry or trade. The organisation pursues the interests of these businesses

EXAM PRACTICE

CASE STUDY: GLOBAL PORTS HOLDING

SKILLS ▷ CRITICAL THINKING, ANALYSIS, INTERPRETATION, ADAPTIVE LEARNING

The company and its products

Turkey-based Global Ports Holding (GPH) is the world's largest cruise ship ports operator. It has developed a business model that generates revenue from passengers using facilities and services. This is in addition to the landing fees paid by the owners of vessels. The products include information services, transport arrangements such as transfers to airports, excursions, hotel and restaurant booking, luggage services, connectivity (to Wi-Fi) and travel services. They are provided by guest information desks and other guest services points located at the GPH ports. In May 2017, GPH obtained a listing on the London Stock Exchange.

Financial performance

In 2017, the company had a 1.3 per cent increase in revenue to $116.4 million. However, despite this increase, GPH made a loss of $14.1 million. This compares with a $4.4 million profit in the previous year. During the year, the company floated on the London Stock Exchange. The flotation was responsible for higher costs which contributed to the year's losses. However, the company raised $154.5 million, of which about a third will be used to finance growth in the business. The company plans to use some of the money to expand in the Mediterranean – where GPH has a 25 per cent market share – and the Caribbean and Asia. Since the flotation, though, the share price has fallen steadily.

GPH markets

GPH operates in some popular and admired ports such as Venice, Valletta, Lisbon, Malaga, Barcelona and Singapore. However, the very important business generated by its operations in its two Turkish ports, Bodrum and Anatalya, has been economically affected by reduced foreign investment in the country. Also, GPH does not operate in the Americas, where cruise holidays are very popular. Passenger numbers using cruise ships rose by 15.2 per cent in 2017 and GPH are hoping to develop operations in the port of Havana, Cuba. Finally, in addition to cruise work, GPH also operates two commercial ports which handled about 16 per cent more cargo in 2017. GPH is trying to expand, but some say it focuses on a very narrow range of products.

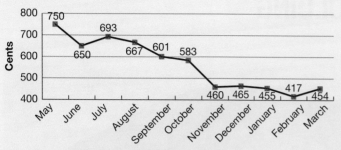

▲ Figure 2 GPH share price since the flotation in May 2017

The future of cruising

The graph in Figure 3 shows that the number of passengers taking cruises has grown slowly but steadily since 2009. The industry is confident about the future. However, the demand for cruises (along with other types of holidays) may fall if global growth slows.

There has also been a rise in the popularity of river cruising in recent years. Cruises along rivers such as the Danube, Nile, Rhine and even the Ganges, are attracting a rapidly growing number of passengers. This is a market that GPH has yet to enter.

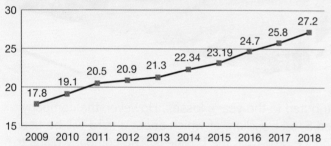

▲ Figure 3 The number of cruise passengers carried (global) 2009–18 (millions)
(NB: 2016, 2017 and 2018 all predicted)

Q

1 Explain how an internal audit might play a role in SWOT analysis. **(4 marks)**
2 Explain how an external audit might play a role in SWOT analysis. **(4 marks)**
3 Discuss how useful a SWOT analysis might be to a business such as GPH if it were planning to expand into a new market. **(8 marks)**
4 Assess the position of GPH by carrying out a SWOT analysis. **(12 marks)**

EXAM HINT

You may get a question that asks you to discuss how useful a SWOT analysis might be for a business when planning a particular project or action. When answering a question where 'Discuss' is the command word, you must remember to use a logical chain of reasoning in context. Your arguments must include causes and effects where appropriate, including a brief assessment to show an awareness of competing arguments and factors.

4 IMPACT OF EXTERNAL INFLUENCES

LEARNING OBJECTIVES

By the end of this chapter you should be able to understand:
- PESTLE (**P**olitical, **E**conomic, **S**ocial, **T**echnological, **L**egal and **E**nvironmental)
- the changing competitive environment
- Porter's Five Forces.

GETTING STARTED

The Kingdom of Bhutan has experienced a sustained period of economic growth in recent years. The future is also bright. The World Bank has predicted GDP growth of 7.7 per cent for the country in 2018, and a huge 10.5 per cent in 2019. However, the mountainous terrain in Bhutan makes the building of roads and other infrastructure difficult and expensive. Therefore, a lot of output (i.e. the amount of something that is produced) is produced using small-scale production. Bhutan relies quite heavily on forestry, agriculture and hydroelectric power generation for employment and business development.

One example of a small agricultural business in Bhutan is the one run by Tshering Wangdi Sherpa. He makes a living from beekeeping in Darachu, Bhutan. When he first started, he maintained a few colonies of honeybees in log hives. However, he attended some training courses run by organisations linked to the government. As a result, Tshering adopted some new beekeeping practices such as using movable frame hives. Tshering has now become a successful beekeeper. Last year, Tshering earned Nu100 000 from selling honey. In addition, he constructed and sold beehives and bee colonies, which earned him Nu50 000. Beekeeping has become his main source of income. In Bhutan, Asiatic honeybee honey sells for Nu1000 per kg, a beehive for Nu3000, and a bee colony for Nu500 per frame, and Tshering says there is a large demand for honey.

There are some barriers to business development in Bhutan. Complicated controls and uncertain policies in areas such as industrial licensing, trade, labour and finance continue to prevent foreign investment and the development of some business activity.

Identify two external factors that may influence the success of Tshering's beekeeping business. Do you think Tshering faces much competition in his line of business? What external factors might affect the performance of businesses in Bhutan in general? What measures might the government in Bhutan take to help businesses?

EXTERNAL INFLUENCES

Sometimes, businesses have to deal with events and issues that are completely beyond their control. These are called external influences and can impact on businesses unexpectedly. They usually mean that businesses have to make changes to the way they operate. The effects of external influences can be both positive and negative.

For example, there have been some important technological advances in the automotive industry. It is likely that many people will replace their petrol and diesel-powered cars for cleaner, and possibly cheaper, electric-powered vehicles. This will have a very positive impact on many electric car manufacturers and their suppliers. There will be a huge global demand for the new products. However, for other businesses there will be a negative impact. For example, suppliers of petrol and diesel vehicles will see demand for their products dwindle.

External influences may fall into a number of different categories which are outlined below.

PESTLE ANALYSIS

The impact of external influences on business can be enormous and can be positive or negative. For example, if interest rates fall, the costs of repaying business loans will fall and profits could rise. Businesses may also be encouraged to invest more. In contrast, if interest rates rise, interest charges will rise, and profits will fall. Also, demand for goods such as cars and houses, which are often funded by borrowing, will fall.

Consequently, it will be helpful to businesses if they can monitor (i.e. watch carefully) and analyse the likely impact of external influences. One approach is to use **PESTLE analysis**. This involves identifying the political (P), economic (E), social (S), technological (T), legal (L) and environmental (E) factors that might influence business activity and performance.

Political: Some parts of the world are politically unpredictable. It is important to pay special attention if businesses try to operate in politically unstable countries. However, political factors can also influence businesses in stable countries. The activities of pressure groups can play a role in influencing business activity. Some examples of political factors include the following.

- Members joining or leaving a trading bloc. This could disrupt financial markets and create a great deal of uncertainty. For example, in 2016, the UK voted to leave the EU.
- The issue of national security has become a priority for many governments. If measures designed to improve national security restrict the movement of goods, people and capital, this could have either a positive or a negative impact on businesses.
- Pressure groups such as trade unions, which aim to protect the rights of workers, can affect businesses. For example, they may be able to force up wages for their members. This will raise business costs.
- Changes in government. For example, a new government may want to introduce laws which might have an impact on some businesses.

Economic: The general state of the economy can have a huge impact on business activity. Since the financial crisis in 2008, a number of countries have suffered a recession. This has made trading conditions very difficult for many businesses. However:

- falling unemployment might help to increase demand for many businesses

- stable prices would create more certainty, which should encourage businesses to invest for the future
- a strengthening exchange rate might make exporting more difficult but it might also make importing cheaper
- lower interest rates would make borrowing cheaper and encourage more investment
- some businesses may suffer badly during a recession.

Businesses that produce goods and services that are income elastic will tend to be worst affected during a recession. These include car producers, house builders, holiday companies, computer games companies and 'white goods' companies (dealing with freezers, cookers and washing machines, etc.). This is because people can postpone purchases of these items until incomes pick up again.

Social: Over time there are likely to be changes in the way society operates. Although social and cultural changes tend to be gradual, they can still have an impact.

- In some countries, greater numbers of people are going to university. This could increase the quality of human resources, which might benefit certain businesses.
- The population in many countries is ageing. This could affect demand patterns and create new opportunities for some businesses.
- Increasing migration (i.e. large numbers of people moving from one place to another) might increase the size of the potential workforce, making recruitment easier. It might also provide a boost to demand.
- People appear to be becoming more health conscious. This might create opportunities for certain businesses, such as those selling healthy foods or running fitness centres.

Technological: The rate of technological change seems to be increasing all the time. Businesses usually welcome technological developments because they can provide new product opportunities or help to improve efficiency.

- Changes in technology can shorten product life cycles. This is because new products are quickly developed to replace ones that use older technology.
- Developments in technology often mean that businesses can replace labour with machines. This is welcomed because human resources are often said to be the most expensive and difficult to manage. New technology also lowers unit costs.
- The development of social media has helped to improve communications between businesses and customers. This allows businesses to keep track of changing consumer needs.

Legal: The government provides the legal framework in which businesses operate. However, it also directs legislation at businesses to protect vulnerable groups (i.e. groups that are easily hurt or damaged) that might otherwise be exploited. EU businesses are also affected by EU regulations.

- EU legislation can affect tax laws. For example, a few years ago the rules changed so that EU VAT (see Student Book 1, Chapter 42) would be charged in the country where products were bought as opposed to the country where they were sold. The legislation only applied to digital products, such as e-books, online courses or downloads.
- Businesses in the food industry are currently under pressure to reduce the amount of sugar and salt they add to products. In some countries, governments have imposed taxes on the use of sugar in certain products
- In some countries, the government states that it wants to reduce the number of rules and regulations addressing business behaviour. This might benefit a wide range of businesses.

Environmental: People are increasingly protective of the environment; for example, because of the threats posed by global warming. Business activities also sometimes threaten wildlife and natural habitats.

- Some people prefer to buy environmentally friendly goods. This provides opportunities for businesses that specialise in these products.
- There are new ways of generating power using renewable sources rather than by burning fossil fuels, such as oil and coal, which are providing new opportunities.
- The trend towards recycling is gathering pace in many countries. By using recycled resources, businesses can cut their costs.

IMPACT OF EXTERNAL INFLUENCES

The impact on businesses of the external influences discussed above could be wide ranging, depending on the nature of the factor. However, some examples are outlined below.

Demand: Businesses will be concerned if external influences reduce demand for their products. This is likely to result in lower revenues, lower profits and weaker cash flows. For example, a sharp rise in the exchange rate will have a negative impact on most businesses that rely heavily on exports. In contrast, importers such as retailers will benefit from the rise. Their purchases will be cheaper and so they may sell more.

Costs: Some external influences are likely to raise costs. This will reduce profit margins or force businesses to raise their prices. For example, a surge in the global oil price will raise costs for many businesses. This is because oil is an important input for many businesses – particularly in manufacturing. However, oil producers will clearly benefit from the price rise.

Operations: Businesses often have to change their operational methods as a result of an external influence. For example, a government may introduce a new minimum wage. This may force a multinational company (MNC) to relocate production to a country with lower wages in comparison to its current location. The development of new technology might force firms to adopt new production methods or risk losing their competitive edge.

ACTIVITY 1   SKILLS CRITICAL THINKING, ANALYSIS, INTERPRETATION

CASE STUDY: GLOBAL SOLAR POWER

There has been global growth in the use of solar panels to generate electricity. One of the reasons for this is the growing awareness of the damage to the environment caused by using fossil fuels. Many people are increasingly concerned about global warming. Some people also see solar power as a status symbol (i.e. it displays their social position or wealth). In addition, many businesses recognise the importance of reducing their carbon footprint. As a result, many are choosing solar power as a source of energy.

One of the barriers to growth in solar power was the performance of the batteries used to store the energy created. Historically, they were huge lead-plate batteries made with sulphuric acid. They were expensive to make and harmful to the environment. Due to advances in technology, newer batteries use saltwater as the only electrolyte. They are also made of lithium iron which is safer because there is less risk of fire.

Another important impact on the solar power industry was the Paris Climate Agreement. In 2015, 195 countries signed a document promising to reduce global warming. The agreement aimed to reduce carbon emissions and limit global warming. It included guidelines suggesting measures that could be taken by developed countries to reduce carbon dioxide emissions. As a result of this agreement, some governments introduced quite generous subsidies and tax benefits. This will help businesses in the solar power industry.

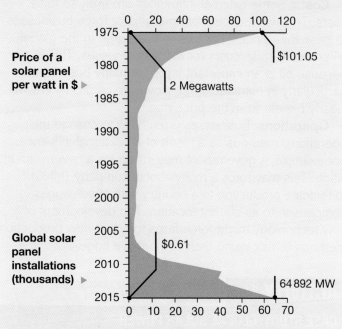

▲ Figure 1 The price of solar power and the growth in solar power installations (1975–2015)

1 Explain how PESTLE analysis might be useful for a business.
2 Consider the impact of (a) political, (b) environmental and (c) technological factors on businesses in the solar energy industry.

THE STRUCTURE OF MARKETS

Competition is the **rivalry** that exists between firms when they are trying to sell goods in a particular market. In some markets, there is a lot of competition. For example, the restaurant market in Los Angeles, USA is very competitive, with more than 36 000 restaurants competing for customers. However, in other markets there is very little competition. For example, SNCF is the sole supplier of rail transport in France. No other rail operator competes with SNCF.

Competitive markets: In a competitive market, there is likely to be a large number of buyers and sellers, and the products sold by each business are close substitutes for each other. Barriers to entry in competitive markets will be low and businesses have very little control over the price charged (see Student Book 1, Chapter 43). For example, if a firm tries to charge more than its rivals, it is likely to lose business. Finally, there will be a free flow of information about the nature of products, availability at different outlets, prices, methods of production and the cost and availability of production factors.

Uncompetitive markets: Some markets are dominated by a single producer or just a few large businesses. In a small number of markets, such as rail travel and water supply, a **monopoly** exists. This means

that just one business supplies the entire market. For example, if you want to get a train from Glasgow to Edinburgh in Scotland, UK, there is only one train service provider – ScotRail. A monopoly might also exist in a local market. For example, a village shop might serve the whole community without any competition from other shops. Monopolies may attempt to exploit consumers by charging higher prices and preventing competition. For example, they may erect barriers to entry. Therefore, the government may choose to monitor the activities of monopolies closely.

A market that is dominated by a few very large producers is called an **oligopoly**. For example, there might be 2000 businesses in a market. If three of the businesses share 70 per cent of the market between them, then it is an oligopoly. One of the key features of an oligopoly is interdependence. This means the actions of one business will affect other businesses. For example, if one business gains an extra 4 per cent of the market, others must have lost the 4 per cent between them. There are usually high barriers to entry in this type of market. The larger firms can exploit economies of scale. Also, because of interdependence, prices tend to remain stable for long periods of time. This is because all firms in the market are afraid of a price war. In an oligopoly, businesses are more likely to engage in non-price competition, such as advertising and promotion. For example, in many countries, car and confectionery (i.e. sweets) production is dominated by just a few large suppliers.

THE CHANGING COMPETITIVE ENVIRONMENT

Over time, the structure of markets is likely to change. In some markets, competition intensifies (i.e. becomes much more extreme) as new businesses enter the market. A new business might have a novel product. Alternatively, the new business might be an established one that wants to diversify (i.e. develop a wider range of products of services) into a different business area.

For a number of years, many governments around the world have tried to make markets more competitive by reducing the amount of regulation. For example, at one time in the UK, only local councils were allowed to operate bus services. However, today it is easier for those who meet the minimum requirements to get a licence and provide bus services on any route they choose.

In contrast, in some markets there has been some consolidation (i.e. the process of joining things together to make one larger or more powerful thing). This means that there are now fewer businesses in the market. This might result from a takeover or merger activity when two or more firms join together. Some examples of changes in the competitive environment are outlined below.

- Retailing has become more competitive due to an increase in the number of consumers using online shopping facilities. For example, people can buy products from all over the world when shopping online, e.g. from Amazon or Ali Baba®.
- There has been a significant consolidation in the global airline industry. For example, in 2005 there were 11 US airlines sharing 96 per cent of the domestic market. In 2016 this had fallen to just seven airlines sharing the majority of the market. In Europe, there were mergers between national airlines. British Airways, Iberian Airlines and several others merged to become IAG, now one of the biggest carriers in the world. Air France and KLM have also merged, as have Swiss Air and Lufthansa.
- In India, the handheld mobile phone market, which was thought to be worth $15 billion in 2017, is expected to consolidate. There were about 100 brands, but intense competition is expected to reduce this number in the near future. Industry analysts say that the market will be consolidated because it is not possible for smaller competitors to survive.

THE IMPACT ON BUSINESSES OF A CHANGING COMPETITIVE ENVIRONMENT

Many markets are dynamic (i.e. continuously changing) and businesses need to be aware of the changes that are taking place. They may have to react to certain changes when they occur.

New entrants: When new entrants in the market increase competition, existing businesses have to consider their position. For example, the growth in online shopping has forced many retailers to offer their own online shopping services. In some cases, retailers have collapsed (i.e. they went out of business) as they failed to compete online. In 2017, an estimated 7795 US retail stores closed down according to research by UBS. This was a record number, and one chain, Radio Shack®, closed down 1470 stores alone. Not all of these closures are due to online shopping; however, retailers may find it hard to survive if they do not offer an online service in the future.

New products: When a new product appears in the market, businesses may be forced to make changes of their own. They might adapt their own products, lower the price of existing products or invest in an aggressive marketing campaign. In the banking industry, a number of new entrants have appeared offering **peer-to-peer (P2P) lending** (the word 'peer' means somebody who is your equal). Traditional banks have noticed this, and some have started to respond. The majority have looked to join up with online services that are already running. However, Lendbox in India plans to pilot a new P2P platform of its own.

Consolidation: When consolidation occurs in markets, the number of businesses in the market falls but some of the existing businesses get bigger. These bigger organisations are likely to be more of a threat to the others; they may be able to lower their costs and they will have a larger market share. Other businesses in the market might respond by organising mergers or takeovers of their own. Alternatively, they may look to develop their products, diversify, or cut their costs in some way. As a last resort, they may continue to operate in much the same way but accept lower profit margins.

Failure to respond effectively to the changing competitive environment could negatively affect the performance of a business. At worst, certain changes may threaten the business's survival.

ACTIVITY 2   **SKILLS**   CRITICAL THINKING, ANALYSIS, INTERPRETATION, COMMUNICATION

CASE STUDY: CONSOLIDATION IN THE EUROPEAN AIRLINE MARKET

In the airline business, the European short-haul market (short flights, such as domestic and to neighbouring countries) has become highly competitive in the last 20 years. This is because of low-cost airlines growing their market share and cheaper aviation fuel. During a six-month period in 2017, three sizable airlines collapsed – Air Berlin, Alitalia and Monarch. Low-cost operators, such as easyJet® and Ryanair have driven airfares down and put pressure on those rivals with a higher cost base. Budget airlines held just 9 per cent of the market 15 years ago. This had grown to 43 per cent in 2017.

The collapse of these three airlines has led to consolidation in the market. In many markets, consolidation results from merger and takeover activity. However, in this case it has been caused by strong airlines growing organically (see Chapter 6) and weaker rivals being forced out.

The strengths and weaknesses of airlines in the European short-haul market are shown in Figure 3. This shows the operating profit margins of all the airlines in the market. Ryanair is clearly the most profitable, with a margin of 23.1 per cent. In second place is Wizz Air, with a margin of 15.7 per cent. Both Alitalia and Air Berlin are at the bottom with negative margins (they made losses).

Finally, there are more airlines operating in the European market than in any other region in the world. According to OAG (a travel intelligence company), Europe has a total of 217, compared with 100 in the USA. Also, US carriers are expected to post a US$15.4 billion net profit in 2017. This is compared with a US$7.4 billion profit for European airlines. It will be interesting to see what happens in the European market in the future.

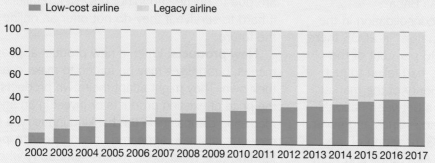

▲ Figure 2 Market shares of the low-cost and legacy airlines* in the European short-haul market 2002–17
* A legacy airline is one that had established routes before the beginning of the route liberalisation which was permitted by new laws.

2016 operating margin (% of revenue)*

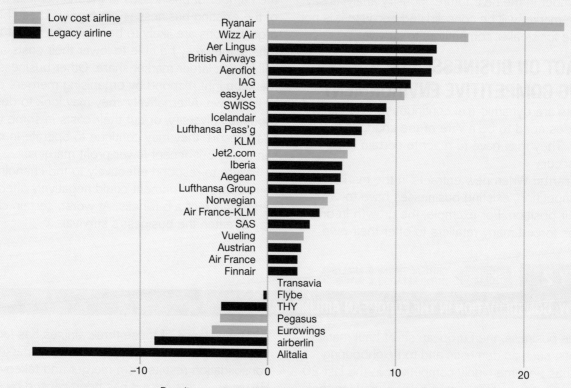

Despite recent negative publicity, Ryanair is still the industry success story

* Before non-recurring items

▲ Figure 3 Profit margins of the airlines in the European short-haul market (2016)

1 What is meant by 'consolidation' in the European short-haul market?

2 Give one reason why the European short-haul market has become more consolidated.

3 What are the factors that might influence the level of consolidation in the European short-haul market?

PORTER'S FIVE FORCES

Another way of looking at the competitive environment is to consider a model put forward by Michael Porter in his book, *Competitive Advantage: Creating and Sustaining Superior Performance* (1985). In the book, he outlines five forces, or factors, which determine the profitability of an industry. He argues that the ultimate aim of competitive strategy is to cope with and ideally change those forces in favour of the business. Where the collective strength of those five forces is favourable, a business will be able to earn acceptable or average returns on their investments. Where they are unfavourable, a business will have low or unpredictable returns.

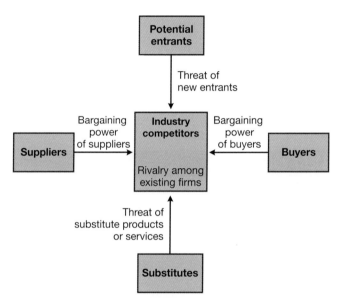

▲ Figure 4 The five competitive forces that determine industry profitability

The five forces, shown in Figure 4, are as follows.

The bargaining power of suppliers: Suppliers, like any business, want to maximise the profit they make from their customers. The more power a supplier has over its customers, the higher the prices it can charge and the more it can reallocate (i.e. move) profit from the customer to itself. Limiting the power of its supplier will therefore improve the competitive position of a business. It has a variety of strategies it can adopt to achieve this. It can grow vertically (backward vertical integration, see Chapter 6), either acquiring a supplier or setting up its own business by growing organically upwards. It can seek out new suppliers to create more competition amongst suppliers. It might be able to engage in technical research to find substitutes for a particular input to broaden the supply base. It may also minimise the information provided to suppliers in order to prevent the supplier realising its power over the customer.

The bargaining power of buyers: Suppliers want to charge maximum prices to customers, and buyers want to obtain supplies for the lowest price. If buyers or customers have considerable market power, they will be able to beat down prices offered by suppliers. For example, the major car manufacturers have succeeded in forcing down the price of components from component suppliers because of their enormous buying power and the small number of major car manufacturers in the world.

One way a business can improve its competitive position with buyers is to extend into the buyers' market through forward vertical integration. A car manufacturer might set up its own dealership, for example. It could encourage other businesses to set up in its customers' market to reduce the power of existing customers. It could also try to make it expensive for customers to switch to another supplier. For example, one way games console manufacturers keep up the price of computer games for their machines (which they receive a royalty fee for) is by making them technically incompatible (i.e. unable to work together) with other machines.

The threat of new entrants: If businesses can easily enter an industry and exit if profits are low, it becomes difficult for existing businesses in the industry to charge high prices and make high profits. Existing businesses are constantly under threat from new suppliers if the profits in an industry rise too much. This is because the new suppliers can undercut their prices.

Businesses can protect themselves from this by erecting barriers to entry to the industry. For example, a business may apply for patents and copyright to protect its intellectual property and prevent other businesses using it. It can attempt to create strong brands which will attract customer loyalty and make customers less price sensitive. Large amounts of advertising can be a deterrent (i.e. something that stops people from doing something) because it represents a large cost to a new entrant, which might have to match the spending to grow some market share. Large sunk costs, costs which have to be paid at the start but are difficult to get back if the business leaves the industry, can deter new entrants.

Substitutes: The more substitutes there are for a particular product, the fiercer the competitive pressure on a business making the product. Equally, a business making a product with few or no substitutes is likely to be able to charge higher prices and make high profits. A business can reduce the number of potential substitutes through research and development, and then patenting the substitutes itself. Sometimes, a business will buy the patent for a new invention from a third party and do nothing with it, simply to prevent the product coming to market. Businesses can also use marketing tactics to stop the spread of substitute products. A local newspaper, for example, might use **predatory pricing** if a new competitor comes into its market to drive it out again.

Rivalry among existing firms: The degree of rivalry among existing firms in an industry will also determine prices and profits for any single firm. If rivalry is fierce, businesses can reduce that rivalry by forming **cartels**, or engaging in a broad range of anti-competitive practices. In many countries this is illegal, but it is not uncommon.

Businesses can also reduce competition by buying up their rivals (horizontal integration, see Chapter 7). Again, competition law may intervene to prevent this happening, but most horizontal mergers are allowed to proceed.

In industries where there are relatively few businesses, often businesses don't compete on price. This allows them to maintain high profitability. Instead, they tend to compete by bringing out new products and increased advertising, thus creating strong brands. As a result, their costs are higher than they might otherwise be, but they can also charge higher prices than in a more competitive market, creating high profits.

LINKS

External influences can have an impact on a wide range of business activities. It is a topic area that allows you to demonstrate your synoptic skills (i.e. your ability to provide a summary). For example, you might need to answer a question explaining the impact of economic growth on a particular business. Or you might need to explain the impact of higher interest rates on a business that is planning to increase investment. Examples of other chapters that could be linked to external influences include: Marketing strategy (Student Book 1, Chapter 9), Business failure (Student Book 1, Chapter 36), Theories of corporate strategy (this book, Chapter 2), Marketing (Chapter 32), Cultural/social factors (Chapter 34), International business ethics (Chapter 36) and Controlling MNCs (Chapter 37). There are many others.

CHECKPOINT

1 Give two examples of political factors that might affect the food industry.

2 Give two examples of economic factors that might affect the holiday industry.

3 Give two examples of technological factors that might affect the motor industry.

4 Give two examples of environmental factors that might affect the chemical-processing industry.

5 How does PESTLE analysis help a business?

6 What is meant by an uncompetitive market?

7 State two possible effects on a business of a strong new entrant in a market.

8 How might the degree of rivalry in a market affect prices and profits?

9 What action might businesses take to deal with the threat of potential entrants?

SUBJECT VOCABULARY

cartel a group of businesses that act together to reduce competition in a market – by fixing prices, for example
monopoly a market dominated by a single business
oligopoly a market dominated by a few large businesses
peer-to-peer (P2P) lending providing loans to individuals or businesses through online services that match lenders with borrowers
PESTLE analysis analysis of the external political, economic, social, technological, legal and environmental factors affecting a business
predatory (or destroyer) pricing setting a low price to force rivals out of business
rivalry the competition that exists between businesses operating in the same market

EXAM PRACTICE

CASE STUDY: RETAILING IN VIETNAM

SKILLS   CRITICAL THINKING, ANALYSIS, INTERPRETATION

Competition in the retailing industry in Vietnam has intensified (i.e. become more extreme) recently. This is due to an increasing number of new entrants that have moved into the market. For example, Vingroup, a major real estate agency in Vietnam, entered retailing in 2015 when it bought a supermarket. Since then it has developed a chain of convenience stores called VinMart+. It now operates 880 stores in Hanoi and Ho Chi Minh City and plans to increase the number of branches by more than 10 000 by 2019.

In the clothing sector, Canifa, which set up as a manufacturer several years ago, began large-scale retailing in 2014. It is targeting the growing number of middle-class customers in the market. Canifa's products are quite expensive for the average Vietnamese customer but the company has managed to develop a chain of over 70 stores.

One of the reasons for the changing competitive environment in retailing in Vietnam is the relaxation of trading rules and regulations. Businesses that want to open a store in Vietnam are required to carry out a review. This is to determine the possible impact of the operation on the local community. It is supervised by the local authorities. However, the review process has now been simplified (i.e. made less complicated) and the criteria (i.e. standards by which something is judged) used in the process are a lot clearer. This has made it easier for businesses to develop a chain of stores. These changes to the law, and others like it, began a few years ago when Vietnam joined the World Trade Organisation. In 2016, the government planned to change the law so that small retailers (with less than 500 m² floor space) would be able to start up without having to get approval from the authorities.

Another reason why competition in the Vietnamese retail market is intensifying is the growing interest from overseas retailers. For example, Japanese retailer Aeon opened a store in Ho Chi Minh City in 2014. Then, Aeon opened three stores in Hanoi and other cities. Also, 7-Eleven, the Japanese-owned US convenience chain, was planning to open its first store in South East Asia in 2018 in Vietnam.

Vietnam has a population of around 93 million and businesses are attracted by the growing number of middle-class consumers. It has been estimated that the retail market reached US$109.8 billion in 2015. However, it is predicted to reach US$179 billion in 2020. Figure 5 shows that Vietnam's GDP more than doubled between 2008 and 2016.

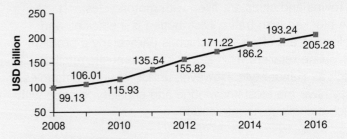

▲ Figure 5 Vietnam GDP 2008–16

A Vietnamese clothing retailer, Hanoi Style, has also benefited from the boom in retailing. The business was started in 2006 by two brothers, Vũ Văn Thanh and Nguyễn Văn Thanh. They designed their own clothes and sold them in a store in Hanoi. Their designs were stylish, popular and priced according to this. The store was successful and within five years the brothers operated six profitable stores under the Hanoi Style brand. In 2013, a large Chinese retailer approached the company asking if they could stock the Hanoi Style brand in their own stores. The offer was financially attractive, but the Chinese company wanted too much control over product development. Vũ Văn Thanh and Nguyễn Văn Thanh believed that this was not the way forward for their business. Instead, the brothers decided to cash in on the recent fall in interest rates and the boom in online retailing. Vietnam's e-commerce market climbed to about $4 billion in 2016. It is one of the fastest-growing markets in the world. Revenue from online retailing in Vietnam is expected to hit US$10 billion by 2020, accounting for 5 per cent of the country's retail market.

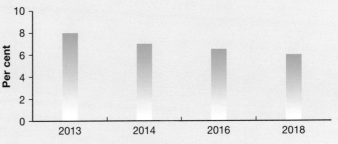

▲ Figure 6 Vietnam interest rates 2013–18

Consequently, the brothers took out a large bank loan and spent 12 months setting up their own online operation. This was expensive because they had to buy and equip an operations centre and employ specialists to deal with the IT. However, things went well for Hanoi Style. Although the costs of going online reduced profits for a couple of years, they soon recovered, and eventually started to rise. Figure 7 shows profits from 2010 to 2018.

However, Hanoi Style has had to deal with some difficulties like other retailers in Vietnam. The country has an underdeveloped logistics network. Narrow streets in towns and cities are filled with motorcycles and are blocked with traffic. Distribution is inefficient, and deliveries are often late, which is particularly a problem for online retailers. This is a risk for domestic retailers such as Hanoi Style. However, unlike foreign companies, they have the local knowledge and capacity to cope with such a challenging infrastructure.

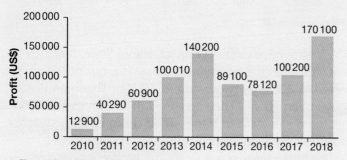

▲ Figure 7 Hanoi Style profits 2010–18

Q

1 Explain one reason why there are changes in the competitive environment of the Vietnamese retail industry. **(4 marks)**
2 Discuss how Porter's five forces analysis might be used by an established business in Vietnam's retail market. **(8 marks)**
3 Evaluate whether or not the success of Hanoi Style is the result of (a) external influences or (b) internal influences. **(20 marks)**

EXAM HINT

When answering a question about factors that might influence business performance or any of its activities, it is good practice to distinguish between internal and external factors. This may provide a useful opportunity to demonstrate your evaluation skills.

Remember that external influences can be positive. For example, if interest rates fall, many businesses will benefit in some way. Also, remember that an external event may have a positive impact on some businesses, but a negative impact on others. For example, if the exchange rate gets stronger, exporters will see a rise in the price of their goods sold abroad. However, importers will be able to buy goods more cheaply.

BUSINESS GROWTH

Many owners want their business to grow. This section explores the objectives of growth such as economies of scale, increased market power, increased market share, increased brand recognition and increased profitability. It also looks at the distinction between organic and inorganic growth. It considers the methods of organic growth and the advantages and disadvantages of this growth strategy. It investigates the reasons for mergers and takeovers, horizontal and vertical integration, conglomerates and the financial risks and rewards of inorganic growth as well as the advantages and disadvantages. Finally, the section looks at the problems arising from (i.e. starting to happen because of) growth such as diseconomies of scale, internal communication difficulties and overtrading.

5 GROWTH

LEARNING OBJECTIVES

By the end of this chapter you should be able to understand:

■ objectives of growth: economies of scale (internal and external), increased market power over customers and suppliers, increased market share and brand recognition and increased profitability
■ the distinction between inorganic and organic growth.

GETTING STARTED

Avanti Feeds is based in Hyderabad in India. About 85 per cent of its output (i.e. of the total amount that it produces) is fish food for shrimps. However, it has a growing interest in shrimp production. In the future, it hopes that this will account for up to 40 per cent of the company's revenue.

The company has seen huge growth in recent years due to expansion in the size of the market. Figure 1 shows revenue growth between 2010 and 2017. In 2017, Avanti's share price also rose by over 300 per cent in the first eight months of the year.

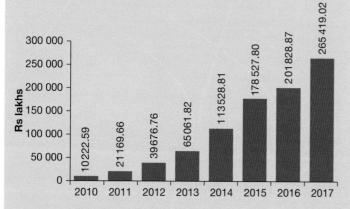

1 Rs Lakh = Rs100 000

▲ Figure 1 Avanti Feeds revenue 2010–17

Adapted from 20th Annual Report 2012-2013, © 2013, Avanti Feeds Ltd

Calculate the percentage growth in revenue for Avanti Feeds between 2010 and 2017. State three benefits of growing the business to Avanti Feeds. Explain one problem that might arise from the growth of the business. Do you think this business will continue to grow? Explain two reasons for your answer.

GROWTH

If a business is growing, it means that it generates more revenue, owns more assets, uses more resources (such as labour and capital) and hopefully makes more profit. Growing businesses are also likely to increase their market share, launch new products and sell into a wider range of markets.

Most businesses start small and then grow. For example, Toronto-based Gillam Group, a Canadian construction company, was set up by Marcus Gillam in 2011. By 2017 Gillam Group was the fastest growing company in Canada. It was ranked first in the PROFIT 500 ranking of Canada's Fastest-Growing Companies. Since 2011, the firm has experienced revenue growth of more than 29 000 per cent. Gillam's revenues doubled in each of its first three years of trading. In 2016, its workforce grew from 60 to 85.

The company is not one of Canada's most well-known construction companies. However, it had sales of between $50–$100 million last year.

When a business grows, the benefits can be very attractive. For example, revenues will be higher and unit costs are likely to be lower. The business will have a higher profile with a larger market share. The specific objectives that a business might have when growing, such as economies of scale and increased market power, are outlined below.

ECONOMIES OF SCALE

The size of a business has a major impact on average costs of production. Typically, there is a range of output over which average costs fall as output rises. Over this range, larger businesses have a competitive advantage over smaller businesses. They benefit from economies of scale. In the long run, a business can build another factory or purchase more machinery. This can cause the average cost of production to fall.

In Figure 2, a firm is currently producing in a small plant (i.e. a factory) and its short-run costs are $SRAC_1$. When it produces an output equal to Q_1, its average cost will be AC_1. If it raises production to Q_2, average costs will rise to AC_2. This is the result of the law of diminishing returns.

If the firm expands the scale of its operations (which it can do in the long run), the same level of output can be produced more efficiently. With a bigger plant, represented by $SRAC_2$, Q_2 can be produced at an average cost of just AC_3. Long-run average costs fall due to economies of scale. They will continue to do so until the firm has built a plant which minimises long-run average costs (i.e. makes the costs as small as possible). In the diagram, this occurs when a plant shown by $SRAC_3$ is built. This is sometimes called the **minimum efficient scale** of plant. When output reaches Q* in this plant, long-run average costs cannot be reduced any further through expansion. The business is said to be productively efficient at this point.

At any output level higher or lower than Q*, the business is productively inefficient because average costs could be lower. For example, if the firm continues to grow, it will experience rising average costs due to diseconomies of scale, as in $SRAC_4$ in Figure 2. This is dealt with in Chapter 8.

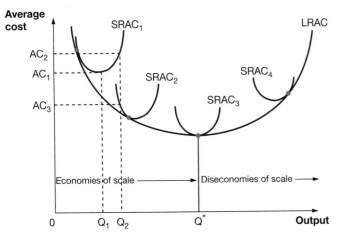

▲ Figure 2 The long-run average cost curve and the effect of economies of scale

INTERNAL ECONOMIES OF SCALE

What are the different economies of scale a firm can gain? **Internal economies of scale** are the benefits of growth that arise within the firm. They occur for a number of reasons.

Purchasing and marketing economies: Large firms are likely to get better rates when buying raw materials and components (i.e. the parts something is made of) in bulk. In addition, the administration costs involved do not rise in proportion to the size of the order. The cost of processing an order for 10 000 tonnes of coal does not double when 20 000 tonnes are ordered.

A number of marketing economies exist. For example, a large company may find it cost-effective to buy its own vans and lorries. The cost to the sales force of selling 30 product lines is not double that of selling 15 lines. Again, the administration costs of selling do not rise in proportion to the size of the sale.

Technical economies: Technical economies arise because larger plants are often more efficient. The capital costs and the running costs of plants do not rise in proportion to their size. For example, the capital cost of a double-decker bus will not be twice that of a single-

decker bus. This is because the main cost (engine and chassis) does not double when the capacity of the bus doubles. Increased size may mean a doubling of output, but not cost. Therefore, the average cost will fall. This is sometimes called the principle of increased dimensions. In addition, the cost of the crew and fuel will not increase in proportion to its size.

Another technical economy is that of **indivisibility**. Many firms need a particular item of equipment or machinery but fail to make full use of it. A small business may pay $400 for a laptop computer. The cost will be the same whether it is used twice a week by a part-time worker or every day. As the business expands, it will be used more and so the average cost of the machine will fall.

As the scale of operations expands, the firm may switch to mass-production techniques. Flow production involves breaking down the production process into a very large number of small operations. It allows for greater use of highly specialised machinery. This results in large improvements in efficiency as labour is replaced by capital.

Businesses often employ a variety of machines which have different capacities. A slow machine may increase production time. As the firm expands and produces more output, it can employ more of the slower machines in order to match the capacity of the faster machines. This is called the law of multiples. It involves firms finding a balanced team of machines so that when they operate together they are all running at full capacity.

Specialisation and managerial economies: A firm can afford to employ specialist managers as it grows. In a small business, one general manager may be responsible for finance, marketing, production and human resources. The manager may find the role demanding. Efficiency may improve and average costs fall if a business employs specialists in these fields. Specialists would be an indivisibility if they were employed in a small firm.

Financial economies: Large firms have advantages when they try to raise finance. They will have a wider variety of sources from which to choose. For example, **sole traders** cannot sell more shares to raise extra funds, but large public limited companies can. Very large firms will often find it easier to persuade institutions to lend them money. This is because they will have large assets to offer as security. Finally, large firms borrowing very large amounts of money can often gain better interest rates. Some governments have recognised the problems facing small firms. A number of schemes have been designed to help small firms raise funds.

Risk-bearing economies: As a firm grows it may well diversify (i.e. develop a wider range of products) to reduce risk. For example, the online retailer Amazon has recently diversified into the operation of supermarkets. Large businesses can also reduce risk by carrying out research and development. The development of new products can help firms gain a competitive edge over smaller rivals (i.e. competing businesses).

EXTERNAL ECONOMIES OF SCALE

External economies of scale are the reductions in costs that any business within an industry might benefit from as the industry grows. External economies are more likely to arise if the industry is concentrated (i.e. if there are a large number of firms) in a particular geographic region.

Labour: The concentration of firms may lead to the build-up of a labour force with the skills required by the industry. Training costs may be reduced if workers have gained skills at another firm in the same industry. Local schools and colleges, or even local government, may offer training courses which are aimed at the needs of the local industry.

Ancillary and commercial services: An established industry tends to attract smaller firms that are trying to serve the particular industry's needs. A wide range of commercial and support services can be offered. Some examples include specialist banking, insurance, marketing, waste disposal, maintenance, cleaning, components and distribution services.

Co-operation: Firms in the same industry are more likely to co-operate if they are concentrated in the same region. They might work together to fund a research and development centre for the industry. An industry journal (i.e. magazine) might be published so that information can be shared.

Disintegration: Disintegration occurs when production is broken up so that more specialisation can take place. When an industry is concentrated in an area, firms might specialise in the production of one component. Then, they would transport it to a main assembly plant (i.e. the place where it is put together). For example, in US film production, many different operations were often done by the same organisation based in Hollywood. However, there are now far more specialist businesses, such as editing, casting, make-up, costume design, special effects, filming, props manufacturing, marketing and distribution.

EXAM HINT

You need to remember that economies of scale are enjoyed in the long term. This means that average costs will fall when a business increases the scale of its operations. This involves changing fixed factors of production, such as machinery or premises (the building or land a business uses). This could be important when evaluating. If you consider, or compare, both short-term and long-term factors, it is regarded as an evaluative skill.

INCREASED MARKET POWER

As businesses get bigger they become more dominant (i.e. more powerful). As a result, rivals are left with a smaller market share and some weaker businesses may be forced to close down. If a business is large enough, it may be able to dominate two particular stakeholders.

- **Customers:** A dominant business may be able to charge higher prices if competition in the market is limited. Customers are forced to pay higher prices when there is less choice. Also, there is less need to develop new products if there is a lack of competition in the market. This means that a dominant firm will not have to meet the costs of expensive and risky innovation (i.e. new ideas). As a result, product choice may remain limited for consumers.

- **Suppliers:** Sometimes a business can dominate its suppliers. For example, it may be able to force the costs of materials and commercial services down if it buys large quantities from smaller suppliers. Dominant businesses will be in a good position if their suppliers rely upon them for their custom. For example, a small supplier is vulnerable if it sells all of its output to just one large business. It may have to accept the prices that the customer is prepared to pay.

However, a business might attract the attention of the authorities if it becomes too dominant. If the dominant business appears to be exploiting consumers or suppliers, there may be an investigation into the industry. In recent years, energy companies in some countries have been criticised for charging high prices. Some supermarkets have also been accused of 'bullying suppliers' (i.e. using their power to hurt the suppliers). For example, suppliers might be threatened with the loss of an order if prices are not reduced. Alternatively, they might be made to wait an unreasonable amount of time for payment.

ACTIVITY 1   SKILLS   CRITICAL THINKING, ANALYSIS
CASE STUDY: MILK PRODUCTION

There is some evidence in the UK dairy industry that larger herds result in higher yields (i.e. higher levels of production) and lower costs. For example, Table 1 shows that when the herd size rises from 85 cows to 339 cows, the average milk yield per cow rises from 6247 litres per year to 8135 litres per year. Figure 3 shows the impact of larger herds on revenue, costs and profit margins.

Summary of milk production quartiles	Quartile 1 (small)	Quartile 2 (small/ medium)	Quartile 3 (medium/ large)	Quartile 4 (large)
Average annual milk production (litres)	531 000	1 033 000	1 535 000	2 758 000
Herd size (number of cows)	85	157	205	339
Average yield (1/cow/ year)	6247	6580	7488	8135

▲ Table 1 The impact of larger herds on milk production and yields

Figure 3 shows that the costs in ppl (pence per litre) fall as herd size gets bigger. There are at least two reasons for this. A farmer with a larger herd will need larger quantities of inputs – cattle feed, for example. Suppliers might offer farmers discounts for buying larger amounts. It is also possible that farmers can make better use of technology with larger herds. For example, automatic milking units are likely to become cost-effective with larger herds.

There is evidence of different farms achieving positive margins whatever their herd size. However, it is worth noting that the lowest herd margins are all among the smaller herds.

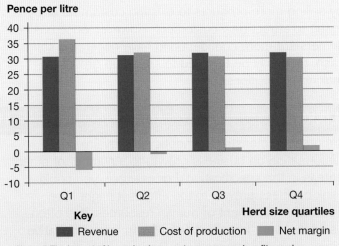

Pence per litre

Key
■ Revenue   ■ Cost of production   ■ Net margin

Herd size quartiles

▲ Figure 3 The impact of larger herds on costs, revenue and profit margins

1 Explain what is meant by economies of scale in the case of the UK dairy industry?
2 Give one example of an internal economy that might account for lower unit costs when larger herds are used in the UK dairy industry.

INCREASED MARKET SHARE AND BRAND RECOGNITION

As businesses grow, their share of the market is also likely to grow. This will give them more power and they may be able to benefit from the advantages previously outlined. However, they will also benefit from having a greater brand recognition (i.e. people remembering and identifying with the brand). As a business gets a larger and larger share of the market, customers become more aware of the brand name because they see the brand advertised and offered for sale in more locations. As the brand becomes stronger, a business may be able to:

- charge higher prices
- make the product distinct from those of rivals
- create customer loyalty
- achieve greater product recognition
- develop an image
- launch new products more easily.

A business with a larger market share is also more likely to attract media attention, which helps to promote the company.

INCREASED PROFITABILITY

One of the main objectives of growth is to make more profit. Larger businesses tend to make bigger profits than smaller ones. As profits grow, returns to the owners will also grow. For example, Arca Continental is a business that manufactures bottles and distributes Coca-Cola® products throughout Mexico, Central America and the USA. It is the second largest Coca-Cola distributor in South America and the third largest in the world. It has a market value of $11.3 billion.

Between 2015 and 2016, its revenues grew 17.8 per cent from MXN1477.7 million to MXN1740.6 million. The benefit to shareholders of this growth was significant. Arca increased its dividend payment to shareholders from MXN1.75 to MXN1.85 per share. Additionally, when a company grows, shareholders are likely to see the price of their shares rise. The Arca share price rose from MXN92 to about MXN105 over the calendar year.

If a business grows and increases its profitability, it will have more profit for investment and innovation. This will allow the business to develop and launch new products and make acquisitions. The business is likely to grow even further if these investments are successful.

ACTIVITY 2

CASE STUDY: RTR LTD

Croatia-based RTR Ltd was set up as a satellite TV company in 1991. Originally most famous for its sports channels, it has since branched out into a range of different services, including broadband and telephony.

In 2012 RTR's revenue was €5200 million. By 2017 it had grown to €7691 million.

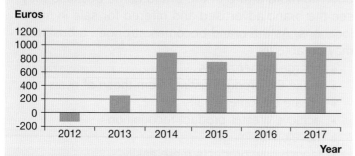

▲ Figure 4 RTR profit after tax 2012–17

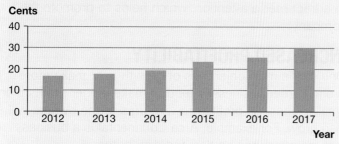

▲ Figure 5 RTR dividends per share 2012–17

1 Calculate the percentage increase in dividend payments between 2012 and 2017.
2 Explain one benefit to RTR shareholders of the growth of RTR.

THE DISTINCTION BETWEEN INORGANIC AND ORGANIC GROWTH

Businesses can choose from two key growth strategies. One strategy is to use mergers and takeovers (see Chapter 7). This type of growth is called external growth or inorganic growth. It involves businesses joining together so that, in theory, they could double in size overnight. For example, in 2016 the Barcelona-based start-up Doctoralia®, an online booking platform for healthcare appointments, merged with the Warsaw-based company DocPlanner. Doctoralia has around 9 million monthly users, while DocPlanner has over 8 million. This means that the new organisation will virtually double in size.

In contrast, internal growth or **organic growth** occurs when a business grows naturally by selling more of its output using its own resources. For example, many top European football clubs have experienced some solid organic growth over the last 10 years or more. German club Bayern Munich has seen its revenues grow from around €166 million in 2003–04 to over €640 million in 2015–16. Clubs have grown by increasing the capacity of their stadiums and attracting new sources of revenue such as income from TV rights, hospitality and other commercial activities.

Speed is one of the key differences between the two growth strategies. Inorganic growth is much faster. As the example above shows, it is possible to instantly double in size as a result of joining with another business. Organic growth is normally much slower. It takes time to develop and grow a business using its own resources.

Another difference is the potential risk involved in the two different strategies. It could be argued that organic growth is a safer strategy because owners expand their businesses by developing their current expertise. They may be growing by 'doing more of the same'. There is not much risk involved in this strategy. In contrast, growing through mergers or acquisitions has risk attached. This is because the process of integrating when two organisations are brought together can create problems. For example, there could be differences between the working cultures that might result in conflict, delays and instability.

In the early stages of business development, after the initial launch and transition period, most owners pursue organic growth strategies. Entrepreneurs are likely to be cautious and grow their businesses gradually, perhaps by selling more products to existing customers or by trying to attract new customers. However, once business owners are more confident and have generated some cash, they may be tempted to speed up growth by making acquisitions.

LINKS

You can demonstrate synoptic skills by linking information on business growth to a number of other areas in the specification. For example, you could link business growth to the effects it might have on the environment or human resources. It is often said that very large businesses can have a negative impact on the environment. Business growth also has important links to the development of multinational companies (this book, Chapter 35), Corporate strategies (Chapter 2), Decision making (Chapter 11), International business ethics (Chapter 36), Human resources (Chapter 19), Key factors change (Chapter 20), International trade and business growth (Chapter 23), Problems arising from growth (Chapter 8) and Business objectives (Student Book, Chapter 21).

CHECKPOINT

1 What is the difference between internal and external economies of scale?

2 What is meant by technical economies of scale?

3 How might a supermarket chain benefit from purchasing economies?

4 What is meant by risk-bearing economies?

5 Give two examples of external economies of scale.

6 What is meant by the minimum efficient scale of plant?

7 How can a business experience market power over its suppliers?

8 Give an example of inorganic growth.

SUBJECT VOCABULARY

diseconomies of scale rising long-run average costs as a business expands beyond its minimum efficient scale

economies of scale the reductions in average costs experienced by a business as output increases

external economies of scale the cost reductions available to all businesses as the industry grows

indivisibility the physical inability, or economic inappropriateness, of running a machine or some other piece of equipment at below its optimal operational capacity

inorganic growth a business growth strategy that involves two (or more) businesses joining together to form one much larger one

internal economies of scale the cost reductions experienced by a single business as it grows

minimum efficient scale the output that minimises long-run average costs

organic growth a business growth strategy that involves a business growing gradually using its own resources

sole trader or sole proprietor a business organisation which has a single owner

venture capitalist provider of funds for small- or medium-sized companies that may be considered too risky for other investors

EXAM PRACTICE

CASE STUDY: CATA COMPANY

Cata Company is a rapidly growing medium-sized technology company based in Florianópolis (Santa Catarina), Brazil. Between 2014 and 2016 the company grew by 4500 per cent, making it the fastest growing small- to medium-sized enterprise in Brazil (according to *Deloitte and Exame* magazine). The company was set up in 2012 when a young Brazilian entrepreneur, Victor Levy, put together a group of talented individuals. They developed electronic cash machines and safes to help transport and circulate (i.e. move around) cash in the country.

In 2013, Cata Company attracted funding from Fundo SC, **venture capitalists** with a particular interest in innovative start-up companies. Some of the money was used to get a patent (i.e. the right to be the only company able to make a certain product) on a new coin machine, which could handle large quantities of coins at the same time. The company's first product, CataCoin®, was developed to provide a client-facing, interactive coin machine that would recirculate coins in Brazil and direct them to locations needed by retailers.

By recirculating coins, Cata Company reduces the need for additional coin production. As a result, this reduces the demand for valuable minerals and helps to prevent damage to the environment caused by mining. The company has received some very positive feedback from environmental groups commenting on the impact of CataCoin machines. Also, retailers can show their adverts on a screen while the user is waiting for coins to be processed. This may attract customers, who then buy something from the store after changing coins.

In 2014, the business developed a control panel that can be used along with all of Cata Company's machines. Cata Company also secured an important partnership with Prosegur, a cash transit service with operations in 18 countries. This was important because it allowed Cata Company to increase the scale of its manufacturing operations and experience some economies of scale.

More recently, Cata Company has introduced two more products. These are CataCash One and CataCash Mille. These are mini-safes designed for cash management.

Cata Company's latest product is a Shielded Vault System. This helps to remove the risk of huge losses resulting from bank and CIT (cash-in-transit) robberies.

Cata Company has also developed a branch in Florida, USA. It is committed to further growth and plans to export its machines to the USA, Peru, Australia and Spain. CataCash machines are being sold in the USA, Mexico, Argentina, Paraguay and Spain. The company also has a number of products being tested on the market. It is developing partnerships with other companies such as Protégé and Preserve.

Q

1 Explain one reason why some of Cata Company's growth may be regarded as inorganic. **(4 marks)**
2 Explain one internal economy of scale Cata Company might benefit from. **(4 marks)**
3 Discuss how Cata Company might be exploiting risk-bearing economies. **(8 marks)**
4 Assess the possible growth objectives of Cata Company. **(12 marks)**

6 ORGANIC GROWTH

UNIT 3
3.3.2

LEARNING OBJECTIVES

By the end of this chapter you should be able to understand:
- methods of growing organically
- the advantages and disadvantages of organic growth.

GETTING STARTED

Alacer Gold is a Canadian gold-mining company with a listing on the Toronto Stock Exchange. Its main source of revenue is from the Çöpler Gold Mine in Turkey near the capital, Ankara. Alacer Gold has an 80 per cent **stake** in the Çöpler Gold Mine. The remaining 20 per cent is owned by Turkish company, Lidya Mining.

Alacer Gold is currently pursuing an organic growth strategy (growing without mergers or takeovers). The Çöpler Gold Mine has been operating since 2010 and produced 168 163 ounces of gold during 2017. In 2018, Çöpler is also forecast to produce 70 000 to 90 000 ounces of oxide ore and 50 000 to 100 000 ounces of sulfide ore. The company's revenue grew from US$141 944 000 in 2016 to US$209 087 000 in 2017.

Alacer Gold hopes to build on this growth by extracting more gold from the Çöpler Gold Mine and developing other interests. Alacer Gold plans to become a sustainable (i.e. where a business is able to meet its needs without preventing future generations from meeting their needs) multi-mine producer in Turkey. It already has a number of exploration projects in the Çöpler region. For example, its exploration activities have already had promising results in the Çakmaktepe and Gediktepe projects.

What might be two advantages to Alacer Gold of growing without mergers and takeovers? What might be the disadvantages of this growth strategy?

METHODS OF GROWING ORGANICALLY

Organic growth usually involves a business growing by building on its strengths to increase sales. However, there are several different approaches to growing organically.

New customers: Perhaps the easiest approach is to rely on driving sales from existing activities. For example, a food processing company that supplies to local shops may gradually increase production to supply to more and more customers. The business can carry on growing organically (by building an extension or moving to larger premises if the factory reaches full capacity). It may be possible to find new customers by exploiting new distribution channels. For example, the food processor above may start selling to supermarkets. This approach to growth may need investment in marketing to increase the customer base.

New products: Some businesses grow by developing new products. They may be very innovative (i.e. good at introducing new ideas) and committed to research and development. For example, a business that designs software for computer games can grow by designing new games. Alternatively, a business might identify customers with slightly different needs. This could require adapting or modifying existing products (i.e. making changes to improve them) to meet these needs. A business might need to invest some of its profit into product development.

New markets: Some businesses grow organically by finding new markets for their products. For example, a hairdresser could open another salon in a different location. The assets, systems and working practices used in the original salon can be copied in another location. New premises (i.e. the building or land that a business uses) can be adapted and decorated in the style that has already been successful. Some businesses may look to overseas markets to grow. However, this approach carries more risk because markets abroad are unfamiliar. Growing by selling in new areas is sometimes called geographic expansion. For example, a number of European and US retailers have opened stores in China, such as Auchan® and Carrefour from France, and GAP® and Bebe® from the USA.

New business model: It is possible to grow organically by using a new business model. Developments in technology or social change may lead to this growth. For example, a retailer selling children's toys may start an online operation. This approach could see the business grow very quickly because the size of the potential market opened up could be considerable, even global.

Franchising: A business might set up a franchising operation to increase the speed of organic growth. This approach allows other entrepreneurs to trade under the name of the original business. The fast-food outlet SUBWAY® is an example of a business that has used this method to grow. Franchising is discussed in detail in Student Book 1, Chapter 26.

ADVANTAGES OF ORGANIC GROWTH

There are many benefits of organic growth. Entrepreneurs should know their business and grow their company by exploiting its own strengths and expertise. For example, they can move quickly by adapting to changes in the market. Entrepreneurs can experience the satisfaction of seeing their business develop and grow. They can also choose the pace of growth – at a rate that is comfortable for their own personal needs. Eventually, owners may choose to sell the business and cash in on their investment and hard work. Some specific advantages are outlined below.

- **Less risky.** Organic growth might be less risky than other growth strategies. Growth can be achieved by extending practices that are well known and understood. This can prevent errors because the culture, norms and practices of the business are already established and effective. Organic growth can also help to avoid the complications that might arise when integrating with another organisation.

- **Relatively cheaper.** Growing organically might be cheaper than using other methods. Organic growth can be financed from retained profit. This is likely to be the cheapest of all sources of finance. There will be an opportunity cost, but the financial cost can be zero. Businesses that grow inorganically often have to borrow money or raise fresh capital. This will add to the costs of growth. Organic growth also avoids the premium prices that can be paid when buying other businesses.

- **Keep control.** A business will keep more control when growing organically. Owners, or the senior management team, will have complete control of the growth process. This is because there are no outsiders with any controlling interest. For example, a retail chain is growing because they are opening a new store in a new location every six months. Therefore, the business will have a team of employees who are experienced at opening new stores. They can go in, recruit and train new staff. They can ensure that the store is run in the way that has proved

successful in the past, then move on to the next. This approach means that the business has full control and is much easier to organise. If growth were achieved by joining with another business, some control would be lost. This is because the other organisation will probably want to keep some control of its own.

- **Better protection.** The financial position of a business might be better protected with organic growth. Since growth is gradual, there is less strain on financial resources. As a result, cash flow is stronger and the business will keep more liquidity. Inorganic growth often requires huge outlays of money. For example, in 2018, US company Keurig Green Mountain Inc. bought Dr Pepper® Snapple Group Inc. for US$18.7 billion in cash. Such high expenditure can put financial pressure on the business.

- **Avoid diseconomies of scale.** A business that grows organically is less likely to experience diseconomies of scale. Sharp increases in unit costs are not likely to occur if growth is steady and measured. It may be easier for a business growing organically to see any possible difficulties resulting from scale increases. This will help to keep costs under control.

ACTIVITY 1   SKILLS   CRITICAL THINKING, REASONING

CASE STUDY: APPicon®

Rufus Storm owns a business called APPicon, which designs icons for apps. He set up APPicon after graduating from art school in 2014. He worked alone at home for two years, but after early successes he opened up an office in Melbourne, Australia. Since then he has taken on four staff. He has designed 25 000 icons that might be used for apps. However, now that the business is established, he is getting enquiries from app developers who want bespoke designs for their icons. This work is more profitable and is helping to increase revenue. In the future, Rufus wants to carry on growing the business organically. The success of the business is reflected by the sales data shown in Figure 1.

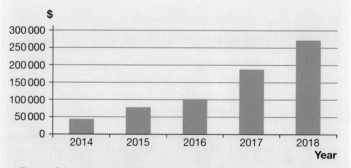

▲ Figure 1 Sales revenue for APPicon 2014–18 (AUS$)

1 How has APPicon achieved organic growth?
2 Suggest one way in which Rufus might continue to grow his business organically in the future.

DISADVANTAGES OF ORGANIC GROWTH

Although there are advantages of organic growth, there is the argument that it prevents a business from reaching its full potential. It may miss out on rewarding opportunities and get left behind in the market. Some specific disadvantages are outlined below.

- **Slow pace of growth.** The pace of organic growth may be too slow for some stakeholders. For example, shareholders in a plc may want the business to provide quicker returns on their investments than organic growth can deliver. Shareholders may sell their shares if they are unhappy with the pace of growth. As a result, the share price can fall. This could make the company at risk of a takeover.
- **Lack of access to resources.** Organic growth may prevent the business from using the resources owned by other businesses. As a result, it might miss out on some profitable developments. For example, a construction firm might want to develop expertise in energy-saving technology. This would help it to build more houses with solar panels. It could do this by gradually developing its own expertise. However, it might be better to buy a company that already does this, rather than trying to do it for themselves. Such companies will be specialists and can provide the knowledge and experience required by the housebuilder.

- **Unable to be competitive.** A business that grows slowly may be left behind in the market. The business may end up feeling small if competitors are growing through mergers and acquisitions. As a result, it may lose its ability to compete effectively. For example, it may not be able to match the advertising budgets of its larger rivals.
- **Unable to fully exploit economies of scale.** A business may be able to exploit economies of scale as it grows. However, if a business is growing organically it may take some time before such economies are fully exploited. This could mean that a business is having to operate with higher costs for longer periods of time. This could lower profit margins and make it less competitive. Also, some businesses, such as shipbuilding, require investment in large-scale production before trading can begin. Businesses that grow organically may be prevented from entering such industries.
- **May be inappropriate.** Organic growth may not be appropriate if a market is growing rapidly. For example, when mobile telephones were first introduced, the market expanded very quickly. Businesses making the best progress were those that were growing through mergers or acquisitions. The three firms now remaining in the UK market are all the result of multiple takeovers and mergers.

ACTIVITY 2   **SKILLS**   CRITICAL THINKING, ANALYSIS

CASE STUDY: KANTUR PALM OIL

Kantur is a medium-sized palm oil producer in Malaysia. The business has grown organically since it was set up in 2001. However, the shareholders have become unhappy because the growth rate has only averaged 3.4 per cent per annum since it was established. In 2018, groups of shareholders said they were dissatisfied at the Annual General Meeting (AGM). These shareholders wanted faster growth to justify their investment in the business. They were critical of the directors for following an organic growth strategy.

In recent years, it was also evident that Kantur was operating with higher costs than many of its rivals. It was argued by some shareholders that this was because the company was growing too slowly and not able to exploit economies of scale. By the end of the AGM in 2018, it was clear that if the directors did not increase the pace of growth, their positions on the board would be under threat.

1 Why are some shareholders unhappy with Kantur's organic growth strategy?
2 Why is Kantur unable to exploit economies of scale?

EXAM HINT

An exam question might ask you to 'evaluate' whether or not the advantages of organic growth outweigh (i.e. are greater than) the disadvantages. After analysing the advantages and disadvantages appropriate to the case, you will need to make a judgement. This means that you will have to say whether or not the advantages of organic growth outweigh the disadvantages. The information that you have to analyse may not be decisive, however, so you must still make a judgement. The important point is that you provide support for your judgement.

LINKS

Organic growth is an example of a growth strategy. The information in this chapter could be used when discussing issues in exam questions such as Business objectives (Student Book 1, Chapter 21), Corporate objectives (this book, Chapter 1), Theories of corporate strategy (Chapter 2), Growth (Chapter 5), Key factors in change (Chapter 20) and International trade and business growth (Chapter 23). For example, in a question on choosing an appropriate corporate strategy for a business, organic growth might be one of the options, or, in a question on key factors in change, a decision to grow organically might be a reason why changes are necessary. In a question on business objectives, organic growth might feature as an option.

CHECKPOINT

1 What is the difference between organic and inorganic growth?

2 Why are businesses likely to grow organically in their early stages of development?

3 Outline two methods of growing organically.

4 Why is organic growth likely to be slower than inorganic growth?

5 Why is organic growth less risky than inorganic growth?

6 Suggest two businesses in your locality that have grown organically.

7 How might shareholders in a plc feel about organic growth?

SUBJECT VOCABULARY

franchising a business model where a business owner (the franchisor) allows another person (the franchisee) to trade under their name
retained profit profit after tax that is 'ploughed back' into the business
stake a financial interest in a business which entitles the investor to part-ownership

EXAM PRACTICE

CASE STUDY: MINDTREE IT SOLUTIONS

SKILLS CRITICAL THINKING, PROBLEM SOLVING, INTERPRETATION, REASONING

MindTree is an IT solutions company based in Bengaluru, India. It was set up in 1999 and has grown very successfully. The company has interests in e-commerce, mobile applications, cloud computing, digital transformation and data analytics. MindTree employs 17 000 people, has around 350 active clients and 43 offices in over 17 countries. The provision of IT solutions involves:

- studying the client's current IT infrastructure
- evaluating the client's needs
- identifying the mix of hardware and software required to meet the client's objectives
- installing the recommended hardware and software.

Also, the 'solution' often includes the provision of staff training and ongoing service and support.

Some of MindTree's current high-profile clients include Toyota®, Kellogg's®, Honeywell®, the BBC and GlaxoSmithKline. One example of some work carried out by MindTree is for a large consumer packaged products company that distributes goods such as food and beverages. The client has an established distribution network but needs to add new distributors across regions such as Vietnam, Thailand, Cambodia and the Philippines. The client uses a SAP system (enterprise resource-planning software) to monitor and manage its network of distributors. Every time a new distributor is identified, the distributor details are entered into SAP. However, the process is manual and very dependent on the client. This can result in errors and delays that reduce revenue.

MindTree's solution to the problem is to automate the distributor creation process using Robotic Process Automation (RPA). (RPA is the application of technology that allows employees in a company to configure computer software or a 'robot'. This allows them to capture and interpret existing applications for processing a transaction, manipulating data, causing responses and communicating with other digital systems.) This helps to reduce the cost of adding new distributors to the network by 70 per cent. It improves the flow of information, improving efficiency and increasing revenues.

Although MindTree was only formed in 1999, it now generates huge revenues and has grown into one of the market leaders. Figure 2 shows MindTree's revenue growth between 2010 and 2017. In 2017, the company generated over INR52 000 million.. The profit before tax for that year was INR5549 million. In the past, a proportion of MindTree's growth has been inorganic. For example, in 2015 it made three significant acquisitions. It bought Discoverture Solutions LCC (USA), Bluefin Solutions Limited (UK) and Relational Solutions Inc. (USA) for $15 million, $42.3 million and $10 million, respectively. In 2016, MindTree bought another company, Magnet 360 (USA) for $50 million.

Acquisitions should help MindTree to offer a wider range of services to a larger number of clients. Examples include:

- **Discoverture** was bought to help MindTree tap into the $1.5 billion global P&C services market. It should help MindTree gain access to 15 high-profile clients and add over 300 experts across the USA, UK, Canada and India.
- **Bluefin** was bought because it had expertise in SAP software. MindTree also said that the acquisition will help boost its European presence and its competencies in a number of fields.
- **Magnet 360** was bought to help MindTree develop more business in the fast-growing cloud computing services area.

There are a number of areas where MindTree can grow organically, such as digital. MindTree has invested in digital and are very focused on the development of this product. The company claims to have delivered some innovative solutions for customers which nobody in their industry has ever done before. In March 2017, the growth rate of the digital market was twice that of MindTree.

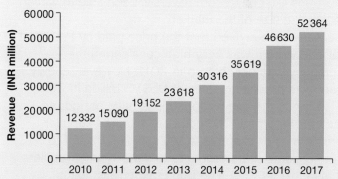

▲ Figure 2 MindTree's revenue, 2010–17 (INR million)

Based on Make Digital Real Annual Report 2014-15, https://www.mindtree.com/sites/default/files/2017-10/mindtree-annual-report-2014-2015.pdf, Mindtree

Q

1 Calculate MindTree's percentage growth rate between 2010 and 2017. You are advised to show your workings out. **(4 marks)**
2 Explain one way MindTree plans to grow in the near future. **(4 marks)**
3 Evaluate whether or not the advantages of organic growth will outweigh the disadvantages to MindTree in the future. **(20 marks)**

7 INORGANIC GROWTH

LEARNING OBJECTIVES

By the end of this chapter you should be able to understand:

■ mergers and takeovers: reasons for mergers and takeovers, distinction between mergers and takeovers, horizontal and vertical integration, conglomerates and financial risks and rewards

■ the advantages and disadvantages of inorganic growth.

GETTING STARTED

PetSmart is a USA-based retail chain selling pet food, pet products and services. This includes pet grooming, pet boarding and pet adoption services. It has more than 1500 stores in the USA, Canada and Puerto Rico. In 2017 it took over (acquired) online pet products retailer chewy.com. The **acquisition** was expected to cost about US$3.3 billion. The main motive for the purchase was to help speed up PetSmart's goal of selling products and services both in stores and online. Retailers are quickly realising that an effective e-commerce strategy is needed to survive in the market. Many store-based chains have increased their size and improved operations. However, e-commerce start-ups like chewy.com have still been able to win an increasing size of the market.

Many have argued that the price paid by PetSmart for chewy.com was very high considering the company was only set up in 2011. However, chewy.com was predicting sales of US$1.5 billion in 2017. Also, since the acquisition, things have not gone well for PetSmart. The company has had supplier problems. For example, a key supplier started to supply some of its products to mass-market retailers. It also lost its CEO. The bonds (specialist loans like debentures – see Chapter 25) used to finance the deal have fallen sharply in price. This has left investors with a large potential loss. PetSmart is also finding that integrating its operations with chewy.com is challenging. Some bond-holders think that chewy.com may have to be sold.

What do you think is meant by a takeover? Why did PetSmart want to buy chewy.com?

State two advantages of inorganic growth. What problems might a business encounter when taking over another?

REASONS FOR MERGERS AND TAKEOVERS

The distinction between organic and inorganic growth was made in Chapter 5. Inorganic growth means that businesses get bigger by joining together. For example, **mergers** and **takeovers** take place when firms join together and operate as one organisation. Why do some businesses act in this way?

● One of the main motives for integration (i.e. joining) is to exploit the **synergies** that might exist following a merger or takeover. This means that two businesses joined together form an organisation that is more powerful and efficient than the two companies operating on their own. Synergy occurs when 'the whole is greater than the sum of the parts'. Synergies may arise from economies of scale, the potential for asset stripping (i.e. removing assets; see below), the reduction of risk through diversification (i.e. providing a wider range of products) or the potential for gains by management.

● It is a quick and easy way to expand the business. For example, if a supermarket chain wanted to open 100 stores in China, it could find sites and build new premises. A quicker way could be to buy a company that already owns a chain of stores and change them.

- Buying another business is often cheaper than growing internally. A business may calculate that the cost of internal growth is $80 million. However, it might be possible to buy another company for $55 million on the stock market. The process of buying the company might inflate its price. But, it could still work out much cheaper.
- Some businesses have cash available which they want to use. Buying another business is one way of doing this. In 2018, in many countries around the world the returns on cash were only about 1 per cent. Many businesses would be keen to generate higher returns than this.
- Mergers take place for defensive reasons. One business might buy another to consolidate its position (i.e. make its position more powerful) in the market. Also, if a firm can increase its size through merging, it may avoid a takeover itself.
- Businesses respond to economic changes. For example, some businesses may have merged to deal with Brexit in the UK. A larger organisation may be able to cope with the uncertainties arising from Brexit.
- Merging with a business in a different country is one way in which a business can gain entry into foreign markets. It may also avoid restrictions that prevent it from locating in a country or avoid paying tariffs on goods sold in that country.
- The globalisation of markets has encouraged mergers between foreign businesses. This could allow a company to operate and sell worldwide, rather than in particular countries or regions.
- A business may want to gain economies of scale. Firms can often lower their costs by joining with another firm.
- Some firms are asset strippers. They buy a company, sell off profitable parts, close down unprofitable sections and perhaps integrate other activities into the existing business. Some private equity companies have been accused of asset stripping in recent years.
- Management may want to increase the size of the company. This is because the growth of the business is their main objective. It may also be because the financial rewards to managers is often linked to growth and the size of the company.

DISTINCTION BETWEEN MERGERS AND TAKEOVERS

Both mergers and takeovers are corporate strategies that aim to improve the performance of a business. However, there is a clear distinction between the two.

Merger: A merger is where two (or more) businesses join together and operate as one. Mergers are usually conducted with the agreement of both businesses. They are generally 'friendly'. The name of the new business is often formed out of the names of the two original businesses. For example, one of the biggest mergers recently was between Swiss-based cement producer Holcim Ltd and French cement company Lafarge SA, forming LafargeHolcim. The merger helped to cut costs and cope better with overcapacity (i.e. when an industry produces more than it is able to sell) and weak demand.

Takeover: A takeover, sometimes called an acquisition, occurs when one business buys another. Takeovers among public limited companies can occur because their shares are traded openly and anyone can buy them. One business can acquire another by buying 51 per cent of the shares. Some of these can be bought on the stock market and others might be bought directly from existing shareholders. When a takeover is complete, the company that has been 'bought' loses its identity and becomes part of the predator company (i.e. the company that 'hunted' the other). However, private limited companies cannot be taken over unless the majority shareholders 'invite' others to buy their shares.

In practice, a firm can take control of another company by buying less than 51 per cent of the shares. This may happen when share ownership is widely spread and little communication takes place between shareholders. In some cases, a predator can take control of a company by purchasing as little as 15 per cent of the total share issue. Once a company has bought 3 per cent of another company, it must make a declaration to the stock market. This is a legal requirement to ensure that the existing shareholders are aware of the situation.

Takeovers of public limited companies often result in a sudden increase in their share price. This is due to the volume of buying by the predator and also speculation by investors. Once it is known that a takeover is likely, investors quickly buy shares, anticipating a quick price rise. Sometimes more than one firm might attempt to take over a company. This can result in very sharp increases in the share price as the two buyers bid up the price. Some of the biggest takeovers in 2017 include:

- CVS Health Corp, a US drugstore chain, agreed to pay US$69 billion to buy Aetna, a health insurer
- Walt Disney bought film and television businesses from 21st Century Fox for US$52 billion.

Figure 1 shows the number and value of worldwide mergers and acquisitions from 1985 to 2018. For example, since 2002 the value of mergers and acquisitions rose sharply until 2007 and then fell just after. The financial crisis, followed by the global recession, was probably responsible for the rapid decline. Since then, the value of merger and takeover activity has risen again, although not consistently.

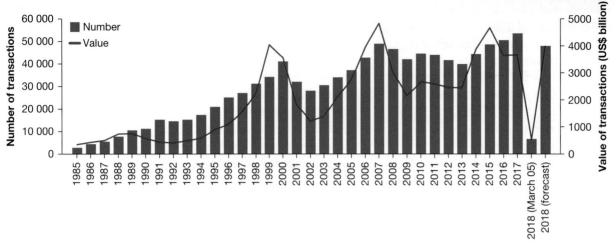

▲ Figure 1 The number and value of global mergers and takeovers 1985–2018
Based on M&A Statistics, https://imaa-institute.org/mergers-and-acquisitions-statistics/, Institute for Mergers, Acquisitions and Alliances

THINKING BIGGER

Takeovers can be hostile or friendly. A hostile takeover means that the victim tries to resist the bid. Resistance (i.e. fighting against it) is usually co-ordinated by the board of directors. They attempt to persuade the shareholders that their interests would be best protected if the company remains under the control of the existing board of directors. Shareholders then have to assess the advantages and disadvantages of a new 'owner'. In 2018, the US President blocked the proposed US$117 billion hostile takeover of Qualcomm Incorporated (a US multinational semiconductor and telecommunications equipment company) by Broadcom Limited (a large US semiconductor business). This was based on a recommendation from the Committee on Foreign Investment in the United States (CFIUS). The government claimed that the takeover could threaten the national security of the USA.

A takeover may be invited, however. A firm might be struggling because it has cash-flow problems, for example. It might want the current business activity to continue, but under the control of another, stronger company. The new company would inject some cash in exchange for control. Such a company is sometimes referred to as a 'white knight'.

ACTIVITY 1   SKILLS   CRITICAL THINKING, ANALYSIS, COMMUNICATION

CASE STUDY: BIDVEST

Bidvest is a services, trading and distribution group based in South Africa. It operates in a number of diverse business sectors. It sells consumer and industrial products, electrical products, financial services, fishing and materials handling services, freight management services, office and print solutions, outsourced hard and soft services, travel and aviation services and automotive retailing. Bidvest has used both organic and inorganic growth strategies to boost its revenues. Some of its acquisitions undertaken in recent years are listed in Table 1.

Year	Company	Business activity(s)
2011	Seafood Holdings	Fish producer & distributor and catering & hospitality
2011	Nowaco Baltics	Food and food products suppliers
2011	Rotolabel	Labelling solutions
2012	Deli Meals	Food services
2013	Home of Living	Household durables
2014	Mvelaserve	Catering, food and hygiene
2014	Brushware	Household brushes, paint brushes and rollers

2015	Compendiom	Financial (insurance)
2015	Bush Breaks	Tour operator (EG Safaris)
2016	Plumblink	Plumbing and bathroom specialist
2016	Glassock	Financial (pensions and life assurance)
2017	Brandcorp	Holding company
2017	Technilamp	Infrared and ultraviolet technology
2017	Eagle Lighting	Domestic and commercial lighting
2018	Noonan	Technical and lighting services

▲ Table 1 Bidvest – a selection of acquisitions made between 2011 and 2018

1 Explain what is meant by 'inorganic growth'.
2 Discuss the possible reasons for Bidvest's numerous acquisitions.

HORIZONTAL AND VERTICAL INTEGRATION

Integration is when businesses join together to form one. It can be classified in a number of ways, although not all mergers and acquisitions fit neatly into these categories.

Horizontal integration occurs when two firms that are in exactly the same line of business and the same stage of production join together. The merger between the two cement producers, Lafarge SA and Holcim Ltd, is an example of a horizontal merger. The benefits of mergers between such firms include:

- a common knowledge of the markets in which they operate
- less likelihood of failure than merging two different areas of business
- similar skills of employees
- less disruption.

Vertical integration occurs when firms in different stages of production join together. **Forward vertical integration** is where a business joins with another that is in the next stage of production. **Backward vertical integration** is where a business joins with another in the previous stage of production.

Consider a business that manufactures mountain bikes. If it bought a supplier of tyres for the bikes, this would be an example of backward vertical integration. The two firms are at different stages of production. The main motive for such a merger would be to guarantee

and control the supply of components and raw materials. Another motive would be to remove the profit margin that the supplier would demand. Forward vertical integration involves merging with a firm that is in the next stage of production. For example, the mountain bike manufacturer might merge with a retail outlet selling bikes. This removes the profit margin expected by the firm in the next stage of production. It also gives manufacturers guaranteed outlets for their output.

CONGLOMERATES

A **conglomerate** is a very large business organisation which owns a number of other businesses. Each business usually operates as a separate entity with its own board of directors. However, each business is still under the control of the owner (conglomerate). The group of businesses are usually acquired through mergers and takeovers. They normally have a wide range of business interests. An example of a conglomerate is Tata, which is based in Mumbai, India. Some of the major companies owned by Tata include Tata Steel, Tata Motors (including Jaguar Land Rover), Tata Consultancy Services, Tata Power, Tata Chemicals, Tata Global Beverages, Tata Coffee, Tata Teleservices, Titan, Tata Communications, and The Indian Hotels Company Limited (Taj Hotels). In 2017, the group's revenue was over $100 billion.

The main advantage of operating as a conglomerate is that these organisations have a very wide range of business interests. This spreads the risk of business enterprise. If one of the businesses is not doing very well, group revenues and profits can be supported by other businesses in the conglomerate. Another advantage is that they are very large and powerful. They can exploit economies of scale and often have influence in markets.

One of the disadvantages of a conglomerate is that diversification can result in difficulties. For example, the specialist skills built up in the original company or group of companies may not be relevant in the new acquisitions. This means the original management team may not fully appreciate the forces that drive success in some of its component parts. Over time, a conglomerate can become a confusing body that fails to maximise its full potential. For example, sometimes a conglomerate may be too slow to get rid of failing companies. This might be due to the fear of losing the required levels of diversification.

ACTIVITY 2   SKILLS   CRITICAL THINKING, ANALYSIS, REASONING

CASE STUDY: FIRST MAJESTIC SILVER AND PRIMERO MINING

First Majestic Silver is a Canadian mining company which operates a number of silver mines in Mexico. In recent years, the company has made several acquisitions, buying up silver mines in Mexico. Majestic is growing quite rapidly and will seek to acquire other similar assets in the future.

In 2018, it announced plans to buy another mining company, Primero Mining, in a deal worth $320 million. Primero owns and operates the San Dimas silver and gold mine in Durango, Mexico. This is a premier low-cost asset with more than 100 years of mine production history. The takeover was friendly, and the shareholders of both companies will benefit. For example, Majestic will get a new mine that builds on the company's strengths and expertise (i.e. specialist knowledge) in Mexico and underground mining. The takeover gives Majestic a well-established mine with low-cost operations which complement (i.e. work well with) First Majestic's existing operations. The new mine will help

to increase output, the value of net assets, cash flow and access to valuable resources. These should bring positive financial benefits to Majestic's shareholders.

Primero's shareholders will also benefit. The deal provides a significant and immediate up-front premium to Primero shareholders. They will be given shares in Majestic that will be 200 per cent more valuable than their current shares in Primero. Figure 2 shows how the share price of Primero has fallen sharply in recent years. These Majestic shares give holders a stake in a well-performing company (Majestic) with a strong balance sheet and diversified portfolio involving seven operating mines with strong growth potential. Primero shareholders will also benefit from Majestic's superior financial strength and ability to support a number of development projects and growth of silver production.

▲ Figure 2 Primero Mining share price 2015–18 (cents)

1 Explain what is meant by 'horizontal integration'. Use the example in this case to support your answer.
2 How might First Majestic Silver benefit from this takeover?
3 Explain how Primero shareholders will benefit from being taken over by First Majestic Silver.

FINANCIAL RISKS AND REWARDS

Financial rewards: The main reason why firms join together is to improve the financial strength of a business and make more money. A number of specific financial rewards are identified below.

- **Stakeholder benefits.** Shareholders in the 'target' company often get an immediate premium when taken over. This is because the share price often rises sharply during the process of a bid. For example, in Activity 2, Primero shareholders received a 200 per cent premium on the share price following the takeover by First Majestic Silver. If an acquisition is successful shareholders

in the 'predator' company (the company making the acquisition) will also benefit. However, their benefits may be long term. It may take a while for the integration process to be completed and there may be a delay in the improvement of financial performance. But if all goes well, shareholders should get higher dividends in the future and the share price should rise. In the long term, job security might also improve as the business becomes stronger due to the merger or takeover. It is also likely that the remuneration packages of some employees (i.e. the money paid to them), particularly senior management, will be better.

- **Stronger balance sheet.** A takeover or merger results in a larger single organisation. As a result, the strength of the balance sheet improves. The company will have more assets which are also likely to be more diverse. It is possible that the cash flow of the company will also improve since greater revenues will be generated by the larger organisation.

- **Lower costs.** One of the main motives for mergers and takeovers is to lower costs. Following acquisitions, corporations will be larger. As a result they will be able to exploit economies of scale and lower their costs.

- **Lower taxes.** It is possible for a company to lower its tax liabilities following a takeover. This is likely to occur if a business acquires another which is located in a 'low-tax' country. Tax liabilities can be reduced by registering all the activities of the business in the country where tax rates are lower.

Risks: Mergers and takeovers are common corporate strategies. They allow businesses to grow quickly and may create financial rewards for a range of stakeholders. However, they can sometimes go wrong and may have a negative long-term financial impact on a business. Some of the key financial risks are outlined below.

- **Integration costs.** After a merger or takeover has been agreed, the next step is to physically integrate the two organisations. This can be a very complex, expensive and time-consuming process, the effects of which may be felt for many years. Some of the costs incurred result from the organisational and personnel changes, severance pay for dismissed workers (i.e. the money paid to workers who are forced to leave), technical changes, systems changes, training and many others. It is not uncommon for businesses to underestimate these costs and encounter problems when carrying out the consolidation process. For example, merging two different cultures can be particularly problematic.

- **Overpayment.** There is some evidence to suggest that businesses often pay too much when making an acquisition. Numerous studies over the years reckon that the failure rate of mergers and acquisitions are somewhere between 70 per cent and 90 per cent. One of the main reasons for this is overpayment. This may be because the financial benefits are overestimated, or the costs of acquisition are underestimated, or both. Therefore, the price that the acquirer is willing to pay is inflated. There are many examples of overpayment. For example, Yahoo!® felt that it paid too much ($1 billion) for social network site Tumblr. Yahoo! said that assessing the value of a fast-growing new business which has only a small amount of revenue can be

difficult. Tumblr's assets were $353 million, and its liabilities were $114 million, according to Yahoo!.

- **Bidding wars.** In some cases, it is possible that one business attracts more than one potential buyer. If this happens the price of the acquisition will start to rise, as it would do in an auction. This makes the takeover more expensive. One example of this was the takeover of the American food company Hillshire Brands Co. by Tyson Foods Inc. Previously another company, poultry producer Pilgrim's Pride, had made an offer of $6.4 billion for Hillshire. However, within 48 hours, Tyson offered $6.8 billion. Pilgrim then raised its bid to $7.7 billion, but this was outstripped by Tyson's further bid of $8.55 billion, which was finally accepted by Hillshire. This case shows how the cost of a takeover can escalate when more than one business is interested in a target. The overall price rose from $6.4 billion to $8.55 billion, an increase of 33.6 per cent.

THE ADVANTAGES OF INORGANIC GROWTH

Some companies may be under pressure to grow quickly. Shareholders often favour quick growth because it usually stimulates a rise in the share price. Inorganic growth can deliver rapid growth but there are other specific benefits which are outlined below.

- **Speedy growth.** Businesses can grow far more quickly through mergers and takeovers than growing organically. This means that the benefits of growth, such as larger market share, lower costs resulting from economies of scale, more market power and higher profitability, can be enjoyed more immediately. This might benefit a range of stakeholders.

- **Strategic benefits.** Acquisitions and mergers can help businesses to improve their strategic position. Firms often join together because their activities may complement each other. For example, if two companies join together, collectively they may have a more balanced and diverse global product portfolio. A business can fill gaps in its product portfolio very quickly by making acquisitions. Inorganic growth often means that strengths in one company can compensate for relative weaknesses in the other.

- **Economies of scale.** An important advantage of inorganic growth is that a company may benefit from economies of scale almost overnight. For example, when two companies join, the new organisation will only need one head office. Therefore, one can be closed down, reducing administration costs significantly. Sometimes, after an acquisition, the size of a business can double. This provides scope for making cost savings in the form of bulk buying, increased specialisation of resources and raising capital.

- **Eliminate competition.** Inorganic growth can help to reduce competition in the market. Clearly, if a company takes over a rival, there will be fewer operators in the market. If the process of acquisitions continues in the same market, competition will decrease. This may lead to one firm (or just a few firms) dominating the market, which might allow the remaining companies to raise prices, restricting consumer choice.

THE DISADVANTAGES OF INORGANIC GROWTH

Businesses that use inorganic growth strategies are usually trying to grow rapidly. Unfortunately, there is risk associated with this and some mergers and takeovers actually fail. If this is the case, failure is probably because the outcomes did not match expectations.

However, occasionally failures can be quite spectacular. For example, Australian conglomerate Wesfarmers bought the UK DIY chain store Homebase® for £340 million in 2016. However, in 2018 Wesfarmers admitted that the takeover had gone badly. Wesfarmers said the 250-store UK business was expected to make an underlying loss of £97 million in the half-year after a £54 million loss in the year to June 2017. As a result, Wesfarmers is taking a £584 million write down on the business, most of which relates to the value of the Homebase brand. A spokesperson for Wesfarmers said the problems were 'through our own doing', as the company had ditched popular lines and removed concessions such as Laura Ashley®, Habitat® and Argos®. Companies that pursue growth through mergers and takeovers have to be cautious. In some cases, if growth is too rapid, serious problems may occur. Some examples are outlined below.

- **Regulatory intervention.** Mergers and takeovers in most countries can attract the attention of market **regulators** (i.e. people or organisations that make sure an industry is being run fairly). If they think that a merger or takeover acts against the interests of the consumer, they have the power to order an investigation. This takes time and may cause delays. After the investigation, the regulator often has the power to recommend that the merger be blocked. Alternatively, it may allow a merger or takeover to go ahead, but with certain conditions. Delays in proceedings and undertakings, such as the sale of assets, take time and cost money.

- **Drain on resources.** Mergers and takeovers can cost a lot of money. For example, in 2017, Aerospace supplier United Technologies Corp paid $30 billion for avionics and interiors maker Rockwell Collins Inc. This is clearly a very large amount of money and companies that spend such sums on mergers and takeovers have to be very well resourced. If a company grows too rapidly by going on an aggressive acquisition trail, it may stretch financial resources and damage other aspects of the business.

- **Culture clash.** When businesses merge, the integration process can be challenging because lots of changes have to be made. One of the main difficulties is merging two different cultures. It can be very difficult to impose a new culture on a business and there may be resistance (e.g. disagreements). For example, a business that prizes flexible working practices and quality of life, may lose important members of staff after merging with a firm where employees are expected to be in the office at all times. If changes are forced through too quickly, without proper discussion for example, this resistance is likely to be stronger. Such problems are likely to be more intense if growth is too rapid and firms are combining two contrasting cultures too quickly.

- **The alienation of customers.** Companies that are growing too fast might lose touch with their customers. Too much attention and resources get focused on the process of growth. As a consequence, the needs of customers can be overlooked. For example, after a takeover or merger the name of a business may change; some consumers may be confused, wondering what the new brand is and what values might be attached to it. Ultimately, this could damage the image of the company and result in the loss of customers.

- **Loss of managerial control.** If growth is too rapid the company might get too big too fast. This can result in a loss of control by the senior executives. A bigger organisation means that additional layers of management are required. This means that communication channels take longer to reach the intended recipient and might impact negatively on the chain of command. As a result, costs may start to rise as diseconomies of scale set in (see Chapter 8).

LINKS

Many businesses pursue growth through mergers and takeovers. To demonstrate your synoptic skills, you could link answers on this topic to a range of other areas covered by the specification. For example, when discussing multinational businesses you might add to your discussion the role played by mergers and takeovers in becoming a multinational. You may link this chapter with others in the book such as Marketing strategy (Student Book, 1 Chapter 9), Business failure (Student Book 1, Chapter 36), Production (Student Book 1, Chapter 37), Legislation (Student Book 1, Chapter 42), Corporate objectives (this book, Chapter 1), Theories of corporate strategy (Chapter 2), Growth (Chapter 5), International business ethics (Chapter 36) and Reasons for global mergers or joint ventures (Chapter 30).

SUBJECT VOCABULARY

acquisition the purchase of one company by another
backward vertical integration joining with a business in the previous stage of production
conglomerate a very large single business organisation made up of many different businesses producing unrelated products
forward vertical integration joining with a business in the next stage of production
globalisation (of a market) where markets become so large that products could be sold anywhere in the world
horizontal integration the joining of businesses that are in exactly the same line of business
integration the joining together of two businesses as a result of a merger or takeover
merger occurs when two (or more) businesses join together and operate as one
regulatory intervention control by the relevant authorities such as the Competition Commission
synergy the combining of two or more activities or businesses which creates a better outcome than the sum of the individual parts
takeover the process of one business buying another
vertical integration the joining of two businesses at different stages of production

CHECKPOINT

1 Give three reasons why two businesses might choose to join together.

2 Give two examples of horizontal integration.

3 Give an example of forward vertical integration in the car industry.

4 Give an example of backward vertical integration in the airline industry.

5 Briefly explain how an acquisition is carried out.

6 Give an example of a problem that a business might encounter when integrating two organisations.

7 State one financial reward of a merger or takeover.

8 Why might job losses result from a takeover or merger?

9 Describe one financial risk of a merger or takeover.

10 Outline two disadvantages of inorganic growth.

EXAM PRACTICE

CASE STUDY: LINDE® AND PRAXAIR® MERGER

SKILLS ▷ CRITICAL THINKING, ANALYSIS, INTERPRETATION, REASONING

In 2017, it was announced that German company Linde and USA-based Praxair would merge to form one company. It was felt that together the company could become a world-class leader in the industrial gas industry. The merged company will generate extra value for shareholders through lower costs and the exploitation of synergies. After three years it is expected that about $1.2 billion would be created for shareholders. The new company will be called Linde because it is a globally recognised and respected brand. Linde will be governed by a 12-member board of directors with equal representation from Linde and Praxair. Linde's Wolfgang Reitzle will become chairman of the new holding company's board and Praxair's chairman and CEO, Steve Angel, will become CEO of the new group and a board member.

From a financial perspective, the merged group would enjoy three key benefits:

- a $1.2 billion increase in shareholder value resulting from lower costs and the exploitation of synergies
- a stronger balance sheet and improved cash flow, providing financial flexibility for future investments
- a combined revenue of $29 billion and market value of $73 billion.

Strategically, the new group would benefit from the following.

- The unique strengths of the two companies will complement each other. Linde's engineering and technology expertise and Praxair's operational excellence will help propel the group into a world leader in the industrial gas market. These strengths are summarised in Table 2.
- The combined group will have a more balanced and diverse global product portfolio.
- Exposure to the long-term growth trends in healthcare, emerging markets, digitalisation and clean energy will be improved.

Although the shareholders of both companies were in favour of the merger, the deal was delayed while an investigation took place. The European Competition Commission said that an in-depth investigation would take place because it felt that the merger threatened the level of competition in the supply of some crucial gases. According to Competition Commissioner Margrethe Vestager, gases like oxygen and helium are crucial inputs for a wide variety of important day-to-day products. She said the commission would assess whether the proposed merger would lead to higher prices and/or less choice in the EU. It was stated that the investigation would be completed by July 2018. In an effort to win favour with the regulators, Linde and Praxair started to sell off assets. The exact scale of the sell-off is still under negotiation. However, both companies have agreed that if they have to sell businesses worth more than $3.7 billion in sales or $1.1 billion in earnings before interest, taxes and depreciation, either party can withdraw from (i.e. decide that they will no longer take part in) the deal without penalty.

	Linde	Praxair
Core expertise	Technology & engineering	Excellent operations
Product lines	HYcO and large ASUs*	Standardises ASUs and non-cryo*
End-markets	Chemicals, energy and healthcare	Petrochemicals and metals
Areas of business	Europe, Africa, Middle East and Oceania	The American continents

*HycO, ASU and Cryo are the names of chemical products

▲ Table 2 The complementary strengths of Linde and Praxair

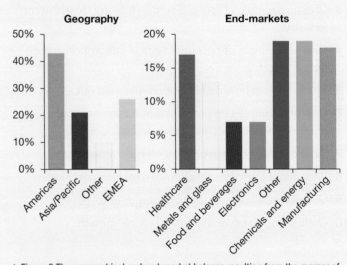

▲ Figure 3 The geographical and end-market balance resulting from the merger of Linde and Praxair

1 Explain one difference between the Linde and Praxair merger and a takeover. **(4 marks)**
2 Explain one financial reward that might arise from the proposed merger between Linde and Praxair. **(4 marks)**
3 Discuss the role played by the Competition Commission in the proposed merger between Linde and Praxair. **(8 marks)**
4 Evaluate whether or not the advantages of the proposed merger between Linde and Praxair outweigh the disadvantages. **(20 marks)**

8 PROBLEMS ARISING FROM GROWTH

LEARNING OBJECTIVES

By the end of this chapter you should be able to understand:
- diseconomies of scale
- internal communication
- overtrading.

GETTING STARTED

The benefits of rapid growth are attractive. These might include lower average costs, greater revenue, higher long-term profits and market control. However, in a small minority of cases, firms might grow too big. If this happens, average costs can start to rise as operational inefficiencies may increase. For example, it has been argued that in the software industry, many large-scale software development projects are not cost-effective. It is also argued that it is better for smaller enterprises to develop software because small teams frequently outperform large teams.

The costs of developing software do not rise in proportion to the size of the project. For example, the size of computer programmes may be measured in lines of code (LOC). If the development of software experienced economies of scale, a 100 000-LOC program would cost less than 10 times that of a 10 000-LOC program. However, in software development, larger projects require a lot of co-ordination among larger groups of people. This results in the need for much more communication which takes time. As the size of a software development project increases, the number of communication lines among different people increases and more people are employed on the project. Therefore, as the size of a software development project increases, the amount of effort (and thus cost) required increases at a faster rate.

Large software development projects are quite likely to suffer from cancellation, running over deadlines and escalating (i.e. rising) costs. In the UK, the National Health Service (NHS) has experienced multiple problems when trying to introduce new computer systems. For example, in 2016, NHS24 (a health information and self-care service in Scotland) admitted that a new IT system to help deal with customer calls was a failure. The system crashed when it went live. It experienced a number of faults and after 10 days it was shut down. In a report by Audit Scotland, the new system, which ended up costing £117.4 million, had exceeded the original cost by 55 per cent.

A number of people now claim that in the development of software, working in small groups promotes clearer, meaningful communication and more productive relationships. This helps to produce better products, improve customer satisfaction, generate more revenue, lower costs and raise profitability.

Explain why costs are expected to rise when developing software projects on a large scale. In groups, try to identify some examples of business costs that might rise when a business gets too big.

DISECONOMIES OF SCALE

Diseconomies of scale may occur if a business expands the scale of its operations further than the minimum efficient scale. This is where long-run average costs rise as output rises. In Figure 1, when the business produces 6 million units the average cost is $10 per unit. This is the minimum efficient scale of operations and all economies of scale have been used up. From this point, higher levels of output result in rising long-run average costs. For example, if the business increases output to 7 million units, average costs rise to $11 per unit. If output is raised to the higher level of 9 million units then, average costs rise to $15 per unit.

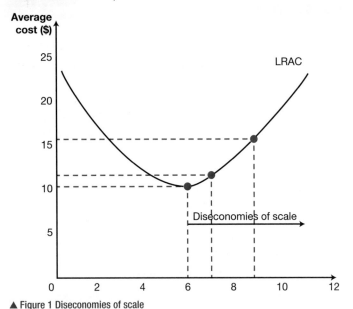

▲ Figure 1 Diseconomies of scale

SOURCES OF DISECONOMIES OF SCALE

There are a number of reasons why long-run average costs might rise as output is pushed above the minimum efficient scale. They fall into two groups – internal diseconomies of scale and external diseconomies of scale.

Internal diseconomies of scale: Internal diseconomies of scale are the rising costs caused by excessive growth in the business. Most internal diseconomies are caused by the problem of managing very large business organisations.

- **Poor communication.** Very large firms often suffer from poor communication. The flow of information between individual employees, departments, divisions or between head office and subsidiaries becomes more difficult to manage when a firm is very large. This is because the chain of command in such organisations may be long. There may be many layers of management in the hierarchical structure (i.e. one that is organised into levels of importance from top to bottom). Both internal and external communication might be affected. In a very large organisation it is possible to lose touch with customers and as a result a business may fail to identify changes in customer needs. Also, large businesses often employ automatic telephone answering services which keep customers waiting, direct them to inappropriate departments or fail to provide a swift solution. Many customers find these answering systems annoying. The problems associated with internal communication in a very large organisation are discussed in more detail below.

- **Control and co-ordination.** The control and co-ordination of large businesses is also demanding. Thousands of employees, large amounts of resources and many different operational locations all mean added responsibility and more supervision. In many cases, businesses have to employ a larger number of managers and supervisors to maintain adequate control. This can result in rising costs. There have been examples where it has been challenging for senior managers in big companies to be in complete control of such a huge quantity of resources spread out all over the world. For example, Volkswagen (VW)®, the giant car manufacturer which employs around 600 000 people worldwide, had problems in 2015. It was discovered that many cars had been fitted with a 'defeat device' to help it pass certain environmental tests. However, when the cars returned to the road, the emissions levels rose again. It is possible that VW had grown too big and unmanageable. It was claimed that the CEO of VW did not know about this activity. In such a large organisation this might be true.

- **Poor worker motivation.** Motivation may suffer as individual workers become a minor part of the total workforce. For example, in an organisation that employs thousands of people globally, each individual worker may feel unimportant. This may lead to an attitude of wanting to 'do the absolute minimum'. There may be higher levels of staff turnover, increased absence and poor time-keeping, which will raise labour costs. There may also be poor relations between management and the workforce in a very large organisation. For example, managers might lose touch with the needs of employees. As a result, conflicts may occur and trying to resolve them may cost money.

- **Technical diseconomies.** Plants, machinery and equipment will usually have an optimum (i.e. most efficient) capacity. If these resources are overused, they are likely to become inefficient. For example, in the agricultural industry, if a tractor is overworked the engine may run 'too hot', causing it to stop working properly. This might reduce its output or result in a breakdown which will cost money to repair. Another example is in the chemical industry, where construction problems often mean that two smaller plants are more cost-effective than one very large one. If a business employs one huge plant and a breakdown occurs production will stop. With two smaller plants, production can continue even if one breaks down.

- **Bureaucracy.** If a business becomes too bureaucratic, it means that too many resources are used in administration. Too much time may be spent filling in forms or writing reports. Also, decision making may be too slow and communication channels too long. If resources are wasted in administration, average costs will start to rise.

External diseconomies of scale: External diseconomies occur when an *industry* grows too big (rather than the individual firm). Rapid growth in an industry can result in the price of production factors rising sharply. This is because growing demand for them drives up the price. For example, the construction industry in Japan has grown as the country develops the infrastructure (e.g. transport networks, water and power supplies) needed to stage the 2020 Olympics. This has driven up the wages paid to construction workers, resulting in all businesses in the Japanese construction industry facing rising labour costs as output expands.

External diseconomies are perhaps most likely to occur when an industry grows in the same geographical location. The price of land, labour, services and materials might rise as firms compete with each other in the same area for a limited amount of resources. Also, congestion (i.e. too much traffic) in the area might lead to inefficiency, as delays are caused to deliveries and employees travelling to work.

INTERNAL COMMUNICATION

Internal communication is the exchange of messages and the flow of information inside a business; for example, between individual workers or between departments. If a business grows too big, there could be a problem with internal communication. This is because the number of layers in the management structure are also likely to grow. As a result, channels of communication get longer and the scope for error in sharing messages increases. Distortions to information may occur (i.e. changes that make the information no longer correct) as it is passed through the managerial hierarchy. At worst, this could lead to misunderstandings and arguments between workers and managers. Such arguments use up resources. Any cost resulting from a misunderstanding or argument will reduce productivity.

With the rapid development in information and communication technology (ICT), some of these problems may have been reduced. For example, any number of people can be copied into an email so that important messages can be shared instantly to thousands of people all over the world. The use of video conferencing might also help internal communication, where members of staff in different geographical locations can communicate face to face. However, it might also be argued that IT has

brought a whole new set of communication problems. For example, communications can be seriously affected when IT systems fail.

Sometimes resources might be wasted due to a lack of effective communication. One problem that might occur is the duplication of resources. This is where two or more identical activities or projects are being followed in the same organisation at the same time. For example, a division of a company in Germany may be writing a new complaints procedure policy. If another division, say the Indonesian division, is doing exactly the same, resources will be wasted. Better communication would ensure that only one new complaints procedure policy is produced.

If communication is poor between different departments, competition between them may have negative effects. As different departments compete for company resources they may adopt a 'silo mentality'. This is where individual departments become reluctant to share information with others in the organisation. This behaviour could lead to conflict between departments and even missed opportunities and higher costs.

In 2014, the large mining company, BHP Billiton, announced that it would sell off about US$20 billion in non-core assets. This was the company's response to its declining productivity. For many years before the announcement, the whole mining industry was increasing the scale of its operations. They thought that costs would continue to fall as individual mines grew.

However, Andrew Mackenzie, Chief Executive at BHP Billiton, said that he was worried about diseconomies of scale at the company. Also, according to a report by consultant Ernst and Young (EY), individual mining operations were sometimes getting too large to manage effectively. This led to lower productivity, 'The industry thought that bigger was always going to be better and it hasn't always worked out that way.' Paul Mitchell, global mining and metals advisory leader at EY, observed, 'It is bad enough [managing a mine] with 100 people on site – with 1000 it becomes much more complex.'

The rapid growth in the size of mines has resulted in several problems. The cost of resources, such as labour and materials, has risen sharply, increasing average costs. The EY report showed how running larger mines is very complex. It said that very high staff turnover in the industry meant that mines were being run by inexperienced managers. They did not have the resources needed to deal with the increased complexity. Executives in the industry said that communication across departments was poor.

1 Explain what is meant by diseconomies of scale and, using the example of BHP Billiton, explain why they occur.
2 Discuss one way in which BHP Billiton has dealt with the problem of diseconomies of scale.

OVERTRADING

If a business grows too fast, there is a danger that it might suffer from **overtrading**. This is more likely to affect young, rapidly growing businesses. Overtrading occurs when a business tries to fund a large volume of new business without sufficient resources. As a result, it runs out of cash and, at worst, it can collapse.

Overtrading is most likely to occur if a business:

- does not have enough capital. It is fairly common for a new business to be undercapitalised. This means that it has started trading with insufficient capital. It does not have enough cash to buy the resources needed to meet the growing orders
- offers too much trade credit to customers. It may be tempting for a new business to allow its customers 90 or 120 days' trade credit. However, this means that the business has to wait that length of time, or more, to be paid. During this time it will be short of cash to buy the resources needed to meet new orders
- is operating with small profit margins. In order to make an impact in the market, a new business may offer its products at lower prices. However, with lower prices (and therefore lower profit margins), it may not generate enough profit to fund the growing volume of business.

Whatever the cause, if a business is overtrading it can run out of cash and this threatens its survival. Therefore, growth has to be managed carefully.

CASE STUDY: CAIRO SA (CAIRO STUDENT ACCOMMODATION)

In 2014, Egyptian entrepreneur Tarek Salah took a risk and bought a three-bedroom apartment in Cairo near the main campus of Cairo University. He paid EGP280 000 and spent a further EGP30 000 refurbishing (i.e. improving and decorating) the property to accommodate three university students. The purchase was funded partly with his own capital. An EGP260 000 commercial mortgage was also needed at an interest rate of 10 per cent. He charged each student EGP2000 per month rent. The total rent for the year of EGP72 000 (3 students x 12 months x EGP2000) easily covered the annual interest payments of EGP26 000.

The project went well and in 2016 he bought two more three-bedroom apartments for EGP280 000 and EGP 300 000. He spent another EGP70 000 on refurbishment. The monthly rents charged on these apartments were EGP2400 per room. However, the total amount borrowed by Tarek's business, now called Cairo SA, rose to EGP750 000. The interest was still 10 per cent.

Inspired by the success of his property business, Tarek decided to go bigger. In 2017, he bought a small 10-bedroom apartment block for EGP800 000. However, interest rates had risen and the commercial rate on all properties rose to 14 per cent. Tarek wasn't too concerned because he was now able to charge EGP2500 each for all of his rooms. This was expected to generate rental income of EGP570 000 per annum (19 rooms x 12 months x EGP2500). The annual interest charges were EGP210 000 (EGP1.5 million x 14 per cent).

However, things started to go wrong in 2018. Interest rates in Egypt rose again and the commercial rate he was required to pay on his mortgages rose to 20 per cent. There was another problem – Tarek had underestimated the cost of refurbishment for the new apartment block. Due to one or two electrical issues, and the need to construct a proper fire escape, refurbishment costs escalated and Cairo SA was forced to go overdrawn. This caused a six-month delay. Then Tarek struggled to fill the rooms. The college year had ended at Cairo University and the supply of student accommodation was greater than demand. Seven of his rooms in the new block were empty and after three months the business collapsed. Tarek tried to sell one of the three-bedroomed apartments to raise cash, but it failed to reach the reserve price at an auction.

Tarek's sister said that he had been foolish to try and grow the business so quickly!

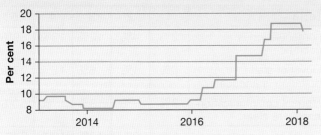

▲ Figure 2 Egypt interest rates 2013–18

1 Calculate the total annual interest payments on all of the properties owned by Cairo SA in 2018 (after the rate rise to 20 per cent).
2 Assess the extent to which the collapse of Cairo SA was the result of overtrading.

LINKS

One way in which you could demonstrate synoptic skills is by linking diseconomies of scale with answers on business performance. For example, when discussing business failure (see Student Book 1, Chapter 36), diseconomies of scale might be a convincing reason for escalating costs resulting in failure. Also, many large companies that might experience diseconomies of scale are multinational corporations (MNCs). In Unit 4, MNCs are discussed in detail in Chapters 35 and 37. For example, one of the impacts of growing MNCs in Chapter 35 is that they put pressure on local resources as their demand grows. This could drive up the rewards to these factors/resources.

EXAM PRACTICE

CASE STUDY: ELS ELECTRONICS

SKILLS CRITICAL THINKING, ANALYSIS, INTERPRETATION, REASONING

ELS Electronics is based in Seoul, South Korea. It is a very large multinational with huge factories in Seoul, Turkey and Chicago. The company manufactures electronic circuit boards for a number of high-profile manufacturers of consumer durables such as washing machines, computers, TVs and security systems. In 2018, the corporation saw a dip in profits. Revenues rose from US$93.1 billion to US$99.3 billion. However, profits before tax fell from US$14.31 billion to US$11.48 billion. Some of the senior management team are worried that profits will fall further next year if they cannot apply more control on costs.

In recent years, the company has grown quite quickly by making a number of strategic acquisitions around the world. However, some of the anticipated cost benefits have not materialised. Indeed, in some areas, costs have actually risen.

Some middle managers from Turkey have complained that the company has become too bureaucratic. They met with some directors in Seoul and explained that too much of their time was being spent writing reports, carrying out risk assessments and documenting operational procedures. The directors explained that the bureaucracy was necessary; it maintained control and ensured that key performance indicators were being watched. However, the managers said that staff turnover in important managerial positions was increasing quickly. They argued that it was raising recruitment and retention costs exponentially (i.e. at a faster rate).

In Chicago, it had been noted that internal communications in the organisation had become worse in recent years. In a staff survey carried out at the Chicago plant, it was found that the majority of staff thought that internal communications weren't clear. An extract from the survey is shown in Table 1.

In relation to internal communications, one of the human resources managers believed that important information was being hidden in the head office. She said that there needed to be more information sharing. For example, it was important to learn from efficient plants that had discovered good working practices.

Finally, in Seoul, due to an increase in demand for the products being manufactured, more components (i.e. parts) were needed from local suppliers. Unfortunately,

Criteria	1	2	3	4	5
The organisation is democratic.	2%	4%	12%	13%	69%
The level of staff consultation is adequate.	0%	1%	6%	16%	77%
The formal communication channels are clear.	3%	7%	13%	17%	60%
The company's goals are clear.	6%	9%	12%	19%	54%
The company's mission statement is clear.	3%	8%	12%	14%	63%
I have enough time to discuss work with colleagues.	0%	2%	7%	12%	79%

1 = Strongly agree, 5 = Strongly disagree

▲ Table 1 Extract from a staff survey carried out at the ELS Chicago plant

most local suppliers were operating at full capacity due to rising demand from a wide range of customers in the electronics industry. When ELS increased demand by 20 per cent, suppliers raised prices by 18 per cent. There was also an increase in labour costs for some skilled electrical engineers. Shortages of certain types of labour in the electronics industry were making wages higher.

1 Explain one difference between internal and external diseconomies of scale. **(4 marks)**
2 Discuss the internal communication problems being experienced at ELS Electronics. **(8 marks)**
3 Assess the disadvantages for ELS Electronics in experiencing diseconomies of scale. **(12 marks)**

DECISION-MAKING TECHNIQUES

Business owners, managers and other employees have to make lots of decisions while carrying out their duties. This section looks at a range of decision-making techniques that they might use. For example, some businesses use quantitative (i.e. measured with numbers) sales forecast techniques. Those addressed here include time-series analysis, moving averages, the use of scatter diagrams and extrapolation. The limitations of these methods are also explored. Some of the different methods of investment appraisal are also covered, such as payback, average rate of return and discounted cash flow. This section looks at how decision trees might be used to make decisions and how critical path analysis can be employed in project management to calculate the earliest start times, the latest finishing times and the total float. The limitations of these two methods are also discussed. Finally, the nature and purpose of contribution is explored. This includes the calculation and interpretation (i.e. the way that something is explained) of contribution and how the concept might be used to make decisions in business.

9 QUANTITATIVE SALES FORECASTING

LEARNING OBJECTIVES

By the end of this chapter you should be able to understand:
- calculation of time-series analysis: moving averages (three period/four quarter)
- interpretation of scatter graphs and line of best fit: extrapolation of past data to future
- limitations of quantitative sales forecasting techniques.

GETTING STARTED

Chapter 30 in Student Book 1 showed how sales forecasting is very important to business and that this process informs key decisions of business. In Unit 3 the aim is to explore and develop an understanding of some of the key statistical tools that are used to make this forecasting as accurate and robust as possible.

Marco Chung, in deciding on his sales forecasts for the coming months and years, has produced a range of **time-series** data that records previous sales and includes a trend analysis. A breakdown of sales, and predictions for coming months is shown in Table 1.

	2018 Q1	2018 Q2	2018 Q3	2018 Q4	Total 2018
Sales (thousands)	17	19	34	16	86

	2019 Q1	2019 Q2	2019 Q3	2019 Q4	Total 2019
Sales (thousands)	18	21	33	16	88

▲ Table 1 Sales breakdown and predictions by quarter

What might Marco's sales forecast be for the first three months of 2020? What is the trend of his sales? Is there any evidence that sales are increasing? To what extent is the business affected by seasonal factors?

CALCULATING TIME-SERIES ANALYSIS

It is often important for businesses to forecast future sales levels. Accurate sales forecasts will help businesses to make a number of key decisions, such as how much stock to hold, how many people to employ, how much cash is needed and what marketing strategies should be used. A business might use some quantitative sales forecasting methods to improve the accuracy of sales forecasts. These are statistical methods which use past sales data to predict future sales. One important quantitative sales forecasting method involves using **time-series analysis**.

The four main components that a business wants to identify in time-series analysis are:
- trend
- seasonal fluctuations
- cyclical fluctuations (i.e. fluctuations that are repeated lots of times in the same order)
- random fluctuations.

(Note: fluctuation refers to frequent changes from one extreme to another.) This chapter is concerned with identifying the trend.

IDENTIFYING THE TREND

An analysis of figures will tell a business whether there is an upward, downward or constant trend. Identifying the trend allows the business to predict what is likely to happen in future. The first step is to 'smooth out' (i.e. make the difficulties disappear from) the raw data. For example, look at the yearly sales of a garden furniture manufacturer over ten years (see Book 1, Chapter 30) shown in Table 2.

Year	2006	2007	2008	2009	2010
Sales ($ 000)	125	130	130	150	140

Year	2011	2012	2013	2014	2015
Sales ($ 000)	155	180	190	210	230

▲ Table 2 Yearly sales of a garden furniture manufacturer

It is possible to calculate a trend by using a **moving average**. The average can be taken for any period the business wants, such as a year, a month or a quarter. For now we will assume the garden furniture manufacturer uses a three-year average.

The average of sales in the first three years was:

$$= \frac{125 + 130 + 130}{3} = \frac{385}{3} = 128.3$$

To calculate the moving average, the first year's sales drop out and the next year's sales (2009) are added. The average for the next three years was:

$$= \frac{130 + 130 + 150}{3} = \frac{410}{3} = 136.7$$

If the business continues to do this, the results will be as shown in Table 3. Notice that the moving average is placed at the centre of the three years (i.e. the average for 2006–08 is plotted next to 2007).

Year	2006	2007	2008	2009	2010
Sales ($000)	125	130	130	150	140
		128.3	136.7	140	148.3

Year	2011	2012	2013	2014	2015
Sales ($000)	155	180	190	210	230
	158.3	175	193.3	210	

▲ Table 3 Three-year moving average for sales of a garden furniture manufacturer

What if the firm had used a four-year period instead of three years? No one year is the centre point, and simply placing the figure in between two years may result in misleading predictions in future. The solution is to use **centring**. This uses a four- and eight-year moving total to find a mid-point, as shown in Table 4.

Year	2006	2007	2008	2009	2010
Sales ($000)	125	130	130	150	140

▲ Table 4 Centring

$$\underset{\text{(Four-year moving totals)}}{535 + 550} = \underset{\text{(Eight-year moving total)}}{1085}$$

Here, the mid-point is 2008. The trend or four-period centred moving average can be found by dividing the eight-year moving total by 8, the number of years, as shown in Table 5.

Year	Sales	Four-year moving total	Eight-year moving total	Trend*
2006	125			
2007	130			
2008	130	535	1085	135.63
2009	150	550	1125	140.63
2010	140	575	1200	150
2011	155	625	1290	161.25
2012	180	665	1400	175
2013	190	735	1535	193.13
2014	210	810		
2015	230			

Trend* (four-year centered moving average = eight-year moving average ÷ 8)

▲ Table 5 Calculating a four-year moving average for a garden furniture manufacturer

Plotting the four-period centred moving average figures onto a graph (as shown in Figure 1) shows the trend in the figures. It is clear to see that sales appear to be rising over the period. The trend line is 'smoother' than the line showing the actual sales figures. It removes any fluctuations in sales each year and gives a more obvious picture of the trend that has been taking place.

ACTIVITY 1 〉 SKILLS 〉 INTERPRETATION, PROBLEM SOLVING

CASE STUDY: MORENO SERVICE CENTRE

Moreno Service Centre, a Colombian car maintenance business, has recently gathered data on its sales revenue as shown in Table 6, and wants to calculate a three- and four-period moving average.

	(COP million)									
Period	1	2	3	4	5	6	7	8	9	10
Sales revenue	100	130	160	175	180	190	190	180	220	250
3-period moving average		130	155							
4-period moving average		151.3								

▲ Table 6 Sales revenue for Moreno Service Centre

1 Calculate the three- and four-period moving averages for as many years as you can to complete the table.
2 Plot the sales figures and both trend lines onto a graph on graph paper and explain the relationship between the trend and the actual sales revenue figures for the Moreno Service Centre.

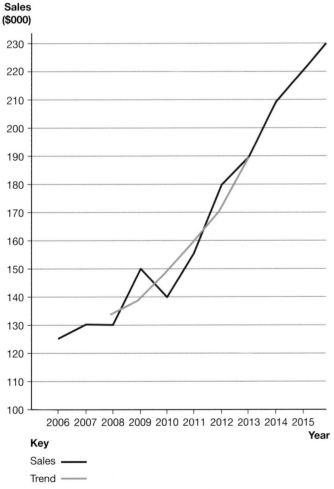

Key
Sales ──────
Trend ──────

▲ Figure 1 Annual sales of a garden furniture manufacturer

PREDICTING THE LINE OF BEST FIT FROM THE TREND

Having identified a trend that is taking place, it is possible for a business to now predict what may happen in future. Consider the business represented in Table 7.

Year	Sales ($000)	Four-year moving total	Eight-year moving total	Trend (four-year centred moving average = eight-year moving total/8)
2006	300			
2007	500			
		1950		
2008	600		4200	525.00
		2250		
2009	550		4750	593.75
		2500		
2010	600		5250	656.25
		2750		
2011	750		6050	756.25
		3300		
2012	850		6800	850
		3500		
2013	1100		7350	918.75
		3850		
2014	800			
2015	1100			

▲ Table 7 Four-year moving average and trend for a toy manufacturer

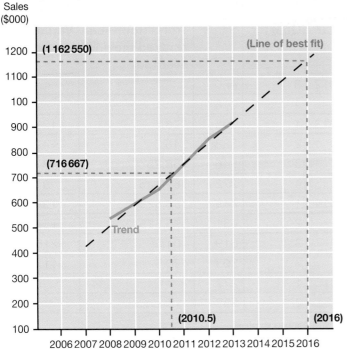

▲ Figure 2 Annual sales of a toy manufacturer

and Y is the average sales. These co-ordinates can be calculated using the figures in Table 7:

$$\bar{X} = \frac{\Sigma X \text{ (the total years)}}{N \text{ (the number of years)}}$$

$$= \frac{2008 + 2009 + 2010 + 2011 + 2012 + 2013}{6}$$

$$= \frac{12\,063}{6} = 2010.5$$

$$\bar{Y} = \frac{\Sigma Y \text{ (the total sales in the trend)}}{N \text{ (the number of years)}}$$

$$= \frac{\$525\,000 + \$593\,750 + \$656\,250 + \$756\,250 + \$850\,000 + \$918\,750}{6}$$

$$= \frac{\$4\,300\,000}{6}$$

$$= \$716\,667$$

Consider the sales of this business during the period 2006–15. These data have been used to calculate four-year moving averages and this information used to calculate the trend. **Extrapolation** involves the use of past sales data to forecast future sales.

Figure 2 shows that sales of the toy manufacturer's goods may reach about $1 160 000. The business has made certain assumptions (i.e. things you think are true without proof) when predicting this figure. Firstly, no other factors were likely to have changed to affect the trend. The prediction is likely to be inaccurate if other factors changed and led to different sales figures. Secondly, the sales figures are predicted by drawing a line through the trend figures and extending it to the year 2016. The broken line through the trend in Figure 2 is called the **line of best fit**. It is the best line that can be drawn that matches the general slope of all points in the trend. The line is an average, where points in the trend on one side of the line are balanced with those on the other. In other words, it is a line that 'best fits' all points in the trend.

It is possible to draw the line of best fit by plotting the trend figures on graph paper accurately and then adding the line of best fit 'by eye'. This is so that the points fit equally either side of the line. You should get a reasonable prediction by extending the line carefully.

To help draw the line, it should pass through the co-ordinates (X,Y) where X is the average of the years

This point is shown on Figure 2. The actual predicted figure for the year 2016 is $1 162 550. This can be found by a method known as 'the sum of least squares'. Computer software can be used by businesses to calculate the line of best fit and to predict from the trend.

VARIATIONS FROM THE TREND

How accurate is the prediction of around $1 160 000 sales of toys by the year 2016? Even allowing for the assumptions on the previous page, the prediction may not be accurate. This is because it is taken from the trend, and the trend 'smoothed out' variations in sales figures. To make an accurate prediction, the business will have to find the average variation over the period and take this into account. We can find how much variation there is from the trend by calculating:

Actual sales − trend

So, for example, the cyclical variation in Table 7 would be as shown in Table 8. The average of the variations over the period 2006–15 is (in $000):

$$= \frac{+75 - 43.75 - 56.25 - 6.25 +/- 0 + 181.25}{6}$$

$$= \frac{+150}{6} = +25 \text{ (or} + \$25\,000)$$

Year	Sales	Trend (four-year centred moving average)	($000) Variation in each year
2006	300		
2007	500		
2008	600	525.00	+75.00
2009	550	593.75	−43.75
2010	600	656.25	−56.25
2011	750	756.25	−6.25
2012	850	850.00	+/− 0
2013	1100	918.75	+181.25
2014	800		
2015	1100		

▲ Table 8 Cyclical variations

Year	Quarter	Sales	Trend (four-year centred moving average)	($000) Variation
2012	3	460		
	4	218		
2013	1	205	328.5	−123.5
	2	388	346.0	+42.0
	3	546	358.25	−187.75
	4	272	369.125	−97.125
2014	1	249	383.625	−134.625
	2	431	396.625	+34.375
	3	619	404.0	+215.0
	4	303	420.5	−117.5
2015	1	277		
	2	535		

▲ Table 9 Seasonal variations

If the predicted value based on the trend was $1 160 000, then adding $25 000 may give a more accurate predicted figure of $1 185 000.

SEASONAL VARIATIONS

It is possible to make predictions from a trend. It is also possible to use seasonal variations to make a more accurate prediction. Table 9 shows sales of a different business over a three-year period, including sales in each quarter. A four-quarter moving average has been calculated and also the variation in each quarter.

Carrying on the trend to predict the sales for the fourth quarter of the year 2015 might give a figure of $470 000. (It would be possible to find this by drawing and extending a line of best fit through the trend.) As we know, this is a 'smoothed out' figure. A more accurate prediction might be to calculate the average seasonal variation in the fourth quarter, for example (in $000):

$$\frac{-97.125 - 117.5}{2} = \frac{-214.625}{2} = -107.313$$

By subtracting $107 313 from the total of $470 000, this gives a more accurate prediction of $362 687.

THE LIMITATIONS OF QUANTITATIVE SALES FORECASTS

Quantitative sales forecasts are powerful tools for businesses and are used to help make important decisions. These methods can still lead to mistakes, even though they use advanced computer models and algorithms and are managed by expert sales analysts – what has gone before is not always the best predictor of what is to come.

Sales forecasts are likely to be more reliable when:
- the forecast is for a short period of time in the future, such as six months, rather than a long time, such as five years
- they are revised frequently to take account of new data and other information
- the market is slow-changing
- market research data, including test marketing data, is available
- those preparing the forecast have a good understanding of how to use data to produce a forecast
- those preparing the forecast have a good 'feel' for the market and can adjust the forecast to take account of their predictions for the future.

No forecaster is accurate all the time. Even in slow-moving markets, sales can change by a few per cent for no apparent reason. One way to take this into account is to produce a forecast range. For example, forecasters might prepare three sets of figures – an optimistic forecast, a pessimistic forecast and a central forecast. The two outlying forecasts would have a low probability of occurring but would give an idea of the best- and worst-case scenarios. The central forecast would be the forecast that had the highest probability of occurring. Supplying these forecasts to other departments, such as production, would give them an idea of the possible variations they might have to face. They could then prepare their own plans for these eventualities. In a very sophisticated forecast, there would be a whole range of possible outcomes each with a probability attached to its occurring.

Even though forecasts are rarely 100 per cent accurate, they do give an idea of likely future trends. As such, they are important tools for any planning or budgeting.

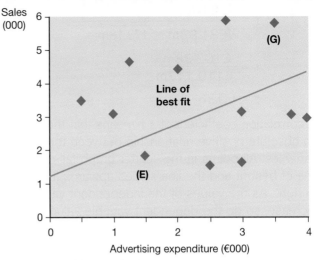

▲ Figure 3 Advertising and sales data

CAUSAL MODELLING AND LINE OF BEST FIT

Time-series analysis only describes what is happening to information. Causal modelling tries to explain data, usually by finding a link between one set of data and another. For example, a business may want to find whether there is a link between the amount that it spends on advertising and its sales.

Table 11 shows data that has been collected about advertising and sales by a business at different times. The data in the table is plotted onto a **scatter graph** in Figure 3.

Advertising (the independent variable) is shown on the horizontal (X) axis. Sales (the dependent variable) are shown on the vertical (Y) axis. The figure shows, for example, that in one period (E) the business had

advertising spending of €1500 and sales of 1800 units. In another period (G) the business had advertising spending of €3500 and sales of 5800 units.

Looking at the graph, there appears to be a positive **correlation** between the two variables (sales and advertising expenditure in this case). The more that is spent on advertising, the higher the level of sales. The line of best fit is drawn through the data to show this relationship better. It is also possible to calculate the extent of the relationship by means of a **correlation coefficient**, using the formula:

$$r = \frac{\Sigma XY}{\sqrt{(\Sigma X^2)\ (\Sigma Y^2)}}$$

Using the data in Table 11, the correlation coefficient for advertising and sales can be calculated as follows.

Period	Advertising expenditure (€ 000)	Sales (000)	(€ million)	(million)	(€ million)
	X	Y	X²	Y²	XY
A	1.0	3.2	1.0	10.24	3.2
B	2.0	4.5	4.0	20.25	9.0
C	3.0	1.8	9.0	3.24	5.4
D	4.0	3.0	16.0	9.0	12.0
E	1.5	1.8	2.25	3.24	2.7
F	2.5	1.6	6.25	2.56	4.0
G	3.5	5.8	12.25	33.64	20.3
H	1.2	4.7	1.44	22.09	5.64
I	2.7	5.9	7.29	34.81	15.93
J	3.0	3.5	9.0	12.25	10.5
K	3.6	3.1	12.96	9.61	11.16
L	0.7	3.5	0.49	12.25	2.45
			ΣX² = 81.93	ΣY² = 173.18	ΣXY = 102.28

▲ Table 11 Advertising and sales data

$$r = \frac{€102.28m}{\sqrt{€81.93m \times 173.18m}}$$

$$r = \frac{€102.28m}{€119.117m}$$

$$r = +0.86$$

- A correlation coefficient of +1 means that there is an absolute positive relationship between the two variables. All points in the scatter graph fall on the line of best fit and the line slopes upwards from left to right. As the values of the independent variable increase, so do the dependent variable values.
- A correlation coefficient of 0 means that there is no relationship between the variables.
- A correlation coefficient of −1 means that there is an absolute negative relationship between the two variables. All points in the scatter graph fall on the line of best fit and the line slopes downwards from left to right. As the values of the independent variable increase, the values of the dependent variable fall.

The formula itself does not show positive and negative values. However, it is easy to see whether the relationship is positive or negative from the graph. A positive coefficient of 0.86 suggests a strong correlation between the spending on advertising and the level of sales. As advertising increases, so do sales. This information could help a business in future when making decisions about its marketing. It is suggested that if the figure falls below 0.7 it becomes difficult to see any correlation from the scatter graph. An example of a negative correlation might be the relationship between prices and customer demand. As prices rise, demand falls. Examples of different correlations are shown in Figure 4.

Businesses must be careful when basing decisions on such calculations.

- A large quantity of sales in any period may be due to factors other than advertising, such as other forms of promotion.
- There are sometimes examples of 'nonsense correlations'. These are correlation coefficients that appear to show a strong relationship between two variables even though the relationship between the figures is pure coincidence.

QUALITATIVE FORECASTING

Qualitative forecasting uses people's opinions or judgements rather than numerical data. A business could base its predictions on the views of 'experts', or on the opinions of experienced managers in the marketing or production department. Such methods are usually used by businesses:

- where there is insufficient numerical data
- where figures date quickly because the market is changing rapidly.

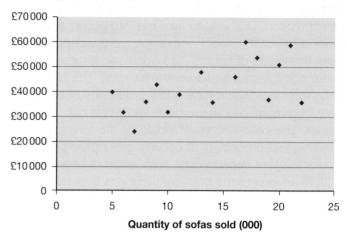

Marketing expenditure

Quantity of sofas sold (000)

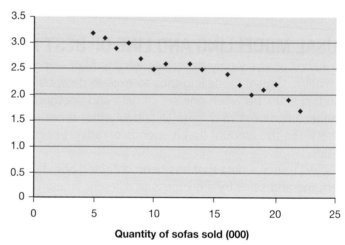

Unemployment (millions)

Quantity of sofas sold (000)

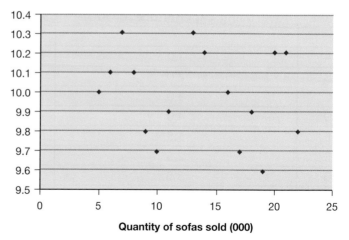

Quantity of baked beans (millions)

Quantity of sofas sold (000)

▲ Figure 4 A weak positive correlation, a strong negative correlation and little or no correlation

THINKING BIGGER

Quantitative sales forecasting is an important technique for businesses, but it is not without disagreement. At some point, the judgement about what the forecast will be needs to be made by a person within a business, even with the most powerful statistical models and forecasts available. From this forecast, decisions will be made concerning staffing, ordering of materials, marketing and so on. Importantly, ultimate decisions are subjective in the sense that they are judgements made by individuals or departments. Individuals may be driven by competing motives. The sales manager may be motivated to have forecasts that paint a positive picture.

This lack of certainty is a good opportunity for the development of balanced arguments in any written response to a question. The statistically produced trend may well point to a particular level of sales. However, wider economic factors might make this forecast unlikely. A rise in average incomes in an economy, combined with a weakening exchange rate, for example, may mean that the forecast is an under-prediction.

The topic lends itself to an evaluative approach. Essentially, avoid basing forecasts on a very small range of factors. Time-series analysis is a useful tool for business, but it is risky to rely heavily on what has gone before.

LINKS

Sales forecasting was discussed in Student Book 1, Chapter 30. However, this chapter focuses on the quantitative techniques that might be used when making future sales forecasts. Although the quantitative techniques in this chapter are very specific, links can be made with other subject areas. For example, a line of best fit might be drawn to show the relationship that exists for other variables such as interest rates and costs (see Student Book 1, Chapter 29) or costs and capacity utilisation (see Student Book 1, Chapter 38). In general, reference to sales forecasting techniques can also be made when discussing the advantages and disadvantages of quantitative techniques in decision making, for example.

CHECKPOINT

1 Why might a business want to predict the future?

2 What are the four components of time-series data that a business will take into account?

3 What does a trend show?

4 How might a business use the calculation of a trend?

5 What does a scatter graph show?

6 What is meant by causal modelling?

7 State two difficulties with quantitative sales forecasting.

8 How would a line of best fit be useful for a business when looking to forecast sales?

SUBJECT VOCABULARY

centring a method used to calculate a moving average, where the average is plotted or calculated in relation to the central figure
correlation the relationship between two sets of variables
correlation coefficient a measure of the extent of the relationship between two sets of variables
extrapolation forecasting future trends based on past data
line of best fit a straight line drawn through the centre of a group of data points plotted on a scatter graph
moving average a succession of averages derived from successive segments (typically of constant size and overlapping) of a series of values
scatter graph a graph showing the performance of one variable against another independent variable on a variety of occasions. It is used to show whether a correlation exists between the variables
time-series analysis a method that allows a business to predict future levels from past figures

EXAM PRACTICE

PROSPER-i

In 2016 Prosper-i, a global electronics company and developer of toys and games, launched the latest version of its popular robot toy. Called the i-do, the robot offered new features such as the ability to be controlled by a smart phone app and could be programmed to play music and video. The new features were designed to appeal to new parts of the market including adults. It was also designed to compete with two main competitors – ChiBot and Pal-i.

i-do was initially well-received by consumers and by reviewers. In the USA the entire stock of over 40 000 units was sold in the first three months of release. Over 300 000 units were sold in 2016. Table 12 summarises sales in 2017.

	2017 Q1	2017 Q2	2017 Q3	2017 Q4
Sales (000)	39	16	30	195

▲ Table 12 i-do sales 2017

From April to June 2017 (Q2), i-do sold only 16 000 units. This was down 59 per cent on the previous three months. Some retailers were considering whether to continue to stock i-do.

	2018 Q1	2018 Q2	2018 Q3	2018 Q4
Sales (000)	31	51	61	191

▲ Table 13 i-do sales 2018

The sales performance led Prosper-i to lower its 2018 sales forecast by 70 per cent from 900 000 units to 280 000. The reported actual sales for 2018 are shown below.

In 2019, Prosper-i reported that sales of i-do were running ahead of its sales forecast.

Q

1 Define the term 'sales forecast'.   **(4 marks)**
2 Explain the extent to which sales of i-do could be described as being influenced by seasonal factors.   **(4 marks)**
3 Assess the extent to which quantitative sales forecasting is useful to Prosper-i.   **(12 marks)**

EXAM HINT

There are lots of opportunities for exam questions requiring analysis and evaluation in this topic. The statistical element of quantitative sales data means that analytical considerations can be made. For example, you may be required to analyse data in tables which represent sales forecasts.

10 INVESTMENT APPRAISAL

LEARNING OBJECTIVES

By the end of this chapter you should be able to understand:

- simple payback
- average (accounting) rate of return
- discounted cash flow (net present value only)

- calculations and interpretations of figures generated by these techniques
- limitations of these techniques.

GETTING STARTED

Durban Recycling is a recycling plant owned by the Mathoho family in Durban, South Africa. In 2017 the business invested ZAR100 million in a new plant designed to convert plastic bottles into plastic flakes and pellets. Table 1 shows the net cash flow the business hoped to receive over the life of the investment (expected to be 10 years). Once the plant was constructed in 2018, at a cost of ZAR70 million, revenue flows were due to begin in 2019. James Mathoho, the managing director, commented that the growth in the recycling of plastic bottles was around 45 per cent and looked to grow in the future. If so, it would be a profitable investment.

The investment would create 20 new jobs at the plant. However, some local residents were worried about the noise the new plant might make and had a meeting with the local council about their concerns.

Calculate the expected net cash flow from the investment over the time period. Investment is often said to be risky. Can you account for this view, using this investment as an example? What non-financial factors might Durban Recycling have to consider when deciding if they should build the new plant?

		2018	2019	2020	2021	2022	2023	2024	2025	2026	2027	ZAR million 2028
Net cash flow		(70)	10	13	20	25	27	30	26	23	21	20

▲ Table 1 Expected net cash flow from the new plant

INVESTMENT APPRAISAL

Investment refers to the purchase of capital goods. Capital goods are used in the production of other goods. For example, a building contractor who buys a cement mixer, some scaffolding, a lorry, a computer, some office furniture and five shovels has invested. These goods will be used repeatedly by the business over a period of time.

Investment might also refer to expenditure by a business that is likely to give a return in the future. For example, a business might spend €20 million on research and development into a new product or invest €10 million in a promotion campaign. In each case, money is being spent on projects now in the hope that a greater amount of money will be generated in the future as a result of that expenditure.

Investment appraisal describes how a business might objectively evaluate an investment project to determine whether or not it is likely to be profitable. It also allows businesses to make comparisons between different investment projects. There are several **quantitative** methods (i.e. measured with numbers) that a business might use when evaluating projects. However, they all involve comparing the **capital cost** of the project with the **net cash flow**.

- The capital cost is the amount of money spent when setting up a new venture.
- Net cash flow is **cash inflows** minus **cash outflows**.

SIMPLE PAYBACK

The **payback period** refers to the amount of time it takes for a project to recover or pay back the initial outlay. For example, an engineer may invest $500 000 in new cutting machinery and estimate that it will lead to a net cash flow over the next five years, as shown in Table 2. Here the payback period is four years. If we add together the net cash flows from the project in the first four years it amounts to $500 000 (i.e. $100 000 + $125 000 + $125 000 + $150 000).

The payback period can also be found by calculating the **cumulative net cash flow**. This is the net cash flow each year, taking into account the initial cost of the machine. When the machine is first bought, in year 0, there is negative cash flow of −$500 000, the cost of the machine. Next year, the net cash flow minus operating costs is $100 000. So, the cumulative net cash flow is −$500 000 + $100 000 = −$400 000. In year 4 it is zero, so all costs have been covered.

						$000
	Yr 0	Yr 1	Yr 2	Yr 3	Yr 4	Yr 5
Net cash flow	(500)	100	125	125	150	150
Cumulative net cash flow	(500)	(400)	(275)	(150)	0	150

▲ Table 2 Expected net cash flow from some new cutting machinery

WORKED EXAMPLE

When using the payback method to choose between projects, you are looking for the project with the shortest payback period. By choosing the project with the shortest payback, the business gets the money invested back more quickly. This money can then be used for other purposes. Assume a business is appraising three investment projects, all of which cost €70 000. The net cash flow expected from each project is shown in Table 3.

	Yr 0	Yr 1	Yr 2	Yr 3	Yr 4	Yr 5	Yr 6	Expected net cash flow	Payback period
									€000
Project A Net cash flow	(70)	10	10	20	20	30	40	60	4yrs 4mths
Project A Cumulative cash flow	(70)	(60)	(50)	(30)	(10)	20	60		
Project B Net cash flow	(70)	20	20	20	20	20	20	50	3yrs 6mths
Project B Cumulative cash flow	(70)	(50)	(30)	(10)	10	30	50		
Project C Net cash flow	(70)	30	30	20	10	10	10	40	2yrs 6mths
Project C Cumulative cash flow	(70)	(40)	(10)	10	20	30	40		

▲ Table 3 Expected net cash flow from three projects

In this example, Project C would be chosen because it has the shortest payback time: two years and six months. How is this calculated? In years 1 and 2 the net cash flow is €30 000 + €30 000 = €60 000. To pay for an investment of €70 000 the remaining €10 000 (€70 000 − €60 000) comes from year 3's net cash flow. This is €20 000, which is more. So, the number of months in year 3 it takes to pay the €10 000 can be calculated as:

$$\frac{\text{Amount required}}{\text{Net cash flow in year}} \times \frac{€10\,000}{€20\,000} \times 12 = 6 \text{ months}$$

Project A's payback is 4 years and 4 months and Project B's is three years and six months. Note that total cash flow is not taken into account in this method. In fact, Project C has the lowest total return over the six years (€40 000).

ADVANTAGES OF THE PAYBACK METHOD

There are certain advantages to a business when using the payback method to appraise (i.e. examine) the potential success of an investment.

- This method is useful when technology changes rapidly, as it is important to recover the cost of investment before a new model or equipment is designed. This is true of the agriculture industry where new farm machinery is designed and introduced into the market regularly.
- It is simple to use.
- Firms might adopt this method if they have cash-flow problems. This is because the project chosen will 'pay back' the investment more quickly than others.

AVERAGE (ACCOUNTING) RATE OF RETURN (ARR)

The **average rate of return** or the **accounting rate of return** method measures the net return each year as a percentage of the capital cost of the investment.

$$\text{Average rate of return (ARR)(\%)} = \frac{\text{Net return (profit) per annum}}{\text{Capital outlay (cost)}} \times 100$$

ACTIVITY 1   SKILLS   ANALYSIS, INTERPRETATION, PROBLEM SOLVING

CASE STUDY: DELLE ROSE ASSOCIATES

Delle Rose Associates is a full-service Italian digital-marketing agency. Their main work is developing targeted campaigns to drive quality traffic to websites using highly cost-effective methods.

In 2015 the managing director of the company recognised the need for a new computer system. They carried out some research into three new systems and put together the financial information shown in Table 4.

Computer system	Capital cost	2015	2016	2017	2018	2019	2020	Total
System A	24 000	6000	6000	6000	6000	6000	6000	36 000
System B	37 000	8000	8000	9000	9000	6000	6000	46 000
System C	12 000	4000	4000	4000	2000	1000	1000	16 000

▲ Table 4 Capital costs and expected net cash flows from three new computer systems

1 Explain what is meant by 'expected net cash flow'.
2 Calculate the payback period for each system and state which system Delle Rose Associates should select.

3 Explain one possible reason why Delle Rose used the payback method of investment appraisal in this case.

WORKED EXAMPLE

The capital cost and expected net cash flow from three investment projects is shown in Table 5.

	Project X	Project Y	Project Z
Capital cost	£50 000	£40 000	£90 000
Return Yr 1	£10 000	£10 000	£20 000
Yr 2	£10 000	£10 000	£20 000
Yr 3	£15 000	£10 000	£30 000
Yr 4	£15 000	£15 000	£30 000
Yr 5	£20 000	£15 000	£30 000
Total net cash flows	£70 000	£60 000	£130 000

▲ Table 5 The capital cost and net cash flow from three investment projects

A business would first calculate the net profit from each project by subtracting its capital cost from the expected net cash flow of the project, i.e. £70 000 − £50 000 = £20 000 for Project X. The next step is to calculate the profit per annum by dividing the total profit by the number of years the project runs for, i.e. £20 000 ÷ 5 = £4000 for X. Finally, the ARR is calculated by using the above formula, i.e.:

$$\text{ARR (Project X)} = \frac{£4000}{£50\ 000} \times 100 = 8\%$$

The results for all three projects are shown in Table 6. Project Y would be chosen because it gives a higher ARR (10 per cent) than the other two.

	Project X	Project Y	Project Z
Capital cost	£50 000	£40 000	£90 000
Total net profit (net cash flow − capital cost)	£20 000	£20 000	£40 000
Net profit p.a. (profit ÷ 5)	£4 000	£4 000	£8 000
ARR	8%	10%	8.9%

▲ Table 6 The ARR calculated for three investment projects

ADVANTAGES OF THE ARR METHOD

The advantage of this method is that it shows clearly the profitability of an investment project. Not only does it allow a range of projects to be compared, the overall rate of return can be compared to other uses for investment funds. In the example in Table 6, if a company can gain 12 per cent by placing its funds in a bank account, it might choose to postpone the investment project until interest rates fall. It is also easier to identify the **opportunity cost** of investment.

ACTIVITY 2   SKILLS ▷ CRITICAL THINKING, PROBLEM SOLVING

CASE STUDY: EC GROUP

The Tokyo-based EC Group focuses on developing, producing and installing electrical, electronic and mechanical components for aircraft and helicopters. The company has a leading position in the field of aircraft and helicopter services, customisation (i.e. making changes to suit the owner) and modification (i.e. making changes to improve something). EC Group's employees are engineers and skilled workers. In 2017 the directors identified three investment projects that would benefit the company:

- research and development (R & D)
- marketing campaign
- some new CNC machinery.

The capital cost and expected cash flows for the investment projects are shown in Table 7.

1 (a) Calculate the average rate of return for each project.
  (b) Explain which project should be selected.

2 Explain the advantages to EC Group of using this method of appraisal.

Investment project	Capital cost	2015	2016	2017	2018	2019	2020	Total
R & D	9 600	0	0	2 500	4 600	5 000	5 500	17 600
Marketing campaign	9 000	5 000	4 000	3 000	2 000	1 000	1 000	16 000
New CNC machinery	7 800	2 000	2 000	2 000	2 000	2 000	2 000	12 000

JPN (million)

▲ Table 7 Capital cost and net cash flow for three investment projects

DISCOUNTED CASH FLOW (NET PRESENT VALUE OR NPV)

Both the payback and the ARR methods of investment appraisal do not take into account the time value of money. When making an investment decision, a business might take into account what cash flow or profit earned in the future is worth at the **present value**. For example, look at Table 8. This shows that US$100 invested today at a compound interest rate of 10 per cent would be worth US$161 in five years' time.

- In one year's time, the investment would be worth US$110. Of this, US$10 would be the interest and US$100 would be the initial investment.
- In two years' time, it would be worth US$121. With compound interest, the interest is based not on the initial investment but on the investment at the end of the first year. So, interest is 10 per cent of US$110, making US$11. Then this has to be added to the US$110 value at the end of the first year to make a total of US$121 for the second year.
- This carries on until the value after five years is US$161.

Year	1	2	3	4	5
Value of US$100	US$110	US$121	US$133	US$146	US$161

▲ Table 8 Value of US$100 invested over five years at 10 per cent per annum compound interest

If US$100 today is worth US$161 in five years' time, it must be true that US$161 in five years' time is worth just US$100 today. This is an example of an important insight of **discounted cash-flow** techniques. Money in the future is worth less than the same amount now (the **present value**). This is because money available today could be invested and it could earn interest.

Note that this is a completely different idea to the fact that money in the future can also become devalued due to the effects of inflation. Inflation does indeed affect future values of money. So there are two effects on the value of future money. Discounted cash-flow techniques just deal with one of these – the effect of interest rates.

Discount tables can be used to show by how much a future value must be multiplied to calculate its present value. Table 9 shows a discount table with five different rates of interest. If an investment project was predicted to give a net cash flow of US$10 000 in three years'

time, and the discount rate was 10 per cent, then reading off the table, the US$10 000 would need to be multiplied by 0.75. To reach its present value the calculation would be:

$$US\$10\,000 \times 0.75 = US\$7500$$

Cash flow or profit of US$15 000 from a project received in five years' time, at a discount rate of 20 per cent, would be worth US$6000 in the present (US$15 000 × 0.40).

The discount table shown in Table 9 also shows two features of discounting.

- The higher the rate of discount, the less the present value of cash flow in the future. This is the reverse of saying that the higher the rate of interest, the greater the value of an investment in the future.
- The further into the future the cash flow or earnings from an investment project, the less is their present value. So, US$71 000 earned in five years' time is worth less than US$71 000 earned in one year's time. Again, this is simply the opposite way of saying that US$71 000 invested today at a fixed rate of interest will be worth more in five years' time than in one year's time.

Rate of discount					
Year	5%	10%	15%	20%	25%
0	1.00	1.00	1.00	1.00	1.00
1	0.95	0.91	0.87	0.83	0.80
2	0.91	0.83	0.76	0.69	0.64
3	0.86	0.75	0.66	0.58	0.51
4	0.82	0.68	0.57	0.48	0.41
5	0.78	0.62	0.50	0.40	0.33
6	0.75	0.56	0.43	0.33	0.26
7	0.71	0.51	0.38	0.28	0.21
8	0.68	0.47	0.33	0.23	0.17
9	0.64	0.42	0.28	0.19	0.13
10	0.61	0.39	0.25	0.16	0.11

▲ Table 9 Discount table

Calculating NPV: The **net present value** method makes use of discounted cash flow. It calculates the rate of return on an investment project taking into account the effects of interest rates and time. Using discount tables, it is possible to calculate the net present value of an investment project.

WORKED EXAMPLE

Table 10 shows three investment projects. The initial cost of each investment project is US$50 000, shown in the Year 0 row. In years 1 to 10, each produces a stream of net cash flow. When added up, these exceed the initial US$50 000. So it might appear that each investment project is profitable. However, if the net cash flow is discounted using a discount rate of 20 per cent, the picture is very different.

- **Project A.** The total of the present values in years 1–10 for Project A is just US$41 700. The net cash flow each year is constant at US$10 000, but the present value of each of those US$10 000 falls the further away it is received. By year 10, the present value of US$10 000 discounted at 20 per cent is just US$1 600. The net present value can be calculated by finding the total of the present value figures in years 0–10 minus the initial cost. Or it can be calculated using the formula:

Net present value = present values − initial cost

= US$41 700 − US$50 000

= −US$8 300

So Project A is unprofitable according to discounted cash-flow techniques.

- **Project B.** The expected net cash flow before discounting is higher than for Project A: US$71 000 compared to US$50 000. But once discounted, there is little difference in the sum of the present values. This is because net cash flow in Project B is weighted towards later years. The net present value of this project is US$42 810 − US$50 000 = −US$7 190. Again, Project B is unprofitable according to discounted cash-flow techniques.

- **Project C.** The expected net cash flow before discounting is the same as with Project B. In fact, the pattern of net cash flow is an exact reverse of those of Project B. Here, the higher net cash-flow figures are concentrated at the start and fall off towards the end. This means that the total present value is much higher than with Project B. The net present value of Project C is US$58 260 − US$50 000 = US$8 260. This is the discounted profit that the business will make on this project.

The net present value method would suggest that a business should go ahead with any investment projects that have a positive net present value. If a business has to make a choice between investment projects, it should go for those with the highest net present value. So in this case it would choose Project C.

| Year | Project A | | Project B | | Project C | | |
	Net cash flow US$	Present value US$	Net cash flow US$	Present value US$	Net cash flow US$	Present value US$	Discount table rate of discount at 20%
0	(50 000)	(50 000)	(50 000)	(50 000)	(50 000)	(50 000)	1.00
1	10 000	8300	5000	4150	20 000	16 000	0.83
2	10 000	6900	8000	5520	16 000	11 040	0.69
3	10 000	5800	10 000	5800	14 000	8120	0.58
4	10 000	4800	12 000	5760	12 000	5760	0.48
5	10 000	4000	12 000	4800	12 000	4800	0.40
6	10 000	3300	12 000	3960	12 000	3960	0.33
7	10 000	2800	12 000	3360	12 000	3360	0.28
8	10 000	2300	14 000	3220	12 000	2300	0.23
9	10 000	1900	16 000	3040	8000	1520	0.19
10	10 000	1600	20 000	3200	5000	800	0.16
Expected net cash flow before discounting	50 000		71 000		71 000		
Present values years 1–10		41 700		42 810		58 260	
Net present value (NPV)		(8300)		(7190)		8260	

▲ Table 10 Net present value of three investment projects discounted at 20 per cent

ADVANTAGES OF THE DISCOUNTED CASH-FLOW METHOD

- The discounted cash-flow method, unlike the payback method and the average rate of return, correctly accounts for the value of future earnings by calculating present values.
- The discount rate used can be changed as risk and conditions in financial markets change. For example, in the 1990s, the cost of bank borrowing for many businesses fell from over 15 per cent to 7–8 per cent. Investment projects therefore did not need to make such a high rate of return to be profitable and so the rate of discount could be lowered. Since 2008 rates have been even lower – as low as 1 per cent in some countries.

EXAM HINT

Remember that discounted cash flow is used to take into account the effect that interest rates have on investment decisions. It *does not* take into account the effects of inflation (see Student Book 1, Chapter 41). This is a common error made by students.

LIMITATIONS OF THESE TECHNIQUES

Each of the three methods of investment appraisal outlined above has some limitations. These are summarised in Table 11.

Appraisal method	Limitations
Simple payback.	Cash earned after the payback period is ignored.
	The profitability of the method is overlooked.
Average rate of return.	The effects of time on the value of money are ignored.
Discounted cash flow.	The calculation is more complex than the other methods.
	The rate of discount is critical – if it is high, fewer projects will be profitable.

▲ Table 11 Limitations of the methods of investment

ACTIVITY 3   **SKILLS**   ANALYSIS, INTERPRETATION, PROBLEM SOLVING

CASE STUDY: MIAH LTD

Miah Ltd is a garment manufacturer in Dhaka, Bangladesh. It is considering making an investment in one of two machines, A and B. The projected net cash flows for each machine are shown in Table 12.

							BDT(million)
Year	0	1	2	3	4	5	6
	Initial cost						
Machine A							
Net cash flow	(600)	100	150	200	300	200	100
Discounted cash flow							
Machine B							
Net cash flow	(600)	200	300	200	150	100	100
Discounted cash flow							

▲ Table 12 Expected net cash flow from two investment projects (BDT million)

1 Calculate the discounted cash flow for each machine and each year using a discount rate of 15 per cent from the discount table, Table 9.
2 Calculate the net present value for each machine.
3 Why might Miah Ltd buy machine B if it uses the net present value method of decision making?

THINKING BIGGER

A number of **qualitative** factors should also be taken into account when appraising investment opportunities. These are non-financial considerations.

- **Human relations.** Some investment projects can have a huge impact on the staff in an organisation. For example, investment in plant automation (i.e. replacing workers with machines) might lead to mass redundancies. A business might decide to postpone plans to automate their plant if it thought the damage to human relations in the organisation would be too severe.
- **Ethical considerations.** Along with many other business decisions, managers are being more ethical (i.e. thinking about what is right and wrong) when choosing courses of action. For example, a chemicals producer might decide to build a new plant in a location that does not minimise financial costs but does reduce environmental damage. This decision might help to further improve the image of a company. Companies are increasingly keen to be seen as 'good corporate citizens'.
- **Risk.** One factor in assessing the risk of an investment project is a business's financial situation. Other factors include the state of the economy and the markets into which a business sells. Investment projects that have long payback periods are also riskier than ones with shorter payback periods.

- **Availability of funds.** Some investment projects do not start because businesses are unable to raise the money needed to fund the project. A large number of these will be small businesses that find it difficult to persuade investors and lenders to provide finance.
- **Business confidence.** Entrepreneurs, managers and businesses tend to have different attitudes and cultures to each other. One aspect of this is confidence or optimism (i.e. a feeling that good things will happen). Some decision makers tend to be very cautious, seeing all the problems that might arise if things go wrong. Some decision makers are confident and optimistic. They see the future as much better and brighter than others. This has a crucial impact on investment. The cautious, unconfident entrepreneur or manager may delay or abandon investment projects. In the same circumstances with the same investment projects, confident and optimistic managers will tend to go ahead and authorise the expenditure. So, the deeply held attitudes of decision makers have an important influence on investment decision making.

CHECKPOINT

1 What is meant by the term 'investment in business'?

2 Describe briefly how a business would appraise investment using the payback period.

3 What are the advantages of the payback method of investment appraisal?

4 What is the formula for calculating ARR?

5 What does the ARR method of investment appraisal aim to measure?

6 Give one advantage of the ARR method of investment appraisal.

7 What is the formula for calculating NPV?

8 Why is the discounted cash flow/NPV method of appraisal used in business?

9 Give one limitation of the payback method of investment appraisal.

10 Describe two qualitative factors that might influence an investment decision.

LINKS

One way you can demonstrate synoptic skills here is to link investment appraisal with a decision to locate a production operation abroad. For example, a business might face a choice between several different overseas locations. It might use one of the investment appraisal techniques discussed in this chapter to help decide which location might generate the best returns. Choosing an overseas location is discussed in Chapter 29. In general, investment appraisal might be used to help make decisions when the costs and expected net cash flows from different options can be clearly identified or estimated – when choosing between different corporate strategies, for example.

SUBJECT VOCABULARY

average rate of return or accounting rate of return (ARR) a method of investment appraisal that measures the net return per annum as a percentage of the initial spending
capital cost the amount of money spent when setting up a new venture
cash inflow the cash coming into the business such as that from sales or bank loans
cash outflow the cash going out of the business when payments are made to workers or suppliers, for example
discounted cash flow (DCF) a method of investment appraisal that takes interest rates into account by calculating the present value of future income
investment the purchase of capital goods
investment appraisal the evaluation of an investment project to determine whether or not it is likely to be worthwhile
net cash flow cash inflows minus cash outflows
net present value (NPV) the present value of future income from an investment project, minus the cost
opportunity cost when choosing between different alternatives, the opportunity cost is the benefit lost from the next best alternative to the one that has been chosen
payback period the amount of time it takes to recover the cost of an investment project
present value the value today of a sum of money available in the future
qualitative represented by words
quantitative represented by numbers

EXAM PRACTICE

CASE STUDY: FLORIpori LTD

SKILLS   CRITICAL THINKING, ANALYSIS, PROBLEM SOLVING, DECISION MAKING

FLORIpori Ltd, based near Lake Naivasha in Kenya, is a large but under performing flower grower. A management team recently bought the company for KES1 million. The company employs 22 staff and grows a range of cut flowers, pot plants, herbs and shrubs.

The new management team believes it can transform the business so that it is profit-making. In the previous year, the company lost KES2.6 million on sales of KES12.56 million. The team believes that the old company hasn't taken enough risks previously. Because of this, they haven't invested in enough new technology and working methods, and have fallen behind their competitors.

Victor Owino, the new managing director, has already decided to use KES50 million as an investment. Initially four investment projects were identified, but two were removed at a preliminary stage using the payback method

of appraisal. The two remaining projects are now being appraised. One of these projects involves constructing some giant, brand-new greenhouses to extend the growing season by up to 25 per cent. The other involves introducing total quality management (TQM) right across the organisation. The capital cost of the two projects and the expected cash flows are shown in Table 13. The present value of KES1 receivable (i.e. not yet received) at the end of five years at 5 per cent is shown in Table 14.

The new owners of the company are very optimistic about its future direction. However, the workforce does not share their enthusiasm. Many of them are worried about the proposed investment plans. The age profile of the workforce is high. More than 50 per cent of the workers are over 55 and have never worked anywhere else. Many of them joined the company when they left school and began their horticulture training. If FLORIpori select the greenhouse project, then eight staff may lose their jobs because of the improved efficiency of the new system.

Investment project	Cost	Year 1	Year 2	Year 3	Year 4	Year 5	Total
Greenhouses (KES million)	50	23	26	28	33	32	142
Introduce TQM (KES million)	44	21	21	23	24	25	114

▲ Table 13 Capital cost and expected cash flows for FLORIpori Ltd investment projects

After	0 yr	1 yr	2 yrs	3 yrs	4 yrs	5 yrs
Present value of KES1	KES1.00	KES0.95	KES0.90	KES0.86	KES0.82	KES0.78

▲ Table 14 The present value of KES1 receivable at the end of five years at 5 per cent

Q

1 Calculate the average rate of return of each investment project. **(4 marks)**
2 Calculate the net present value of each investment project. **(4 marks)**
3 Explain one advantage of the net present value method of investment appraisal to FLORIpori Ltd. **(4 marks)**
4 Assess which investment project FLORIpori should select. **(12 marks)**

11 DECISION TREES

LEARNING OBJECTIVES

By the end of this chapter you should be able to:
- construct and interpret simple decision tree diagrams
- understand the calculations and interpretations of figures generated by these techniques
- understand the limitations of using decision trees.

GETTING STARTED

When making a business decision it is helpful to use a quantitative decision-making technique if possible. This involves the application of numerical values (i.e. numbers), which can be compared easily. For example, Latika Naidu runs a successful import business, Gujurat Craftwork, based in Paris, buying craft products from India. The company sells the items to a network of retailers in the EU. Latika wants to expand the business and has identified two clear options:
- begin importing products from the Middle East to expand the product range
- set up an online operation to sell more widely.

Latika paid a business consultant €1000 to help make the decision. This was quite helpful. The consultant said the probability of success for the first option was 0.5, or 50 per cent. In contrast, the probability of success for the second option was 0.72, or 72 per cent. The cost of both options is very similar, but Latika will only choose one option.

Which option do you think Latika should choose? Explain your answer. Why might using a quantitative decision-making approach improve the quality of decision making? What might be the disadvantages of this approach if it is used?

MAKING DECISIONS

Every day, businesses make decisions. Most, if not all, involve some risk. This could be because the business has limited information on which to base the decision. Furthermore, the outcome of the decision may be uncertain. Launching a new product in a market abroad can be risky because a firm may not have experience of selling in that market. It may also be unsure about how consumers will react.

When faced with a number of different decisions a business will want to choose the course of action which gives the most return. What if a printing company had to decide whether to invest $750 000 in a new printing press now or wait a few years? If it bought now and a more efficient machine became available next year, then it might have been more profitable to wait. Alternatively, if it waits it may find the old machine has problems and costs increase.

When the outcome is uncertain, **decision trees** can be used to help a business reach a decision which could minimise risk and gain the greatest return.

WHAT ARE DECISION TREES?

A decision tree is a method of thinking about the alternative outcomes of any decision and presenting these in a diagram. The results can then be compared so that the business can find the most profitable alternative. For example, a business may be faced with two alternatives – to launch a new product in Europe or in the USA. A decision tree may show that launching a new product in Europe is likely to be more successful than launching a new product in the USA.

It is argued by some that decision making is more effective if a **quantitative** approach is taken. This is where information on which decisions are based, and the outcomes of decisions, are expressed as numbers. In a decision tree, numerical values are given to such information. The decision tree also provides a pictorial approach to decision making because a diagram is used which resembles the branches of a tree. The diagram maps out different courses of action, possible outcomes of decisions, and points where decisions have to be made. Calculations based on the decision tree can be used to find the 'best' likely outcome for the business and therefore the most suitable decision.

FEATURES OF DECISION TREES

Decision trees have a number of features. These can be seen in Figure 1, which shows the decision tree for a Japanese business that has to decide whether to launch a new advertising campaign or retain an old one.

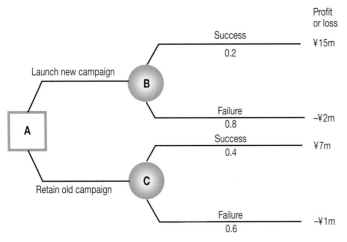

▲ Figure 1 A simple decision tree, based on a decision whether to retain an existing advertising campaign or begin a new one

Decision points: Points where decisions have to be made in a decision tree are represented by squares and are called decision points. The decision maker has to choose between certain courses of action. In this example, the decision is whether to launch a new campaign or retain the old one. The square labelled 'A' represents this point.

Outcomes: Points where there are different possible outcomes in a decision tree are represented by circles and are called **chance nodes**. At these chance nodes it can be shown that a particular course of action might result in a number of outcomes. In this example, at 'B' there is a chance of failure or success of the new campaign.

Probability or chance: The likelihood of a possible outcome happening is represented by **probability** in a decision tree. The chance of a particular outcome occurring is given a value. If the outcome is certain then the probability is 1. Alternatively, if there is no chance at all of a particular outcome occurring, the probability

will be 0. In practice, the value will lie between 0 and 1. In Figure 1, at 'B' the chance of success for the new campaign is 0.2 and the chance of failure is 0.8.

It is possible to estimate the probability of events occurring if information about these events can be found. There are two sources of information which can be used to help estimate probabilities. One source is **back data**. For example, if a business has opened 10 new stores in recent years, and 9 of them have been successful, it might be reasonable to assume that the chances of another new store being successful are 9/10 or 0.9. Another source is research data. For example, a business might carry out market research to find out how customers would react to a new product design – 80 per cent of people surveyed may like the product and 20 per cent may dislike it.

Expected monetary values: This is the financial outcome of a decision. It is based on the predicted profit or loss of an outcome and the probability of that outcome occurring. The profit or loss of any decision is shown on the right-hand side of Figure 1. For example, if the launch of a new campaign is a success, a ¥15 million profit is expected. If it fails, a loss of ¥2 million is expected.

CALCULATING EXPECTED MONETARY VALUES (EMV)

What should the firm decide? It has to work out the **expected values** of each decision, taking into account the expected profit or loss and the probabilities. So, for example, the expected value of a new campaign is:

$$\text{Success} \qquad\qquad \text{Failure}$$
$$\text{Expected value} = 0.2 \times ¥15m \qquad +0.8 \times (-¥2m)$$
$$= ¥3m - ¥1.6m$$
$$= 1.4m$$

The expected value of retaining the current campaign is:

$$\text{Success} \qquad\qquad \text{Failure}$$
$$\text{Expected value} = 0.4 \times ¥7m \qquad +0.6 \times (-¥1m)$$
$$= ¥2.8m - ¥0.6m$$
$$= 2.2m$$

From these figures the firm should continue with the existing campaign because the expected value is higher.

NUMEROUS OUTCOMES

It is possible to have more than two outcomes at a chance node. For example, at point 'B' in Figure 1 there might have been three outcomes.

- The probability of great success may be 0.2 with a profit of ¥15 million.
- The probability of average success may be 0.4 with a profit of ¥6 million.
- The probability of failure may be 0.4 with a loss of −¥2 million.

The expected value is now:

$$= (0.2 \times ¥15m) + (0.4 \times ¥6m) + (0.4 \times -¥2m)$$

$$= ¥3m + ¥2.4m - ¥0.8m$$

$$= ¥4.6m$$

ACTIVITY 1   **SKILLS** ▶ ANALYSIS, INTERPRETATION, PROBLEM SOLVING, DECISION MAKING

CASE STUDY: SWIFTHAIR

SwiftHair owns a chain of 65 hair salons in Sweden. Due to very strong competition, revenue has fallen in the last couple of years. As a means of boosting revenue it has been suggested that the chain, like many retailers, should use a 'special offer' to attract more customers. SwiftHair plans to offer a half-price hair treatment all day on one of the days in the working week. However, SwiftHair is not sure which day would be best to make the half-price offer.

In order to help make the decision, an investigation was carried out in a sample of salons. Different salons would make the offer on different days. But, salons are closed on Sundays and it was decided not to target Saturdays because it was traditionally a busy day. The data gathered during the investigation is shown in Table 1.

Special offer day	Probability of success	Estimated effect on profit (SEK)	Probability of failure	Estimated effect on profit (SEK)	Expected monetary value
Monday	0.5	+1300	?	−200	?
Tuesday	0.5	+1700	?	−400	?
Wednesday	0.7	+400	?	−1200	?
Thursday	0.6	+1000	?	−800	?
Friday	0.6	+1100	?	−400	?

▲ Table 1 Special offer data gathered by SwiftHair

1 Complete Table 1.
2 On financial grounds (i.e. for financial reasons), which day should the special offer be arranged?

DECISIONS, OUTCOMES AND COSTS

In practice, businesses face many alternative decisions and possible outcomes. For example, consider a farmer from the UK who has inherited some land, but does not wish to use it with his existing farming business. There are three possible decisions the farmer could make.

- Sell the land. The market is depressed and this will earn £0.6 million.
- Wait for one year and hope that the market price improves. A land agent has told the farmer that the chance of an upturn in the market is 0.3, while the probabilities of it staying the same or worsening are 0.5 and 0.2 respectively. The likely proceeds from

a sale in each of the circumstances are £1 million, £0.6 million and £0.5 million.
- Seek planning permission to develop the land. The legal and administration fees would be £0.5 million and the probability of being refused permission would be 0.8, which means the chance of obtaining permission is 0.2. If refused, the farmer would be left with the same set of circumstances described in the second option.

If planning permission is granted, the farmer has to make a decision (at node E in Figure 2). If the farmer decides to sell, the probability of getting a good price, i.e. £10 million, is estimated to be 0.4, while the probability of

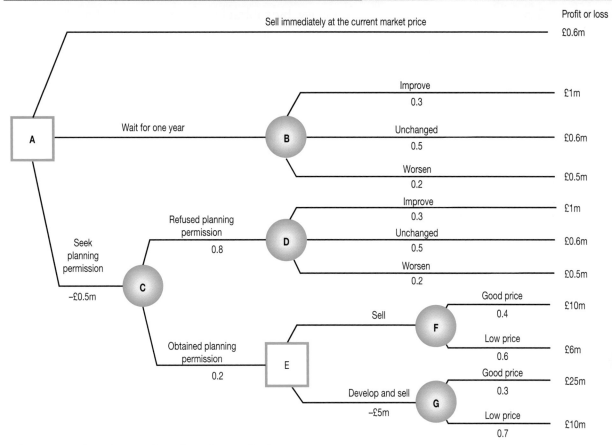

▲ Figure 2 The decisions faced by a farmer in the disposal of land

getting a low price, i.e. £6 million, is 0.6. The farmer could also develop the land himself at a cost of £5 million. The probability of selling the developed land at a good price, i.e. £25 million, is estimated to be 0.3 while the chance of getting a low price, i.e. £10 million, is 0.7. The information about probability and earnings is shown in Figure 2.

What decision should the farmer make? The sale of the land immediately will earn £0.6 million.

The expected monetary value of the second option, waiting a year, is:

0.3 × £1m + 0.5 × £0.6m + 0.2 × £0.5m

= £0.3m + £0.3m + £0.1m

= £0.7m

Since this earns more than the first option, it would be a better choice. We could show this in Figure 3 by

crossing the 'selling immediately' path with a //, indicating that the first option will not be taken up. The expected value of the second option (£0.7 million) is shown in Figure 3 at node B.

A **rollback technique** can then be used to work out the expected value of the third option – seeking planning permission. This means working from right to left, calculating the expected values at each node in the diagram. The expected value at node D is:

Expected value = 0.3 × £1m + 0.5 × £0.6m + 0.2 × £0.5m

= £0.7m

The expected monetary value at node F is:

Expected value = 0.4 × £10m + 0.6 × £6m

= £4m + £3.6m

= £7.6m

The expected value at node G is:

Expected monetary value = 0.3 × £25m + 0.7 x £10m

$$= £7.5m + £7m$$

$$= £14.5m$$

At node E, a decision node, the farmer would choose to develop the land before selling it. This would yield an expected return of £9.5 million (£14.5 million − £5 million) which is higher than £7.6 million, i.e. the expected return from selling the land undeveloped. Thus, in Figure 3 the path representing this option can be crossed. The expected value at node C is now:

Expected monetary value = 0.2 × £9.5m + 0.8 × £0.7m

$$= £1.9m + £0.56m$$

$$= £2.46m$$

Finally, by subtracting the extra cost of seeking planning permission (£0.5 million), the expected value of the final option can be found. It is £1.96 million. Since this is the highest value, this would be the best option for the farmer. This means a // can be placed on the line to node B as £0.7 million is lower than £1.96 million. All of the expected values are shown in Figure 3.

Figure 3 shows profit or loss (taking into account costs) and then the extra costs of planning permission are subtracted in the calculation. However, a decision tree may show revenue in the final column on the right hand side instead of profit, and all costs indicated on the diagram must be subtracted. Whichever is shown, the method of calculation is the same.

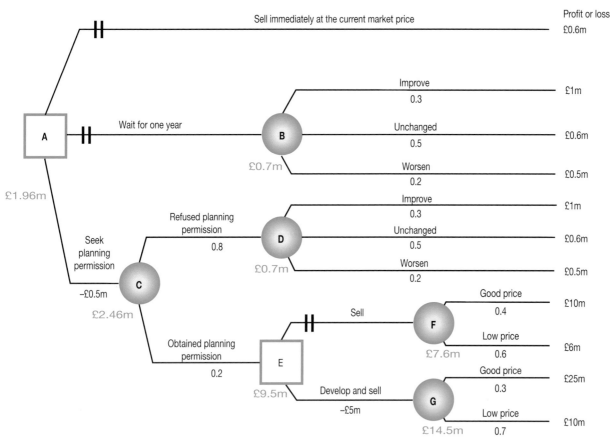

▲ Figure 3 The solution to the farmer's decision problem (all expected values and unused routes are shown)

ACTIVITY 2   SKILLS   ANALYSIS, PROBLEM SOLVING, DECISION MAKING

CASE STUDY: ISAAC CHAILA, MUTANDA IN ZAMBIA

Isaac Chaila is the owner of a smallholding (i.e. a small piece of land used for farming) near Mutanda, Zambia. He specialises in vegetable crops and allocates about 400 acres of land each year to the production of potatoes and swedes. He decides what crops to plant in October each year.

If Isaac plants potatoes, he estimates that the probability of a good crop is 0.3, which will generate ZK50000 profit. The probability of an average crop is 0.3, which would result in ZK30000 profit. The probability of a poor crop is 0.4, which would result in ZK10000 profit.

If swedes are planted, either a good crop or a bad crop will result. He estimates that the probability in each case is 0.5. A good crop will generate a profit of ZK40000 and a poor crop only ZK10000. Figure 4 is a decision tree which shows this information.

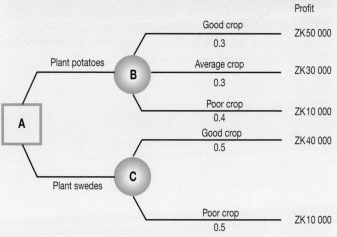

▲ Figure 4 The alternative courses of action faced by Isaac Chaila

1 What is happening at points B and C in the decision tree?
2 Calculate the expected values of each course of action and decide, on financial grounds, which course Isaac should take.

MATHS TIP

Probability can be expressed as a decimal, a fraction or a percentage. For example, the probability of an event might be 0.8, or 80 per cent. They all mean the same. However, when using decision trees it is common to use decimals to represent probability.

EXAM HINT

It is important to recognise that once a particular course of action has been chosen, the profit or revenue generated by that choice is not the same as the expected value. In the first example shown by the decision tree in Figure 1, the expected value of the best option (retain the old campaign) was ¥4.6 million. However, the profit resulting from the decision will be either ¥7 million, or a loss of ¥1 million – it depends on the success of the campaign. But it is not ¥4.6 million, which is the expected value. Expected values are used to make the choice but they do not represent the actual amount of money made.

ADVANTAGES OF DECISION TREES

Decision trees can be applied to much more complicated problems. They have some major advantages.

- Constructing the tree diagram may show possible courses of action not previously considered.
- They involve placing numerical values on decisions. This tends to improve results.
- They force management to take account of the risks involved in decisions and help to separate important from unimportant risks.
- People can often get a better idea of what is involved in a particular decision if the choices are laid out clearly in a diagram.
- They involve placing numerical values on decisions. This tends to improve results. This is because it is far easier to make comparisons between different outcomes if they are presented quantitatively.
- They force management to take account of the risks involved in decisions and help to separate important from unimportant risks. For example, outcomes with low probabilities are less likely to happen than those with higher probabilities.

LIMITATIONS OF DECISION TREES

The technique also has some limitations.

- The information gathered when using the technique is not exact. It is based on probabilities which are often estimated.
- Decisions are not always concerned with quantities and probabilities. For example, they often involve people and are influenced by legal constraints or people's opinions. These factors cannot always be shown by numerical values. **Qualitative** data may also be important.
- Time lags often occur in decision making. By the time a decision is finally made, some of the numerical information may be out of date.
- The process can be quite time-consuming, using up valuable business resources. However, computerised decision-making models can be used to analyse decision trees which can save some time.
- It is argued that decision makers, in an attempt to encourage a particular course of action, may manipulate the data. For example, a manager might be 'biased' when attaching probabilities to certain outcomes. This will change the final results.
- Decision trees are not able to take into account the dynamic nature of business. For example, a sudden change in the economic climate might make a decision based on a decision tree outdated.

ACTIVITY 3   SKILLS ▶ ANALYSIS, INTERPRETATION, PROBLEM SOLVING, DECISION MAKING, INNOVATION

CASE STUDY: TRUMED INC

Trumed Inc. is a US medical company based in Illinois that carries out research into new treatments for colds and influenza. It has won a contract from a large pharmaceuticals corporation to carry out research into new treatments. Trumed has identified three distinct research programmes to develop a vaccination to combat the strain. The code names for each programme are VAC1, VAC2 and VAC3. The cost of the programmes, the expected returns and the probabilities of success and failure are illustrated in the decision tree in Figure 5.

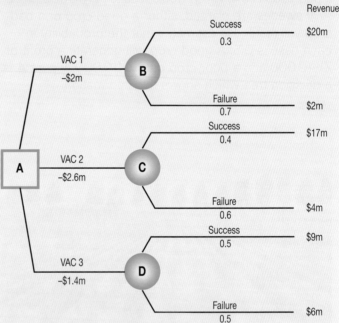

▲ Figure 5 The costs, revenues and probabilities of success and failure of each research programme for Trumed Inc

1 Calculate the expected values of each research programme and advise Trumed which is the best option.

LINKS

Decision trees are quite a useful decision-making technique. They can be used in a variety of circumstances. Consequently, it will be easier to demonstrate synoptic skills when discussing decision trees. For example, a business might use decision trees to help find which course of action to take when deciding upon a price change, or which marketing strategy to select. Links can be made to a range of different areas in the specification – wherever a business might need to make a decision. Some examples of links between this chapter and others include Pricing strategies (Student Book 1, Chapter 12), Marketing strategy (Student Book 1, Chapter 9), Business choices (Student Book 1, Chapter 22), Internal finance (Student Book 1, Chapter 24), External finance (Student Book 1, Chapter 25), Theories of corporate strategy (this book, Chapter 2), Investment appraisal (Chapter 10) and Assessment of a country as a production location (Chapter 29). Finally, Chapter 22 in Student Book 1 looked at the choices and trade-offs that business often face. Decision trees may be helpful when trying to weigh up the trade-offs between different options.

SUBJECT VOCABULARY

back data data obtained from a previous time period
chance node a point on a decision tree diagram (represented by a circle) where a number of outcomes are possible
decision tree a technique which shows all possible outcomes of a decision. The name comes from the similarity of the diagrams to the branches of trees
expected value the numerical value of an outcome multiplied by the probability of that outcome happening
probability the chances of an event happening
rollback technique the process of working back through a decision tree (from right to left) calculating the expected values at each node

CHECKPOINT

1 Why are decision trees useful when a business has to make important decisions?

2 What is meant by a quantitative approach to decision making?

3 What is meant by probability in a decision tree?

4 What is the difference between chance nodes and decision nodes?

5 How is the expected value of a course of action calculated?

6 What are the limitations of using decision trees?

7 State three situations where a business might make use of a decision tree.

EXAM PRACTICE

OPAL MEDIA

SKILLS CRITICAL THINKING, ANALYSIS, INTERPRETATION, PROBLEM SOLVING, DECISION MAKING

Opal Media publishes a number of consumer magazines in Dublin, Ireland. In 2018, the company was concerned that one of its magazines, *Squash Monthly* was not performing well enough. Its circulation figures had dwindled slowly but consistently over the last ten years. The board at Opal Media asked the head of marketing to look into the situation and make a recommendation. He identified a number of options open to the company.

1 Withdraw *Squash Monthly* from the market and replace it with a new magazine.
The marketing department believed there might be a gap in the market for a magazine devoted entirely to the World Cup 2022. Obviously, this would have a short life cycle because once the event was over sales would fall to zero. However, the amount of publicity the event would get suggested that the potential for high sales levels for a short period of time could be enormous. It was also felt that competitors would not be interested in a magazine with such a short life cycle.

- With a thorough development programme, the new magazine, called *World Cup '22*, could be launched in September 2020. The cost of thorough product development would be €400 000 and, once launched, net revenue of €3.5 million would be generated if the magazine was a complete success. The chances of this were estimated to be 0.5. If the magazine flopped (i.e. failed), sales would only be €900 000. The chances of this were thought to be 0.2. If the magazine had moderate success (0.3 chance), sales of €1.8 million would be generated.
- If the product was launched with a rapid development programme it could come out in December 2019. This would cost €100 000. However, with a short development programme, the quality would not be as good and as a result advertising revenue would be lower. If the launch was a complete success (0.6 chance), sales revenue of €2.8 million would be generated. If the magazine flopped (0.2 chance), revenue would be €500 000. With moderate success (0.2 chance), revenue would be around €1.2 million.

2 Retain *Squash Monthly* in its existing form and invest €500 000 in an above-the-line promotion.
This strategy would generate €3.9 million if successful and the chances of success were 0.4. If the investment failed to be a success only €700 000 would be generated.

3 Retain *Squash Monthly* and develop some extension strategies.
Two alternative extension strategies were identified by the marketing department.
- Relaunch the magazine with new features, articles and some below-the-line promotion. The cost of this strategy would be €300 000 and if successful would generate revenue of €3 million. The probability of this was estimated at 0.5. If the strategy was unsuccessful only €600 000 would be generated.
- Launch *Squash Monthly* in Canada and America. This would be risky and more expensive, but the rewards potentially higher at €8 million if completely successful. The costs would be €600 000 and the chance of complete success was estimated to be 0.3. If the magazine flopped in the new markets, the revenue would only amount to €800 000.

The costs, revenues and probabilities of success and failure of Opal Media's options are shown in Figure 6.

1 Calculate the expected values for withdrawing and replacing *Squash Monthly*. **(4 marks)**
2 Calculate the expected values of retaining *Squash Monthly* and (a) investing in above-the-line promotion and (b) developing some extension strategies. **(4 marks)**
3 Explain, on financial grounds only, one option Opal Media should select. **(4 marks)**

Just before the final decision was made by Opal, it was brought to the attention of the marketing department that future exchange rate forecasts would have an impact on the revenues earned in Canada and the USA. It was estimated that the euro would rise against the dollar over the next few years and the revenues earned could fall to €6.5 million and €0.6 million (depending on the success of the launch).

4 Explain one reason why this might affect the decision. **(4 marks)**
5 Assess the limitations to Opal Media of using decision trees to make a decision about the future of *Squash Monthly*. **(12 marks)**

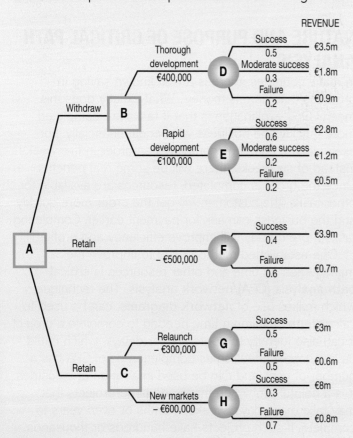

▲ Figure 6 The costs, revenues and probabilities of success and failure of the options open to Opal Media

12 CRITICAL PATH ANALYSIS

LEARNING OBJECTIVES

By the end of this chapter you should be able to understand:
- the nature and purpose of critical path analysis
- how to complete and interpret simple networks to identify the critical path
- how to calculate earliest start time, latest finish time and total float
- the limitations of using critical path analysis.

GETTING STARTED

Sometimes business activity involves project management. Project management is the organisation and supervision (i.e. being in charge) of processes and resources to achieve a specific outcome or goal. A project could be planning a product launch, improving some premises, installing some new machinery, moving to a new location or constructing a factory. These projects are 'big jobs' – they involve lots of different tasks and might use a wide range of business resources. It is important to calculate how much time it will take to complete such a project and whether or not the completion time will be extended if a particular task is delayed. Look at the example below.

Scotnect+ provides a connection service for the supply of electricity. It currently has a job connecting a new hotel to the national grid in a remote part of Scotland, UK. The tasks required in the connection, and the order in which they should be completed, are as follows.

- Task A   Clear land   (3 days)
- Task B   Erect ten pylons   (6 days)
- Task C   Fit cabling   (4 days)
- Task D   Fit fuse box, junction and meter (2 days)
- Task E   Safety testing   (1 day)

In this project, Task C and Task D can be done at the same time.

What is meant by project management? How many days will it take Scotnect+ to complete the project? If Task D were delayed by one day what impact would this have on the completion time? Why is it important to know how long a project will take to complete before starting?

NATURE AND PURPOSE OF CRITICAL PATH ANALYSIS

In many countries, there is a well-known saying in business that 'time is money'. What exactly does this mean? One explanation is that if tasks are completed more quickly, the business will benefit financially. For example, if a company completes an order in five weeks instead of six weeks, there will be some real benefits. Once the order is completed, resources are available for other tasks, the customer will get the order more quickly and the business can ask for payment earlier. Completing tasks more quickly will improve efficiency and profitability.

One established method used to improve the management of time and other resources is **critical path analysis (CPA)/network analysis**. The technique, which makes use of **network diagrams**, can be used to calculate the minimum time needed to complete a project. It can also identify the potential for delays, which could have a crucial effect on its completion date. CPA has a number of uses and can be used in a range of industries. It is a helpful tool when managing large projects that may take many days, weeks, months or even years to complete. If such projects have hundreds or thousands of tasks, CPA can aid planning, organisation and resource management. It is commonly used in construction, engineering, product development, software design, plant maintenance, aerospace and defence industries.

Efficiency: Producing a network diagram can help a business to operate efficiently. For example, a network shows those tasks that can be carried out at the same time. This can help save production or installation time and the use of resources. Highlighting exactly which delays are crucial to the timing of the project can help a business to meet deadlines. Inability to meet a deadline can be costly for a business. Orders may be lost if goods are not produced on time. In the construction industry, clients sometimes have penalty clauses in contracts. These are costs payable by the building company if it does not meet its deadlines. Sometimes building firms earn bonuses for coming in on time or beating deadlines.

Decision making: The use of business models, such as network analysis, is argued to be a more scientific and objective method of making decisions. It is suggested that estimating the length of time a project will take based on past information and an analysis of the tasks involved should lead to deadlines being met more effectively. This is because the implications of delays can be assessed, identified and prevented.

Time-based management: Some businesses operate time-based management systems. These are techniques to minimise the length of time spent in business processes. Identifying tasks that have to be done in order, tasks that can be done together and tasks that may delay the whole project if not completed on time, will all help to ensure that the least time is taken to complete an operation.

Working capital control: Identifying when resources will be required in projects can help a business to manage its working capital cycle. Network diagrams allow a business to identify exactly when materials and equipment will be used in a project. For example, materials can be purchased when required, rather than holding costly stocks. This is especially important if a business operates a just-in-time system of stock control. If a business has to borrow to purchase materials, then charges or interest costs may be reduced (if materials are only bought when required). If delays are identified and taken into account, then resources can be allocated to other operations until they are needed.

MATHS TIP

The arithmetic needed for critical path analysis is very basic – just adding and subtracting. However, to avoid mistakes it is important that your network diagram is big enough to contain all the information needed and is also clearly labelled. Try to draw all arrows with straight lines. It might also be helpful to use more than one colour.

NETWORKS

Many of the operations carried out by businesses are made up of a number of tasks. The operation is only complete when all of the tasks have taken place. For example, the tasks involved in changing a set of strings on a guitar for an instrument repairer might include:

- slackening the strings (i.e. making them looser)
- attaching new strings
- removing the strings
- retuning the strings
- cleaning the fretboard.

These tasks must be carried out in order for the operation to take place. Each task will take a certain amount of time. The operation is shown in Figure 1 on a network diagram. The operation takes 20 minutes to carry out (1 minute + 1 minute + 5 minutes + 10 minutes + 3 minutes).

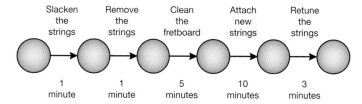

▲ Figure 1 A simple network

Some operations are less simple, with many tasks involved. Figure 2 shows a network diagram for an operation carried out by a cake manufacturer to make cakes for a wedding reception. In this operation, some of the tasks can be carried out at the same time. So, for example, some of the ingredients can be prepared at the same time. Ingredient A takes 10 minutes to prepare, which is longer than any of the other ingredients. So, the whole operation must take 30 minutes (5 mins + 10 mins + 15 mins). This assumes tasks A, B and C can be carried out at the same time.

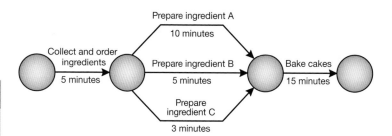

▲ Figure 2 A more complex network

ACTIVITY 1

SKILLS ▸ ANALYSIS, INTERPRETATION, PROBLEM SOLVING

CASE STUDY: INDAIR

IndAir, an Indonesian airline company, is considering improvements to its turnaround time for planes from the moment a plane arrives at the airport terminal to the time it leaves. Figure 3 shows a network diagram for the turnaround.

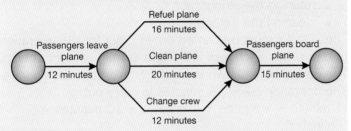

▲ Figure 3 Turnaround time for a passenger aircraft

1 What is the minimum amount of time it takes for the turnaround of the aeroplane?

2 Would the time be affected if the company cut the time it takes to clean a plane from 20 minutes to 14 minutes?

NETWORK ANALYSIS

Businesses often have to complete large projects that involve a series of complicated tasks or activities which must be carried out in a certain order. The use of networks helps a business to manage these projects effectively.

It is vital that a business knows the minimum length of time a project will take to complete. It is also important to know whether a delay in completing individual tasks in an operation will delay the whole project. Network analysis allows a business to find the sequence or 'path' of tasks which are critical to the project and which, if delayed, will cause delays in the entire operation. In practice, businesses may use computers to manage large projects, such as the construction of a road system or hospital, or the manufacture of a large urgent overseas order of new machinery.

Before any project starts, it is important that networks are planned. This involves identifying the tasks that are to take place, how long each will take and the order in which they will take place. This information may be based on previous experience of projects or from research carried out by the business.

Figure 4 shows a network diagram for a construction company that is renovating a home. There are certain features to note about the network.

- Arrows and lines show the tasks or activities to be carried out to complete the project. For example, Task B involves removing and replacing brickwork and flooring in the home.
- Some tasks can be carried out at the same time. For example, Tasks B and C can take place together, but only after Task A has been completed.
- Arrows and lines cannot cross.
- Each task takes a certain amount of time. For example, the business plans to take four days to complete Task B (removing and replacing the brickwork and flooring in the home).
- Tasks must be completed in a certain order. Certain tasks are dependent on others being completed. For example, Task D (fitting new windows) and Task E (rewiring) cannot begin until Task B (removing and replacing brickwork and flooring) has taken place.
- Circles on the diagram, called **nodes**, show the start and finish of a task or activity. For example, Task A, preparing and organising materials, starts at Node 1 and ends at Node 2.
- There is always a node at the start and end of the project.
- Nodes contain information about the timing involved in the project.

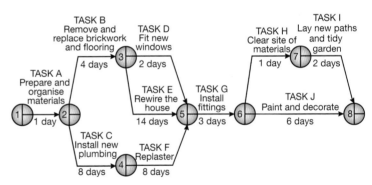

▲ Figure 4 Network for a home renovation

CALCULATING THE EARLIEST START TIMES

The first stage in finding the **critical path** in the network is to calculate the earliest time at which each of the tasks or activities can start, called the **earliest start time** (EST). These are shown in the top right of the nodes. Figure 5 shows the earliest start times for all tasks in the renovation of the home.

Node 1: Task A can begin immediately. So 0 is placed in the EST in Node 1.

Node 2: Task A takes one day to complete. Tasks B and C, which can be carried out at the same time, can only begin after Task A is completed. So they can only begin after 1 day. This is placed in the EST in Node 2.

Node 3: Task B takes 4 days to complete. Together with the day to complete Task A, this means that Tasks D and E can't start until after 5 days (4 days + 1 day). This is placed in the EST in Node 3.

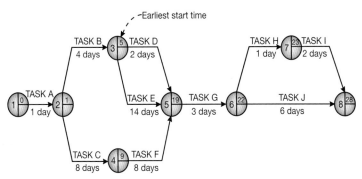

▲ Figure 5 Network showing the earliest start times for the home renovation

Node 4: Task C takes 8 days to complete. Together with the 1 day to complete Task A, this means that Task F can't start until after 9 days (8 days + 1 day). This is placed in the EST in Node 4.

Node 5: What will be the earliest start time for Task G which begins at Node 5?

- Tasks A, B and D take 7 days to complete (1 day + 4 days + 2 days)
- Tasks A, C and F take 17 days to complete (1 day + 8 days + 8 days)
- Tasks A, B and E take 19 days to complete (1 day + 4 days + 14 days)

Task G can only begin when all tasks that come before are completed. It is dependent on earlier tasks. The longest time to complete these tasks is 19 days. So the EST in Node 5 is 19 days and Task G can't start until after 19 days. This highlights an important rule when calculating earliest start times. Always choose the longest amount of time when placing the ESTs in nodes.

Node 8: Another example of this can be found when calculating the final node, Node 8. Tasks up to Node 6 have taken 22 days to complete. So Tasks H and J can only begin after 22 days. The time taken to complete Task J is 6 days. This is longer than the time taken to complete Tasks H and I, which is 3 days (2 days + 1 day). So the EST placed in Node 8 is 22 days + 6 days = 28 days.

As Node 8 is the final node, then 28 days is the time taken to complete the entire project.

ACTIVITY 2

SKILLS ANALYSIS, INTERPRETATION, PROBLEM SOLVING

CASE STUDY: FLEUR ROUGE

Fleur Rouge, a French advertising agency, is working on a campaign for a large client for the launch of a new product. It has constructed a network showing the earliest start times for the different phases of the campaign.

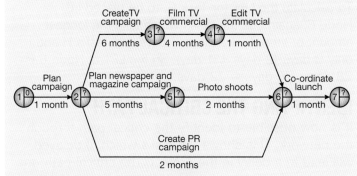

▲ Figure 6 Network for an advertising campaign

1 Copy out the network in Figure 6 and fill in the earliest start times marked by '?'.
2 What is the minimum amount of time the campaign will take to complete?
3 In the one month taken to plan the campaign at the start, the advertising agency revises its estimate of the time taken to plan the newspaper and magazine campaign to 10 months. How will this affect (a) the earliest starting times and (b) the overall time taken to complete the campaign?

CALCULATING THE LATEST FINISH TIMES

The next step involves calculating the latest times that each task can finish without causing the project to be delayed. The **latest finish times (LFTs)** of the project to renovate a home are shown in Figure 7. They appear at the bottom right of the nodes.

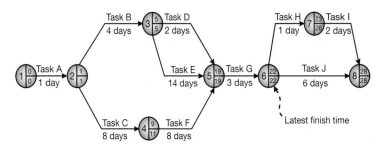

▲ Figure 7 Network showing latest finishing times for the home renovation

Calculating the latest finish times begins at the final node, Node 8. It has already been calculated that the project will take 28 days. This is placed in the LFT of Node 8. To calculate the LFTs of earlier nodes, use the formula:

LFT at node − time taken to complete previous task
LFT at Node 7, for Task H =
28 days − 2 days = 26 days.

To calculate the LFT for Task G, to be placed in Node 6, again use the tasks which take the longest amount of time. Task J takes 6 days and Tasks H and I only 3 days (2 days + 1 day). So the LFT at Node 6 is 28 days − 6 days = 22 days.

IDENTIFYING THE CRITICAL PATH

It is now possible to identify the critical path through the network. This shows the tasks which, if delayed, will lead to a delay in the project. The critical path on any network is where the earliest start times and the latest finish times in the nodes are the same. But it must also be the route through the nodes which takes the longest time.

Figure 8 shows the critical path and the tasks which can't be delayed if the renovation of the home is to be completed on time. These are tasks A, B, E, G and J. The critical path can be indicated by a broken line or crossed lines, or by some other method, such as highlighting the line in colour, by pen or on computer. Other tasks in the network do not lie on the critical path.

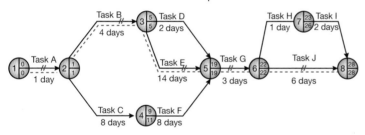

▲ Figure 8 Critical path for the home renovation

CALCULATING THE FLOAT

A business can use the information in the network to calculate the float time in the project. This is the amount of time by which a task can be delayed without causing the project to be delayed. For example, Task I takes 2 days to complete. However, as it does not lie on the critical path, it is possible that some delay can take place in this task without delaying the whole project. A delay of 1 day, for example, would not lead to the project taking longer than 28 days.

How much delay can there be in tasks which do not lie on the critical path?

Total float: The **total float** is the amount of time by which a task can be delayed without affecting the project. It can be calculated as:

LFT of activity − EST of activity − duration

So, for Task B in Figure 8, for example, it would be:

5 days − 1 day − 4 days = 0 days

Activities which lie on the critical path will always have a zero total float value. For Task C, which does not lie on the critical path, the total float is:

11 days − 1 day − 8 days = 2 days

Table 1 shows the total float for all tasks.

Free float: The **free float** is the amount of time by which a task can be delayed without affecting the following task. It can be calculated by:

EST start of next task − EST start of this task − duration

So for Task C it would be:

9 − 1 − 8 = 0 days

Task/activity	LFT	EST	Duration	Total float	EST next	EST this	Duration	Free float
								(days)
A	1	0	1	0	1	0	1	0
B	5	1	4	0	5	1	4	0
C	11	1	8	2	9	1	8	0
D	19	5	2	12	19	5	2	12
E	19	5	14	0	19	5	14	0
F	19	9	8	2	19	9	8	2
G	22	19	3	0	22	19	3	0
H	26	22	1	3	23	22	1	0
I	28	23	2	3	28	23	2	3
J	28	22	6	0	28	22	6	0

▲ Table 1 Float

ACTIVITY 3   SKILLS ANALYSIS, INTERPRETATION, PROBLEM SOLVING

CASE STUDY: HURFORD'S

Chilean-based Hurford's is a specialist zinc galvanising business, coating steel components with zinc to prevent them from rusting. A network for one of its processes is shown in Figure 9.

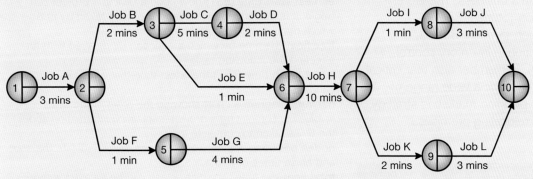

▲ Figure 9 Network for Hurford's

1 Copy out Figure 9 and fill in the earliest start times for each job on your diagram.
2 Fill in the latest finishing times on the diagram.
3 Show the critical path on the diagram.

LIMITATIONS OF CRITICAL PATH ANALYSIS

Critical path analysis has a number of clear advantages which are summarised in Table 2.

However, a business must not assume that because it produces a network its project will be completed without delay. There are some limitations that businesses need to be aware of when using this technique.

- Information used to estimate times in the network may be incorrect. For example, management might have estimated times based on past performance, but a new project could have special requirements that take longer.
- Changes sometimes occur during the life of the project. For example, construction companies may need contingency plans to deal with unforeseen events, such as bad weather delaying operations. These need to be taken into account when producing a network.
- Although critical path analysis identifies times when resources might be used somewhere else in the business, these resources may be inflexible. For example, a giant crane may be identified as being available for a few days. However, if it takes several days to dismantle the crane, move it and reassemble it, it may not be feasible to use it at another location.
- With very large projects, such as building a skyscraper, network analysis can become complex with hundreds of thousands of tasks to consider. However, the use of a computer may simplify the whole approach.

Critical path analysis	Advantages
Identifies the minimum completion time.	CPA enables managers to minimise the project length by monitoring the critical path.
Improves efficiency.	CPA helps to improve resource use. For example, it shows which tasks have 'float' which allows a business to use resources in alternative locations for a period without holding up the completion of the project. Time can also be saved when certain tasks are completed at the same time.
Helps decision making.	CPA is a quantitative technique and can be used to help managers make decisions about resource use, for example.
Helps project management.	Some projects are very large and complex. CPA helps to make clear the order in which tasks must be completed. This reduces the risks and costs associated with such projects.
An aid to planning.	CPA is carried out before work on a project is started. This helps to prepare more thoroughly for a large project. It identifies problems that might occur, so they can be dealt with in advance.

▲ Table 2 Advantages of critical path analysis

LINKS

To demonstrate your synoptic skills when discussing critical path analysis in an exam, you could make relevant links to a number of areas in the specification. For example, critical path analysis is used to improve efficiency and reduce waste in a business. Therefore, it could be linked to Production (Student Book 1, Chapter 37), Capacity utilisation (Student Book 1, Chapter 38) and lean production in Inventory control (Student Book 1, Chapter 39). Remember also that critical path analysis can be used to manage a wide range of projects in business, such as planning marketing strategy, planning a product launch or relocating premises.

CHECKPOINT

1 Why is network analysis also known as 'critical path analysis'?

2 What is shown by a node on a network diagram?

3 What is the difference between the earliest start time (EST) and the latest finish time (LFT)?

4 What is the difference between the total float and the free float?

5 Why can network analysis help improve the efficiency of a business?

6 What are the implications of network analysis for working capital control?

SUBJECT VOCABULARY

critical path the tasks involved in a project which, if delayed, could delay the project
critical path analysis (CPA)/network analysis a method of calculating the minimum time required to complete a project, identifying delays which could be critical to its completion
earliest start time (EST) how soon a task in a project can begin. It is influenced by the length of time taken by tasks which must be completed before it can begin
free float the time by which a task can be delayed without affecting the following task
latest finish time (LFT) the latest time that a task in a project can finish
network diagram a chart showing the order of the tasks involved in completing a project, containing information about the times taken to complete the tasks
nodes positions in a network diagram which indicate the start and finish times of a task
total float the time by which a task can be delayed without affecting the time needed to complete the project

EXAM PRACTICE

CASE STUDY: MANGUXI HOLDINGS

SKILLS   CRITICAL THINKING, ANALYSIS, INTERPRETATION, PROBLEM SOLVING, REASONING

Angolan company Manguxi Holdings manufactures electronic components for domestic appliances. The company has received some large orders recently after a successful sales drive. However, to increase capacity and improve productivity it must replace the entire assembly line with up-to-date technology. The directors are keen to

go ahead with the investment but are worried about the disruption that will be caused. During the construction of the new assembly line, production will be zero. The company can hold up to 30 days of stocks, so the new line must be working within one month. If the new line is not ready, Manguxi Holdings will lose approximately AOA70 000 per day. This will be unacceptable to the directors.

Figure 10 shows the network diagram for the installation of the new technology and Table 3 shows the tasks, task order and task times required to construct the new assembly line.

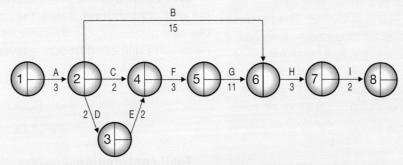

▲ Figure 10 Network diagram for the installation of new technology at Manguxi Holdings

Task	Description	Order/dependency	Duration
A	Dismantle old line	Must be done first	3 days
B	Retrain staff	Must follow A	15 days
C	Position lifting gear	Must follow A	2 days
D	Remove roof panels	Must follow A	2 days
E	Lower in new plant	Must follow D	2 days
F	Replace roof panels	Must follow C and E	3 days
G	Install new plant	Must follow F	11 days
H	Test run	Must follow B and G	3 days
I	Safety checks	Must follow H	2 days

▲ Table 3 The tasks, task order and task times required to construct the new assembly line

Q

1 Calculate the earliest start times (ESTs) for the activities required to install the new technology. **(4 marks)**
2 Calculate the latest finish times (LFTs) for the activities required to install the new technology. **(4 marks)**
3 Explain what is meant by the critical path and state the minimum amount of time in which this project can be completed. **(4 marks)**
4 Explain one reason why the construction time will be affected if Task B is delayed by four days. **(4 marks)**
5 Assess the advantages and disadvantages to Manguxi Holdings of using critical path analysis (CPA). **(12 marks)**

EXAM HINT

Drawing network diagrams, calculating ESTs, LFTs and floats may be challenging. However, with practice it becomes a lot easier. It is also important not to neglect your understanding of the nature, purpose and limitations of critical path analysis. It is possible for exam questions to focus on this and/or calculations.

13 CONTRIBUTION

LEARNING OBJECTIVES

By the end of this chapter you should be able to understand:
■ the nature and purpose of contribution
■ calculation and interpretation of contribution
■ the use of contribution as a decision-making technique.

GETTING STARTED

Kostas Retsos is the manager of a small hotel with 20 rooms in Paphos, on the island of Cyprus. The hotel is very busy and often operates at full capacity during the summer months. In August 2018, the hotel was full every single day. Guests pay €100 per night to stay in the hotel which includes breakfast. The variable costs per room in August are €40 per night. This includes cleaning, other housekeeping costs, breakfast, electricity and other variable costs (see Student Book 1, Chapter 29).

How much money is left over per room after variable costs have been covered? How much money will be left over after all variable costs have been covered for the whole of August (remember: there are 31 days in August)? If fixed costs are €2000 for August, how much profit would be made by the hotel in that month?

WHAT IS CONTRIBUTION?

In business, the word **contribution** has a specific meaning. It is the amount of money left over from a sale after variable costs have been covered. For example, Varinder Patel owns a second-hand bicycle shop in Hyderabad. If he buys a second-hand bicycle for INR5500 and sells it for INR8000, the difference between the selling price and the amount he paid for the bicycle is INR2500 (INR8000 − INR5500). This is the contribution made by the sale. However, this is not the same as profit. The INR2500 will contribute to the fixed costs or **overheads** of the business and profit.

A business can calculate the contribution made by the sale of a single unit. It can also calculate the contribution made by the sale of a much larger quantity, such as a big order or a whole month's sales.

Unit contribution: In the example, we have calculated the **unit contribution**. It was the contribution made by the sale of one bicycle by Varinder Patel. The formula for calculating unit contribution is given by:

$$\text{Contribution per unit} = \text{selling price} - \text{variable cost}$$
$$= \text{INR8000} - \text{INR5500}$$
$$= \text{INR2500}$$

Total contribution: It is possible to calculate the **total contribution** made by a large order. For example, an Indian textile company sells 500 000 T-shirts to a customer for INR120 each. The variable cost for each T-shirt is INR90. The total contribution made by the order is given by:

$$\text{Total contribution} = \text{total revenue} - \text{total variable cost}$$
$$= \text{INR120} \times 500\,000 -$$
$$\text{INR90} \times 500\,000$$
$$= \text{INR60 million} \times \text{INR45 million}$$
$$= \text{INR15 million}$$

In this example, the INR15 million total contribution will contribute to the manufacturer's fixed costs and profit. We can also calculate the total contribution by multiplying the unit contribution by the number of units sold. In this example, the total contribution made by the T-shirt order would be given by:

$$\text{Total contribution} = \text{unit contribution} \times \text{number of units sold}$$
$$= (\text{INR120} - \text{INR90}) \times 500\,000$$
$$= \text{INR30} \times 500\,000$$
$$= \text{INR15 million}$$

ACTIVITY 1   SKILLS   PROBLEM SOLVING

CASE STUDY: HAMZA JOBE

In the Republic of The Gambia, around three-quarters of the population rely on agriculture for their livelihoods (i.e. their means of earning money in order to live). The Jobe family rent some land and grow peanuts. Bags of peanuts (1 kg) are sold in a local market for GMD15. The variable costs of a 1 kg bag are estimated to be GMD10. In October 2018, Hamza Jobe sold 210 bags of peanuts at the local market.

1 Explain what is meant by contribution.
2 Calculate the unit contribution of a 1 kg bag of peanuts.
3 Calculate the total contribution for sales in October.

THE NATURE OF CONTRIBUTION AND ITS CALCULATION

Contribution has a number of purposes in business. We can use contribution to help make decisions and calculate some key financial values. For example, we can use it to:

- calculate the break-even level of **output** (see Student Book 1, Chapter 31)
- calculate the amount of profit made by a business
- calculate the amount that needs to be sold to reach a specific profit target
- help a business to decide which order to accept when faced with a choice
- help a business decide what price to charge for a product.

Contribution and break-even: The break-even level of output is given by:

$$\text{Break-even} = \frac{\text{fixed costs}}{\text{contribution}}$$

Take the example of the Indian T-shirt manufacturer, where the unit contribution is INR30. If fixed costs are INR6 million, the break-even level of output is given by:

$$\text{Break-even output} = \frac{\text{INR6 million}}{\text{INR30}} = 200\,000 \text{ T-shirts}$$

Contribution and profit: Profit can be calculated using the formula below.

$$\text{Profit} = \text{total contribution} - \text{fixed costs}$$

If the Indian T-shirt manufacturer produces 700 000 T-shirts and fixed costs are INR6 million, the amount of profit made at this level of output is given by:

$$\begin{aligned}\text{Profit} &= \text{INR30} \times 700\,000 - \text{INR6 million} \\ &= \text{INR21 million} - \text{INR6 million} \\ &= \text{INR15 million}\end{aligned}$$

Contribution and profit target: Contribution can be used to work out how much a business needs to sell to reach a specific profit target. The formula needed to do this is given by:

$$\text{Output} = \frac{\text{fixed costs} + \text{profit target}}{\text{contribution}}$$

For example, if the Indian T-shirt manufacturer wanted to make a profit of INR12 million, the level of output that must be sold to reach this target is given by:

$$\text{Output} = \frac{\text{INR6 million} + \text{INR12 million}}{\text{INR30}}$$

$$= \frac{\text{INR18 million}}{\text{INR30}}$$

$$= 600\,000 \text{ T-shirts}$$

We will discuss the role of contribution in decision making and other financial calculations later in the chapter.

INTERPRETING CONTRIBUTION

Contribution margin ratio: Contribution is the amount of money left over from a sale after variable costs have been covered. This means that any money left over can be used to pay fixed costs and contribute to profit if there is enough left. We may interpret contribution as the gross profit margin and can be expressed as a percentage. For example, if a firm's annual sales are US$1.68 million and its total variable costs for the year are US$1.02 million, then the total contribution for the year will be US$660 000 (US$1.68 million − US$1.02 million). This means that the gross profit margin (sometimes called the contribution margin ratio) is 39.3 per cent (US$660 000 ÷ US$1.68 million × 100).

The contribution margin ratio can also be calculated for a unit of output. For example, if unit contribution is US$2 and price is US$4, the contribution margin for a single unit will be 50 per cent (US$2 ÷ US$4 × 100).

Contribution, fixed costs, variable costs and profit: The value of contribution can be illustrated in relation to variable costs, fixed costs and profit using a pie chart. In the example, assume that in November 2018, Varinder Patel's:

- total revenue is INR105 300
- total variable costs are INR64 200
- fixed costs are INR10 000.

Figure 1(a) shows how the total revenue of INR105 300 is divided between total variable cost (INR64 200) and contribution (INR41 100).

Figure 1(b) shows how the same total revenue is divided between variable costs (INR64 200), fixed costs (10 000) and profit (INR31 100). Note that the value of contribution (INR41 100) is equal to the value of fixed cost (INR10 000) and profit (INR31 100) added together.

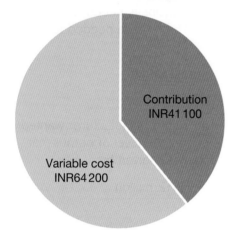

▲ Figure 1(a) Total revenue INR105 300 divided between total variable cost (INR64 200) and contribution (INR41 100)

▲ Figure 1(b) Total revenue INR105 300 divided between variable costs (INR64 200), fixed costs (INR10 000) and profit (INR31 100)

CONTRIBUTION AND DECISION MAKING

Contribution costing: A business might use contribution when making certain types of decision. For example, sometimes a business will have to decide which order(s) or contract(s) to accept when faced with a choice from different customers. This may be because the business does not have enough capacity to accept all the orders it receives. Or it may be that they are not all financially viable (i.e. capable of financial success). **Contribution costing** can help here.

For example, Lee Chang Engineering receives the three orders shown in Table 1. Total fixed costs for the period are $50 000. Lee Chang only has enough capacity to complete one of these orders. By calculating the total contribution made by each order, it will be easier to decide which order to accept. Table 2 shows the unit contributions and total contributions for each order. Financially, Lee Chang should accept the order for the 7000 brackets. This order generates a total contribution of $91 000. If the fixed costs are subtracted from the total contribution, the business will make a profit of $41 000 ($91 000 − $50 000) on the order.

Order	Variable costs ($ per unit)	Price ($ per unit)
5000 drive shafts	20	35
12 000 mountings	13	18
7000 brackets	16	29

▲ Table 1 Three orders received by Lee Chang Engineering

	Variable costs ($ per unit)	Price ($ per unit)	Unit contribution ($)	Total contribution ($)
5000 drive shafts	20	35	15	75 000
12 000 mountings	13	18	5	60 000
7000 brackets	16	29	13	91 000

▲ Table 2 Unit contribution and total contribution for the three orders received by Lee Chang Engineering

Contribution pricing: A business may use contribution when deciding what price to charge. This involves setting a price that exceeds the value of variable cost. This means that a particular order or product will always make a contribution when sold. This approach ignores fixed costs because a single order or product may not generate enough contribution to cover fixed costs. This approach needs to be used carefully. Obviously, to make a profit fixed costs have to be covered. Contribution pricing is more likely to be used when fixed costs are low or when a business, through experience, knows that fixed costs will be covered.

Table 3 shows some financial information for Rossi Shoes, an Italian shoemaker that receives four big orders in a particular month. The table shows the price charged for each order, the variable costs and the total contribution made by each. The total contribution for all four orders is also given as €35 500. Through experience, Rossi Shoes knows that these prices will cover fixed costs. Fixed costs are €10 000, so the monthly profit from these four orders is €25 500 (€35 500 − €10 000)

	Price (€)	Variable cost (€)	Contribution (€)
Order 1	45 000	32 000	13 000
Order 2	23 000	21 000	2 000
Order 3	49 000	39 500	9 500
Order 4	58 000	47 000	11 000
Total	175 000	139 500	35 500

▲ Table 3 Financial information for Rossi Shoes

THINKING BIGGER

The use of contribution to help make business decisions is a quantitative approach to decision making. The method ignores qualitative issues. In practice, qualitative issues may be important and therefore would have to be taken into account. For example, when a business uses contribution to select which orders to accept, it is possible that they might choose to accept an order, even though the total contribution fails to cover fixed costs entirely. There may be several reasons for this.

- A business may accept an order with a low contribution from a new customer. It may do this in the hope that in the future it will receive more profitable orders from this customer.
- If a business is quiet, it may accept orders with low contributions in order to reduce the burden of fixed costs. If an order makes a contribution to fixed costs, losses will be lower, even though it may not be profitable overall.
- Orders with low contributions may be accepted in order to keep resources occupied in a business. For example, a business may accept unprofitable orders to keep employees busy. It may not be a good idea to make workers redundant because they may be needed in the future when trading conditions improve. A business may also want to resist making staff redundant because it has invested in their training.

ACTIVITY 2   SKILLS   INTERPRETATION, PROBLEM SOLVING

CASE STUDY: FREDRIKKE HOLMGAARD

Fredrikke Holmgaard runs a catering company in Odense, Denmark. She provides dinner parties for people in their own homes. Fredrikke has built up an excellent reputation in the local area and only has to work four nights a week to make a comfortable living. In the first year of trading she incurred quite high fixed costs. Now, however, most of her costs are variable. These include the costs of food, dining accessories such as napkins, flower decorations and the hire of glassware and eating utensils when necessary. Fredrikke normally uses her client's kitchen and cooking utensils when working. Fixed costs are currently DKK1000 per week and Fredrikke uses contribution pricing. The price is determined by the number of diners in the party and the choice of client menu. Table 4 shows some financial information for a typical week.

Dinner party	Price (DKK)	Variable cost (DKK)	Contribution (DKK)
1	2400	1550	850
2	1400	700	700
3	3200	1800	1400
4	2000	600	1400

▲ Table 4 Financial information for Fredrikke Holmgaard's business

1 Explain what is meant by 'contribution pricing'.
2 Calculate the week's profit made by Fredrikke's business using the information in Table 4.
3 Why should contribution pricing be used carefully?

EXAM HINT

When answering calculation questions, it is always important to show the units. The units might be, for example, £, $, millions, 000s, tonnes or product names. It is also important to state the formula that you are using in calculation questions. This means that if you make a mistake with the calculations, you are still likely to be awarded some marks for showing that you understand the question.

SUBJECT VOCABULARY

contribution the amount of money left over from a sale after variable costs have been subtracted from revenue. The money contributes to fixed costs and profit
contribution costing the use of contribution to help make decisions based on costs, such as which order to accept
contribution pricing a pricing strategy that involves setting a price that exceeds the value of the variable cost
overheads an overhead cost or expense, for example lighting, equipment and any extras paid for out of a centralised budget
total contribution the amount of money left over from the sale of several units, or an order, after variable costs have been covered
unit contribution the amount of money left over from the sale of a single unit after variable costs have been covered

CHECKPOINT

1 A product sells for $10 and the variable costs are $8.50. What is the contribution per unit?

2 A clothes retailer buys 20 000 garments from a Bangladeshi supplier for BDT2.5 million. The garments are sold for BDT200 each. What is the total contribution made by the sale of the garments?

3 What is the formula for calculating profit using contribution?

4 If the total contribution is €120 000 and fixed costs are €96 000, what is the profit?

5 If total variable costs are AUD450 000 and contribution is AUD225 000, what is total revenue?

6 State three ways in which contribution can be used to help make business decisions.

EXAM PRACTICE

CASE STUDY: CHENGDU PLASTIC CONTAINERS

SKILLS INTERPRETATION, PROBLEM SOLVING

Chengdu Plastic Containers is a family business based in Chengdu, China. It was set up in 2010 when Deng Xuri, a plastics factory manager, decided that he no longer wanted to work for someone else. He felt that he could set up a small production facility to manufacture plastic containers for storage.

His main customers were office suppliers and large businesses. However, an increasing number of customers were buying them to store belongings outside because the containers are weatherproof. By 2018 the business offered quite a wide range of plastic containers such as those shown in the photograph below.

Sales have grown strongly from CNY41 million in 2015 to CNY82 million in 2018. Chengdu Plastic Containers is operating at almost full capacity, but the Xuri family has no plans to expand. They are happy with the current profit levels. However, the business does have to refuse work. When faced with a choice of orders, Deng only accepts those which make the largest contribution. In February 2018, the business received four orders in one week as outlined in Table 5. The factory could only meet the demands of two.

	Wong & Co	BNY Stores	VC Singh	Chow Ltd
Number of units	20 000	30 000	25 000	20 000
Contract price per unit (CNY)	800	850	700	1050
Material costs per unit (CNY)	220	200	240	300
Labour costs per unit (CNY)	340	420	210	380
Other variable costs per unit (CNY)	100	140	120	130
Fixed costs (CNY)	500 000	500 000	500 000	500 000

▲ Table 5 Details of four orders for Chengdu Plastic Containers

Q

1 Explain one difference between unit contribution and total contribution. **(4 marks)**

2 Calculate the total contribution made by each of the four orders. **(4 marks)**

3 Explain which two orders should be accepted by Chengdu Plastic Containers. **(4 marks)**

4 Calculate the profit made from the two orders accepted by Deng Xuri. **(4 marks)**

5 Discuss the qualitative factors that might be taken into account by Chengdu Plastic Containers when using contribution to help make business decisions. **(8 marks)**

INFLUENCES ON BUSINESS DECISIONS

Many business decisions are likely to be influenced by the culture of an organisation, the relative power of stakeholders and the moral position a business takes. This section looks at how organisational culture might be strong or weak, the classification of company cultures (i.e. how they can be grouped) such as power, role, task and person, how corporate culture is formed and the difficulties a business might have establishing a culture. It also addresses the role of internal and external stakeholders, their objectives and whether or not businesses take a stakeholder approach or a shareholder approach when making decisions. The potential for conflict between shareholders and other stakeholders is explored. Finally, the section investigates the ethics of strategic decisions and the trade-offs between profit and ethics. This includes a focus on pay and rewards and corporate social responsibility.

14 CORPORATE CULTURE

UNIT 3
3.3.4

LEARNING OBJECTIVES

By the end of this chapter you should be able to understand:

■ strong and weak cultures
■ classification of company cultures: power, role, task, person
■ how corporate culture is formed
■ the difficulties in changing an established culture.

GETTING STARTED

Warren Buffett has been the CEO and chairman of Berkshire Hathaway, a multinational conglomerate since 1970. The company has stakes in many famous brands, such as Heinz®, American Express® and Coca-Cola. In 2018, aged 88, he was personally worth $87 billion. As a philanthropist (i.e. a rich person who helps those in need), Buffet spends a large portion of his money on good deeds. Buffett is regarded as one of the most generous philanthropists in the world. He has given more than $27 billion to 'good causes' in the last decade. Buffet believes that a business should have strong moral principles; for example, treating suppliers, employees and customers well. He thinks that a business with strong moral principles will win more interest and co-operation among stakeholders compared to competitors who do not. He also has a reputation for buying businesses with a strong leader and allowing them high levels of autonomy (i.e. the freedom to make their own decisions).

What sort of businesses does Warren Buffet prefer to buy? Explain how he expects the businesses he buys to behave in the commercial world. How might stakeholders respond to leaders who treat them well? How might such an esteemed leader influence the values and norms in a corporation?

WHAT IS CORPORATE CULTURE?

Every place of work has a slightly different atmosphere. Some are busy, some are friendly, some are disorganised and others are challenging. This reflects the **organisational culture** (sometimes also called the **organisation, corporate or business culture**) of a business. The organisational culture is the values, attitudes, beliefs, meanings and norms (i.e. typical behaviour) that are shared by people and groups within an organisation.

For example, in some companies there may be very strict rules and regulations. Workers might be tightly controlled. They may not be allowed to make decisions for themselves and supervision levels may be very high. In others, the atmosphere may be more relaxed. Interaction between workers may be permitted or even encouraged. Supervision levels will be lower and workers may be expected to think for themselves.

Many different types of culture exist and it might be rare to find two or more firms with identical cultures. Cultures are often described as strong or weak. These are discussed below.

Strong corporate cultures: A strong culture is one that is deeply fixed into the way a business or organisation does things. It is argued that there are certain advantages to a business of establishing a strong corporate culture.

- It provides a sense of identity for employees. They feel part of the business. This may lead workers to be flexible when the company needs to change or is having difficulties.
- Workers identify with other employees. This may help with aspects of the business such as teamwork.
- It increases the commitment of employees to the company. This may prevent problems such as high labour **turnover** or industrial relations problems.
- It motivates workers in their jobs. This may lead to increased productivity.

- It helps employees understand what is going on around them. This can prevent misunderstanding in operations or instructions passed to them.
- It helps to reinforce the values of the organisation and senior management.
- It acts as a control device for management. This can help when setting company strategy.

Weak corporate cultures: In comparison to a strong culture, a **weak culture** exists where it is difficult to identify the factors that form the culture or where a wide range of subcultures exist, making the culture difficult to define.

In an organisation with a weak culture, the beliefs, behavioural rules, traditions and rituals are not easily adopted by workers. This means the business has to set up systems to make worker alignment (i.e. where all employees are pulling in the same direction) happen. Businesses with a weak culture tend to struggle. For example, workers may be resistant to change or there might be too much **bureaucracy**. There may also be inconsistent behaviour which results in inconsistent and poor performance. This can reflect badly on a company. Companies with a weak culture are likely to have higher costs as they implement a range of systems to help align workers with a better culture.

Companies with a weak culture can often be identified by their poor quality of customer service. For example, customers may be kept waiting, staff may be inflexible, phones may not be answered and mistakes are more likely to happen.

Finally, although a strong corporate culture may be preferable to a weak one, it does not guarantee success. For example, if a culture is too rigid, a business may not be able to respond quickly to a sudden change in the market. In such a case, a weak culture may be more flexible.

There are certain factors that are likely to lead to a strong or weak culture in a business.

- **Surface manifestations (i.e. appearances).** These include:
  - artefacts, such as furniture, clothes or tools – wearing a uniform would be an example
  - ceremonials, such as award-giving ceremonies or the singing of the company song at the start of work
  - courses, such as induction courses, or ongoing training courses for workers which are used to instil the organisational culture
  - heroes of the business, living or dead, such as Bill Gates, Richard Branson or Walt Disney, whose way of working provides a role model within the business
  - language used in a business-specific way, such as referring to workers as 'colleagues' or calling workers 'crew members' or associates
  - mottoes, which are short statements that never change, expressing the values of an organisation

  - stories, which tell of some important event that exemplifies the values of the business, such as the history and role of the founders
  - myths, which are frequently told stories within a business about itself, but are not necessarily true
  - norms, which are the ways in which most workers behave, such as worrying if you turn up for work late, always being prepared to cover for workers who are off sick, or not using the company's telephone to make personal calls
  - physical layout of premises, such as open plan offices, 'hot desking', or allocating the size of an office according to a manager's place in the hierarchy
  - rituals, which are regular events that reinforce the culture of an organisation, such as always supporting charity or fundraising events ('we are a caring organisation'), having a weekly 'dress down day' ('we are a relaxed organisation'), or holding an annual end-of-year party ('we are a sociable organisation').
- **Core organisational values.** Core values are the most important or central values. They are located below the surface manifestations of organisational culture. They are consciously expressed in words and policies, such as mission statements. Core organisational values can reflect the actual culture of a business, but, equally, they might not. Workers at the bottom of the hierarchy might have very different values from the ones that senior management want them to possess.
- **Basic assumptions.** Basic assumptions are the unspoken beliefs and ways of working. The workforce may share a general attitude which affects how they behave. These beliefs are 'invisible' and therefore often difficult to see, understand and change.

In practice, there may be differences between the three levels of surface manifestations, core organisational values and basic assumptions. For example, a company might organise regular social events for employees (a surface manifestation). It might say in documents that it is a 'friendly and caring employer' (its organisational values), but there might be a competitive culture in the organisation that tends to make people 'look out for themselves' and be distrustful of everyone else. In this situation, the actual organisational culture is different from the surface manifestation and the organisational values.

In contrast, another organisation might call its employees 'partners' (the surface manifestation). Its mission statement may say that it is committed to 'rewarding employees as well as shareholders' (its organisational values). It may then pay employees above the average for the industry and give regular annual bonuses based upon how much profit the business has made during the year (the organisational culture). Here, the organisational culture fits with the stated values and the surface manifestation. There is a culture of rewarding employees because they are stakeholders. For example, the John Lewis Partnership based in the UK operates a supermarket chain and a department store. It has an excellent reputation for the way it treats employees. Employees are part-owners of the business and receive a share of the profits each year.

CLASSIFICATION OF COMPANY CULTURES

There are many ways of classifying (i.e. putting into groups) organisational culture. One attempt was made by Charles Handy in *Understanding Organisations* (1993). He argued that there were four main types of organisational culture.

Power culture: A power culture is one where there is a central source of power responsible for decision making. There are few rules and procedures within the business and these are rejected by the individuals who hold power when it suits them. There is a competitive atmosphere among employees. Among other things, they compete to gain power because this allows them to achieve their own objectives. This creates a political atmosphere within the business. Relatively young, small-to medium-sized businesses, where a single owner founded the firm and is still very much in control could typically have power cultures.

Role culture: In a role culture, decisions are made through well-established rules and procedures. Power is associated with a role, such as marketing director or supervisor, rather than with individuals. In contrast to a power culture, influence and control lies with the roles that individuals play rather than with the individuals themselves. An organisation with a role culture will have a tall hierarchy with a long chain of command. Role cultures could be described as bureaucratic cultures. Local government departments responsible for administering community services are examples of role cultures.

Task culture: In a task culture, power is given to those who can complete tasks. Power therefore lies with those with expertise rather than a particular role, as in a role culture. In a task culture, teamworking is common, with teams made up of the experts needed to get a job done. Teams are created and then taken apart as the work changes. Adaptability and dynamism are important in this culture.

Person culture: A person culture is one where there are a number of individuals in the business who have expertise, but who don't necessarily work together particularly closely. The purpose of the organisation is to support those individuals. The business will be full of people with a similar backgrounds, skill sets and training. Examples of person cultures could be firms of accountants, lawyers, doctors or architects.

ACTIVITY 1　　SKILLS　CRITICAL THINKING, ANALYSIS

CASE STUDY: TOP 10 BEST COMPANIES TO WORK FOR IN CANADA

In some countries, surveys are carried out to identify the best business to work for. Companies sign up to enter the survey and in 2018, in Canada, more than 600 businesses registered to take part. All of the data is based on employee opinions given through a questionnaire. The questionnaire is updated each year to reflect current workplace concerns. Below is the Top 10 of the '25 Best Big Companies' to work for from the 2018 list.

Rank	Company	Industry
1	SAP	Computer hardware and software
2	Paysafe® Group	Financial transaction processing
3	Shopify®	Internet
4	Microsoft®	Computer hardware and software
5	Salesforce	Computer hardware and software
6	Lululemon	Department, clothing and shoe stores
7	Apple®	Computer hardware and software
8	Ciridian	Enterprise software and network solutions
9	Hydro One	Energy
10	Starbucks®	Fast food & quick service restaurants

▲ Table 1 The Top 10 of the '25 Best Big Companies' to work for in Canada (2018)
Adapted from https://www.glassdoor.ca/Award/Best-Places-to-Work-Canada-LST_KQ0,26.htm

1 Discuss the cultural factors that may have led to these companies being voted into the Top 10 'Best Big Companies' to work for. You could pick two companies and carry out your own research.

THINKING BIGGER

In the 1970s and 1980s, Dutch psychologist Professor Geert Hofstede conducted research into how culture differs between organisations across international barriers. (Geert Hofstede, Comparing Values, Behaviors, Insititutions and Organizations Across Nations, Second Edition, 2003) He examined these **cultural dimensions** by studying work-related values and identified five key variables, or dimensions, that vary across businesses in different countries. These variables impact organisational culture and how the business may react in certain circumstances.

Power distance

This is the distance between managers and subordinates. A high-power distance culture suggests that managers will have significantly more power and privileges than their subordinates. They probably will not socialise and communication is generally top down. A lower-power distance culture has greater collaboration and discussion between employees of different rank.

Individualism

This is how people see themselves within their organisation. Where individualism is high, people tend to focus on their own success above that of the organisation or their team. The level of individualism versus collectivism within a culture can determine organisational structure, motivation and internal competition.

Masculinity versus femininity

Hofstede theorises the management style in a masculine organisation might be described as competitive and assertive. Its counterpart approach might be described as caring and co-operative. According to him, this could influence how people respond to targets and goals, and relate to one another in the business.

Uncertainty avoidance

This is the level at which an organisation will accept risk. A high level of uncertainty avoidance suggests a business will want evidence, security and proof before acting. By contrast a business with a low uncertainty avoidance might take 'a long shot' if it believes the rewards are worthwhile. Organisations with low uncertainty avoidance are more entrepreneurial and agile in their decision making.

Long-term versus short-term orientation

This addresses a culture's 'time horizon' and the basis on which decisions are made. A high score indicates business decisions are made to achieve success in the long term. A low score suggests an organisation makes decisions to achieve short-term rewards and immediate gratification in terms of shareholder value.

Hofstede's cultural dimensions go beyond simply identifying behavioural differences – they present a useful framework for understanding the cultural setting of a business. This is particularly useful when analysing businesses across borders and interpreting how international businesses might react and interact in different circumstances, such as international trade, partnerships, mergers and takeovers.

EFFECTS OF ORGANISATIONAL CULTURE

Organisational culture affects a business in a wide variety of ways. Three of these ways are motivation, organisational structures and change (for example, new management and mergers and takeovers).

Motivation: Organisational culture affects the motivation of staff. It can have a direct effect because the way in which staff treat each other impacts on motivation. For example, motivation is likely to be greater if the culture of the organisation respects individual workers and their achievements. A highly competitive culture might motivate some workers and demotivate others. Organisational culture can also indirectly affect motivation. An organisational culture which leads to a successful business is likely in itself to motivate staff because they feel part of the successful business.

Organisational structures: Organisational culture can affect the organisational structure of a business. In a person culture the hierarchy is likely to be fairly flat. For example, in a doctors' practice, there are unlikely to be many layers of management. This is because a number of key workers share the senior management roles. In contrast there are likely to be more layers of management in a large multinational business as they have regional and divisional managers and multiple product teams. There are likely to be more layers in larger businesses' hierarchy as specialist roles are assigned.

New management: A business could change the way that they choose new management. The greater the change needed, the more likely it is that the new management will have to challenge the existing organisational culture. The organisational culture is likely to be part of the problem that needs addressing if the business is to change.

Mergers and takeovers: When two businesses merge or one takes over another, each business is likely to have a different organisational culture. The process of creating a single business out of the two organisations will therefore involve changing organisational culture. In a takeover, one simple way of making that change quickly is for the senior management in the company being taken over to be made redundant. Without powerful advocates at the top of the organisation, those lower down will find it difficult to resist the change that will be imposed upon them. However, motivation and morale is often low in a company that has been taken over for the first year or so because they are being forced to change.

As you might identify a patent on an invention or an established brand as an asset, culture can be a distinctive and sustainable competitive advantage. Chapter 2 discussed distinctive capabilities as a route to achieving competitive advantage for a business. John Kay (1993) referred to 'architecture' as one of the types of distinctive capability that could lead to competitive advantage. Architecture refers to the relationships and networks within an organisation and those that it develops with its external stakeholders – corporate culture would be included. We should consider corporate culture as an asset that can be used to add value and compete in the market. However, we must remember that culture is very difficult to operate and shape in order to meet the changing needs of the business. Figure 1 shows how Hofstede's cultural dimensions vary in a small sample of different countries/regions. This can be used in your answer in Activity 2.

ACTIVITY 2   SKILLS   ANALYSIS, INTERPRETATION

CASE STUDY: TAKEOVER OF ISTA INTERNATIONAL

In recent years, a number of Chinese companies have made **acquisitions** in Germany. Indeed, Chinese buyers invested a record sum of $13.7 billion in German companies in 2017. For example, the biggest deal in 2017 was the purchase of Ista International (a Germany-based energy service provider) by billionaire magnate Li Ka-shing's Cheung Kong Property Holdings for $6.7 billion. Li Ka-shing is the richest person in Hong Kong, China and is also a famous philanthropist.

Ista, which is based in Essen in the Rhine-Ruhr region of Germany, runs the submetering business, measuring energy and water consumption (i.e. how much is used) and the cost allocation (i.e. how much is given) for properties. It also sells a range of meters and provides a number of other services such as maintenance, meter reading, data processing and billing. Ista has interests in Germany, Denmark, the Netherlands, France, Italy and Spain. It has been reported that Ista has a sound growth record and generates steady and strong cash flows.

Cheung Kong Property Holdings changed its name to CK Asset Holdings Limited later in 2017. The purpose of this was to better reflect the company's strategy also in **infrastructure** investment and aircraft leasing. The company has a number of diverse operations and the takeover of Ista reinforces the organisation's growth strategy.

1 Assess the factors that CK Asset Holdings and Ista International may have to consider to ensure their cultural differences impact in a successful way following the takeover.

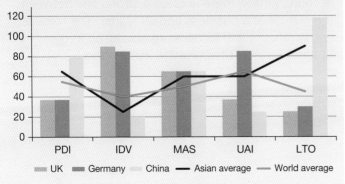

▲ Figure 1 Hofstede's five cultural dimension comparison of China and Germany

HOW CORPORATE CULTURE IS FORMED

Many factors contribute to how corporate culture is formed. These include the role of the founding members of the organisation, their personalities and beliefs. Often a strong leader's attitudes will affect the organisation. For example, Jan Koum, the CEO of WhatsApp®, has refused to let advertisers buy space on the WhatsApp application. His belief has influenced the strategy and values of the company.

Another factor that will impact on the organisation's culture are the environmental factors when a business is first formed. For example, the history or traditions of a business may control certain values and norms because they form part of what employees 'buy into'. However, this factor may not be applicable to a new company such as Otto, a US company developing self-driving technology set up in 2016. In a similar way, the success of a company will play a big part in setting the values and expectations of staff.

The type of product is another factor in creating culture. For example, how technically complex a product is may determine the skill and expertise of the workforce (perhaps contributing to a role culture) and the speed of change or need for innovation (i.e. coming up with new ideas).

Figure 2 shows the factors that form the culture of an organisation. These factors play a part in forming the culture in every business. However, each business is unique, and the factors will have varying levels of influence and connection. As you can see, the leader in Business A has a big influence on how the overall culture is formed. However, in Business B it is the well-established values that play a significant role in defining the culture.

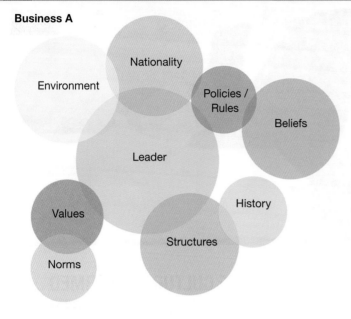

Business A

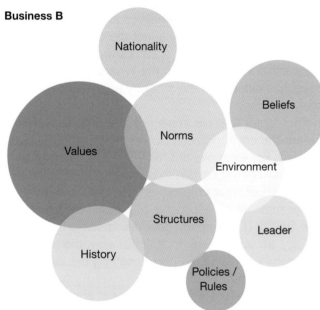

Business B

▲ Figure 2 Factors that affect the culture of an organisation

The problem with organisational culture is that although it may be easy to describe, identifying the factors that contribute towards that culture and how significant they are is very difficult. Even changing one of these factors may not have a significant influence on changing the culture. Furthermore, most organisations have subcultures within specific teams or functions.

Some aspects of organisational culture might also be easier to change than others. For example, it might be easy to change the policies, rules and working practices within a firm – these are tangible factors (i.e. clearly seen to exist). However, it is much harder to manipulate people's attitudes and beliefs.

Managers will be very keen to align workers with the culture of a company. This is a difficult task, but may be achieved if a company has a strong and respected leader. For example, if a CEO acts as a good example, others in the organisation may be happy to adopt the norms and attitudes used by that leader. It may also be possible to train workers to adopt the required culture. This training is likely to be more successful if the benefits of the required culture are emphasised in the training sessions.

Overall, culture can be changed if the right factors are influenced and the leaders within the organisation are strong, but changing culture is not easy and can be a long process. Many factors contribute to how the corporate culture is formed. It is important for the directors of a company to understand these factors and the role they play before they can hope to manage cultural change.

DIFFICULTIES IN CHANGING AN ESTABLISHED CULTURE

Chapter 20 explores the causes and effects of change on a business. From time to time it might be desirable for a business to change its culture to one that is stronger and more productive. A firm's culture can provide it with an advantage over its competitors.

LINKS

The culture of a business can have an impact on a wide range of business issues. For example, if a business has a strong culture, the financial performance of the business might be improved. In contrast, if a business develops a weak or 'rotten' culture, the performance is likely to be adversely affected. When analysing the financial performance of a business, such as in Chapters 17 and 18, the culture of a business is a factor that needs to be taken into account. Finally, there is often a strong link between the culture of a business and its leader. The roles of entrepreneurs and leaders are discussed in detail in Student Book 1, Chapters 19, 20, 21 and 22.

CHECKPOINT

1 What is the difference between surface manifestations, organisational values and basic assumptions of corporate culture?

2 What are the differences between power culture, role culture, task culture and person culture?

3 How can an organisational culture give a business a competitive advantage?

4 How might Hofstede's cultural dimensions influence the culture of international businesses?

5 Outline the possible impact of organisational culture on (a) staff motivation and (b) the organisational structure of a business.

6 State five advantages of a strong organisational culture.

7 Can an organisation's culture be changed?

SUBJECT VOCABULARY

bureaucracy the system of rules

cultural dimensions a set of characteristics that form the international context of business culture

infrastructure the basic physical and organisational structures and facilities (e.g. buildings, roads, power supplies) needed for the operation of a society or enterprise

multinational a business organisation operating in several countries

organisational culture (also organisation, corporate or business culture) the values, attitudes, beliefs, meanings and norms that are shared by people and groups within an organisation

strong culture a culture where the values, beliefs and ways of working are deeply fixed within the business and its employees

labour turnover the rate at which employees leave a business

weak culture a culture where workers are not fully aligned to the values, beliefs and ways of working of an organisation

EXAM PRACTICE

CASE STUDY: MOSAIC®

SKILLS CRITICAL THINKING, ANALYSIS, REASONING

Since 2000, Mosaic has grown from two to over 25 000 employees. Mosaic Ltd has an organisational culture that encourages employees to be creative and loyal. It encourages innovation and, as a result, has created some leading products, including an advanced Mosaic® search engine, a leading smartphone and a music-streaming service.

The founders of Mosaic, Dominic Moore and Rita Singh, brought flexible and hard-working approaches to Mosaic, and these qualities have survived as the business has grown. There has been a purposeful emphasis within the company on developing a corporate culture that is open and creative.

At Mosaic's head office, known as 'Mosaic Towers', employees are encouraged to keep fit and healthy through heavily subsidised membership of the next-door gym. A free healthy breakfast is also provided for all employees, and on-site childcare facilities are part of a supportive package for parents. These benefits are designed to build a happy and healthy company where employees can focus on productivity and innovation.

Dominic Moore places an emphasis on ability and creativity when the company finds new employees, not only on experience. All new employees are invited to become a member of the 'Mosaicians' – a company social and sports club that builds a sense of belonging and networking within the organisation.

Mosaic continues to be flexible with its corporate culture. Each week, in addition to working on given projects, half a day is devoted to new ideas on existing products, and research and development of new projects, reflecting individual interests. Dominic Moore suggests that this creates key opportunities for innovation and is also motivating for employees. Every other month there is a meeting between employees and the executive team, where new ideas and concepts can be suggested and discussed.

Mosaic has an informal motto created by a young employee: 'Live to give'. In addition to the business decisions that are focused on strong revenue growth, the company philosophy is to work creatively to build success and to develop products that improve people's lives.

Q

1 Explain one reason why Mosaic's corporate culture could be referred to as a 'strong culture'. **(4 marks)**
2 Assess the benefits for Mosaic of fostering a creative culture. **(12 marks)**
3 Evaluate whether or not a strong corporate culture is important to the long-term success of Mosaic. **(20 marks)**

EXAM HINT

When reading through a case study there may be indications of a firm's culture, or at least signs that it is a weak culture or a strong culture. These signs may be surface manifestations, values or beliefs. You might also be able to identify the culture by the influence of the CEO (power culture), the nationality of the business, or different dimensions and structures.

15 STAKEHOLDER MODEL VERSUS SHAREHOLDER MODEL

LEARNING OBJECTIVES

By the end of this chapter you should be able to understand:

■ internal and external stakeholders
■ stakeholder objectives
■ stakeholder influences: that the business considers all of its stakeholders in its business decisions/objectives
■ shareholder influences: that the business should focus only on shareholder returns (increasing share price and dividends) in its business decisions/objectives
■ the potential for conflict between profit-based (shareholder) and wider (stakeholder) objectives.

GETTING STARTED

Identify the two groups of people in the photograph who have an interest in this business. Identify another group that might have an interest in this business. What might be the objectives of the groups that you have identified? Do you think these groups have all the same objectives? If they differ, why? To what extent might each of these groups influence decision making in the business?

INTERNAL AND EXTERNAL STAKEHOLDERS

A stakeholder is a person, group or organisation who can affect or be affected by the actions, objectives and policies of a business. Stakeholders can be directors, employees, owners, suppliers, unions and customers. The interest each stakeholder has will vary according to the nature of their stake; for example, whether they are inside or outside the business.

INTERNAL STAKEHOLDERS

Some groups of people inside the business have a direct interest in its survival and well-being. These may be referred to as **internal stakeholders**.

Business owners: A business is the property of the owners. Owners are stakeholders because they may gain, or lose, financially from the performance of the business. If the business does well, they will enjoy a share of the profit. They will also benefit if the value of business increases. However, if the business fails, owners may lose the money they invested in the business. With larger companies, such as large public limited companies (plcs), the shareholders may be internal and external.

Internal shareholders may be directors, managers and sometimes employees. External shareholders may be individuals, financial institutions or other companies. Most are likely to be external because the majority of large plcs are owned by financial institutions, such as pension **funds**, investment banks and insurance companies. Their interests are discussed later.

However, in most large plcs, some of the senior managers and members of the board are likely to own shares. One reason for this is because part of their **remuneration** often consists of shares. In some companies, employees may own a small number of shares. For example, one company in Kenya has given its employees shares for a number of years. In 2017, it was reported that the workforce of ARM Cement limited, which makes the Rhino Cement brand, had a 15 per cent stake in the company. It was estimated that each of the

3000 workers had an average of nearly Sh1 million shares. These employees were some of the richest workers in Kenya. Owning shares in companies they work for exposes employees to the upsides and downsides of the decisions they make. Consequently, the quality of their performance can influence their earnings.

Employees: Employees are internal stakeholders because they work for businesses. Employees depend on businesses for their livelihood (i.e. their means of earning money in order to live). Most employees have no other sources of income and rely on wages to live on. Some employees are represented at work by trade unions. If this is the case, then trade unions also become stakeholders. The needs of employees are often in conflict with those of other stakeholders, such as owners and managers. This is discussed later in the chapter.

Managers and directors: In small businesses, managerial tasks, such as organising, decision making, planning and control, are carried out by the entrepreneur themselves. However, in large businesses, the key decisions relating to company policy and strategy are made by the board of directors. It is then the responsibility of managers to ensure that the policies and strategies are implemented. Large businesses employ specialists in managerial positions. For example, managers are often employed to run the different departments in businesses, such as marketing, production, finance and human resources. They are responsible for the work carried out in their departments and for the people employed to do the work.

Managers have to show leadership, solve problems, make decisions, settle disputes and motivate workers. Managers are likely to help plan the direction of the business with owners. They also have to control resources, such as finance, equipment, time and people. Managers are also accountable. This means they are responsible for their actions and the actions of their subordinates. Managers are accountable to senior managers in the managerial hierarchy. The board of directors is accountable to the shareholders.

EXTERNAL STAKEHOLDERS

A range of groups outside a business may have an interest in its activities. Such groups are called **external stakeholders**.

Shareholders: Most shareholders in large companies are not involved in the day-to-day running of the business. They are investors and only have a financial interest. External shareholders might be individuals or large financial institutions who invest their money to get a financial return. Shareholders are also allowed to vote at the AGM of a plc. They can vote to re-elect or replace the current board of directors. However, many external shareholders do not take up this right. In some cases, it is possible for senior managers in an organisation to have more control over the direction of a company than its shareholders. However, if they are not happy with the way the company is being run, or the return they get is inadequate, external shareholders can sell their shares and invest their money elsewhere.

Customers: Customers buy the goods and services that businesses sell. Through their purchases, they provide the revenue and profit that businesses need to survive. However, customers need businesses because they provide the goods and services they require and want. Most customers are consumers (individuals and families) who use or 'consume' products. However, some may be other businesses. For example, JCB manufactures a range of construction machinery that it sells to other businesses.

Creditors: Creditors lend money to a business. They may be banks, but could also be individuals, such as family members, or private investors, such as venture capitalists. Clearly these stakeholders have a financial interest in a business and will be keen for it to do well. Creditors will expect their interest payments to be met and their money returned at the end of the loan period. They will also want clear communication links with the business.

Suppliers: Businesses that provide raw materials, components, commercial services and utilities to other businesses are called suppliers. Relations between businesses and their suppliers need to be good because they rely on each other. Businesses want good-quality resources at reasonable prices. They also want prompt delivery, trade credit (buy now pay later) and flexibility. In return, suppliers require prompt payment and regular orders. As with customers and businesses, there is a mutual dependence (i.e. each needing the other in order to survive) between suppliers and businesses.

Pressure groups: Pressure groups such as trade unions or environmental groups like Greenpeace may try to influence business activities. They may do this if specific activities threaten the interests of that group. Pressure groups can exert influence by finding allies in the media, by organising protest marches, and by running marketing campaigns to express their concerns. For example, Greenpeace might publish an article in the media that draws attention to a business which is threatening a wildlife habitat.

The local community: Most businesses are likely to have an impact on the local community.

- **Positive impact.** A business may employ local people and if the business does well the community may benefit. There may be more jobs, more overtime and perhaps higher pay. This will then have an effect in the community. For example, shops, restaurants and cinemas may benefit from extra spending.

- **Negative impact.** A business may be criticised by the local community. For example, if a factory is noisy, polluting or if there are works at night there may be complaints from local residents. If a business that employed a lot of local people closes down, the impact on the community can be devastating. For many years in Nigeria, the activities of oil company Shell have affected' the lives of many locals. A consultant carried out a study into the impact of oil spills for shell following a clean-up after years of damage. According to a study, very high levels of pollution remained in swamps, mangroves and creeks (in the Niger Delta) years after oil spills, endangering the community. The study said there was a need for health screenings. The author of the study said that Shell denied him permission to publish the study's results in a scientific journal to show that the area had been exposed to dangerous levels of toxins.

The government: Governments have an interest in all businesses and want them to be successful. They provide employment, generate wealth and pay taxes. Taxes from businesses and their employees are used to fund government expenditure. It helps to pay for welfare benefits, state-funded healthcare, schools and other services. If businesses fail, the government loses tax revenue and has to pay benefits to the unemployed. However, the government will also require businesses to comply with (i.e. follow) the law. A significant amount of legislation exists to protect those who might be exploited by businesses if they were too powerful.

The environment: Business activity can have an impact on the environment. For example, if a business releases toxic waste into the waterway system, wildlife and its habitats could be destroyed. Thus, representatives of the environment have an interest in business activity. These representatives may be individuals or environmental groups, such as Friends of the Earth and Greenpeace. An increasing number of people are concerned about environmental issues; consequently, environmental groups are becoming more influential in business decision making.

ACTIVITY 1 — SKILLS ▸ CRITICAL THINKING, ANALYSIS

CASE STUDY: NIKE®

US multinational corporation Nike® designs, produces and markets a wide range of sports footwear, equipment and accessories. In 2017, Nike said that it plans to automate more of its production (i.e. to use machines to do a job instead of people). Flex, the high-tech manufacturing company, is one of Nike's important suppliers. Nike is working with Flex to introduce more automation into shoe production which is currently very labour intensive. Flex's factory in Mexico has become one of Nike's most important factories.

Greater automation in production will help Nike to lower its costs and drive up profit margins. It will also speed up the delivery of brand-new designs to Nike's fashion-conscious customers at a premium, such as Nike's 2017 Air Max® shoes, one of its top-selling lines. It is estimated that the involvement of Flex using automated processes will lower labour costs by 50 per cent and material costs by 20 per cent. This could help to increase gross profit margins by 12.5 per cent. If Flex were to make 30 per cent of Nike's US footwear, the company could save US$400 million. This would add 5 per cent to earnings per share. Greater automation in shoe production would also speed up lead times from several months to three to four weeks for a customised pair of training shoes.

Nike's worldwide workforce of over 1 million are afraid of automation. According to the UN's International Labour Organisation, in the next decade or two, about 56 per cent of jobs in Cambodia, Indonesia, the Philippines, Thailand and Vietnam could be lost to automation. Clothing and footwear manufacturing jobs are particularly at risk. More than 75 per cent of footwear line workers for Nike work in Vietnam, Indonesia and China. However, Nike has suggested that employees should not be worried. Jobs lost to automation will be made up in other parts of the supply chain assuming that sales grow.

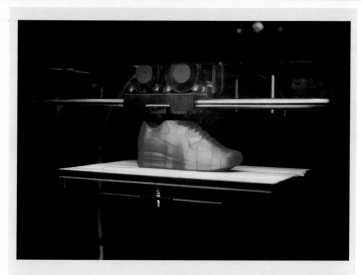

1 What is the difference between 'internal' and 'external' stakeholders? Use examples from this case.
2 Explain how two groups of stakeholders in this case might be affected by Nike's plans to increase automation.

STAKEHOLDER OBJECTIVES

Many stakeholders have common objectives. For example, most stakeholders will want a business to survive and be successful. However, each group of stakeholders is likely to have some of their own specific objectives.

Shareholders: The majority of shareholders will want the business to maximise **shareholder value**. This is a measure of company performance that takes into account the size of **dividends** and the share price. Over time, shareholders want this to grow. If the growth in shareholder value is not to the satisfaction of external investors they may sell their shares. This could result in a fall in the share price, which might make the company at risk of a takeover.

Employee objectives: Employees want the business that they work for to succeed. If a business is growing and profitable, employees are likely to get higher wages, more benefits and perhaps a bonus. They will also feel more secure in their jobs. It could be argued that, according to Herzberg, employees *expect* good pay and comfortable working conditions. However, they will also *want* responsibility, interaction with colleagues, to be valued, personal development, fair and honest treatment, and opportunities for promotion. Safety at work is also important, as are issues to do with equal opportunities. Employees will want to maximise their financial rewards and welfare.

Managerial objectives: Managers and directors are likely to have similar needs to those of employees. Many managers (and employees) have part of their remuneration linked to the performance of the business and will therefore want the business to perform well. Managers may also press for other benefits, for instance bonus payments if they perform well, expense allowances when travelling on company business, and benefits such as a company car, free health insurance and more flexibility. Some senior executives may see power as an objective. As a result, the shareholders may lose the ability to influence key decisions in the organisation.

Customer objectives: Customers want good-quality products at a fair price. They also want clear and accurate information about products and high-quality customer service. They may also want choice, innovative products and flexibility. For some products, such as machinery, electrical goods and children's products, safety is an important issue. If these needs are not met, customers will spend their money elsewhere. Customers have a powerful influence on businesses. They are also more aware today about the range of products available and about their rights as consumers. In competitive markets only those businesses that meet customer needs are likely to survive.

Supplier objectives: Suppliers want to be treated fairly by businesses. They would prefer to have long-term contracts and regular orders. They will also want a fair price for their goods or services and to be paid in reasonable time. Recently, it was suggested in the media that some businesses might 'bully' suppliers. Some retail businesses might put pressure on suppliers and demand price cuts because of falls in commodity prices. They might threaten to withdraw orders if suppliers refuse to comply. In cases such as these, an investigation might take place by the authorities. For example, in 2017, the UK supermarket Asda was found to be treating some of its suppliers badly. About 12 per cent of Asda's suppliers said that the supermarket rarely or never complied with the Grocery Supply Code of Practice. This covers dealings by 10 retailers that sell over £1 billion of groceries a year.

Government objectives: Governments will want businesses to grow and make more profit. They will also want them to comply with legislation and not exploit groups that are at risk.

Environmental objectives: Environmental groups will want businesses to avoid having any negative impact on the environment. For example, they will demand that business activity does not damage wildlife and its habitats, pollute the atmosphere or waste resources.

Local community objectives: Local communities will want businesses to contribute to the success of the community and be good corporate citizens. Communities would also want businesses to create employment and, depending on their size, nature of business and abilities, build links with schools and charities, maintain open communications, and avoid or minimise congestion and pollution in the area.

STAKEHOLDER INFLUENCES – STAKEHOLDER MODEL

Some corporations take into account the objectives of a wider group of stakeholders in addition to shareholders when making business decisions. According to the Clarkson Principles (www.cauxroundtable.org), this means that corporations should:

- recognise the interests of other stakeholders and take their views into account when running the business and making decisions
- maintain open communication channels with other stakeholders and consult with them before making radical changes
- recognise the mutual dependence that exists between different stakeholders, ensuring that the benefits of enterprise are distributed fairly after considering the level of effort and risk each group contributes
- minimise or remove the negative effects of business activity. If such effects cannot be avoided, then those affected should be adequately compensated.

Some businesses might claim to have adopted this stakeholder model. Part of the reason for this is that corporations are coming under pressure from stakeholders, the media and the wider public to be more socially responsible. It might be argued that some businesses like to show that they consider the needs of a wider range of stakeholders, but in reality, they are still more focused on shareholder needs. For example, a business might claim to adopt an ethical stance, so they can increase sales, revenue and profit. Corporate social responsibility is discussed in Chapter 36.

STAKEHOLDER INFLUENCES – SHAREHOLDER MODEL

Traditionally, many corporations focus on growth or profit when making important business decisions. The objectives of shareholders have more influence on decision making than those of other stakeholders. This model is based on the idea that directors and managers are employed by shareholders and should serve their interests. This means that they should make as much money as possible for the owners of the business as long as they follow the law. Some businesses still adopt this model. Their main objective is to maximise shareholder returns by raising both dividends paid to shareholders and the share price.

THE POTENTIAL FOR CONFLICT BETWEEN SHAREHOLDERS AND STAKEHOLDERS

Problems are likely to arise between shareholders and other stakeholders when their objectives are in direct conflict. Some examples of this conflict are outlined below.

Shareholders and employees: Meeting the objectives of employees in terms of higher wages, better conditions, more benefits and bonuses, providing training and improving employee welfare comes at a cost. If the needs of employees are met in full there is likely to be a negative impact on profit and dividends. Conflict will arise if shareholders insist that the rewards to employees should not come at the expense of dividends. Employees may try to put pressure on the business to ensure their objectives are met by threatening industrial action. However, if this action causes too many problems, it might risk the survival of the business, so employees have to be careful not to push their claims too far.

In 2018, some McDonald's® employees at several branches in the UK received a wage increase after taking industrial action in 2017. Staff demanded more secure working patterns and a minimum wage of £10 an hour. The new rates of pay offered by McDonald's were £5.75 to £7 for 16–17-year-old crew members; £8 to £10 for crew members over 25; and £9.50 to £11.75 for a floor manager running shifts. McDonald's also agreed to make extra payments to employees who worked between midnight and 6.00 a.m.

Shareholders and customers: Conflict between shareholders and customers is most likely to occur if a business charges prices that are too high. Higher prices will help to increase shareholder returns but reduce the buying power of customers. Customers might also enter into conflict with businesses if levels of customer service are poor or if businesses fail to invest in research and development and bring out new products. However, if businesses can reduce research and development spending, they can pay shareholders higher dividends.

In 2017, many customers of mobile phone operators Digicel® and Flow® in Jamaica complained about rising prices and poor customer service. The large number of complaints resulted in a meeting between the Consumer Affairs Commission (CAC) in Jamaica and representatives from Jamaica's two major telecommunication service providers. One topic of discussion during the talks was how clear the information over charges was. After the talks, the CAC said that Digicel had promised to address the complaints about charges quickly. Digicel said they would inform customers about how mobile data charges are determined 'in a way and a methodology that anybody practically can understand'.

Shareholders and directors and managers: Senior managers and directors are employed to further the interests of shareholders. However, conflict might arise if they start to prioritise their own objectives, such as maximising remuneration, expenses and other benefits. If these are too high, profit and dividends may suffer. This is most likely to happen if shareholders lose some of their control over the business. There may be a 'divorce of ownership and control'. This can happen if shares are held by a very large number of different shareholders where no single shareholder has any significant control. A common conflict between shareholders and directors is the balance between paying dividends and retaining profit for investment. Shareholders may prefer to have higher dividends while the directors may prefer to retain more profit for investment.

Shareholders and the environment: In an effort to maximise profit, a business might forget its responsibilities towards the environment. One very serious concern is the impact some business activity is having on the environment, such as global warming. For example, in the palm oil industry every year, illegal forest-clearing practices cause devastating fires that impact on the forest ecosystems. This affects the lives of millions of people across South East Asia. One example is Indonesian plantation owner PT Agra Bumi Niaga (ABN). Activities such as these may attract the attention of the media and environmental groups, resulting in conflict between the company and environmentalists.

Shareholders and the government: Conflict between shareholders and the government is likely if businesses break the law. However, the judicial system should help to solve such conflicts. Recently there has been growing uneasiness between governments in some countries and large corporations. A number of large multinationals such as Apple, Amazon, Google® and Facebook® have been accused of avoiding the payment of tax in a number of countries. For example, in 2017 the European Commission wanted to take Ireland to court for failing to collect around €13 billion in taxes from Apple. The Commission ruled that Apple should hand over unpaid taxes, saying it had received illegal state aid – a judgement criticised by the Irish authorities. If corporations can reduce the amount of tax they pay, then the shareholders will enjoy bigger profits. However, if businesses are able to avoid paying taxes the government is likely to be criticised.

ACTIVITY 2 SKILLS CRITICAL THINKING, ANALYSIS

CASE STUDY: TAKEOVER OF MONSANTO® BY BAYER®

In 2018, German chemical company Bayer won approval for its takeover bid for the seed and weed-killer giant Monsanto. The US$66 billion takeover deal creates one of the world's largest agriculture conglomerates. Agricultural groups in the USA expressed their concerns about the takeover. They said it could have devastating impacts on farmers, consumers and the economy. The groups, including Friends of Earth, the Northeast Organic Dairy Producers Alliance, Northeast Organic Farming Association of New York and others, said that the merger would decrease competition in the seed and agrochemical markets.

The National Farmers Union said the merger would mean that three companies would have more than 80 per cent of US corn seed sales market and 70 per cent of the global pesticide market. They were concerned because the market was already highly consolidated. They feared that the takeover would raise seed prices for farmers and limit their seed choices. For example, while the price of corn seed has nearly quadrupled in the last 20 years, the price farmers get for their output is roughly the same as it was at in 1996. However, these costs may be partly due to the greater use of genetically modified (GM) seeds (which have increased from 25 per cent of all US corn seed planted in 2000 to 92 per cent of all corn seed in 2016). The agricultural groups also said that the lack of competition in the market would reduce the incentive (i.e. motivation) to innovate.

Monsanto shareholders will benefit from the takeover. They will get US$128 per share – a 44 per cent premium over the company's closing price before rumours of a takeover surfaced. The merger was expected to generate cost savings for the combined company, although the companies would not discuss potential job cuts. However, job losses are inevitable (i.e. very likely to happen) after big mergers. After three years, the companies predict about 80 per cent of the US$1.5 billion in synergies will be cost cuts in administration, sales and marketing.

1 What are likely to be the main objectives for customers as stakeholders in the market for seeds?
2 Discuss the conflict between stakeholders that exists in this case.

LINKS

The experiences of stakeholders could be linked to most topics in the specification. This is because stakeholders are at the heart of business activity. Any decision made by a business is likely to have an impact on at least one stakeholder. For example, pricing decisions affect customers and shareholders. Location decisions affect communities and employees. Marketing decisions will affect customers and employees. Wage negotiations will have an impact on employees, shareholders and managers. It is not difficult to identify links. And do not forget, decisions are also made by stakeholders.

CHECKPOINT

1   Give two examples of internal stakeholders in a business.

2   Give two examples of external stakeholders in a business.

3   How might employees become shareholders?

4   What are the objectives of suppliers as stakeholders?

5   What are the objectives of the government as a stakeholder?

6   What is the difference between the 'shareholder approach' and the 'stakeholder approach' when running a company?

7   How might the objectives of shareholders and employees enter into conflict?

8   How might the objectives of shareholders and the local community enter into conflict?

EXAM HINT

Do not confuse stakeholders with shareholders. When you write the word shareholders, make sure that you mean shareholders. These are the owners of the business who hold shares in it.

SUBJECT VOCABULARY

dividend a sum of money paid regularly (typically annually) by a company to its shareholders out of its profits (or reserves)
external stakeholders groups outside a business with an interest in its activities
fund(s) a sum of money saved or made available for a particular purpose
internal stakeholders groups inside a business with an interest in its activities
remuneration the reward for work in the form of pay, salary or wages, including allowances and benefits, such as company cars, health insurance, pension, bonuses and non-cash incentives
shareholder value a measure of company performance that combines the size of dividends with the share price

EXAM PRACTICE

CASE STUDY: MASDAR BEVERAGES

SKILLS | CRITICAL THINKING, ANALYSIS, INTERPRETATION, REASONING

Masdar Beverages is a popular brand of drinks based in the UAE. It sells and distributes its own range of beverage brands in the Middle East, Africa and parts of Europe such as Turkey, Greece and some Baltic states. The company was founded in 1996 with the aim of supplying customers with premium-quality soft drinks and alternative beverages at an affordable price, such as carbonated soft drinks, fruit juices and bottled water. In recent years, the company has grown rapidly and now dominates many of its markets. It invests very heavily in marketing and strengthening its brand. In 2018, the company generated AED6.588 billion in net revenue and made a profit of AED501 million before tax and interest. Figure 1 shows the returns enjoyed by shareholders between 2013 and 2018.

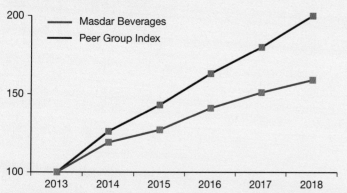

▲ Figure 1 Return to shareholders 2013 to 2018 (stock price plus reinvested dividends)

Masdar Beverages claims that it engages with a wide range of stakeholders. The frequent communication with stakeholders provides important information which is used in Masdar's decision-making process. This helps the company to continuously improve and make progress toward their 2025 sustainability goals. For example, it uses hotlines, local websites, plant tours, research, surveys, social channels and focus groups to engage with consumers. To get feedback from local communities it holds community meetings, encourages plant visits, develops partnerships on common issues, uses sponsorships and organises visits to local schools and colleges. To monitor the views of employees, Masdar uses staff surveys, senior executive business updates, regular meetings, employee communications, individual development plans, health and safety communications programmes, community and employee well-being projects and an ethics hotline (to report 'bad' behaviour).

One example of Masdar's commitment to the community is their 'Business Skills' programme, designed to help young entrepreneurs overcome the problems they face when setting up and running a business. Masdar offers access to training, financial services and connections with peers and mentors. At the moment, their focus is in the Middle East and a number of African states.

Finally, one area where Masdar Beverages has been criticised in their stakeholder approach is their failure to address the problem of plastic waste in their environmental plan. According to some environmental groups, Masdar Beverages sells 4 billion single-use plastic bottles every year. In 2018, Masdar announced a goal to help to collect and recycle a bottle or can for every one it sells by 2040 as part of its 'Save our Seas' programme.

1 Assess the possible benefits to a business like Masdar Beverages of adopting a stakeholder approach to decision making. **(12 marks)**
2 Evaluate whether Masdar Beverages has adopted **(a)** the stakeholder approach, or **(b)** a shareholder approach to business. **(20 marks)**

16 BUSINESS ETHICS

LEARNING OBJECTIVES

By the end of this chapter you should be able to understand:
- the ethics of strategic decisions: trade-offs between profit and ethics
- pay and rewards
- Corporate Social Responsibility (CSR).

GETTING STARTED

There have been growing concerns about the collection and use of personal data by businesses. It seems that a wide range of organisations are collecting personal data without the permission of individuals. Data harvesting is being used by both businesses and governments to track what we do, who we know and where we go. The methods and purposes of data collection seem to be expanding all the time. For example, they might include:

- WhatsApp sharing your name and phone number with Facebook to assist with targeted advertising
- a device that uses your phone's battery status as a 'fingerprint' to track your online activities
- using surveillance systems, such as Baltimore police in the USA using aerial surveillance systems to watch and record the city
- the creation of individual personalised profiles by data agents. These profiles are then sold and used to avoid consumer protection legislation.

It has been argued that data harvesting is a form of consumer exploitation. This is because businesses and other organisations may use data to create value without compensating those who unknowingly provide the information. However, it is also argued that social media companies, such as Google and Facebook, provide users with 'free' services in return for this data. But this does not explain the behaviour of data agents. They do not provide anything to the users.

Capturing data from people without consent and compensation is an ethical issue. If people are unhappy with the practice, then it may need to be outlawed (i.e. made illegal). However, this would require international co-operation and a need for new models of data ownership and protection that reflect the role information has in society.

What is meant by data harvesting? Do you think data harvesting is morally wrong? Explain your answer. What is most important for a business – looking after its stakeholders or looking after its shareholders? Do you think a business has a moral obligation to consider the views of all stakeholders when making strategic decisions?

ETHICS

Ethics, in the context of **business ethics**, considers the moral 'rights and wrongs' of a decision. It focuses more on a strategic level, rather than the decisions made by individual employees, for example. All businesses have to make **ethical decisions**. Some are affected by the law. For example, in most countries, it is illegal for businesses to discriminate against a person (i.e. treat them differently) based on their gender, or build a factory without planning permission. However, many ethical decisions have to be made without the help of the law. For example, should an employer allow a worker to take a day off work to look after a sick child and still pay them? Should a company stop buying goods from a factory in certain countries where it knows that work conditions are poor, and wages are very low?

Every business should have a stated code of conduct within which employees operate in respect of ethical business decisions, although at a senior level and on a personal level some employees might have differences of opinion. For example, some individuals may argue that it is wrong for businesses to manufacture make-up to sell to children. Others may suggest that it does no real harm. Despite these differences, in many situations most people often take the same ethical stance (i.e. the opinions somebody holds and expresses) and are anyway required to operate within the business code of conduct and mission statements (see Chapter 1). For example, most would agree that a company should not use employees' money saved in a pension fund to help out the business if it is making a loss.

ETHICS OF STRATEGIC DECISIONS

Strategic decisions are those that affect how a business operates in the long term. All businesses have to make ethical decisions as part of their corporate strategy and these are usually the responsibility of senior management. These decisions then affect the direction of the business, with medium-term tactical decisions usually the responsibility of middle managers. For example, should a finance manager delay sending payments to a supplier if the business has cash-flow difficulties? Should a self-employed plumber charge a senior citizen extra when a job takes longer than estimated? Over the past 20 years, large corporations have experienced a large number of issues that require strategic decisions based on ethics.

The environment: In many countries, the law limits the amount of pollution or environmental damage a business can do. However, businesses must decide whether to adopt stricter measures to protect the environment. For example, should a business recycle materials, especially if this will lower profits? Multinational businesses often face lower environmental standards in developing countries. Should they lower their own environmental standards in such locations to take advantage of this?

Animal rights: Some companies, such as pharmaceutical companies or cosmetics manufacturers, might use animals to test products. Animal rights groups argue this is unethical. Other companies, such as food manufacturers or oil businesses, can destroy habitats and endanger animals. Wildlife conservation groups argue against farming activities that destroy forests or other habitats and oil installations that can pollute the environment, leading to the destruction of animal and plant life.

Workers in developing countries: A number of companies have been criticised for exploiting workers in developing countries. Companies manufacture in countries with **emerging economies** because production costs are much lower. However, there is an ethical question about the extent to which low costs should be at the expense of workers.

Corruption: In some industries, **bribes** (i.e. money paid to persuade somebody to do what you want them to) might be used to persuade customers to sign contracts. It is argued this takes place in certain emerging economies, where civil servants or government ministers want money from big business deals. The ethical question is whether it is right to use bribes even if a business knows that its competitors do.

New technologies: Most new products, such as mobile phones or a new chocolate bar, do not cause ethical problems. But some technological developments can be controversial. For example, nuclear power generation has been an issue since the 1950s. More recently, genetically modified (GM) crops have also been controversial due to their potential health risks and damage to the environment. In the future, other biological processes, such as cloning, could also lead to strong ethical reactions.

Product availability: If a person cannot afford an expensive car or some other luxury goods, most would not see this as an ethical issue. But if someone is seriously ill and cannot afford drugs for treatment because pharmaceutical businesses charge such a high price, many would argue that this is an ethical issue. The direction of research is also important. Companies might research new drugs for complaints suffered by only a few in the industrialised world. Or they might research illnesses such as malaria, which kills millions each year in many developing counties. The choice that businesses make is an ethical issue.

Trading issues: Some countries have been condemned (i.e. judged as wrong or very bad) internationally for the policies followed by their governments. They may even have had **sanctions or trade embargoes** placed upon them. Companies must decide whether to trade with or invest in these countries.

ACTIVITY 1 · SKILLS › CRITICAL THINKING, REASONING

CASE STUDY: ANIMAL TESTING

Globally, animal experiments are permitted to help develop new medicines and to test the safety of products before being marketed to humans. Many people would argue that allowing animals to feel pain and suffering, which is often associated with animal experimentation, is morally wrong. Even the majority of scientists who carry out the experiments are aware of the ethical issues involved. They also believe that if experiments are necessary they should be undertaken as humanely as possible. Many also believe that animal testing should not be used if other methods are available.

Companies involved in the development and manufacture of pharmaceuticals, cosmetics, household goods and food are most likely to use animal testing. They might argue that animal testing is justifiable if:

- suffering is minimised in all experiments
- humans will benefit and the gains from animal testing could not be achieved in any other way.

Those who oppose all animal testing argue that:
- it causes pain and suffering to defenceless animals
- the benefits to humans are not clearly proven
- any benefits that humans do enjoy can be achieved using other methods.

For cosmetics, the argument against animal experimentation might be very strong as they may be considered unnecessary. However, it might be less strong when used to test the safety and effectiveness of drugs and medicines. If tests on animals were outlawed scientists say that there would be an end to testing new drugs, or that humans would be used for tests instead. Animal experiments are not used to show that drugs are safe and effective in human beings because that is not possible. Instead, they help to decide whether a particular drug should be tested on people. Animal experiments are used to determine whether drugs are either ineffective or dangerous on humans. Only if a drug passes the animal test is it then tested on humans.

1 What is meant by an ethical issue in business?
2 Discuss whether animal testing is justifiable in business.

TRADE-OFFS BETWEEN PROFIT AND ETHICS

A conflict can exist between ethical objectives and profitability and a trade-off occurs when the selection of one choice results in the loss of another. This applies at all levels, from individuals through to the largest corporations and even governments. If I choose to buy a new car, the trade-off might be that I cannot have a holiday. The trade-off of a government decision to increase the income tax personal allowance might be that it cannot afford to spend more money on a high-speed rail upgrade.

Similarly, for businesses, trade-offs exist with any decision. Investing in a new production facility may mean that new vans cannot be purchased. The idea of such trade-offs is particularly apparent when considering ethics. Is the cost of acting ethically an acceptance of lower profit?

For businesses, acting ethically when not required to do so by the law can have a negative impact on profit in a number of ways. The result can be a trade-off.

- It can raise costs. For example, paying higher wages than is necessary to overseas workers increases costs. Having to find other ways than animal experiments to test a new drug might add to costs. Adopting an ethical code of practice can raise costs. Staff have to be made aware of the code and trained to implement it. It takes management time to prepare a code of practice. Paying workers more than a legal minimum directly increases costs.
- It can reduce revenues. A business might lose a contract if it refuses to give a bribe. Selling medicines to emerging economies at low prices might increase sales, but total revenue is likely to be lower. Refusing to develop GM crops might mean a competitor getting into the market first and becoming the market leader. Acting ethically might even mean the destruction of the company. For example, if a business failed to develop GM crops, it might struggle to survive if all other businesses in the market were selling higher yielding GM products.

However, adopting an ethical stance can produce benefits.

- Some companies have used their ethical stance for marketing purposes. For example, in 2017 the financial investment industry reported that **sustainable and ethical investment** was booming (i.e. having a period of great prosperity or rapid economic growth). There had been an increase in the number of investors who were interested in more than just financial returns. A survey showed that more than 54 per cent of people wanted their investments to have a positive social impact in addition to a satisfactory financial return. In 2016, 70 per cent of investors approached by the financial institution Morgan Stanley said they were interested in sustainable investments. Among **millennials** (the generation who became adults around the year 2000), this figure was even higher at 84 per cent.

- Some businesses promote their positive ethical beliefs when marketing their products. Businesses face problems if they behave unethically and they face serious penalties for breaking the law. They don't want sales to fall as customers protest against this behaviour. In the past, companies have experienced negative effects for reported unethical behaviour. For example, Enron, a large US energy trading company, collapsed. It was found to have changed its accounts to inflate its profits. Senior management was reported as acting unethically by hiding this from shareholders and government. This also led to the collapse of one of the world's top five accounting firms, Arthur Andersen. It had **audited** Enron's accounts and was accused of hiding the irregularities. As a result, it began to lose its major customers and decided to close down.

Large companies need to take the consequences of their behaviour and decision making seriously. Customers and society have become less tolerant (i.e. less able to accept something they disagree with) of businesses that behave in a way they regard as unethical. However, most companies follow trends and adopt ethical policies that will prevent them from being harmed in the marketplace or by law. Often, small to mediumsized businesses do not have management time or resources to prepare an ethical code of practice. Their ethical stance and behaviour is more organic, and influenced by the society in which they operate.

CODES OF PRACTICE

In recent years, some large businesses have adopted **ethical codes of practice**. These explain how employees in the business should respond in situations where they encounter ethical issues. Ethical codes will differ from one business and one industry to another. However, they may contain statements about:

- environmental responsibility
- dealing with customers and suppliers in a fair and honest manner
- competing fairly and not engaging in practices such as collusion or destroyer pricing
- the workforce and responding fairly to their needs.

CASE STUDY: SPOTIFY'S CODE OF CONDUCT AND ETHICS

Swedish company Spotify® is a music, podcast and video streaming service. Users of the service may have an app which allows them to browse and search for music from Spotify's bank of over 30 million tracks. Users can also create and share playlists on social media and generate playlists with other users. Like most companies, Spotify has a formal code of conduct and ethics.

Their code is based on three key rules and how to make sure employees do not break them. These rules are:

1 Do the right thing. Always act with honesty, integrity (i.e. strong moral principles), and reliability. Maintain high moral and ethical standards.
2 Be nice. Treat all people with dignity and respect. Ensure that all relationships are conducted with decency and courtesy.
3 Play fair. Do not cheat. Be sure to balance the interests of stakeholders, artists, users, employees and the general public, in your role as an employee.

The code is quite detailed and covers a range of areas such as:

- compliance with the law
- full, fair, accurate, timely and understandable disclosure
- conflicts of interest
- confidentiality
- insider trading
- competition and fair dealing
- anti-corruption and bribery
- gifts and entertainment
- discrimination and harassment
- health and safety
- user and IT security
- protection and proper use of Spotify assets and record keeping.

The code of practice provides employees with guidelines on how to follow the rules with regard to each specific issue. All employees such as board members, officers, employees, consultants and others working on Spotify's behalf are expected to know the code. Failure to follow the code may lead to disciplinary action, or even termination of employment.

1 Explain what is meant by an ethical code of practice.
2 Assess the possible advantages to Spotify of having an ethical code of practice.

PAY AND REWARDS

An important issue in the area of business ethics relates to pay and rewards. **Remuneration** is the reward for work, such as pay, wages or salary. Businesses use pay and rewards for different purposes:

- to attract employees with the right skills, experience and knowledge. Jobs that are less skilled may have a high number of available workers, which means pay can be low. Jobs that need rare skills, for example with top Premier League footballers, pay rates need to be very high to attract the best.
- to reward and motivate existing staff. The ultimate aim of businesses is to make profit. Rather than pay the lowest possible rates of pay, to keep costs down and profit margins high, businesses need to pay their staff enough money so that they to work to the best of their ability. The link between pay and motivation is discussed in detail in Student Book 1, Chapter 17.
- maximise productivity levels. Pay is an important motivator and highly motivated staff are more productive.

Businesses need to make a profit if they are to survive. Therefore, they will try to minimise costs. This will extend to labour costs and most firms are not likely to pay higher wages if they can avoid it. However, although higher profits can be achieved by reducing the pay of employees within legal limits, is this ethical?

Generally, it is the role of individual businesses to decide on rates of pay. An exception to this relates to low pay. In some countries, such as the USA, Australia and India, a **national minimum wage exists**. In others, such as Canada, there are legal minimum wages, but they may vary between different regions. Figure 1 shows the minimum wage rates in different Canadian provinces. The differences might be explained by variations in the cost of living and the different labour market conditions in each province.

This type of government regulation forces businesses to pay their workers a fair rate of pay. It is a legal limit on what can be paid and means that businesses cannot pay very low wages. However, some argue that the national minimum wage is not high enough to provide

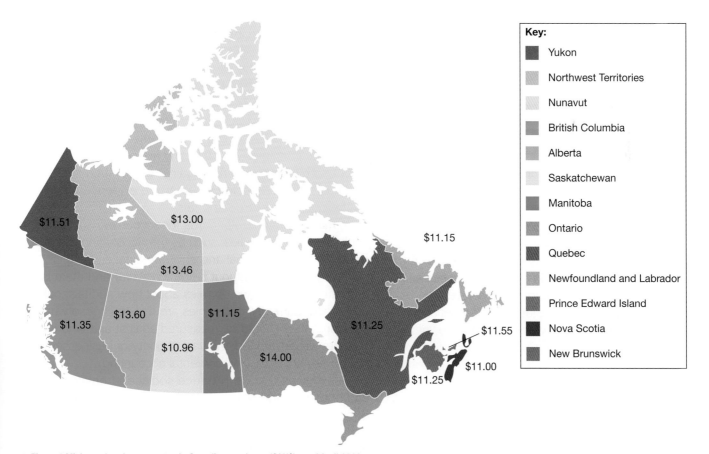

Key:
- Yukon
- Northwest Territories
- Nunavut
- British Columbia
- Alberta
- Saskatchewan
- Manitoba
- Ontario
- Quebec
- Newfoundland and Labrador
- Prince Edward Island
- Nova Scotia
- New Brunswick

▲ Figure 1 Minimum hourly wage rates in Canadian provinces (CAN$) as of April 2018 a satisfactory standard of living. In some countries, this means that the government has to provide a range of financial benefits to the very low paid. Effectively, the government is making up the difference between the wages paid by a business and the amount needed for a person to live on. In some countries, groups have argued that workers should be paid a **living wage**. This would be set higher than the national minimum wage and covers the basic cost of living.

Remuneration is extremely important for a business. The extent to which decisions on pay are an ethical matter depends on which perspective this is being considered from. Supporters of the free market would argue that decisions on pay should be left to businesses to decide. The aim of business is to maximise profits and returns for owners/shareholders. To achieve this aim, if a business needs to pay millions to attract the most highly skilled staff, then this is their decision. According to *Forbes*, Real Madrid striker Cristiano Ronaldo earned more than any other athlete in the world in 2017 at $93 million. Is it 'right' that one person can earn so much money, while others have to manage with the minimum wage? From a business perspective, it makes sense to pay the highest salaries to the most highly skilled people. If Real Madrid did not buy the best players, it would not be able to compete for league titles and other trophies.

ACTIVITY 3 SKILLS CRITICAL THINKING, PROBLEM SOLVING

CASE STUDY: MINIMUM WAGES IN AUSTRALIA

In 2017, the Fair Work Commission (FWC) in Australia increased the national minimum wage by 3.3 per cent. This means that Australian workers will be entitled to at least AUS$694 per week – an increase of AUS$22.20. The increase was higher than in the previous year but less than the AUS$45 per week demanded by trade unions.

Business representatives said that the increase was too high and could result in job losses. However, the FWC said that the increase was justified since inflation was lower, labour productivity was higher and business profits had grown. These favourable economic conditions had provided the opportunity to reward the 2.3 million Australians who relied on national minimum wages. The FWC also said that international research had not provided very much evidence, if any, that modest and regular wage increases result in unemployment.

Finally, the FWC said that profit growth had been particularly strong recently, above the five- and 10-year average for most industries, and that wage increases had been few.

But, the Australian Chamber of Commerce and Industry said that the job prospects of the 744 000 unemployed were 'at risk from minimum wage increases beyond what is affordable for small and award-reliant businesses'. The Chamber said that wage rises across the rest of the economy have been lower than the increase in the minimum wage, which means the commission has increased the burden on the small and medium-sized businesses who rely on awards. It argued that this will make it harder to compete.

An Australian chain store employs 2100 people on the minimum wage across the country.

1 Calculate the annual increase in total wages paid to this group of employees.
2 How might an increase in the national minimum wage benefit the government?
3 Discuss whether the increase in the minimum wage in Australia will result in job losses.

CORPORATE SOCIAL RESPONSIBILITY (CSR)

Corporate social responsibility (CSR) is a form of self-regulation. It involves a business ensuring that its activities consider the interests of all stakeholders. Some large businesses have responded to concerns about CSR by auditing relevant activities. These audits may then be made available to the public in a corporate social responsibility report, in the same way that the financial accounts of the company are published. Auditing involves checking evidence against established standards. Auditors can then decide whether the evidence presented by the business is 'true and fair'.

In many countries, standards for accounting audits are set by accounting bodies, such as the Accounting Standards Board. In contrast, social and environmental auditing is voluntary (i.e. done without being forced to) and there is no official body that draws up rules about how audits should take place. Currently, companies are free to choose what standards they should be measured against and who the auditors will be. Indeed, the vast majority of businesses do not do any social or environmental accounting.

Businesses that do produce social and environmental audits use a wide range of measures, which differ from business to business. For example, an oil company may measure the number of oil spills for which it is responsible. This would not be appropriate for a drinks company, which might use other indicators, such as the levels of air pollution created by its breweries and distilleries. Social and environmental audits might include some of the following.

Employment indicators: How well does the business treat its staff? This might include indicators about pensions, healthcare benefits, union representation, training and education, the number of accidents involving staff, payment of minimum wages, equal opportunities and the number of women in higher management or director positions.

Human rights indicators: How well does the company perform on human rights issues? For example:

- Does the company have works councils?
- Do its suppliers use child labour?
- Does it operate in, buy supplies from or sell products to countries that have a poor human rights record?
- Does the company discriminate on grounds of race, gender or age when recruiting or promoting staff?

The communities in which the business operates: What impact does the business have on the life of the communities in which it operates? For example, how much does it give to charities? How much is spent on local schools, hospitals and housing?

Business integrity and ethics: How ethical is the business in its activities? For example, has the company been involved in any cases of trading that break legislation? Does the company make political contributions and to whom? Has the company been involved in cases associated with unfair competition?

Product responsibility: What is the social impact of the products sold by the business? For example, are there health and safety issues? Is after-sales service adequate? Is advertising true and fair? Does the company manage its information on customers and suppliers in such a way as to preserve their privacy?

The environment: These indicators can form a separate environmental audit. Some businesses may only produce an environmental audit and not include any of the other social indicators described above. Indicators might include:

- the amount of energy or other raw materials used by the business, such as water or pesticides
- how much waste or effluent was produced
- the levels of greenhouse gases or ozone-depleting emissions
- what percentage of materials used were recycled
- the company's impact on biodiversity
- what impact it had on protected and sensitive areas
- how many times it was fined during the period for failure to comply with environmental regulations, and the total level of fines.

Some of these measures are financial, i.e. they are measured by money. However, many are non-financial. For this reason, it is difficult to get a quick and easy overall measure of how well a business is doing from its social and environmental audit. In contrast to a financial audit, the data from social audits are more difficult to assess and compare from year to year. This is because with a set of financial accounts, it is possible to look at the profit and loss account and say that the business has performed better or worse in terms of revenues, costs and profit.

THINKING BIGGER

There is a lot of conflict and controversy in business ethics. What factors does a business need to consider, as it assesses what is 'good' and being profitable as part of its decision-making process? Is this a 'zero-sum' game (where one person's gain is equivalent to another's loss), or can one improve the other? What considerations influence decision making? For example, is the priority to drive down costs or to encourage professional development to upskill a workforce?

It is a good idea to think about your own beliefs in this area. These views can be used in constructing arguments one way or the other. On the one hand, being ethical can increase the costs of a business. This might have implications for prices and thus competitiveness. It may mean that a business loses market position due to its ethical stance. Equally, being ethical can have positive implications for a business. For example, The Body Shop® is a soap and cosmetics manufacturer that refuses to test on animals. It supports various campaign organisations, such as Cruelty Free International and the World Bio-Bridges Mission that commits to protect and regenerate endangered species in rainforest areas. It tries to use only natural ingredients and most things are made locally. In the past the business has enjoyed rising sales and profits, part of which it attributed to its ethical stance.

CHECKPOINT

1 Give two examples of ethical decisions an oil production company might have to make.

2 What is meant by a trade-off?

3 Which types of companies might be particularly affected by ethical issues relating to: (a) the environment; (b) animal rights issues; (c) workers in developing countries; (d) bribery; (e) new technologies; (f) access to products; (g) trading with politically unstable countries?

4 What might be contained in an ethical code of practice?

5 How are the national minimum wage and the living wage different?

6 To what extent can businesses increase profits by becoming more ethical?

7 'Businesses should not be expected to act ethically.' Explain the two sides to this argument.

8 To whom might a business have social responsibility?

SUBJECT VOCABULARY

audit an official inspection of an organisation's accounts, typically by an independent body

bribe money paid to persuade somebody to do what you want them to

business ethics the moral principles that guide the way in which a business behaves

Corporate Social Responsibility (CSR) a business assessing and taking responsibility for its effects on the environment and its impact on social welfare. It involves the idea that businesses are responsible for more than their shareholders

data harvesting the process of extracting information from websites automatically and using it for other purposes

emerging economy used to describe a developing country, in which investment would be expected to achieve higher returns but would be accompanied by greater risk

ethical codes of practice statements about how employees in a business should behave in particular circumstances where they experience ethical issues

ethical decision a decision which considers what is morally right or wrong

ethics moral rules or principles of behaviour that should guide members of a profession or organisation and make them deal honestly and fairly with each other and with their stakeholders

living wage an hourly rate of pay based on the basic cost of living, set independently of government and updated annually

millennials people reaching adulthood in the early 21st century (there are no specific dates)

national minimum wage the minimum pay per hour all workers are entitled to by law

sanctions (or trade embargoes) sanctions are restrictions (i.e. limits) that are used in trade or investment with the aim of influencing a policy change in another country. Trade embargoes can be included in sanctions, where commercial shipments are banned in and out of a particular country, or where an embargo is placed on a particular product

sustainable and ethical investment where investments are made in companies with a strong ethical stance

EXAM PRACTICE

CASE STUDY: SUPERMARKET PACKAGING

SKILLS   CRITICAL THINKING, ANALYSIS, BUSINESS ETHICS

In recent years, there has been a lot of publicity about the amount of plastic that is in the world's seas and oceans. Businesses use a huge variety of plastics in the packaging of their products that cannot be recycled. It is these single-use plastics that cause the most problems, especially plastic shopping bags and drinks bottles. Unfortunately, a lot of this waste plastic is entering the world's seas and oceans. For example:

- at least 8 million tons of plastic enter the oceans each year
- more than 50 per cent of sea turtles have consumed plastic
- only 25 per cent of the plastic bottles consumed in the USA are recycled
- in the next 10 years the amount of plastic in the world's oceans could increase tenfold.

In 2017, a 6-ton, 33-foot-long sperm whale found dead in southern Spain was discovered to have swallowed 64 pounds of plastic rubbish. This is just one example of the damage inflicted on marine life by plastic in the seas and oceans. The marine species at most risk from plastic pollution are sea turtles, seals and sea lions, seabirds, whales and dolphins and fish.

Globally, plastic is often used to package many of the products sold in supermarkets. In some countries, laws have been passed to make retailers charge for single-use plastic bags. Indeed, this has been quite successful. For example, the use of single-use plastic bags has fallen by between 80 and 90 per cent in some countries after the introduction of modest charges such as 5 cents.

Some supermarkets have promised to cut the use of plastic in their CSR reports. Maruetsu, a Japanese supermarket, said it was working together with customers to reduce the amount of plastic bags used. Each customer who presents his or her T card (loyalty card) earns two T points when declining to use plastic bags. Maruetsu also encourages shoppers to bring their own shopping bags in their 'Bring a Shopping Bag Campaign'. According to their Corporate Social Responsibility report there has been a 19 per cent decline in plastic bag use between 2013 and 2015.

Despite the measures discussed above, many believe that supermarkets need to do a lot more. For example, Greenpeace has suggested that supermarkets and other retailers stop using non-recyclable and single-use plastics in their own brand products, and try out dispensers and refillable containers for products like shampoo, cleaning products and beverages. They also recommend putting water fountains and water refill stations in their stores and operating deposit return schemes (where customers get cash back if they return a water bottle). They want supermarkets and retailers to encourage national brands to stop using non-recyclable and single-use plastics.

Q

1 Explain one purpose of a corporate social responsibility report. **(4 marks)**
2 Analyse the possible impact on the environment of the increasing use of plastic made by businesses. **(6 marks)**
3 Evaluate whether or not supermarkets are likely to take a stronger ethical stance and reduce the amount of plastic packaging they use in the future. **(20 marks)**

EXAM HINT

Exam questions on this topic offer opportunities for analysis and evaluation. It is possible to consider the extent to which a business decision is the right one from different perspectives. For a typical question in this area there will not be a right or a wrong answer, and marks will be based on the strength and quality of your arguments.

In short, if you are asked whether a business decision is an ethical one, the answer will probably be 'it depends'. It depends on the type of business, the market it operates in, economic conditions, staff recruitment and retention, and so on. Using this 'it depends' approach is useful when answering questions around ethics. This will help you to focus on the need for evaluation and give some structure to a response in the exam.

ASSESSING COMPETITIVENESS

Businesses may wish to assess their competitiveness using financial information and/ or indicators relating to human resources. This section looks at how key information in the statement of comprehensive income and the statement of financial position can be used to assess competitiveness and stakeholder interest. It explores the use of financial ratios such as profit margins, liquidity ratios, gearing ratios and the return on capital employed (ROCE) when assessing competitiveness. This includes how such ratios can be used to make business decisions and the limitations of their use. The section also looks at how labour productivity, labour turnover and absenteeism can be calculated and interpreted, including the limitations of these calculations. Finally, it investigates the strategies a business might use to improve the performance of human resources such as financial rewards, employee share ownership, consultation and empowerment.

17 INTERPRETATION OF FINANCIAL STATEMENTS

LEARNING OBJECTIVES

By the end of this chapter you should be able to understand:
- statement of comprehensive income (profit and loss account): key information and stakeholder interest
- statement of financial position (balance sheet): key information and stakeholder interest.

GETTING STARTED

Walmart is one of the biggest corporations in the world. It is a retail giant that operates a chain of supermarkets, hypermarkets and discount department stores. Walmart owns over 11 700 stores under 65 banners in 28 countries and e-commerce websites. The organisation currently employs about 2.3 million people globally, with 1.5 million in the USA alone. Tables 1 and 2 show some financial information for Walmart.

	2017 (US$ million)	2016 (US$ million)
Revenue	485 873	482 130
Cost of sales	361 256	360 984
Gross profit	124 617	121 146
Selling and admin expenses	101 853	97 041
Operating profit	22 764	24 105
Profit for the year	13 643	14 694

▲ Table 1 Extracts from Walmart statement of comprehensive income, 2017

	2017 (US$ million)	2016 (US$ million)
Non-current assets	141 136	139 342
Current assets	57 689	60 239
Current liabilities	66 928	64 619
Non-current liabilities	51 362	51 351
Share capital	80 535	83 611
Retained earnings	89 354	90 021

▲ Table 2 Extracts from Walmart statement of financial position, 2017

What is the key information in tables 1 and 2? Comment on the performance of the business between 2016 and 2017. Why might shareholders be interested in this information?

FINANCIAL STATEMENTS

All companies are required by law to produce financial statements at the end of the financial year – although many public limited companies (plcs) produce them on a quarterly basis (i.e. four times per year). According to the International Accounting Standards Board, the body responsible for developing and approving international financial reporting standards, the following statements are required.
- A statement of financial position (balance sheet), which shows the assets, liabilities and capital of the business.
- A statement of comprehensive income (profit and loss account), which starts with the profit or loss for the year and then shows other items of comprehensive income, such as gains made on currency transactions.

Sole traders and partnerships also produce financial statements. They are usually less complex than those of companies and may be presented in a slightly different style. However, the majority of small businesses produce a balance sheet and a profit and loss account (or an income and expenditure account). The focus in this chapter is on the statement of financial position (balance sheet) and the statement of comprehensive income (profit and loss account).

THE STATEMENT OF COMPREHENSIVE INCOME

The statement of comprehensive income is used by most plcs to show the income and expenditure of the business for a period of time (usually one year) and calculate the profit made by the business. The financial information has to be presented in a standard way. An example for a limited company, Cattle Snaffle Ltd, is shown in Table 3. Cattle Snaffle Ltd supplies cattle and sheep feed to farmers in the EU.

	2017 (€m)	2016 (€m)
Revenue	25.4	21.2
Cost of sales	12.3	11.7
Gross profit	13.1	9.5
Selling expenses	3.2	2.3
Admin expenses	6.4	5.2
Operating profit	3.5	2.0
Finance costs	0.4	0.4
Profit for the year (net profit)	3.1	1.6
Taxation	0.6	0.3
Profit for the year (net profit) after taxation	2.5	1.3

▲ Table 3 Extract from the statement of comprehensive income for Cattle Snaffle Ltd, year ending 31/12/17

Key information:

The statement of comprehensive income contains the following information.

- **Revenue.** This is the money the business receives from selling goods and services. It is sometimes called turnover. Revenue must not include VAT. This is because VAT does not belong to the business. The revenue for Cattle Snaffle Ltd in 2017 was €25.4 million.
- **Cost of sales.** This refers to the production costs of a business. It relates to direct costs in particular, such as raw materials and labour. In the case of Cattle Snaffle Ltd, the cost of sales would be the cost of grain, nutrients, electricity, wages to factory workers and any sales taxes paid such as VAT. For a retailer, it will be the cost of direct labour and buying in stock to re-sell. For a service provider it will include the direct costs of providing a service, such as labour. In 2017, the cost of sales for Cattle Snaffle Ltd was €12.3 million.
- **Gross profit.** This is the cost of sales subtracted from the revenue. It is the profit made before the deduction of general overheads. The gross profit made by Cattle Snaffle Ltd in 2017 was €13.1 million (€25.4 million − €12.3 million).
- **Selling expenses.** A business is likely to have a range of expenses from the selling of its products. Examples might include sales commissions, advertising, distribution and promotional costs. In 2017, Cattle Snaffle Ltd spent €3.2 million on selling expenses.
- **Administrative (admin) expenses.** These are the general overheads or indirect costs of the business. Examples might include office salaries, expenses claimed by senior staff, stationery supplies, IT expenses, accountancy fees and telephone bills. Cattle Snaffle Ltd incurred **administrative expenses** of €6.4 million in 2017.

- **Operating profit.** The operating profit is gross profit minus selling and administrative costs. It is the profit generated from the firm's core activities. It does not include any income from financial investments made by the business. Cattle Snaffle Ltd made an operating profit of €3.5 million in 2017.
- **Finance costs.** If a business borrows money, it will have to pay interest to the lender. The amount paid will be entered in the statement of comprehensive income as a **finance cost**. However, a business may also receive interest if it has money in deposit accounts. This will appear as **finance income** in the accounts. In 2017, Cattle Snaffle Ltd paid €400 000 in interest.
- **Profit for the year (net profit).** The net profit for the year is operating profit minus the cost of finance. This is the profit before taxation. Cattle Snaffle Ltd made a profit for the year (net profit) of €3.1 million in 2017.
- **Profit for the year (net profit) after tax.** This is the amount of money that is left over after all expenses, including taxation, have been deducted from revenue. It is often referred to as the 'bottom line'. The money belongs to the owners of the business. In the case of a limited company, it belongs to the shareholders. However, it may not necessarily be distributed to the shareholders. Some of it may be retained . This is discussed later in the chapter. Cattle Snaffle Ltd made a profit for the year (net profit) after tax of €2.5 million in 2017.

The extract from the statement of comprehensive income for Cattle Snaffle Ltd in Table 3 shows figures for both 2017 and the previous year. This is standard practice and helps to make comparisons over time. For example, the performance of Cattle Snaffle Ltd has improved over the two years. Its profit for the year (net profit) after tax (the 'bottom line') has nearly doubled from €1.3 million in 2016 to €2.5 million in 2017.

WORKED EXAMPLE

Vũ Minh Tuấn runs a bicycle manufacturing company in Hanoi, Vietnam. At the end of the financial year in 2018, revenue was VND980 000, cost of sales were VND430 000, selling expenses were VND110 000, admin expenses were VND130 000 and finance costs were VND80 000. We can use a statement of comprehensive income to calculate gross profit, operating profit and profit for the year (net profit). It is shown in Table 4.

	2018 (VND)
Revenue	980 000
Cost of sales	430 000
Gross profit	**550 000**
Selling expenses	110 000
Admin. Expenses	130 000
Operating profit	**310 000**
Finance costs	80 000
Profit for the year (net profit)	**230 000**

▲ Table 4 Example statement of comprehensive income

STAKEHOLDER INTEREST

The statement of comprehensive income can be used to help evaluate (i.e. form an opinion after careful thought) the performance of a business. It is therefore likely to be of interest to a range of stakeholders.

Shareholders: Obviously, the owners of a business are interested in its performance. Shareholders are likely to be interested in the profit made by the business, particularly the profit for the year (net profit) after tax. This is an effective guide to the performance of a business but not the only guide. Rising profits suggest improving performance. It is possible for shareholders, or their representatives, to calculate profit for the year (net profit) and gross profit margins using information from the statement of comprehensive income to assess performance more thoroughly. This is discussed in Student Book 1, Chapter 34.

It is also possible to assess the growth of the business by looking at the statement of comprehensive income. If the revenue is rising, it suggests that the business is growing. In the Cattle Snaffle Ltd statement, revenue rises from €21.2 million in 2016 to €25.4 million in 2017. This is an increase of 19.8 per cent and indicates a growth rate of nearly one-fifth.

Managers and directors: Since managers and directors are responsible for running the business, they are likely to use key information in the statement of comprehensive income to monitor progress. For example,

they might be setting annual targets for growth in revenue or profit for the year (net profit). Changes in the revenue will show how fast a company has grown and whether targets have been met.

Employees: If employees (or their representatives) want a wage increase, it may be helpful to have access to some of the information in the statement of comprehensive income when presenting a claim. For example, if Cattle Snaffle Ltd employees wanted a 5 per cent wage increase, they might use the following figures as an argument that the company could afford it: a 92 per cent increase in profit for the year (net profit) from €1.3 million in 2016 to €2.5 million in 2017.

Suppliers: Before a supplier accepts an order from a new customer on trade credit, it is sensible to check their creditworthiness (i.e. their ability to pay for what they have bought on credit). One way to do this is to look at the trading history of the customer. If the customer can provide several years of authenticated (i.e. proved to be genuine) accounts, this might help to show whether the customer is able to pay what is owed at the end of the credit period. If the statement of comprehensive income shows that a customer is always profitable, this might be enough proof for the supplier.

The government: Companies have to produce a statement of comprehensive income by law. It is needed by the tax authorities to help assess how much tax a business has to pay. The tax authorities collect taxes on behalf of the government and require all business owners to provide documentary evidence of the profits or losses made by the business every year. Also, government statistics agencies may have an interest in business accounts because they collect economic data for public use.

ACTIVITY 1 SKILLS CRITICAL THINKING, PROBLEM SOLVING

CASE STUDY: MOOSEWEAR LTD

A Danish company called Moosewear Ltd operates an online shopping site. It sells winter clothing imported from Alaska and Canada. The majority of its products are made from fake fur. In 2016 it launched a range of furry 'onesies' (a loose-fitting garment which covers the entire body), which sold very well. An extract from the statement of comprehensive income for Moosewear Ltd is shown in Table 5.

	2017 (DKK 000)	2016 (DKK 000)
Revenue	3450	2980
Cost of sales	1210	990
Gross profit	2240	1990
Selling expenses	760	560
Admin expenses	780	870
Operating profit	700	560
Finance costs	80	70
Profit for the year (net profit)	620	490
Taxation	120	110
Profit for the year (net profit) after taxation	500	380

▲ Table 5 Extract from the statement of comprehensive income for Moosewear Ltd, 31/12/17

1 What is meant by 'cost of sales'? Use examples from this case to illustrate your answer.
2 Calculate the percentage increase in (a) revenue and (b) profit for the year (net profit) after tax for Moosewear Ltd from 2016 to 2017.
3 Discuss whether shareholders are likely to be happy with the performance of Moosewear Ltd in 2017.

STATEMENT OF FINANCIAL POSITION

The statement of financial position (balance sheet) provides a summary of a firm's assets, liabilities and capital. It is like a photograph of the financial position of a business at a particular point in time.

- **Assets.** Assets are the resources that a business owns and uses. Assets are usually divided into current assets and non-current assets. Current assets are used up in production, such as stocks of raw materials. They can also be money owed to the business by **debtors**. Non-current assets, such as machinery, are used again and again over a period of time.
- **Liabilities.** Liabilities are the debts of the business, i.e. what it owes to other businesses, individuals and institutions. Liabilities are a source of funds for a business. They might be short term, such as an overdraft, or long term, such as a mortgage. In the balance sheet, liabilities are divided into current liabilities and non-current liabilities.
- **Capital.** This is the money introduced by the owners of the business, for example when they buy shares. It is another source of funds and can be used to purchase assets.

In all balance sheets, the value of assets (what a business uses or owns) will equal the value of liabilities and capital (what the business owes). This is because any increase in total assets must be funded by an equal increase in capital or liabilities. For example, a business wanting to buy extra machinery (an asset) may need to obtain a bank loan (a liability). Alternatively, a reduction in credit from suppliers (a liability) may mean a reduction in stocks that can be bought (an asset). So:

$$\text{Assets} = \text{capital} + \text{liabilities}$$

WORKED EXAMPLE

A business has assets of $437.6 million, its capital is $250.1 million, therefore its liabilities must be $187.5 million ($437.6 million − $250.1 million).
If this business took out a $15 million mortgage to pay for a new building, liabilities would rise by $15 million and the value of assets would also rise by $15 million. As a result, the business's assets would be $452.6 million and its liabilities would be $202.5 million. Capital and liabilities added together would be $452.6 million (exactly the same as total assets).

KEY INFORMATION

The key information that is likely to be listed in a statement of financial position is shown in Table 6. It shows the assets, liabilities and capital of Cattle Snaffle Ltd, the cattle and sheep feed producer mentioned earlier.

Non-current assets: Non-current assets are any assets that are not expected to be sold within 12 months. They are the long-term resources of the business. A number of entries are likely to be found in this section of the balance sheet.

- **Goodwill.** This is an example of an intangible asset. This is a non-physical asset of a business (i.e. it is not a visible asset). It is the amount the business is worth above the value of net assets. Goodwill exists if a company has built up a good reputation and its customers are likely to return. The goodwill for Cattle Snaffle Ltd in 2017 was valued at €30.5 million.
- **Other intangible assets.** These may appear in some plc balance sheets. Examples include brand names, copyrights, trademarks and **patents** (see Student Book 1, Chapter 42). The value of other intangible assets for Cattle Snaffle Ltd in 2017 was €15.2 million.
- **Property, plant and equipment.** These are the tangible assets that the business owns. Tangible assets are the physical assets of a business. Examples for Cattle Snaffle Ltd might be a factory, and the machinery and equipment used to process cattle feed from raw materials. In 2017, Cattle

Snaffle Ltd had €97.7 million in tangible assets. The total for non-current assets is also shown in the balance sheet – it was €143.4 million.

- **Investments.** These are the financial assets owned by the company. An example might be shares held in other companies. If investments are listed under non-current assets, it means that they are not expected to be sold for at least 12 months. If investments are likely to be sold within 12 months, they should be listed under current assets. According to the balance sheet in Table 6, Cattle Snaffle Ltd does not own any investments.

	2017 (€m)	2016 (€m)
Non-current assets		
Goodwill	30.5	27.8
Other intangible assets	15.2	11.6
Property, plant & equipment	97.7	94.1
Total non-current assets	**143.4**	**133.5**
Current assets		
Inventories	8.6	6.7
Trade and other receivables	3.4	3.1
Cash and cash equivalents	3.1	2.7
Total current assets	**15.1**	**12.5**
Total assets	**158.5**	**146.0**
Current liabilities		
Trade and other payables	5.5	5.1
Dividends payable	1.2	0.8
Current tax liabilities	6.7	5.7
Total current liabilities	**13.4**	**11.6**
Non-current liabilities		
Borrowings	24.5	26.1
Provisions	4.1	3.4
Pensions	7.8	6.7
Total non-current liabilities	**36.4**	**36.2**
Total liabilities	**49.8**	**47.8**
Net assets	**108.7**	**98.2**
Shareholders' equity		
Share capital	30.0	30.0
Other reserves	17.7	9.7
Retained earnings	61.0	58.5
Total equity	**108.7**	**98.2**

▲ Table 6 Statement of financial position for Cattle Snaffle Ltd, as at 31/12/17

Current assets: Current assets are the liquid assets that belong to the business. Liquid assets are either cash or are expected to be converted into cash within 12 months.

- **Inventories.** This refers to stocks of raw materials and components, stocks of finished goods and work

in progress. For Cattle Snaffle Ltd, examples might be grain, such as barley and wheat, nutrients and packaging. The value of Cattle Snaffle's inventories in 2017 was €8.6 million.

- **Trade and other receivables.** These are trade debtors, prepayments and any other amounts owed to the business that are likely to be repaid within 12 months. If Cattle Snaffle Ltd gives its customers trade credit, the money owed by customers would be an example. In 2017 Cattle Snaffle Ltd was owed a total of €3.4 million by debtors.

- **Cash at bank and in hand.** This is the money held by a business on the premises or in bank accounts. Cattle Snaffle Ltd had €3.1 million in cash or cash equivalents in 2017. Also, Cattle Snaffle's current assets totalled €15.1 million and the value of total assets for the business (current + non-current) was €158.5 million.

Current liabilities: Any money owed by the business that is expected to be repaid within 12 months is called a current liability. Some examples are outlined below.

- **Borrowings.** Any short-term loans or bank overdrafts taken out by the business. In this case, Cattle Snaffle does not have any short-term loans.

- **Trade and other payables.** Trade creditors and other amounts owed by the business to suppliers of goods, services and utilities (such as electricity, gas, water, cable and telephone), for example. Table 6 shows that Cattle Snaffle owed €5.5 million to its suppliers in 2017.

- **Dividends payable.** It is possible that the company has decided how much it will pay to the shareholders in dividends when the balance sheet is prepared. However, the money has not yet been paid so it appears in the balance sheet as dividends payable. Cattle Snaffle Ltd owed €1.2 million in dividends to shareholders on 31/12/17.

- **Current tax liabilities.** Corporation tax, employees' income tax and any other tax owed by the business that must be repaid within 12 months. Cattle Snaffle Ltd owed €6.7 million to the tax authorities on 31/12/17. The total value of Cattle Snaffle's current liabilities in 2017 was €13.4 million.

Non-current liabilities: These are the long-term liabilities of a business. Any amount of money owed for more than one year will appear in this section of the balance sheet.

- **Other loans and borrowings.** Money owed by the company that does not have to be repaid for at least 12 months. Examples would be long-term bank loans and mortgages. Table 6 shows that Cattle Snaffle Ltd owed €24.5 million in 2017.

- **Retirement pension obligations.** Companies need to show any money owed to past employees in the form of pension obligations. In 2017 Cattle Snaffle Ltd had €7.8 million in pension commitments.

- **Provisions.** Provisions have to be made if a company is likely to incur (i.e. owe) expenditure in the future. Such expenditure might occur as a result of agreements in contracts or warranties. An example for Cattle Snaffle Ltd might be a possible bad debt that it may incur. If these provisions are short term they will appear under current liabilities. In 2017 Cattle Snaffle Ltd had €4.1 million in provisions. The total value of its non-current liabilities was €36.4 million. Its total liabilities (current + non-current) were €49.8 million.

Net assets: Net assets is the value of all assets minus the value of all liabilities. It will be the same value as shareholders' equity at the bottom of the balance sheet. The value of Cattle Snaffle's net assets in 2017 was €108.7 million. The net assets provide a guide to the value of a business.

Equity: The bottom section of the balance sheet shows the amounts of money owed to the shareholders. It will contain details of share capital and reserves.

- **Share capital.** The amount of money paid by shareholders for their shares when they were originally issued. It does not represent the current value of those shares on the stock market. Share capital is not usually repaid to the shareholders in the lifetime of a company. The value of Cattle Snaffle's issued share capital in 2017 was €30 million.
- **Share premium account.** This shows the difference between the value of new shares issued by the company and their nominal value. For example, the nominal value of a share may have been €1. The company may decide to issue 2 million new shares. If the company sold them for €3, each new share is now worth €2 more than the nominal price. In total, this would be €4 million (€2 × 2 million). This €4 million would be entered on the share premium account in the balance sheet. Cattle Snaffle Ltd does not have any share premium.
- **Other reserves.** Refers to any amounts owing to the shareholders not covered by the other entries under equity. Cattle Snaffle Ltd had €17.7 million in other reserves in 2017.
- **Retained earnings.** The same as retained profit. It is the amount of profit kept by the business to be used in the future, for example to fund investment projects. Cattle Snaffle Ltd had €61 million retained profit in 2017.

The total value of shareholders' equity, €108.7 million in the case of Cattle Snaffle Ltd, is the same as net assets. This will always be the case and explains why the statement of financial position is sometimes called the balance sheet. Company law requires companies to show both this year's and last year's figures in published accounts. This allows comparisons to be made.

ACTIVITY 2   SKILLS   PROBLEM SOLVING, ANALYSIS

CASE STUDY: GROSICKI & CO

Polish baker, Grosicki & Co, makes cakes and biscuits for supermarkets and large retailers. Table 7 shows the statement of financial position for the company as at 31/12/18.

	2018 (PLN 000)	2017 (PLN 000)
Non-current assets		
Intangible assets	8667	8009
Property and equipment	11 987	12 134
	20 654	20 143
Current assets		
Inventories	4501	4511
Trade and other receivables	3444	4100
Cash and cash equivalents	1200	1300
	9145	9911
Total assets	**29 799**	**30 054**
Current liabilities		
Trade and other payables	4888	4976
Current tax liabilities	?????	2009
	6009	6985
Non-current liabilities		
Borrowings	4222	4777
Pensions	1233	1341
	5455	6118
Total liabilities	11 464	13 103
Net assets	**??????**	**16 951**
Shareholders' equity		
Share capital	10 000	10 000
Retained earnings	8335	6951
Total equity	**18 335**	**16 951**

▲ Table 7 Statement of financial position for Grosicki & Co, as at 31/12/18

1 Complete the balance sheet by calculating the missing values for (a) net assets and (b) current tax liabilities.
2 Give two possible examples of trade and other payables for Grosicki & Co.
3 Explain the difference between current liabilities and non-current liabilities.
4 What has happened to the value of Grosicki between 2017 and 2018?

STAKEHOLDER INTEREST

The statement of financial position can be used to help evaluate the performance of a business. It shows different information from that of the statement of comprehensive income, and stakeholders are likely to be interested in both statements together.

Shareholders: Shareholders might use the balance sheet to analyse the asset structure of the business. This shows how the funds raised by the business have been put to use. For example, shareholders in Cattle Snaffle Ltd in Table 6 can see that more than 60 per cent of the assets (€97.7 million) are invested in property, plant and equipment. The balance sheet also shows the capital structure of the business, i.e. the different sources of funds used by the business. For Cattle Snaffle Ltd, nearly 67 per cent of the firm's funding comes from the shareholders.

The balance sheet can also be used to assess the **solvency** of the business. A business is **solvent** if it has enough liquid assets to pay its bills. The value of working capital will help to assess solvency. The working capital of a business can be calculated by subtracting current liabilities from current assets. For Cattle Snaffle Ltd, the value of working capital is €1.7 million (€15.1 million − €13.4 million). This might be considered inadequate because the value of current liabilities is only just covered by current assets.

WORKED EXAMPLE

Hassani Ltd is an Algerian manufacturer of sweets and desserts. It supplies supermarkets and other large retailers. Table 8 shows some financial information taken from its statement of financial position.

	2018 (DZD million)
Current assets	
Inventories	34.9
Trade and receivables	28.6
Cash and equivalents	31.8
Current liabilities	
Trade and other payables	25.1
Borrowings	32.1
Other tax liabilities	11.9

▲ Table 8 Extract from statement of financial position for Hassani Ltd, 2018

The working capital for Hassani Ltd is given by:

$$\text{Working capital} = \text{current assets} - \text{current liabilities}$$
$$= \text{DZD95 300 000} - \text{DZD69 100 000}$$
$$= \text{DZD26 200 000}$$

In this example, Hassani Ltd has DZD26 200 000 of working capital. This may be an adequate amount of working capital for the business because current assets exceed current liabilities by about 1.5 times. Working capital is discussed in more detail in Student Book 1, Chapter 35.

The value of a business is roughly equivalent to the value of net assets in the business. This means that shareholders can use the balance sheet to see if their investment is growing. Between 2016 and 2017 the value of Cattle Snaffle Ltd grew from €98.2 million to €108.7 million.

Managers and directors: The balance sheet might be used by the management of a business. For example, it is important for senior managers to be aware of the firm's financial position at all times. It will need to monitor working capital levels to ensure that the business does not overspend. Also, if the business is considering raising some more finance, it will have to consider the current capital structure before choosing a suitable source. For example, it might want to avoid borrowing more money if the business is already in debt. Raising fresh capital might be a better option.

Suppliers and creditors: Suppliers will be most interested in the solvency of the business. Suppliers are not likely to offer trade credit to a business that only has a limited amount of working capital. Cattle Snaffle Ltd only has a small amount of working capital; as a result, it might struggle to get generous trade credit terms. However, this will also depend on Cattle Snaffle's trading history and its past credit record. Banks and other lenders will be interested in the balance sheet for the same reasons.

Others: It is possible that employees might use the balance sheet to assess whether a business can afford a pay rise or whether their jobs are secure. Government agencies responsible for gathering statistics might also extract information from the balance sheet to compile national statistics.

LINKS

Information in this chapter could be used in a range of answers. For example, if you are discussing sources of finance for a business you could explain how the capital structure of the business might influence the decision. Businesses that already have a large quantity of borrowings might be better to raise fresh capital, for example. This chapter could also be linked with Internal finance (Student Book 1, Chapter 24), External finance (Student Book 1, Chapter 25), Planning (Student Book 1, Chapter 23), Break-even (Student Book 1, Chapter 31), Profit (Student Book 1, Chapter 34), Liquidity (Student Book 1, Chapter 35), SWOT analysis (this book, Chapter 3), Decision trees (Chapter 11), Ratio analysis (Chapter 18) and Global expansion and uncertainty (Chapter 31).

SUBJECT VOCABULARY

administrative expenses costs relating to running a business
debtors people or businesses that owe money
finance cost interest paid by a business on any borrowed money
finance income interest received by a business on any money held in deposit
patent a government authority or licence for a right or title for a set period of time. This involves the sole right to exclude others from making, using or selling a product, service or idea
solvency (solvent) the ability of a business to meet its debts

CHECKPOINT

1 How is gross profit calculated in a statement of comprehensive income?

2 How is operating profit calculated in a statement of comprehensive income?

3 Give three examples of selling expenses for a business.

4 What is meant by finance costs in a statement of comprehensive income?

5 What is the difference between non-current assets and current assets?

6 Give two examples of intangible assets.

7 What information is needed from the balance sheet to calculate working capital?

8 Give two examples of non-current liabilities.

9 What is meant by retained earnings?

10 Give two reasons why shareholders might be interested in company accounts.

11 Why might the government be interested in company accounts?

EXAM PRACTICE

CASE STUDY: MALAGA MARINE PARK

SKILLS CRITICAL THINKING, ANALYSIS, INTERPRETATION, REASONING

Malaga Marine Park on the Costa del Sol, Spain, has experienced difficult trading conditions since 2014. The business has also been criticised by groups representing animal rights. Despite the marine park's good reputation, there has been negative publicity about the captive environment in which the animals, such as dolphins, seals, sharks and other sea creatures are kept. This has has affected the park's popularity. However, in 2018, as economies in the EU grew strongly, the park experienced a return to profit as visitor numbers rose sharply. The marine park hopes to improve its image in the future by emphasising the work it does protecting the environment and saving rare marine species. An extract from the statement of comprehensive income is shown in Table 9 and statement of financial position for the business is shown in Table 10.

	2018 (€ 000)	2017 (€ 000)
Revenue	6110	4180
Cost of sales	4210	2990
Gross profit	1900	1190
Selling expenses	460	470
Admin expenses	380	480
Operating profit	1060	240
Finance costs	500	600
Profit/loss for the year (net profit/loss)	560	(360)
Taxation	110	0
Profit for the year (net profit) after tax	450	(360)

▲ Table 9 Extract from statement of comprehensive income for Malaga Marine Park, year ending 31/12/18

	2018 (€ 000)	2017 (€ 000)
Non-current assets		
Intangible assets	1100	900
Property and equipment	8556	7986
	9656	8886
Current assets		
Inventories	1200	1170
Trade and other receivables	780	750
Cash and cash equivalents	600	200
	2580	2120
Total assets	**12236**	**11006**
Current liabilities		
Trade and other payables	1091	1136
Current tax liabilities	1400	1750
Current tax liabilities	60	76
	2551	2962
Non-current liabilities		
Borrowings	2050	2160
Pensions	833	841
	2883	3001
Total liabilities	**5434**	**5963**
Net assets	**6802**	**5043**
Shareholders' equity		
Share capital	3000	3000
Other reserves	2348	1039
Retained earnings	1454	1004
Total equity	**6802**	**5043**

▲ Table 10 Statement of financial position for Malaga Marine Park as at 31/12/18

1 Explain one reason why suppliers might want access to the statement of financial position for Malaga Marine Park. **(4 marks)**

2 Explain one reason why managers and directors might want access to the statement of comprehensive income for Malaga Marine Park. **(4 marks)**

3 Evaluate whether or not there has been an improvement in the financial performance (profitability and liquidity) of Malaga Marine Park between 2017 and 2018. **(20 marks)**

18 RATIO ANALYSIS

LEARNING OBJECTIVES

By the end of this chapter you should be able to:
- calculate profitability (gross profit margin and profit for the year margin), liquidity (current and acid test ratios), gearing ratio and return on capital employed (ROCE)
- interpret ratios to make business decisions
- understand the limitations of ratio analysis.

GETTING STARTED

Businesses need to know what returns they are getting on the money invested in the business and whether the business is financially strong. They also like to make comparisons with their rivals. For example, Zahid Ltd, a small Pakistani property developer (a company that makes money by building houses or renovating existing properties for sale), made a profit of PKR4.6 million while a much larger rival, Karachi Properties, made PKR23.4 billion. But which of these companies has performed the best? Clearly one has made more profit than the other, but it does not necessarily mean it has performed the best.

What other information might be needed to determine the best-performing company in the above example? Explain your answer. If Zahid Ltd has borrowed 25 per cent of its finance while Karachi Properties borrowed a much larger 86 per cent, to which business is a bank most likely to lend more money? Explain your answer.

FINANCIAL RATIOS

It is possible to find important information from the statement of comprehensive income and the statement of financial position to help assess the performance of a business. This approach was used in Chapter 17. However, a more thorough approach is to use **ratio analysis**. We can calculate and use financial ratios to analyse the performance of businesses more precisely. A financial ratio is one number divided by another or one number expressed as a percentage of another. There are different types of ratio, which address different aspects of financial performance.

PROFITABILITY RATIOS

Profitability or performance ratios help to show how well a business is doing. They may be used by senior managers, the finance department and investors to help assess the performance of the business. They might be used to make comparisons with previous time periods or other businesses, for example. They usually focus on profit, capital employed and revenue.

The profit figure alone is not a useful **performance indicator**. We must look at the value of profit in relation to the value of revenue or the amount of money that has been invested in the business. A business can use a variety of different profitability ratios.

Gross profit margin: The gross profit margin shows the gross profit made on sales turnover/revenue. It is calculated using the formula:

$$\text{Gross profit margin} = \frac{\text{Gross profit} \times 100}{\text{Revenue}}$$

Profit for the year (net profit) margin: The profit for the year (net profit) margin or net profit margin takes into account all business costs, including finance costs, other non-operating costs and exceptional items. It is also usually calculated before tax has been subtracted. This may be because businesses can sometimes alter the payment of tax so that the profit shown does not accurately reflect the company's performance for that year. The profit for the year (net profit) margin can be calculated by:

$$\text{Profit for the year (net profit) margin} = \frac{\text{Net profit before tax} \times 100}{\text{Revenue}}$$

WORKED EXAMPLE

	2017 (£ 000)	2016 (£ 000)
Revenue	48660	48050
Gross profit	21890	19700
Operating profit	6570	5430
Profit for the year	3940	3460
Non-current assets	21900	20100
Current assets	5430	4300
Current liabilities	3333	3100
Inventories	1900	1800
Non-current liabilities	6900	5490

▲ Table 1 Selective financial information for Washytree Holdings, 2016 and 2017

Washytree Holdings is a farm machinery repair and maintenance company based in Llangollen, Wales. Using the information in Table 1, the gross profit margin is given by:

For 2017:

$$\text{Gross profit margin} = \frac{\text{Gross profit} \times 100}{\text{Revenue}}$$

$$= \frac{£21\,890\,000 \times 100}{£48\,660\,000}$$

$$= 45\%$$

For 2016:

$$= \frac{£19\,700\,000 \times 100}{£48\,050\,000}$$

$$= 41\%$$

Using the information in Table 1, the profit for the year (net profit) margin is given by:

For 2017:

$$\frac{\text{Profit for the year}}{\text{(net profit) margin}} = \frac{\text{Profit for the year} \times 100}{\text{Revenue}}$$

$$= \frac{£3\,940\,000 \times 100}{£48\,660\,000}$$

$$= 8.1\%$$

For 2016:

$$= \frac{£3\,460\,000 \times 100}{£48\,050\,000}$$

$$= 7.2\%$$

INTERPRETING PROFITABILITY RATIOS

Gross margin: Higher gross margins are preferable to lower ones because it means that more gross profit is being made per £1 of sales. The gross profit margin will vary between different industries. The quicker the turnover of inventory, the lower the gross margin that is needed. For example, a supermarket with a fast inventory turnover is likely to have a lower gross margin than a car retailer with a much slower inventory turnover. Some supermarkets are therefore very successful with relatively low gross profit margins because of the regular and fast turnover of inventory.

In this case, the gross profit margin for Washytree Holdings has increased from 41 per cent to 45 per cent over the two years. The managers and owners of the company are likely to be pleased with this.

Gross profit margins may be used by businesses to help make decisions. For example, if gross margins are below the industry average, action might be needed. The business may look for new suppliers of key raw materials or find new working practices to improve efficiency in production. Alternatively, a business may decide to raise the price of the product – if the market can stand such an increase.

Profit for the year (net profit) margin: Again, higher margins are better than lower ones. The profit for the year (net profit) margin focuses on the 'bottom line' in business. The bottom line refers to the very last line in the statement of comprehensive income. It shows the profit that is left after all deductions have been made, i.e. the final amount of profit left over for the owners. In this case, the net profit margin for Washytree Holdings has increased from 7.2 per cent to 8.1 per cent over the two years. There is no reason why the managers and owners of the company should not be pleased with this unless rivals are enjoying much higher margins.

LIQUIDITY RATIOS

Information contained in the balance sheet can be used to measure the liquidity of a business. It is important that a business is able to meet its short-term debts. This means that a business must have enough liquid resources to pay its immediate bills. If it doesn't, it might result in the financial collapse of the business. Two financial ratios can be used to measure liquidity.

Current ratio: The current ratio is a liquidity ratio and focuses on the current assets and current liabilities of a business. It can be calculated using the formula:

$$\text{Current ratio} = \frac{\text{Current assets}}{\text{Current liabilities}}$$

Acid test ratio: The acid test ratio is a more severe test of liquidity. This is because inventories are not treated as liquid resources. There is no guarantee that inventories can be sold, and they may become outdated (i.e. no longer useful after a certain period of time) or decline in quality. They are therefore excluded from current assets when calculating the ratio. The acid test ratio can be calculated using the formula:

$$\text{Acid test ratio} = \frac{\text{Current assets} - \text{Inventories}}{\text{Current liabilities}}$$

WORKED EXAMPLE

Table 1 shows current assets, current liabilities and inventories for Washytree Holdings. The current and acid test ratios for Washytree Holdings are given by:

For 2017:

$$\text{Current ratio} = \frac{\text{Current assets}}{\text{Current liabilities}}$$

$$\text{Current ratio} = \frac{£5\,430\,000}{£3\,333\,000}$$

$$= 1.63$$

$$\text{Acid test ratio} = \frac{\text{Current assets} - \text{Inventories}}{\text{Current liabilities}}$$

$$\text{Acid test ratio} = \frac{£5\,430\,000 - £1\,900\,000}{£3\,333\,000}$$

$$= 1.06$$

For 2016:

$$\text{Current ratio} = \frac{£4\,300\,000}{£3\,100\,000}$$

$$= 1.39$$

$$\text{Acid test ratio} = \frac{£4\,300\,000 - £1\,800\,000}{£3\,100\,000}$$

$$= 0.81$$

INTERPRETING LIQUIDITY RATIOS

Current ratio: A business is said to have enough liquid resources if the current ratio is between 1.5:1 and 2:1. If the current ratio is below 1.5 then the business may not have enough working capital. This might mean that a business is over-borrowing or overtrading (doing more business than can be supported by the resources available). However, some businesses, such as retailers, often have very low current ratios, such as 1:1 or below. This is because they hold fast-selling stocks and generate cash from sales. In contrast, operating above a ratio of 2:1 may suggest that too much money is being used unproductively. For example, money in stocks does not earn any return.

In this case, between 2016 and 2017 the current ratio for Washytree Holdings has improved from 1.39 to 1.63. It has moved into the 'safe' range for the ratio.

Acid test ratio: If a business has an acid test ratio of less than 1:1, it means that its current assets minus stocks do not cover its current liabilities. This could indicate a potential problem. However, as with the current ratio, there is variation between the typical acid test ratios of businesses in different industries. Again, retailers with strong cash flows may operate comfortably with an acid test ratio of less than 1.

In this case, the acid test ratio for Washytree Holdings has also improved. It has increased over the two years from 0.81 in 2016 to 1.06 in 2017. It is now close to 1, but in the previous year it was a little bit below 1. There has been an improvement in the liquidity of Washytree Holdings.

ACTIVITY 1 · SKILLS · PROBLEM SOLVING, ANALYSIS

CASE STUDY: HILDRA COMMS

Based in Cairo, Egypt, Hildra Comms is a telecommunications company with over 100 million customers in a range of international markets. It provides mobile, wireless, wireline and content services in the Middle East, North Africa and South East Asia. Its main aim is to make Egypt one of the best-connected places in the world. Table 2 shows some financial information for Hildra Comms for 2016 and 2017.

	2017	2016
Current assets	27 244 075	24 747 230
Current liabilities	24 048 281	20 447 298
Inventories	679 623	581 144
Revenue	32 735 032	32 503 259
Profit before tax	3 196 699	3 126 759

▲ Table 2 Financial information for Hildra Comms, 2016 and 2017 (EGP 000)

1 Calculate (a) the current ratio and (b) the acid test ratio for Hildra Comms for 2016 and 2017.
2 Calculate the profit for the year (net profit) margin for Hildra Comms in 2016 and 2017.
3 Discuss the liquidity and profitability of Hildra Comms over the two years.

GEARING RATIOS

Gearing ratios show the long-term financial position of the business. We can use them to show the relationship between loans on which interest is paid, and shareholders' equity on which dividends might be paid. There are several different versions of the gearing ratio. One connects the non-current liabilities (total long-term loans) to the capital employed. If not stated clearly, the capital employed can be determined by subtracting current liabilities from total assets. The formula is:

$$\text{Gearing ratio} = \frac{\text{Non-current liabilities}}{\text{Capital employed}} \times 100\%$$

WORKED EXAMPLE

The gearing ratio for Washytree Holdings is given by:

$$\text{Gearing ratio} = \frac{\text{Non-current liabilities}}{\text{Capital employed}} \times 100\%$$

For 2017

$$= \frac{£6\,900\,000}{(£21\,900\,000 + £5\,430\,000) - £3\,333\,000} \times 100$$

$$= \frac{£6\,900\,000}{£27\,330\,000 - £3\,333\,000} \times 100$$

$$= \frac{£6\,900\,000}{£23\,997\,000} \times 100$$

$$= 28.8\%$$

For 2016

$$= \frac{£5\,490\,000}{(£20\,100\,000 + £4\,300\,000) - £3\,100\,000} \times 100$$

$$= \frac{£5\,490\,000}{£24\,400\,000 - £3\,100\,000} \times 100$$

$$= \frac{£5\,490\,000}{£21\,300\,000} \times 100$$

$$= 25.8\%$$

INTERPRETING THE GEARING RATIO

Creditors are likely to be concerned about a firm's gearing (i.e. the ratio of a company's loan capital to its share capital). For example, loans have interest charges that must be paid. Dividends do not have to be paid to ordinary shareholders. As a business becomes more highly geared (loans are high relative to share capital), it is considered riskier by creditors. The owners of a business might prefer to raise extra funds by borrowing. They might not want to issue more shares and share control of the business.

Gearing ratios can be used to analyse the capital structure of a business. They compare the amount of capital raised from ordinary shareholders with that raised in loans. This is important because the interest on loans is a fixed commitment, but the dividends for ordinary shareholders are not. Gearing ratios can assess whether or not a business is burdened by its loans. This is because highly geared companies must still pay their interest even when trading becomes difficult.

The gearing ratio for Washytree Holdings has risen slightly from 25.8 per cent in 2016 to 28.8 per cent in 2017. This is a relatively low gearing ratio. It is not until the gearing ratio reaches 50 per cent that concerns are raised. A gearing ratio of around 25 per cent means that the business is not overburdened with long-term debt. Higher gearing ratios mean that a much larger proportion of the business's finance is borrowed. With low-geared companies a greater proportion of finance is provided by shareholders (the owners).

	2017 (AED million)	2016 (AED million)
Non-current assets	2054	2602
Current assets	1551	1726
Current liabilities	268	153
Non-current liabilities	150	533

▲ Table 3 Selective financial information for Al Faqar Energy, 2016 and 2017

1 Calculate the gearing ratio for Al Faqar Energy in 2017 and 2016.
2 Assess the extent to which Al Faqar Energy is low geared.

MATHS TIP

You need to be careful when calculating ratios to ensure that the correct units are used. For example, financial information might be measured in 100s, 1000s, 100 000s, millions or billions. You need to make sure that decimal points are in the right place or you could end up with miscalculations. As a result, you might make some inaccurate conclusions from your calculations. This could have an adverse impact on your answer.

ACTIVITY 2   SKILLS   CRITICAL THINKING, PROBLEM SOLVING

CASE STUDY: AL FAQAR ENERGY

Dubai-based Al Faqar Energy is an oil company. It owns oil wells in and around the UAE. In 2015 it sold some key assets for AED3.5 billion to help reduce the amount owed by the company.

RETURN ON CAPITAL EMPLOYED (ROCE)

One of the most important ratios used to measure the profitability of a business is the return on capital employed (ROCE). This is sometimes referred to as the primary ratio. It compares the profit, i.e. return, made by the business with the amount of money invested, i.e. its capital. The advantage of this ratio is that it shows the connection between profit and the size of the business. When calculating ROCE, it is standard practice to define profit as operating profit (net profit before tax and interest). This is sometimes described as earnings before interest and tax (EBIT). Tax is ignored because it is determined by the government and is therefore outside the control of the company. Interest is excluded because it does not connect to the business's ordinary trading activities. The capital employed can be determined by subtracting current liabilities from total assets. ROCE can be calculated using the formula:

$$\text{ROCE} = \frac{\text{Operating profit}}{\text{Capital employed}} \times 100\%$$

WORKED EXAMPLE

For Washytree Holdings the return on capital employed is given by:

For 2017

$$= \frac{£6\,570\,000}{(£21\,900\,000 + £5\,430\,000) - £3\,333\,000} \times 100$$

$$= \frac{£6\,570\,000}{£27\,330\,000 - £3\,333\,000} \times 100$$

$$= \frac{£6\,570\,000}{£23\,997\,000} \times 100$$

$$= 27.4\%$$

For 2016

$$= \frac{£5\,430\,000}{(£20\,100\,000 + £4\,300\,000) - £3\,100\,000} \times 100$$

$$= \frac{£5\,430\,000}{£24\,400\,000 - £3\,100\,000} \times 100$$

$$= \frac{£5\,430\,000}{£21\,300\,000} \times 100$$

$$= 25.5\%$$

INTERPRETING ROCE

The ROCE will vary between industries. However, higher ratios are better. Over the two years, Washytree Holdings has seen its ROCE increase from 25.5 per cent to 27.4 per cent. This appears to be an impressive performance. However, to decide whether Washytree Holdings has performed well, this would have to be compared with another business in the same industry. An investor might also compare the ROCE with the possible return if the capital was invested elsewhere. For example, if £23 977 000 was placed in a bank account in 2017, it might have earned a 1.5 per cent return. So the 27.4 per cent ROCE in 2017 seems very impressive. However, an investor in the company will also want to be rewarded for the risk involved. The £23 977 000 invested by shareholders in Washytree Holdings is at risk if the business fails. So, for the investment to be worthwhile, the ROCE must be far greater than the return that could be earned in a 'safe' investment such as a bank deposit account.

ACTIVITY 3   SKILLS   PROBLEM SOLVING, ANALYSIS

CASE STUDY: ARDU

Ardu is an online retailer based in Manilla, Philippines, which delivers to over 40 different countries. Ardu is rapidly growing its market share and sells clothes, fashion accessories, household items and furniture. But the market is becoming more and more competitive. Ardu has been forced to cut the prices of many of its product lines since entering the Australian market. Ardu also had to spend money on some high advertising costs when breaking into this new market. Table 4 shows some financial information for Ardu.

	2017 (PHP million)	2016 (PHP million)
Revenue	2313	2282
Operating profit	106	139
Non-current assets	1662	1662
Current assets	486	471
Current liabilities	758	742
Non-current liabilities	623	646

▲ Table 4 Selective financial information for Ardu, 2016 and 2017

1 Calculate the ROCE for Ardu for 2017 and 2016.
2 Discuss the performance of Ardu between 2016 and 2017.

LIMITATIONS OF RATIO ANALYSIS

Unfortunately, there are problems with ratio analysis, so it must be used carefully. Some of the key limitations are outlined here.

The basis for comparison: We must be careful making comparisons using ratios. It is very important to compare 'like with like'.

- **Comparisons over time.** Care must be taken when comparing ratios from the same company over time. Many companies remain in the same industrial sector over time, but others can become more varied and change quickly. Equally, some companies remain the same size over time, while others grow or shrink quickly. There are factors that can affect the way in which ratios can be used as a measure of performance. For example, the measures of performance of a small company that starts off in the defence sector and grows rapidly to become a leading telecommunications equipment manufacturer will change over time. The value of a particular ratio that is appropriate for the company will therefore change. We must take this into account when comparing ratios.

- **Inter-firm comparisons.** We must be careful as we compare ratios between companies at a point in time. Comparing the ratios of two companies that make the same products is likely to say something about their relative performance. But comparing the ratios of a supermarket chain with those of a cement manufacturer is unlikely to be helpful. For example, the two companies will have different working capital needs and different profit margins. Even companies operating in the same industry can have subtle differences. For example, Safeway® and Whole Foods® are both supermarket chains in the USA. However, Safeway sells a wider range of products – for example, it has an in-store pharmacy. This makes a direct comparison less meaningful because the profit margins on non-food items might be different from those on groceries.
- **Other differences.** Even when companies have similar activities and operating circumstances, there may be other differences between them. For example, two similar companies may use different accounting techniques, different methods to calculate depreciation or different stock valuation methods. If the same accounting conventions have not been used, comparisons may be misleading. Companies can also have different year ends. For example, one company might end its financial year on 31 December and the other on 31 July. Although their accounts should be for the same year, the financial information would look different as they are two quite different time periods. In this case, only six months of the year would be truly suitable for comparison.

The quality of final accounts: Ratios are based on financial accounts, such as the statement of statement of comprehensive income and the statement of financial position. Therefore, ratio analysis is only useful if the accounts are accurate. One factor that can affect the quality of accounting information is the change in monetary values caused by inflation. Rising prices can misrepresent (i.e. represent something in a misleading way) comparisons made between different time periods. For example, in times of high inflation, asset values and revenue might rise quickly in monetary terms. However, when the figures are adjusted for inflation, there might be no increase in real terms. There is also the possibility that the accounts have been **window dressed**. We will discuss this in more detail below.

Limitations of the balance sheet: The balance sheet is an outline of the business at the end of the financial year. This means it might not be representative of the business's circumstances throughout the whole of the year. For example, if a business experiences its peak trading activity in the summer, and it has its year end in January when trade is slow, figures for stock and debtors will be unrepresentative.

Qualitative information is ignored: Ratios only use quantitative information. However, some important qualitative factors may affect the performance of a business that are ignored by ratio analysis. For example, in the service industry, the quality of customer service may be an important performance indicator. However, ratio analysis cannot isolate the impact that good customer service might have on sales. Sales might be higher as a result of good customer service, but there might be other factors that have helped to increase sales, such as advertising.

Window dressing: Accounts must represent a 'true and fair record' of the financial affairs of a business. Legislation and financial reporting standards place limits on the different ways in which a business can present financial information. These limits are designed to stop **fraud** and misrepresentation once accounts are to be presented. However, businesses can adjust their accounts legally to present different financial pictures. This is known as window dressing. Businesses may want to window dress their accounts for a variety of reasons.

- Managers of companies might want to put as good a financial picture forward as possible for shareholders and potential shareholders. Good financial results will attract praise and perhaps rewards. They might also prevent criticism from shareholders and the media.
- If a business wants to raise new capital from investors, then it will want its financial accounts to look as good as possible.
- If a business has experienced severe difficulties during the accounting period, it may decide to take action. The action might make the financial position look even worse now, but it will improve figures in the future.
- Making the financial picture look worse may also be a way of lowering the amount of tax that is paid.
- If the owners of a business want to sell it, the better the financial position shown on the accounts, the higher the price they are likely to get.

There are several ways of window dressing accounts. For example, a business may adjust its sales by increasing the level of revenue recorded in the statement of comprehensive income. This will increase profit in that accounting period. It may be able to hide costs by changing its accounting policies or choosing when to 'write off' (i.e. cancel) unprofitable activities. It can also write off bad debts, revalue property, increase liquidity through the sale and leaseback of assets, and adjust current assets and current liabilities. The methods required to do these transactions are beyond the scope of this book, but you should be aware such methods exist.

LINKS

In addition to assessing the performance of a business, ratio analysis might also be used when making decisions. Therefore, you can demonstrate synoptic skills by linking ratio analysis to answers that involve making business decisions, such as whether to start exporting, investing in growth or launching a new product. Ratio analysis might be linked to Internal finance (Student Book 1, Chapter 24), External finance (Student Book 1, Chapter 25), Planning (Student Book 1, Chapter 23), Break-even (Student Book 1, Chapter 31), Profit (Student Book 1, Chapter 34), Liquidity (Student Book1, Chapter 35), Theories of corporate strategy (this book, Chapter 2), SWOT analysis (Chapter 3) and Decision trees (Chapter 11).

SUBJECT VOCABULARY

fraud the illegal act of cheating somebody to get money
gearing the ratio of a company's loan capital to its share capital
gearing ratios explore the capital structure of a business by comparing the proportions of capital raised by debt and equity
performance indicator a type of performance measurement that evaluates the success of an organisation or of a particular activity
profitability or performance ratios illustrate the profitability of a business compared to other business
ratio analysis to investigate accounts by comparing two connected figures
return on capital employed (ROCE) the profit of a business as a percentage of the total amount of money used to generate it
window dressing the legal adjusting of accounts by a business to present a financial picture that is to its benefit

CHECKPOINT

1 What is the difference between liquidity ratios and gearing ratios?

2 How can capital employed be calculated using information from the balance sheet?

3 What is meant by a highly geared company?

4 A business has a gearing ratio of 76 per cent. Comment on this.

5 What is the formula for calculating return on capital employed?

6 Why is the return on capital employed (ROCE) an important ratio?

7 When using ratios it is important to compare 'like with like'. What does this mean?

8 Why does ratio analysis ignore qualitative information?

9 Why might businesses use ratios to make comparisons over time?

10 Outline three reasons why a business would choose to window dress its accounts.

EXAM PRACTICE

CASE STUDY: HASARANGA COCONUT PRODUCTS (HCP)

SKILLS CRITICAL THINKING, ANALYSIS, PROBLEM SOLVING

Hasaranga Coconut Products (HCP) processes coconuts and produces a range of products such as liquid coconut milk, coconut milk powder, defatted coconut and coconut cream. The company has a number of factories and processing plants around Sri Lanka. It is one of the country's largest employers in the private sector. In 2017, the company took out a substantial loan to help pay for an export drive. A large block of shares in HCP have been sold to new owners and institutional investors who wanted higher returns on their investment. The current board of directors had been given three years to improve profitability. If they did not, it would result in their removal.

HCP is an established company and has grown by serving the national market and developing small export volumes close to home in countries like India, Bangladesh and the Maldives. However, the pressure is now on to grow overseas markets such as the EU where there is a growing demand for Asian foods. This has resulted in growing demand for coconut milk and similar products. Some financial information for HCP is shown in Table 5.

Q

1 Calculate the gearing ratios for HCP for the years between 2015 and 2018. **(4 marks)**
2 Calculate the return on capital employed for HCP for the years between 2015 and 2018. **(4 marks)**
3 Discuss the performance of HCP between 2015 and 2018. **(8 marks)**
4 Assess the usefulness of ratio analysis to a company like Hasaranga Coconut Products. **(12 marks)**

EXAM HINT

It is very important that you show the units used when calculating ratios. For example, you may lose a mark if you miss out the percentage sign when calculating the gross profit margin.

	2015	2016	2017	2018
Revenue	560	598	670	918
Operating profit	78.4	89.7	56.9	165.2
Non-current assets	211	231	289	301
Current assets	45.1	43.9	47.1	55.3
Current liabilities	39.1	38.1	44.2	51.4
Non-current liabilities	49.9	52.1	119.7	106.7

▲ Table 5 Financial information for Hasaranga Coconut Products (LKR million)

19 HUMAN RESOURCES

LEARNING OBJECTIVES

By the end of this chapter you should be able to:
- calculate and interpret the following to help make business decisions: labour productivity, labour turnover and retention, and absenteeism
- understand the limitations of these calculations
- understand the human resources strategies to increase productivity and retention, and to reduce turnover and absenteeism: financial rewards, employee share ownership, consultation strategies and empowerment strategies.

GETTING STARTED

The amount of output that workers produce in different jobs around the world varies. Over time, it is usual for the rate of output produced by workers to rise. One reason is because they may have better tools and equipment to work with. Figure 1 shows the growth in productivity (i.e. the rate at which a worker produces goods) for a selection of five countries.

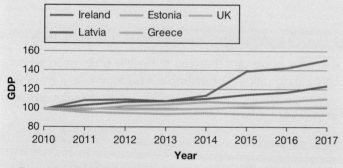

▲ Figure 1 Growth in GDP per hour worked in a selection of five European countries

In which one of the countries in Figure 1 might a labour-intensive business choose to locate a new factory? Explain your answer. Give one reason for the pattern of labour productivity in Greece. How might labour productivity be measured in a car factory? How might labour productivity be improved using financial methods?

LABOUR PRODUCTIVITY

Labour productivity is defined as output per worker over a given period of time. As a formula:

$$\text{Labour productivity} = \frac{\text{Total output (per period of time)}}{\text{Average number of employees (per period of time)}}$$

Labour productivity is an important measure of the efficiency of a workforce. For example, imagine there are two teams of workers in a factory with identical equipment and the same number of workers. The team with the highest productivity could be identified as the most effective team.

Figures for labour productivity need to be used carefully. For example, there might be differences in labour productivity between factories because the equipment is different rather than because of the efficiency of the workforce. A plant with newer equipment is likely to have higher labour productivity than one with old equipment. Equally, productivity differs between processes within and between businesses in different industries. A highly automated section of a factory will have a much higher labour productivity than a labour-intensive packing section in the same factory using little capital equipment. The manufacturing industry may have a higher average labour productivity than service industries because more capital is used per employee in manufacturing.

We might assume that an increase in how competitive a business is will lead to an increase in labour productivity. Higher labour productivity should make average costs lower. This allows a business to either lower its prices (and so gain higher sales) or keep its prices the same (and so increase its profit margins).

However, businesses sometimes find that they become less competitive despite increasing their labour productivity. This may happen for a number of reasons.
- Rival businesses may increase their productivity at an even faster rate.
- New rival businesses may set up and pay lower wages. Many European manufacturing businesses have become less competitive over the past ten years. This is due to the rise of competition

from low-wage, low-cost businesses in countries such as Thailand, Bangladesh, India, Vietnam and China.

● Other factors apart from cost may affect a business. For example, a rival business may release a better new product. However productive the workforce, and however low the cost, customers may prefer to buy the new product rather than a cheaper, older product.

WORKED EXAMPLE

Massamore Ltd operates a call centre in the Philippines where customer service is provided for a large energy company. One week in October 2017, a total of 157 500 calls were handled by the centre's 140 staff. Labour productivity at the call centre is given by:

$$\text{Labour productivity} = \frac{\text{Total output}}{\text{Average number of employees}}$$

$$= \frac{157\,500}{140}$$

$$= 1125 \text{ calls per employee}$$

This means that during that week in October each employee took 1125 calls (on average).

ACTIVITY 1   SKILLS   PROBLEM SOLVING, ANALYSIS

CASE STUDY: JENGRIL LTD

Jengril Ltd manufactures and distributes household appliances. In one of its Asian factories it has a production line making kettles. Table 1 shows the total output of kettles and staffing levels on the production line, between 2014 and 2018.

	2014	2015	2016	2017	2018
Total output (number of kettles)	23 200	24 800	24 700	25 300	24 900
Average number of employees	11	12	13	14	14

▲ Table 1 Total output and staffing levels on the kettle production line, 2014–18

1 Calculate the labour productivity on the kettle line at Jengril Ltd for each year between 2014 and 2018.
2 Explain one possible reason for the pattern of labour productivity on the kettle production line between 2014 and 2018.

LABOUR TURNOVER

Labour, or staff, turnover is another measure of how effective personnel is. **Labour turnover** is the proportion of staff leaving a business compared to the number of staff staying over a period of time. It is measured by the formula:

$$\text{Labour turnover} = \frac{\substack{\text{Number of staff leaving} \\ \text{(over a time period)}}}{\substack{\text{Average number of staff in post} \\ \text{(in the time period)}}} \times 100\%$$

As with other measures of personnel performance, labour turnover differs from department to department within a business, from business to business within an industry and from industry to industry within an economy. High labour turnover is caused by a number of factors.

● Low pay leads to higher labour turnover as workers leave to get better-paid jobs.
● Having few training and promotion opportunities will encourage workers to leave their current jobs.
● Poor working conditions, low job satisfaction, bullying and harassment in the workplace are other factors.
● Some businesses are poor at selecting and recruiting the right candidates for positions. There is more chance that workers will leave quickly if they are not suited to their jobs.

- In a recession, labour turnover often falls as the number of vacancies falls. Workers may worry that if they leave their job without having another one to go to, they will be unemployed for a long time. In a boom, there are far more vacancies due to labour shortages and so labour turnover may rise.

Disadvantages of high labour turnover: High labour turnover is usually seen as a problem for businesses for a number of reasons.

- Recruiting new staff can be costly.
- It takes time for new staff to become familiar with their roles and how the business operates. High labour turnover is likely to reduce the human process advantage of a business.
- Larger companies may put on induction programmes to welcome employees, which adds to the costs.
- If the post is filled from within the business, there may be training needs for the worker who gets the job.

Advantages of high labour turnover: Despite the drawbacks outlined above, some labour turnover is beneficial to a business.

- New staff can bring in fresh ideas and experience from their work with other businesses.
- Some workers may be ineffective in their current job and need to be encouraged to leave. Getting rid of ineffective staff leads to labour turnover.
- If a business is shrinking in size, reducing the size of the workforce will lead to higher labour turnover.
- Where a business pays low wages, or where conditions of work are poor, it may be more profitable to have a constant turnover of staff rather than raise wages or improve conditions of work.

WORKED EXAMPLE

During 2017, 60 staff left Massamore Ltd, the business in the example. Therefore, labour turnover is given by:

$$\text{Labour turnover} = \frac{\substack{\text{Number of staff leaving} \\ \text{(over a time period)}}}{\substack{\text{Average number of staff in post} \\ \text{(in the time period)}}} \times 100\%$$

$$= \frac{60 \times 100}{140}$$

$$= 42.9\%$$

This means that during the year, 42.9 per cent of staff left Massamore Ltd.

LABOUR RETENTION

Labour retention and labour turnover are related. This is because labour turnover looks at the rate at which employees leave a business, while labour retention looks at the rate at which they stay with the business. Therefore, labour retention is the opposite of labour turnover. It can be calculated using the following formula:

$$\text{Labour retention} = \frac{\substack{\text{Number of staff staying} \\ \text{(over a time period)}}}{\substack{\text{Average number of staff in post} \\ \text{(in the time period)}}} \times 100\%$$

The benefits to a business of a high retention rate are the same as the advantages of a low staff turnover rate, such as lower recruitment and selection costs, more continuity and a stable workforce.

WORKED EXAMPLE

During 2017, there were 60 staff who left Massamore Ltd. This means that 80 (140 − 60) staff stayed. Therefore, the retention rate is given by:

$$\text{Retention rate} = \frac{\substack{\text{Number of staff staying} \\ \text{(over a time period)}}}{\substack{\text{Average number of staff in post} \\ \text{(in the time period)}}} \times 100\%$$

$$= \frac{80}{140} \times 100$$

$$= 57.1\%$$

This means that during the year, 57.1 per cent of staff stayed with Massamore Ltd.

ABSENTEEISM

Absenteeism is a problem for all businesses for a number of reasons.

- Staff who are absent often claim to be ill so that, normally, the business then has to pay sick pay.
- If temporary staff are brought in to cover for absent staff, this leads to increased costs. Equally, costs will increase if permanent staff have to work overtime. They are often paid at higher rates than their basic rate of pay.
- Output may suffer if workers are expected to cover for sick colleagues or if temporary staff are not as productive as the absent workers.
- Continued absences can cause problems if the worker is very important to a particular area of work or a new project.

- Customers can be lost if production is delayed or there are problems with quality.
- Absenteeism can demotivate the staff (i.e. make them feel like it is not worth making an effort) who are left to cope with problems.
- The higher the rate of absenteeism, the more likely it is that workers will report ill. This is because a culture of absenteeism will develop, making it acceptable for workers to take extra days holiday by reporting in sick.

The rate of absenteeism: The rate of absenteeism (absenteeism rate or absentee rate) can be calculated by dividing the number of staff who are absent by the total number of staff employed. The rate is expressed as a percentage. It can be calculated as a daily rate using the formula:

$$\frac{\text{Number of staff absent on a day}}{\text{Total number of staff employed}} \times 100$$

WORKED EXAMPLE

On 24 October 2017, eight staff were absent from work at Massamore Ltd. Therefore, the rate of absenteeism is given by:

$$\text{Absenteeism rate} = \frac{\text{Number of staff absent on a day}}{\text{Total number of staff employed}} \times 100$$

$$= \frac{8}{140} \times 100\%$$

$$= 5.7\%$$

This means that on 24 October 2014, 5.7 per cent of Massamore staff were absent from work.

Annual rate of absenteeism: It is also possible to calculate the annual rate of absenteeism. Rates of absenteeism can be calculated for a business as a whole and compared to industry averages or national averages. They can also be compared between one part of a business and another or compared over time. Differences in rates of absenteeism occur for a number of reasons.

- Small businesses tend to have lower rates of absenteeism than larger businesses. This is because there is much more commitment and teamwork in a small business than in a large business. Workers in large businesses can feel that no one will suffer if they take a day off work and so absenteeism is acceptable.

- Health and safety is a factor. Businesses that have good health and safety procedures will tend to suffer less illness-related absenteeism than those with poor procedures. Equally, some jobs are more dangerous to health than others and so absenteeism is more likely.
- The nature of the tasks given to workers is another factor. For example, tasks that are repetitive lead to low job satisfaction and to workers not feeling motivated. This encourages them to report sickness. Workers in jobs which are interesting and rewarding tend to have lower absentee rates.
- The culture of a workplace can cause absenteeism. If workers are overworked, with bosses who make them feel nervous or frightened and ignore workers' needs, work-related stress is much more common. Workers who are off through stress are a problem because they often take months off work at a time.
- Stress-related illness is also more common where workers are over-supervised. They feel that they are not trusted by their bosses to carry out tasks.
- Workers who feel that they are not paid enough are more likely to take time off work. They may see it as compensation (i.e. something that makes a bad situation better) for the lack of money they receive. Low pay can also demotivate workers and so contributes to absenteeism.

WORKED EXAMPLE

During 2017, a total of 1000 staff days were lost through staff absence at Massamore Ltd. Each of the 140 staff should have worked 240 days during the year. So, the total number of staff days that should have been worked was 33 600 (140 × 240). Therefore, the rate of absenteeism for the year is given by:

$$\text{Annual absenteeism rate} = \frac{\text{Total number of staff absence days over the year}}{\text{Total number of staff days that should have been worked}} \times 100\%$$

$$= \frac{1000}{33\,600} \times 100\%$$

$$= 3\%$$

This means that the absenteeism rate throughout 2017 was 3 per cent. Note that this annual rate for Massamore Ltd is lower than the absenteeism rate on 24 October 2017, when it was 5.7 per cent.

LIMITATIONS OF LABOUR PRODUCTIVITY CALCULATIONS

Labour productivity: The method used to calculate labour turnover may not be very effective as it can be difficult to measure the output of workers accurately. This is particularly the case when trying to measure the output of some service providers. For example, how do you measure the output of those working in research and development, product creation, healthcare and maintenance? Their output is often intangible (i.e. not a physical thing) and so very difficult to quantify. There may also be problems in manufacturing when several people are involved in the production of a single unit. For example, how do you measure the output of a dozen different workers all contributing to the construction of a house?

Calculating labour productivity is also limited in highly automated businesses that employ large quantities of plant and machinery. One problem is that different plants are likely to be at different technological stages. Labour productivity in a brand-new car plant will be much higher than that in an old plant. Labour productivity is not likely to be very meaningful in business activities such as oil refining, chemical processing and food processing.

Another problem with measuring labour productivity is that it usually ignores the quality of work. Workers may be able increase their output by working faster. However, if they make mistakes then the quality of output declines. This is likely to have a negative impact on sales.

Labour turnover and retention: The method used above to calculate labour turnover may be limited. One reason is because of the difference in labour turnover between part-time and full-time workers. Labour turnover amongst part-time workers will be higher than that of full-time workers, even when doing the same job. This may be because many part-time workers are looking for a full-time job and will leave as soon as they get one. Alternatively, some part-time workers leave their part-time jobs regularly. One example might be students at the end of the college year. This means the labour turnover for businesses that have more part-time workers will be distorted.

Similar distortions may arise if businesses use more temporary or seasonal staff. These workers are only employed for short periods. This means that the labour turnover of seasonally or temporary workers will be high.

Absenteeism rate: Absenteeism rates can become distorted very easily. For example, a small business may have a very low rate of absenteeism. However, if a single member of staff is off on long-term sickness due a serious illness, this will raise the absenteeism rate.

The way absenteeism is defined or recorded by a business may also distort calculations. For example, if an employee leaves work at lunchtime to collect a sick child from school, some businesses might ignore that absence. However, others might record this as a half day absent. This means an employer's policy or culture will have an effect on the official absenteeism rates.

ACTIVITY 2   SKILLS ▸ PROBLEM SOLVING, ANALYSIS

CASE STUDY: OXCENT.COM

Oxcent.com is an online business based in the UAE. It sells toys, gifts, gadgets and small electronic goods. Orders are packed at and dispatched from a warehouse in the Khalifa Industrial Zone in Abu Dhabi.

In 2016, a new warehouse manager was employed who introduced some new working practices. However, there was a three-month consultation process before the new arrangements were introduced. This gave all staff the opportunity to express their views and preferences about the new arrangements. Table 2 shows the average number of staff employed at the warehouse, the number of staff leaving each year, and the total number of days missed through absence between 2014 and 2018.

The human resources manager at oxcent.com thought that the average staff turnover rate was about 16 per cent in 2015. According to a survey, the rate of absenteeism in 2015 was about 1.8 per cent.

	2014	2015	2016	2017	2018
Average number of staff employed	1590	1610	1620	1670	1710
Average number of staff leaving	410	440	500	410	310
Total number of staff absences (in days)	5760	5890	6180	5200	4200

▲ Table 2 Staffing information for oxcent.com's warehouse, 2014–18

1 Calculate the annual staff turnover at oxcent.com's warehouse between 2014 and 2018.
2 Calculate the annual absenteeism rate at oxcent.com's warehouse between 2014 and 2018 (assume that each employee can work 240 days per year).
3 Assess whether the decision to change working practices in 2016 was a good one for oxcent.com.

STRATEGIES TO INCREASE PRODUCTIVITY AND RETENTION AND TO REDUCE TURNOVER AND ABSENTEEISM

If businesses can raise productivity and retention rates, and reduce staff turnover and absenteeism, the benefits will be significant. Here are a couple of reasons why.

- If productivity rises, output per employee will be higher so there is more output to sell. This will raise revenue and profit.
- If staff turnover can be reduced, money will be saved on recruitment, selection and training. This will help to cut costs and again increase profit.

A number of human resources strategies might be used to help achieve these aims.

FINANCIAL REWARDS

According to some theories of motivation, if financial rewards are increased, employees will work harder and produce more. For example, F.W. Taylor (an American engineer and businessman), outlined his theory of scientific management. Taylor suggested identifying the best way to carry out a task then paying workers according to what they produce. He suggested that people should be paid 'a fair day's pay for a fair day's work'. He argued that people are motivated mainly by money and would work harder to earn more. Therefore, employees should be paid piece rates (i.e. an amount of money paid for the amount of work produced). The main benefit of piece rates for businesses is that it rewards productive workers. Slow or lazy workers will not earn as much as those who work hard and are more productive. This system helps to motivate workers, and businesses are likely to get more out of their employees.

Other ways of improving the performance of workers using financial rewards might be to adopt:

- performance-related pay
- bonus systems
- profit-related pay
- commission systems.

All of these methods reward employees for their effort – both in terms of results and attendance. It is unlikely that staff will want to leave a business if the financial rewards are large, so staff turnover will be lower. For example, bonuses can be paid in addition to the basic wage or salary. Operatives may be paid a bonus if they reach a weekly production target. The main advantage to businesses of bonus payments is that they are only paid if targets are met. This means that money is only paid if it has been earned. Some businesses pay their staff loyalty bonuses that are usually paid annually. Such bonuses are not necessarily linked to productivity but they are designed to reward workers for their loyalty and to help to reduce staff turnover.

Finally, some businesses use financial rewards to reduce absenteeism rates. This is not surprising, given the huge costs to businesses of absenteeism. For example, in Australia absenteeism is a major problem. In 2016 it was estimated that the cost to the Australian economy of lost productivity through absenteeism was AUS$33 billion. A total of 92 million working days were lost through unexpected absences. Some businesses set targets for attendance and reward staff with a bonus for good attendance – where targets are met or exceeded.

EMPLOYEE SHARE OWNERSHIP

Some businesses reward employees by giving them company shares. These schemes are often used to reward senior managers and executives in plcs. The idea is that certain employees will be paid a portion of shares (sometimes in addition to cash bonuses). This happens if the business reaches important performance targets, such as growth in turnover, profit or share price.

Some businesses offer shares to a wider range of employees. A common method of share distribution is to use a **sharesave scheme**, sometimes called a savings related share option scheme. These involve employees saving some of their monthly pay for a fixed number of years. At the end of the period, employees can use the money saved to buy shares at a price that was fixed from the beginning, often at a discount. If the share price has increased over the time period, employees can often make a **capital gain**. However, if the share price has fallen to below the price that was fixed at the outset, employees get their cash back, perhaps with a small cash bonus. Such schemes are considered to be safe and so are very popular with employees.

Employee share schemes are popular in many countries around the world. For example, in India, where they are called employee stock option plans (ESOPs), they may be used to encourage people to get involved in business start-ups.

The benefit to employers is that workers are likely to be better motivated and more loyal to the company if they own shares. They may work harder, take less time off sick and are less likely to leave. For example, once staff have signed up for a five-year sharesave scheme, they may not want to leave halfway through the term and miss out on possible gains.

CONSULTATION STRATEGIES

Employees are likely to be better motivated and more productive if they are involved in decision making. Staff often complain when changes are made and they are not consulted. For example, if a business introduced new working practices to improve the level of customer service without consulting staff, they may feel upset. If staff are consulted by employers when changes are proposed they are more likely to see their views as being valued. Three different types of **consultation** can be identified.

Pseudo-consultation: Pseudo-consultation is where management makes a decision and informs employees of that decision through their representatives. Employees have no power to influence these decisions. Some have suggested that it would be more accurately described as 'information giving'.

Classical consultation: Classical consultation is a way of involving employees, through their representatives, in discussions on matters which affect them. This allows employees to have an influence on management decisions. For example, trade unions may be involved in any decisions relating to changes in the legal, ownership, operational or any other structures in the business.

Integrative consultation: Pseudo and classical consultation do not directly involve employees in decisions which affect them. Integrative consultation is a more democratic method of decision making. Some say it is neither consultation nor negotiation. Management and unions discuss and explore matters which are of common concern, such as ways of increasing productivity or methods of changing work practices. The two groups come to a joint decision, often using problem-solving techniques. An example of an integrative approach to consultation might be the use of **quality circles** in businesses around the world.

EMPOWERMENT STRATEGIES

Empowerment (i.e. giving somebody more power and control) involves making better use of the knowledge, experience and creative talents of employees. It is achieved by granting employees more authority in the workplace. Empowering staff may be a way of creating a positive working environment. This can help to engage employees, so they are happy, motivated and productive. The following strategies might be used to help empower employees.

- **Training.** It is not really possible to empower staff effectively without first preparing them with the skills needed to take on more advanced tasks. A business needs to identify any skills gap. This is the difference between an employee's current skills and those needed to complete new tasks. Training can help employees to learn new skills.
- **Provide the necessary resources.** To be empowered, staff need resources and information to complete more complex tasks. For example, an employee is tasked with leading a small team

to solve a problem. This could be to improve the response time to customer complaints. They will need a range of information and enough resources to make the improvements.

- **Hand over authority.** Once employees have been empowered they must be confident that they have complete authority to make decisions. The methods they choose and approaches they take must not be questioned. Empowerment often won't work if employees are asked to explain themselves each time they make a decision.
- **Inspire confidence.** If employees are being empowered, it is important that they feel confident about their new role. A lack of confidence can cause anxiety, make decision making difficult and lead to mistakes. Senior managers can help to inspire confidence by emphasising the strengths that an individual has. This shows trust by recognising and praising achievements.
- **Provide feedback.** It is necessary to provide positive feedback to empowered workers at appropriate times. Workers need to know how they have performed in their new roles. Feedback will help to guide them in the future and build more confidence.

Giving people more control over their own work role should help to improve their motivation and productivity. They will feel valued, more loyal and less likely to leave an organisation. It may also help to reduce absenteeism because empowered staff may have a greater sense of responsibility.

LINKS

To demonstrate your synoptic skills you could link information in this chapter to answers relating to global competitiveness. For example, businesses trying to compete globally may try to improve productivity and staff retention to gain a competitive edge. Information in this chapter might also be linked with issues covered in Motivation in theory and practice (Student Book 1, Chapter 17), Business objectives (Student Book 1, Chapter 21), Production (Student Book 1, Chapter 37) and Corporate culture (this book, Chapter 14).

CHECKPOINT

1 The factory output for a manufacturer in 2018 was 2.4 million units. The business employed 1200 people in the factory. Calculate the labour productivity.

2 How is labour turnover calculated?

3 Give three reasons why staff might be absent from work.

4 How is the daily absenteeism rate calculated?

5 Outline one way a business might reduce absenteeism.

6 What is meant by labour retention?

7 Suggest one advantage of having a high labour retention rate.

8 Give two financial methods that a business might use to raise productivity.

9 Outline one advantage of giving employees shares.

10 Describe how empowerment might help improve productivity.

SUBJECT VOCABULARY

absenteeism where workers fail to turn up for work without good reason

capital gain the profit made from selling a share for more than it was bought for

consultation listening to the views of employees before making key decisions that affect them

labour productivity output per worker in a given time period

labour retention the number of employees who remain in a business over a period of time

labour turnover the rate at which staff leave a business

quality circles where workers are given time to meet regularly to discuss work issues such as solving problems

rate of absenteeism (absenteeism rate or absentee rate) the number of staff who are absent as a percentage of the total workforce. It can be calculated for different periods of time, e.g. daily or annually

sharesave scheme also known as a savings related share option scheme. Employees save some of their monthly pay for a fixed number of years. At the end of the period employees can use the money saved to buy shares at a price that was fixed at the outset, often at a discount

EXAM PRACTICE

CASE STUDY: THE SEAVIEW RESTAURANT, LIMASSOL

SKILLS PROBLEM SOLVING, ANALYSIS, INTERPRETATION

The Seaview restaurant is located by the sea front in Limassol, Cyprus. In recent years, the financial performance of the restaurant has declined and the parent company wants to see improvement. In 2018 a new manager, Christina, was appointed. She studied a large sample of restaurant reviews and carried out a staff survey.

The reviews indicated poor service and lack of staff commitment. The employee records, shown in Table 3, were very bad. Wage rates paid to staff were slightly above the average for the industry, so it was unlikely that lack of money was a staff issue. However, this would need to be confirmed.

	2014	2015	2016	2017
Average no. of staff	65	61	63	62
Average no. of staff leaving	19	24	28	37
Total no. of staff absences (days)	1755	2196	2835	3534

▲ Table 3 Staff information for the Seaview restaurant, Limassol

Results from the survey suggested that there was a lack of consultation, a lack of training and many staff felt there was a lack of clear leadership. Most of the junior chefs were unhappy because they had no control over the daily menus. The maître d' (the front-of-house manager) said that there was no time made for proper staff training. There was also a lack of communication between staff. Christina also thought that the balance between part-time and full-time staff was wrong. Of the 62 employees in 2017, 48 were part-time.

Christina was given a budget to deal with the staff problems. One approach was to offer staff more financial rewards. Some financial options included:

- an attendance bonus where staff received a three-monthly cash bonus if their attendance was 92 per cent or more. The bonus was doubled for 100 per cent attendance.
- sharing the 10 per cent service charge with all staff in the restaurant. This would be an additional payment on top of tips. It would also be payable to kitchen staff and would reward all staff for their efforts – since good service would help attract repeat customers.

An alternative approach was to use some non-financial methods to improve staff turnover and reduce absenteeism. These included:

- an induction training programme for all new members of staff and any specialist training if required
- the scheduling of regular weekly meetings in work time to discuss work issues, solve problems and generate new ideas for the development of the restaurant
- empowering staff. For example, the junior chefs would be allowed to design their own dishes and contribute to the design of the daily menu.
- redesigning and upgrading the roles of the executive chef and the maître d'. These two important members of staff would receive special training to understand the importance of team working, staff empowerment and consultation.
- providing free group staff meals to encourage teamwork and help bond staff members.

The cost of the financial measures to deal with staff problems was calculated to be €134 000 per annum. This compared to the €187 000 per annum for the introduction of the non-financial measures. The parent company had kept €150 000 to deal with the problem. If Christina spent any more, she would have to use money from other budgets. Christina also decided to change the ratio of part-time to full-time staff. She wanted to reduce the total number of staff and employ 75 per cent full time. However, she knew that this would take time. She was not prepared to make current employees redundant because she thought this would send out the wrong message.

Q

1 Calculate the labour turnover rate for the Seaview restaurant between 2014 and 2017. **(4 marks)**
2 Calculate the absenteeism rate for the Seaview restaurant between 2014 and 2017. Assume that each employee (full-time equivalent) works 300 days a year. **(4 marks)**
3 Explain one limitation of using labour turnover rates to help assess performance at the Seaview restaurant. **(4 marks)**
4 Explain one reason why it might be difficult to calculate labour productivity at the Seaview restaurant. **(4 marks)**
5 Evaluate whether Christina should use (a) financial or (b) non-financial methods to improve aspects of staff performance at the restaurant. **(20 marks)**

MANAGING CHANGE

Businesses operate in a dynamic environment and have to cope with a lot of changes. This section looks at the key factors in change, such as organisational culture, the size of the organisation, the time and speed of change, managing resistance to change and transformative leadership. It also explores the way in which businesses identify through assessment the key risks, such as natural disasters, IT systems failures and the loss of key staff. Finally, it addresses how businesses deal with risk.

20 KEY FACTORS IN CHANGE

LEARNING OBJECTIVES

By the end of this chapter you should be able to understand the key factors in change, including:

- organisational culture
- the size of the organisation
- the time/speed of change
- managing resistance to change
- transformative leadership.

GETTING STARTED

The United Kingdom joined the European Commission (EC) in 1973. The EC later became the EU, a body of 28 European countries with shared political and economic interests. In June 2016, the people of the UK voted to leave. The process of leaving the EU has been called **Brexit**.

One of the main advantages of the UK belonging to the EU is access to a large European single market of around 350 million people. Trade between EU members is tariff free. Free trade encourages businesses to sell overseas which helps them to generate more revenue, profit and employ more people. Trade also helps the economy to grow and improve people's living standards. There is also a free movement of labour which means that businesses in all EU countries can recruit staff from any of the 28 member countries. About half of the UK's international trade is conducted with the EU.

After the results of the Brexit referendum, the value of the pound fell sharply on international exchanges (see Student Book 1, Chapter 41). In 2017 and 2018, many businesses began preparations for a new, unknown trading environment. A number of high-profile businesses operating in the UK have started to take action in their response to Brexit. For example:

- financial services company Visa said it was considering job cuts in the UK and relocation to another European country
- car maker Nissan has delayed some investment decisions
- retailer John Lewis warned that it would be necessary to raise some prices
- telecoms company Vodafone has warned that it might have to move its head office from the UK
- Virgin has cancelled a deal that might have been worth 3000 jobs in the UK
- **management consulting** firm, Oliver Wyman, said that the outcome of the Brexit negotiations would impact on 70 million jobs and around £10 billion in investment funds.

It has been reported that the number of **insolvencies** will rise as a result of Brexit. Figure 1 shows the expected **insolvency** rates between 2016 and 2019.

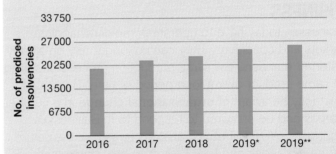

2019* Soft Brexit (UK leaving with a favourable deal)
2019** Hard Brexit (UK leaving with no deal or an unfavourable deal)

▲ Figure 1 Number of predicted insolvencies in the UK as a result of Brexit

One of the main problems of Brexit for businesses is the level of uncertainty. Businesses do not like uncertainty because it makes it harder to plan for the future.

However, there are also potential benefits of leaving the EU. For example, the UK will be free to negotiate its own trade deals with other countries, such as exploring multibillion-pound free trade deals with China. China would also benefit from having greater access to the UK's manufactured goods and investment. Brexit will further reduce barriers to the UK's service industries like banking and insurance, along with other UK goods. Also, companies that do business overseas have reported stronger earnings.

Whilst the pound has declined, it means that international firms have also been investing in the UK. Some examples are listed below.

- Softbank®, a Japanese Internet conglomerate, agreed to buy ARM Holdings, a British designer of semiconductors.
- Qatar Airways increased its stake in the parent company of British Airways, citing 'an attractive opportunity'.
- The Chinese company that owns AMC Entertainment® bought a cinema chain based in the UK.

Comment on the scale of the change to businesses caused by Brexit. How might (a) UK businesses and (b) businesses using the euro be affected by the fall in the value of the pound? Identify four ways in which businesses in the UK might be affected by Brexit.

THE POSSIBLE CAUSES OF CHANGE IN BUSINESS

Businesses today have to operate in rapidly changing markets and conditions. They can no longer rely on steady customer numbers, the same production process or selling the same product over a long period of time. They must constantly be aware of **organisational change** in a number of areas and be prepared to respond to it. Businesses might use SWOT or PESTLE analysis to assess the nature of future changes and how likely they are. These methods are discussed in detail in Chapters 3 and 4.

Business size: Businesses vary considerably in size. For example, some sole traders may employ one person and turn over just $50 000 in revenue. In contrast, a giant multinational may employ over 100 000 people and turn over $50 billion or more. The size of a business can be measured in terms of revenue, the number of employees or capital employed (the amount of money invested in the business).

One of the main causes of change for a business is its size. The size of an organisation will naturally change as it seeks to grow. Growth is a key corporate objective as it allows a firm to satisfy shareholders and create security for a wider range of stakeholders. One of the most significant drivers (i.e. influences) of change as a business grows is the need to restructure. A business will need to start using new policies and processes as it grows.

Sometimes a business will grow externally by merging or taking over another business. This can bring very sudden change to all aspects of the business. How an organisation manages growth can be the difference between success and failure. Most businesses are unable to operate as they once did when they were a small business. There are particular advantages to being a small business, which can be lost as companies grow.

Poor business performance: The poor performance of an organisation will result in a period of change as the company tries to regain customers, sales, profit or reputation. Often the change after a period of poor performance will happen quickly. This is because the business leaders try to improve the company before failure and possibly closure. For this reason, change will often be very quick and may focus on the corporate objectives (Chapter 1) or change in corporate strategy (Chapter 2).

Sometimes, when a large business has a period of poor performance, changes are made to the senior management team. New leadership usually brings significant change as the new boss attempts to create a new plan for the business. For example, in 2017, American International Group (AIG) appointed 70-year-old Brian Duperreault as CEO in the hope that he would turn around the company's fortunes.

Market changes and other external factors (PESTLE): Chapter 4 explores in detail the external influences on a business. These include political, economic, social, technological, legal and environmental – PESTLE). Companies will often be required to adapt and change in line with these external influences. An important example is outlined above in 'Getting started'. A lot of businesses in the UK, but also those in the EU, will have to adapt to a new trading environment after Brexit.

Changes in external factors can be particularly difficult to manage. They are often unexpected, sizable and very difficult to plan for.

Changes in ownership: The change in ownership of a business may come from internal growth. For example, the transition from a private limited company to a public limited company, or the flotation of a firm's shares on the stock market. With the flotation of a business on the stock market comes the opportunity to raise capital for further investment and expansion. This leads to more change. A change in ownership may also become necessary as a business goes through the process of a merger or acquisition (Chapter 7). This can bring very sudden change to a company.

MANAGING CHANGE

Change management is the process of organising and introducing new methods of working in a business. These changes can be driven from within the business or as a result of responding to the external environment caused by PESTLE factors. The **management of change** in business is becoming increasingly important. Many international firms have developed company-wide change programmes because of pressure from competitors, higher costs and tougher economic conditions. Some firms have only made small changes to their business operations and stayed successful. However, the pace of change is getting faster in many areas and businesses are under more pressure to expect changes and prepare for them. The key factors in change are discussed in this chapter.

ORGANISATIONAL CULTURE

Organisational culture can be described as 'the way things are done around here'. This is a simplistic (i.e. less complicated) view of a powerful concept that plays a significant role in the success of a business. Resistance to change may often be found in the culture of an organisation. Customs and practices are fixed in systems that reflect the norms (i.e. the usual way things are done), values and beliefs of the organisation. This gives the organisation stability, but it can also be inflexible, so becomes a problem when a business *needs* to change. Chapter 14 describes how corporate culture is made by many factors, which can be very different from business to business. An organisation's culture may be based on a strong leader – an example is Microsoft's founder, Bill Gates. Or it could be due to a particular operational principle, such as in the John Lewis Partnership in the UK, which has a culture of sharing profits with its employees.

Although a strong culture may give a company a competitive advantage, it can also be a weakness. For example, a management team could be too strong, independent-minded and overconfident. They might not notice, or they might ignore, the impact of important changes.

One of the most significant drivers for organisational change is external growth as a result of a merger or acquisition. Two organisational cultures will come together and their compatibility will often be the key factor that leads to success or failure. A business might avoid the harmful effects of a 'culture clash' (i.e. when two cultures don't get along) by taking the following measures.

1 Identify and analyse cultural differences before a merger goes ahead. This might be done by analysing process flow charts to see how work is done; interview customers to see how they view the two businesses; interview managers to find out about their styles; and get feedback from the workforce to identify norms and beliefs.
2 Communicate with employees to explain the purpose of the merger and its possible effects, but also gather feedback from the workforce to identify their concerns and feelings.
3 Define and implement a new culture by clarifying behavioural norms, the structure of the organisation and the organisation's strategy. Ideally, the new culture should make employees feel that they are starting a new and better job.

4 Celebrate and accept change by emphasising the benefits and the opportunities that staff might enjoy. For example, if workers can learn new skills they will be happier and more employable in the future.

ACTIVITY 1

SKILLS CRITICAL THINKING, ANALYSIS, PROBLEM SOLVING

CASE STUDY: CULTURE CLASH AT KLM AND AIR FRANCE

A few years ago, two large European airlines merged – Air France and KLM. A year after the merger things seemed to be going well. The merged airline increased its annual pre-tax profits by 33 per cent to €455 million. It was estimated that €115 million of this resulted from cost savings – for example, not having more resources than necessary after the merger. Despite an increase in oil prices, the following factors helped to increase profits: cost-cutting, the merger synergies and an 8.9 per cent increase in passenger traffic.

However, several years later it became known that some cultural differences were having a negative impact on business performance. A leaked (i.e. where secret information is shared) document said that Air France-KLM was very difficult to manage. This was apparently due to a national culture clash and a failure to understand each other's languages. The French workers claimed that their Dutch colleagues were only concerned with profit. The Dutch workers said their French colleagues were unfriendly. One minor source of dissatisfaction was that French and Dutch employees were paying different prices for their lunch in the canteen (in Paris). KLM workers were paying €10 while the French were only paying €4.

The leaked report said that employees were very upset. They were negative, frustrated and stressed because no one listened to their concerns. It was also claimed that Air France managers focused on the needs of the whole company, while the Dutch were more concerned about KLM. KLM managers were accused by the French of thinking that they were more professional. In contrast, KLM managers thought that the French were mostly concerned about their job security at Air France. Also, Dutch managers were worried about the French economy and saw Air France as a potential problem.

Although Air France-KLM had a difficult 2016, the CEO said that there were cultural differences and different visions for the future. However, there was also a united desire to find solutions that would benefit everyone.

1 Discuss the problems that Air France-KLM have encountered as a result of the changes that occurred when the two companies merged.
2 Explain how the problems associated with merging two different cultures may be minimised.

SIZE OF THE ORGANISATION

Growth is a key objective for most businesses. Organisational change may be a result of mergers and acquisitions, change in organisational structure, strategic direction or a change in ownership. However, the size of a business may significantly affect its ability to manage successful change.

It is said that the larger an organisation gets, the less flexible it becomes. This could be because there is more change to manage on a larger scale. But it could also be because decision making takes longer in firms with a longer chain of command (i.e. the system where orders are passed from one person to another) and lots of subdivisions. The organisation will have to communicate with lots of people, train them or involve them in the decision-making process. In contrast, smaller businesses are far more flexible because decisions can be taken quickly. The decisions can be implemented without the involvement of a large number of stakeholders.

As companies expand, it is also necessary for them to change the way decisions are made. Multinational, or even regional, businesses may be required to adapt their approach to suit the local context. For example, Starbucks® uses a 'glocalised' approach (based on

the phrase 'think global, act local') with a number of its franchise stores (see Student Book 1, Chapter 26). Instead of having a standardised format, it has adapted some of its franchises to meet local contexts to capture the feel of a local coffee shop. The decisions in these areas are then given to local store and regional managers. Where it is necessary for a business to move from a centralised decision-making approach (or 'top down' structure) to a decentralised strategy (i.e. where local managers are given more control) (see Student Book 1, Chapter 16), change management may be more difficult to implement. Culture is a key factor in any change process. However, it is also true that in large organisations it is easier for subcultures to develop. It is more difficult to manage multiple cultures through any change than just one.

ACTIVITY 2 SKILLS CRITICAL THINKING, ANALYSIS, REASONING

CASE STUDY: CUERO D'IVANA

Ivana Putellas owns a shop in Torremolinos on the Costa del Sol, Spain. The shop sells expensive leather goods to both tourists and local customers. In 2017 it made a profit of €110 400. The business employs 11 staff. Due to her recent success, Ivana wants to grow the business. She has ambitions to start a small chain of shops by finding more locations along the Costa del Sol.

Ivana found a small leather goods shop in Estepona that she plans to buy. The shop employs nine staff and sells a wider range of goods than Ivana's current shop in Torremolinos. Some changes will have to be made. Ivana wants to train the staff in Estepona so that they can match the high-quality customer service provided by her employees in Torremolinos. Ivana wants to target her goods at the high end of the market. The stock in the current Estepona shop will have to be replaced with better-quality merchandise. Ivana also plans to change the name of her shops to Cuero D'Ivana. Her shop in Torremolinos is currently called Putellas – named after her family, who started trading in the 1970s.

1 Discuss the advantages of being a small business when managing change.
2 Explain one benefit of operating a larger business.

TIME/SPEED OF CHANGE

Size is one factor that can affect the pace of change in a business. For example, in some contexts, change can take time and happen organically. This might happen if a business is successful or even leading the market. The development of new products, technology and processes can then progress, knowing that the business is in a safe position. Over the past 10 years, Apple has been at the forefront of innovation in the personal computing market through a lot of changes at a steady, but regular pace.

By contrast, other organisations have to go through change very rapidly. An example is the fashion industry. It is always involved in product development and innovation. Similarly, crisis can also lead to very fast change. For example, Brexit is a very unexpected and rapid change. Businesses need time to prepare for when the UK officially plans to leave the EU in March 2019, but this can be challenging, as the terms on which the UK would leave have not been decided. To make the process more manageable, the UK and the EU agreed to have a transitional period. This means the UK will still comply with EU legislation and benefit from free trade until December 2020. The idea is that the transitional period will provide British businesses, multinationals operating in the UK and businesses in EU countries with more time to prepare.

MANAGING RESISTANCE TO CHANGE

Businesses are likely to face a certain amount of resistance to change from parts of the workforce for a number of reasons.

- Fear of the unknown. People often feel safe with familiar work practices, conditions and relationships.
- Employees and managers may fear that they will be unable to carry out new tasks, may be made redundant or may face a fall in earnings.
- Individual workers might be worried that they will no longer work with their preferred colleagues or may be moved to a job that they dislike.

If change is to be carried out effectively, the businesses must consider their employees' fears. Businesses will have to ensure their employees feel that they can cope with the change in order to operate to its optimum potential.

Owners: Owners of businesses may also be resistant to change for similar reasons. They might fear operating in unknown markets and conditions. They might not want the cost of any changes. They may also fear that they might not be able to adjust to new situations and be forced out of business.

Customers and suppliers: These too may resist change. They may be unwilling to change their own practices when the business they are dealing with changes. For example, a company may reorganise its sales force and decide that it will no longer visit clients that give it less than $5000 worth of orders per year. Instead, it will develop a website and telesales operation to deal with small customers. The company will lose some customers who are not prepared to place orders in this new way.

Generally, stakeholders in a business may resist change for any of the following reasons:

- disagreement with the reasons for or the necessity to change
- fear of the impact
- lack of understanding
- disagreement with the process involved in delivering the change
- lack of involvement
- general inertia – satisfaction with the current situation/way of working.

Harvard Business School Professor John Kotter proposed in *Leading Change* (1996) that eight steps are necessary to manage successful change in a business. The first step is to create a sense of urgency – getting people to actually see and feel the need for change. Stakeholders must understand the need for change through effective communication if anger and fear are to be overcome and the management of change has any chance of succeeding.

TRANSFORMATIVE LEADERSHIP

Occasionally change occurs as a result of a change in management or leadership. When a business appoints a new CEO, it is often because the previous CEO has retired, left or been replaced due to poor performance. In these circumstances, the new CEO will bring in new ideas and changes to the company. This **transformative leadership** might lead to a new vision or strategic direction for the business. If the new CEO has been brought in following a challenging period of performance, they might have been chosen specially to bring in new and fresh ideas. For example, in 2017 Boye Olusanya was appointed CEO of Nigerian telecoms group, Etisalat Nigeria. The company nearly collapsed earlier in the year and one of Boye Olusanya's first jobs was to raise some much-needed capital for the business.

New leaders can have a very positive impact on a company. They may have been appointed because they have a proven track record. They are expected to inspire the whole organisation. They are likely to make big changes and motivate the workforce. For example, new managers are appointed by the owners of football clubs on a very regular basis. This is with the aim of turning the club round and winning trophies.

THINKING BIGGER

This chapter has examined some of the factors that can affect the success of change. However, does the level of success of a business influence the success of change? Can a very successful business become so satisfied when things are going well that it stops trying to improve? Can failure be a good thing? Businesses that have made mistakes build a certain strength that makes them more prepared for the next round of change. For example, in 2017, Amazon CEO Jeff Bezos suggested that a lot of the company's success was the result of its failures.

It is also worth considering the nature of the industry when discussing change. Are some industries more adaptable because of their context and the nature of their product? Fashion and information technology are two industries that are always changing. Change management must be an essential characteristic of any business that operates within these industries. However, there is much to be said for keeping things the same. Change can bring about new opportunities, but long periods of stability and consistency (i.e. things not changing) can help a business to improve and build efficiencies.

CHECKPOINT

1 How might change affect (a) the motivation of employees and (b) the financial performance of a business?

2 What changes might a business go through when merging with another company?

3 What changes might a business face as it moves from being a private limited company (ltd) to a public limited company (plc)?

4 Why might a business replace its CEO?

5 How might poor performance affect a business?

6 State four factors that may have an impact on the success of organisational change.

7 Why might a large firm find change more difficult to manage than a small business.

8 How are culture and change management linked?

9 Why do people resist change?

10 How might a business implement effective change management?

SUBJECT VOCABULARY

Brexit the informal term relating to the UK leaving the EU ('British exit')

insolvency the state of being unable to pay the money owed, by a person or company, on time

management consulting the practice of helping organisations to improve their performance

management of change the process of organising and introducing new methods of working within a business

organisational change a process in which a large company or organisation changes its working methods or aims, for example in order to develop and deal with new situations or markets

transformative leadership where new leadership, such as a new CEO, brings about change with the purpose of improving business performance

EXAM PRACTICE

CASE STUDY: NEW CEO AT VOLKSWAGEN® (VW)

SKILLS CRITICAL THINKING, ANALYSIS, REASONING, DECISION MAKING

In 2015, the giant German car maker Volkswagen® (VW) was caught changing emissions data on its diesel cars. It was alleged that VW had been fitting some special software in its diesel vehicles called a 'defeat device'. This scandal had a very negative impact on the organisation. For example, the value of the company fell by around €30 billion following a flood of bad publicity across the globe.

A number of theories were suggested to explain why this happened. Some analysts say that the company was too big and suffering from diseconomies of scale. Giant companies, like VW, which employs over 600 000 employees, become huge bureaucracies rather than commercial organisations. It is a challenge to control and monitor such vast operations, with factories, offices, warehouses and other operational facilities all over the world. It was claimed that the CEO of VW did not know

about this activity. In such a large organisation, this might be plausible. It is unlikely that any CEO could be in complete control of so many resources all over the world.

In 2018, VW appointed a new CEO, Herbert Diess who was promoted from within the organisation. He was asked to address any alleged poor corporate governance, low profit margins and the sales slowdown in emerging markets such as Russia, Brazil and China. Previously, Mr Diess was employed by BMW Motorcycles to monitor the company's supply chains. In this role, he earned the nickname 'Kostenkiller' as he managed to make €4 billion of cost savings from suppliers.

The appointment of Mr Diess to CEO was well received by the markets. The VW share price rose by 9 per cent the following day. One of his first jobs will be to restructure the organisation in order to speed up decision making across the group. The 12 VW brands will be reorganised into three new groups: mass-market, premium and super-premium.

In a press conference in 2018, Mr Diess said that he will 'forcefully and with focus press ahead' with the VW's strategic plan. In addition to the restructuring programme, he will:

- oversee VW's shift away from diesel cars to electric cars
- embrace developments in autonomous driving technology, such as driverless models operated by ride-sharing services such as Gett®
- make the organisation more manageable by selling off some sizable assets
- develop partnerships to exploit new technology such as that with Toyota's Hino subsidiary, which was announced in 2018
- continue cost-cutting. In 2017, VW employed over 642 000 people worldwide compared to Toyota's 364 000, yet they both produce roughly the same number of cars.

In transforming the organisation, Mr Diess has the full support of chairman, Hans Dieter Pötsch. He said that he welcomed 'the speed and rigour with which Mr Diess can implement the transformation process' to bring about the long-awaited far-reaching changes needed at VW.

Q

1 Explain one reason why transformative leadership may be important to VW. **(4 marks)**
2 Discuss the factors that are enabling the changes at VW. **(8 marks)**
3 Evaluate whether or not the changes proposed by VW's new CEO are likely to improve the performance of the business. **(20 marks)**

EXAM HINT

Change management needs to be approached with care in any examination because it can incorporate all aspects and functions of a business. It is therefore worth examining change and the management of change in a systematic way using a plan, such as:

- What are the driving forces behind the change? Are these internal or external?
- What is the likely impact of the change?
- What factors might affect its success? Think about the issues covered in this chapter.
- What are the key steps the business must take to ensure the change is successful? This will often come from the context of the business you are analysing.

21 CONTINGENCY PLANNING

LEARNING OBJECTIVES

By the end of this chapter you should be able to understand:

- identifying key risks through risk assessment: natural disasters, IT systems failure and loss of key staff.
- planning for risk mitigation: business continuity and succession planning.

GETTING STARTED

Ooops, your files have been encrypted!

Your files will be lost

Time left:

59:59:59

Send $600 worth of bitcoin to this address:
XXXXXXXXXXXXXXXXXXXXXXXXXXXXXXXX

In May 2017, individuals, businesses, governments and others in over 100 countries were hit by an international cyberattack called 'WannaCry' ransomware. This is an attempt by computer hackers to damage or destroy a computer network or system. It was spread around the world using an exploit (i.e. software that exploits weaknesses in computers, causing them to behave in unexpected ways) known as EternalBlue. The crisis affected a number of organisations such as the UK's National Health Service, FedEx®, Russia's Ministry of the Interior, Renault, Telefonica®, Hitachi® and PetroChina®.

WannaCry sent out e-mails with attachments that appeared to contain information such as job offers and invoices. When users opened these attachments, they saw a message like the one in the photo. The message demanded payment in cryptocurrency to regain control of the computer and restoration of lost data.

(Cryptocurrency is a form of electronic money which is not regulated by authorities.)

Car maker Renault, and its partner Nissan®, temporarily had to close down a number of factories in France, Slovenia and Romania because of the attack. Describe the possible impacts of a cyberattack on businesses such as Renault. Could these events have been predicted? What measures might businesses take to prepare for such events?

WHAT IS CONTINGENCY PLANNING?

Unexpected events may happen to businesses and could obstruct their activities. Such events may be called 'crises'. Examples might be a fire that destroys premises, a breakdown in the internal back-up system that stores business information, or the sudden retirement of a CEO.

Many businesses use **contingency planning** in an effort to deal with these crises. Contingency planning is not about trying to predict future events. It is a strategic planning method designed to identify potential crises that a business might experience. It will work out how to protect the business from their worst consequences. It will also help to prepare businesses to exploit any opportunities. It is a disciplined approach to dealing with uncertainty in the future. Contingency planning helps to:

- make clear some of the future uncertainties in business, identify risks and opportunities, and prepare for their eventuality (i.e. something that may happen)
- teach managers how crises may occur, develop and affect the business
- understand the causes and effects of change in business and how to manage it.

There may be different approaches to contingency planning, but there are a number of important steps in the process.

1. **Identify trends and issues.** This involves checking the internal and external environment in an effort to identify any emerging (i.e. starting to happen) threats that might impact on the business. PESTLE analysis might be used to help this process (see Chapter 4).
2. **Identify possible crises.** Businesses need to imagine a range of crises that might affect their operations. The background for these crises will be provided by the information gathered in the previous stage. These crises will

vary between different businesses. This is because different businesses are likely to be presented with different threats. For example, a prolonged drought is more likely to have a serious impact on the agriculture industry than an airline.

3. **Plan a response.** This involves identifying the exact impact crises will have on the business and developing plans to deal with them. This is a lengthy process because such impacts might be numerous and complex.

4. **Identify the most likely crises.** A business may identify a wide range of crises that could affect it. However, there are different probabilities for how likely something is to happen. A business is not likely to have enough resources to plan responses to every single crisis. Therefore, it will be necessary to prioritise (i.e. put things in order of importance) the most likely ones. This allows a business to plan responses to each potential crisis.

5. **Capitalise on crises.** This involves applying the planned responses if crises happen. Not all crises have negative outcomes, however. For example, if the global economy goes into recession, some firms may do very well by providing for new needs that arise from the recession. Those that are prepared for such a crisis may be very successful.

1 Describe how just-in-time manufacturing can lead to a crisis which shuts down a factory.
2 Discuss whether manufacturers, such as the International Motor Corporation, should hold large inventories of components and raw materials to avoid the problem experienced in this case.
3 Explain how contingency planning may have helped the International Motor Corporation.

ACTIVITY 1   SKILLS ▸ CRITICAL THINKING, ANALYSIS

CASE STUDY: ALPHA INFOTAINMENT SYSTEMS

Alpha Infotainment Systems (AIS) is a Swedish manufacturer of motor car 'infotainment' systems. In 2018, the factory was completely destroyed by fire. AIS was the sole supplier to several factories belonging to the International Motor Corporation in Europe. The motor car manufacturer used a 'just-in-time' approach to inventory management for most of the parts in the assembly process. Within hours of the fire, the factories were running out of infotainment systems. After 18 hours, five of the assembly plants belonging to the motor car manufacturer had to shut down for three weeks. The value of lost sales resulting from the closure was estimated to be €560 million.

The International Motor Corporation resolved the problem in the short term by finding a new supplier – one that supplied the International Motor Corporation's rivals. Fortunately, the new supplier was able to deliver infotainment systems at competitive prices. In the long term, the International Motor Corporation subsequently decided to use a wider range of suppliers for each part in the assembly process. This meant that its factories were no longer as likely to experience a break in production if one supplier failed.

RISK ASSESSMENT

A business might use **risk assessment** to attempt to identify the possible crises it might face in the future. This involves examining what might cause harm to people. Businesses need to identify a plan to protect workers from harm. One of the main purposes of risk assessment is to help comply with health and safety laws. Workers have a legal right to protection in the workplace. However, the use of risk assessment might be extended to assess risks to the business in general. Therefore, it is useful in contingency planning. It can be used to help identify potential risks, decide who might be harmed and estimate the probability of events occurring. Possible trends and issues are identified, and this will help in the first stage of contingency planning.

POSSIBLE CRISES

The range of possible crises facing a business is huge. However, some are more likely than others. Three of the most likely scenarios are discussed below.

Natural disasters: Natural disasters are extremely bad events that usually happen suddenly. They are caused by factors beyond our control. Examples include floods, hurricanes, volcanic eruptions, tsunamis, earthquakes, forest fires, snowstorms and epidemics. Such events can result in high levels of damage, death and disruption (i.e. when things are unable to happen in the normal way). Many firms are multinationals with operations in places where some of these events are more likely to occur. So, multinationals are likely to be more exposed to the risk of natural disasters.

One example of a natural disaster that causes difficulties for some businesses around the world is the threat from fire. Bush fires are common in countries such as Australia, the USA, Canada, Ecuador and New Zealand. In 2017, the USA experienced the worst wildfire season in modern history. Woodland fires were responsible for almost 2 million acres of destruction. Another common problem around the world is flooding. In recent years, flooding in the USA has been responsible for reduced shipping, damaging crops and shutting down ports. Last year, three-quarters of Louisiana's rice fields were affected by flooding. It was estimated by experts that the cost to Louisiana rice fields alone would be approximately US$14.3 million.

Volcanic eruptions can cause large-scale disruption to business. If a volcano erupts, business activity in the immediate area will be affected by lava (extremely hot liquid rock) and huge clouds of ash. However, the clouds of ash can sometimes be so large that flight paths are made unusable. In 2010, Eyjafjallajökull volcano in Iceland erupted, sending millions of cubic feet of ash over Europe. This posed a threat to aircraft and many airports in Europe were closed for a period of time. Estimates suggested that the cost of grounded flights to the global airline industry was over £1 billion. However, some businesses actually benefited from the closure of European airspace. Airport hotels were full of travellers who were unable to leave, and trains, buses and coaches were extremely busy. Eurostar trains between London and Paris or Brussels were sold out. More recently in 2017, businesses were affected by the eruption of Bali's Mount Agung volcano. This forced the only airport on the island to close.

IT systems failure: Most businesses employ IT systems in their organisation. The extent to which businesses depend on such systems will vary. Generally, the larger the business, the more investment it will have in IT. This means that an IT systems failure or a cyberattack could be a serious disaster. Many small businesses may have only modest investments in IT systems. For example, computers are used for data storage, email communication, research and website display. However, even smaller businesses are increasing their reliance on IT, such as for online sales and other transactions. This makes them more likely to experience breakdowns.

In 2016, Delta Airlines in Atlanta reported a computer outage (i.e. a period of time when the computers stopped working) at the company's headquarters. This forced the airline to cancel about 2300 flights. This delayed the journeys of hundreds of thousands of passengers. The outage caused up to three days of chaos. The problem was caused by an ageing piece of equipment at Delta's data centre. It had caused a fire that brought down its primary and back-up systems. Delta said that the failure in IT systems reduced revenues by US$100 million. In 2017, Delta experienced another, but smaller, computer outage which also resulted in flights being cancelled and lost revenue.

Businesses and the public are becoming more and more concerned about the threat of cyberattacks. Most people don't know the consequences of such attacks. However, as the number of attacks increases, awareness of their effects is being raised. One problem is personal data being stolen by hackers from businesses. It has been reported that these 'data breaches' happen on a daily basis, but most of the incidents are small. However, some are large and worrying. Figure 1 shows some of the largest examples of data breaches in the 21st century.

Finally, IT systems can be attacked by hackers that use ransomware. This is where the control of a computer is lost to a hacker. The only way users can get back control and recover all their stolen files is to pay a ransom. This is discussed in the 'Getting started' section.

Loss of key staff: People leave businesses all of the time. This may not be a problem but losing key members of staff can cause difficulties – especially if the business has not prepared well enough for it. It can also be a very serious problem in small businesses, which are often dominated by a single person. It has been reported in the past that around 55 per cent of businesses would stop trading if they lost one or more key people. Unexpected losses through illness, long-term incapacity or death are the most common causes of such an event. In a small business, where the owner employs only a few other people, the loss of the owner could result in the closure of the business. This is because the other employees may not have the resources or the desire to take ownership of the business. Finding an outsider (i.e. somebody who is not already part of the business) to take over the business might also be difficult.

In 2017, it was widely reported that Australian group, Ardent Leisure, lost its CEO, Simon Kelly when he left suddenly. His departure was unexpected, and shares fell by 2.2 per cent when he left. Kelly had only been at the company for six months and the departure threw the company into chaos.

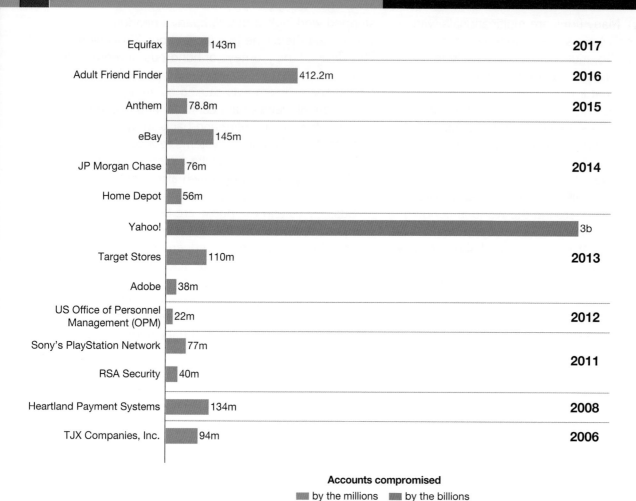

▲ Figure 1 Largest data breaches in the 21st century

Contingency planning has some obvious benefits as it forces decision makers to consider the future and plan for possible changes. But it does have some disadvantages. It is time-consuming and expensive. As a result, there is a risk that a business may not dedicate sufficient resources to it and so fail to carry out the process effectively. Also, some people might argue that preparing for events that may never happen is a waste of money. Another problem might be finding people in the business who have a deep enough understanding of the potential crises. Therefore, it might be necessary to invite external agents to help, which will add to the cost. Finally, only large corporations are likely to have the resources to do full-scale contingency planning. Most small businesses have much less to lose and would probably see the opportunity cost of contingency planning as too high.

PLANNING FOR RISK MITIGATION

Risk mitigation plans identify, assess and prioritise risks. They also plan responses to deal with the impact of these risks to business operations. Generally, a business can use a number of mitigation (i.e. to reduce how bad something is) strategies to reduce the damage caused by serious disruptive events. For example, it can:

- set up in a location that is not likely to experience flooding, earthquakes, bush fires and other potential natural hazards
- ensure that premises are constructed according to building codes that are designed for safety and protection
- take out insurance policies that cover losses resulting from disasters – for example, it may be possible to take out **business interruption cover**
- ensure that data stored on computers is as secure as possible and that back-up systems are adequate
- organise back-up power, such as a generator, to ensure that important machinery and other equipment can still be used if the power is interrupted
- ensure that valuable assets, such as expensive machinery and tools, are protected as much as possible
- ensure that there is access to emergency funding

- ensure that adequate communication channels are set up to deal with crises
- produce a **business continuity plan** to deal with crises. This is discussed next.

Business continuity: A business will want to minimise disruption if an incident happens. After taking care of human life, one of the most important priorities is to get the business 'up and running' again. Some firms produce business continuity plans. These show how a business will operate after a serious incident and how it expects to return to normal in the quickest time possible. There may be four stages in such a plan.

1. **Carry out a business impact analysis.** This will identify those functions and processes that are essential to the running of the business. This involves gathering information so that appropriate recovery strategies can be designed. The process also involves identifying the financial consequences of such incidents, like loss of revenue, customer defection, increased costs, penalties and disruption to business plans. This information may be gathered by using questionnaires and workshop sessions with appropriate employees. Once the information has been gathered it must be analysed, reviewed and updated to reflect changing circumstances.

2. **Formulate recovery strategies.** These are the actions taken to restore the business to a minimum acceptable level after an incident. This will involve identifying the resources needed, such as people, facilities, equipment, utilities, IT and materials to aid recovery. Examples of recovery strategies that might be used include:
   - setting up agreements with another business to share resources and support each other should they face disruption
   - planning to adapt resources for new usages – for example, a canteen might be used as office space
   - contracting out work to third parties (a person or business besides the two primarily involved)
   - prioritising production – perhaps according to customer value
   - maintaining higher stock levels
   - placing restrictions on orders
   - shifting production from one plant to another.

3. **Plan development.** This involves developing a detailed plan to ensure that the recovery strategies are carried out in an organised way. A business is likely to set up recovery teams, develop plans to move to a different location, and document recovery strategies and procedures. This is to ensure that key staff are aware of what is expected of them.

4. **Testing and training.** Once the recovery plan has gained approval, it is necessary to design testing exercises. Staff will have to be trained and the recovery teams will be the main focus of such training.

After testing and training, the business continuity plan will be updated to take into account any discoveries made during this process. Finally, the plan may be reviewed and updated on a regular basis. This is to take into account any changes that have happened in the business, such as changes to key workers, equipment or premises.

Succession planning: Part of risk mitigation involves identifying current employees who have the potential to play key roles in the future and helping them develop their skills. This is called **succession planning**. It is important because it will help a business deal with the problem of losing key staff. However, succession planning will also help to develop the staff needed to fill posts as the business expands. Without succession planning, a business might promote a person who is not equipped to do the job, or the business might end up recruiting an unknown outsider at greater risk and expense. Some research suggests that CEOs appointed from internal sources tend to outperform those from outside.

Some key steps involved in a succession planning process are outlined below.

1. **Identify the characteristics a successor should possess.** This task can be done by looking at the job description and developing a person specification giving the characteristics of the person who currently occupies the key role and identifying any new skills and traits that may be required.

2. **Decide how the successor will be found.** This might involve examining the abilities of every potential internal candidate. Alternatively, a specialist agency might be employed to find possible candidates from outside the business.

3. **Have a rigorous selection process.** Examine the strengths and weaknesses of all the candidates. It is important to involve several key workers and other specialists to gain a broad view of the candidates.

4. **Make the decision.** The people with this duty must analyse and evaluate the performance of each candidate. It is important to reach a conclusion and make an appointment. Not doing this might demotivate (make somebody feel like it isn't worth making an effort) and undermine internal candidates – they may think that they are not valued by the business.

5. **Communicate the decision.** It is important for everyone affected by the decision to be informed about the appointment.

6. **Implement a training and preparation plan.** The person appointed will need to be trained and prepared for the final transition into the post when needed. This may involve 'shadowing' (learning from somebody else by watching them) the person who currently occupies the position for a period of time. It might also involve going on specialist courses to enhance the skills and knowledge needed.

In some countries, regulators have expressed their concern about the poor quality of the succession planning done by corporations. The criticism came after the UK-based supermarket chain Tesco® left the post of financial director vacant for several months and, at one stage, it only had one board member with retail experience. Succession planning should play a very important role in business.

ACTIVITY 2

SKILLS ▶ CRITICAL THINKING, ANALYSIS, CREATIVITY

CASE STUDY: UBER®

Uber Technologies is famous for its app that connects private cab drivers with passengers wanting a ride to a selected destination. In 2017, the company generated revenues of $7.5 billion and had a market valuation of $48 billion.

That same year, Uber's founder and CEO, Travis Kalanick, suddenly resigned. The resignation also followed the announcement that Uber's market share in the USA alone had fallen from 84 per cent to 77 per cent. Uber had been planning a stock-market floatation (IPO), but after Kalanick resigned, the timing was not right for the company.

It was not clear whether Kalanick's resignation was good or bad for Uber. One very important investor in Uber, Tusk Ventures, was worried. It said that Uber would soon find a capable CEO to deal with the HR problems that were affecting the company. However, it said that Uber would need to do more if it was going to influence the future of global transportation and compete with companies like Google, Apple, Tesla® and Facebook. Uber needed someone brilliant – with vision and strong determination – to compete with such high-profile operators.

1 Discuss the possible impact that the sudden loss of CEO, Travis Kalanick, might have on Uber.

2 Analyse how a business such as Uber might protect itself from the sudden loss of an important member of staff.

LINKS

There may only be limited opportunities to show synoptic skills using information about contingency planning and risk mitigation. This is because it is quite a specialised topic. However, chances might arise when you are writing answers about Demand (Student Book 1, Chapter 4), Business failure (Student Book 1, Chapter 36), Economic influences (Student Book 1, Chapter 41) and SWOT analysis (this book, Chapter 3). There may be a particularly strong link with Chapter 4, which is about the impact of external influences on a business.

CHECKPOINT

1 Outline the important steps in a contingency plan.

2 Give three specific benefits of contingency planning.

3 Give three examples of natural disasters that could impact on a business.

4 What role might risk assessment play in contingency planning?

5 How might the loss of key staff impact on a business?

6 Give three examples of problems that a breakdown in IT systems might cause a business.

7 What is meant by risk mitigation planning?

8 Outline the four stages in a business continuity plan.

9 Give four examples of recovery strategies that a business might employ.

10 Describe briefly the key steps in succession planning.

SUBJECT VOCABULARY

business continuity plan shows how a business will operate after a serious incident and how it expects to return to normal in the quickest time possible

business interruption cover a type of insurance that covers the loss of income that a business suffers after a disaster

contingency planning the creation of plans for how particular crises might affect a business in some way, such as a fire which destroys the premises or a cyberattack

risk assessment identifying and evaluating the potential risks that may be involved in an activity that a business proposes to do, and then ensuring compliance with health and safety laws

risk mitigation plans identify, assess and prioritise risks, and plan responses to deal with the impact of these risks on the operation of the business

succession planning identifying and developing people who have the potential to occupy key roles in a business in the future

EXAM PRACTICE

CASE STUDY: THE EDO OIL COMPANY (EOC)

SKILLS   CRITICAL THINKING, INTERPRETATION, REASONING

The Edo Oil Company (EOC) is a large oil production company based in Nigeria. It employs around 21 000 people in Africa and has five refineries (factories for making the oil 'pure') and several exploration operations. In 2017, its revenue was NGN489 billion. It made a profit of NGN24.12 billion and invested NGN19.3 billion in capital expenditure.

In common with many other large oil producers, EOC is exposed to a wide range of global uncertainties. Therefore, EOC uses contingency planning. It helps to prepare the company to deal with crises resulting from a wide range of external influences that might affect the business and the petrochemicals industry as a whole.

In 2018, the company carried out an analysis of external factors that might impact on the company in the future. These are summarised below.

Threats:

- **Cyberattacks.** In recent years, there has been an increasing number of cyberattacks around the world. There have also been problems with personal data being stolen from businesses.
- **Increase in sales of electric cars.** Around the world, many large car manufacturers are making preparations to meet the expected increase in demand for electric vehicles. If this happens, the demand for gasoline for cars is likely to fall sharply. This is shown in Figure 2.

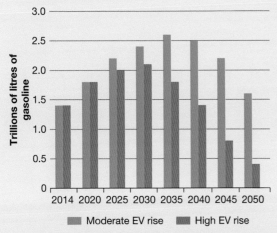

▲ Figure 2 Impact on gasoline consumption due to the growing sales of electric vehicles

- **Volatile oil prices.** The global price of oil has fluctuated (i.e. gone up and down several times) in recent years. These fluctuations impact heavily on those operating in the oil industry. Sharp price fluctuations make it very difficult to predict future revenues and cash flows. This has a disruptive effect on planning and investment decisions. Figure 3 shows the volatility (i.e. something being likely to change suddenly) in the oil price between 2008 and 2018.

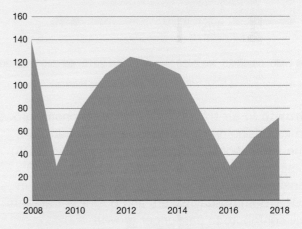

▲ Figure 3 Oil price between 2008 and 2018 (US$)

- **Global pressure for greater environmental and social responsibility.** There are increasing concerns about the impact that burning fossil fuels has on the environment. This includes global warming and its effect on climate and weather patterns. As a result, many businesses have preferred to use energy that comes from cleaner and renewable sources. For example, in many countries, governments have given subsidies to the solar power industry.

Opportunities:

- **Growth in emerging countries.** Economic growth in a number of emerging economies such as China, Brazil, Russia, Mexico and India will help to boost the demand for energy. For example, Chinese GDP will reach $20 000 per capita by 2025. There will be an increase in the global demand for energy, which will be needed to power industrial development and business growth.
- **Growth in car ownership.** As emerging economies grow, the standard of living in those countries will improve. Car ownership will also become more affordable. This is expected to increase the global demand for cars. It has been estimated that the number of cars in India will reach 500 million eventually. Figure 4 compares sales of new cars in two developed countries (Japan and Germany) with that of two emerging countries (India and Brazil). The expected growth in the two emerging countries is significant.

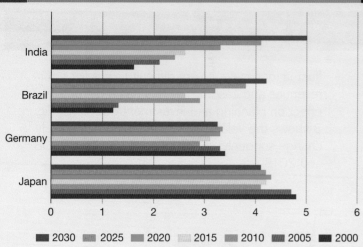

▲ Figure 4 New car sales in two developed and two developing countries

- **Growth in air travel.** As the global economy grows, an increasing number of people use air transport. The International Air Transport Association (IATA) expects 7.2 billion passengers to travel in 2035, a near doubling of the 3.8 billion air travellers in 2016. Both holidaymakers and business travellers will contribute to passenger growth.

Adapted from https://evobsession.com/electric-vehicle-revolution-scenarios/ and https://moneyweek.com/prices-news-charts/oil/ and https://blog.euromonitor.com/wp-content/uploads/2015/07/6a01310f54565d970c01bb0826a907970d-580wi.png/l/g

Q

1 Explain what is meant by contingency planning.
(4 marks)

2 Discuss the possible reasons why EOC demanded a review of its contingency planning. **(8 marks)**

3 Assess the importance of a risk mitigation plan to a company such as EOC. **(12 marks)**

EXAM HINT

You need to remember that contingency planning can be used to prepare for uncertain events that may also provide a business with opportunities. It is not just about planning for disasters. For example, an increase in demand as the global population booms (it is expected to double by 2050) can provide many opportunities for businesses around the world.

GLOBALISATION

Increasingly, many businesses are operating in a global environment. This section looks at the characteristics of developed, developing and emerging economies, the growing economic power of countries within Asia, Africa and other parts of the world, the implications of growth for individuals and businesses and the indicators of growth such as GDP per capita and the human development index (HDI). It also explores the role played by international trade and business growth, including exports and imports, increasing business specialisation and foreign direct investment (FDI), along with the factors that have contributed to increased globalisation such as trade liberalisation, increased flows of FDI, political change, lower transport costs and the growth in the global labour force. It investigates the reasons for protectionism, the different barriers to trade that countries might use (such as tariffs and quotas) and the impact of protectionism on businesses. Finally, it addresses the nature of trading blocs such as the EU, ASEAN and NAFTA, and the impact that the formation of these blocs has on businesses.

22 GROWING ECONOMIES

LEARNING OBJECTIVES

By the end of this chapter you should be able to understand:
- the characteristics of developed, developing and emerging economies
- the growing economic power of countries within Asia, Africa and other parts of the world
- implications of economic growth for individuals and businesses: trade opportunities for businesses and employment patterns
- indicators of growth: gross domestic product (GDP) per capita and the human development index (HDI).

GETTING STARTED

True Indulgence is a holiday company based in the Maldives. It offers high-quality luxury accommodation on an island in the Maldives. A two-week holiday would cost two people up to $20 000. Two popular features of the holiday are scuba diving and fine dining.

The company is planning some advertising campaigns. It is in the process of deciding which countries to target. It can afford campaigns in three different countries. Table 1 shows the GDP (income) per capita and the population size in a selection of countries.

Country	GDP per capita (US$)	Population
Argentina	12 440.30	43 847 430
Australia	49 755.30	24 210 810
Bangladesh	1358.80	162 951 560
Brazil	8649.90	207 652 860
Canada	42 348.90	36 264 600
Costa Rica	11 824.60	4 857 270
Iceland	60 529.90	335 440
India	1709.60	1 324 171 350
Luxembourg	100 738.70	582 010
Switzerland	79 887.50	8 372 410
USA	57 638.20	323 127 510
Spain	26 616.50	46 484 530

▲ Table 1 GDP (income) per capita and total population in a selection of countries (2016)

Which three countries might True Indulgence target with their advertising campaigns? Explain your answer. What other information might be useful for True Indulgence to know before finalising the decision? Suggest three types of business that might be interested in selling goods or services to India. Explain your answers.

CHARACTERISTICS OF ECONOMIES AT DIFFERENT STAGES OF DEVELOPMENT

There is a vast difference between the welfare and prosperity (i.e. success in making money) of people around the world. People experience a comfortable existence in only a minority of countries. They have access to good healthcare, education, housing and high-quality food. They may also have spare income to spend on non-essential items such as holidays, entertainment and leisure activities.

In contrast, large numbers of people struggle to gain enough food, safe accommodation and clean water. They may have little or no education and very limited access to healthcare. They would never take a holiday and often have low life expectancy. Other large groups of people fall in between these two extremes. Economies where these different groups of people live are defined as follows.

Developed economies: In many European countries, the USA, Canada, Japan and Australia most people experience a good standard of living. They live in developed economies, which have the following characteristics.

- **High income levels.** In developed economies, the average income level is relatively high. According to the World Bank, in 2016, high-income economies were those with an income **per capita** of $12 476 or more.

- **High literacy rate.** The majority of people in developed countries can read and write. For example, literacy rates in Germany, the USA and Canada are close to 100 per cent.

- **High life expectancy.** People in developed countries expect to live for over 60 years. For example, the life expectancy is 85.3 years in Japan, 80 years in the USA and 82.3 years in Italy.

- **Good infrastructure.** The majority of people in developed countries have access to schools, colleges, healthcare and varying degrees of welfare support (e.g. monetary payments, housing assistance, etc.). There are railway networks, motorways, sewerage systems, electricity grids and telecommunication systems.

- **Highly industrialised.** Developed economies tend not to rely on the **primary sector** and to rely more heavily on the **tertiary sector**. For example, in France the proportion of the working population employed in the tertiary sector is 79.3 per cent, in Japan it is 69.3 per cent and in Australia it is 70.3 per cent (all 2017 est. – i.e. all of the figures are estimates from 2017).

- **Low levels of unemployment.** Most people in developed economies can find work. There are laws to protect employees from being exploited and working conditions are generally safe and clean. However, in a minority of developed countries, **unemployment** has been a problem. For example, in 2017, the unemployment rates in Spain and Greece were much higher than average at around 17 per cent (Spain) and 22.3 per cent (Greece) respectively. (The average unemployment rate for the EU in 2017 was 7.3 per cent.)

Developing economies: There are more than 100 developing or less-developed countries in the world. Although most of them are in the southern hemisphere, they are not all the same. However, they do share some common characteristics.

- **Low income levels.** Income levels in developing countries are low or lower middle. According to the World Bank, low-income economies are defined as those with an income per capita of $1025 or less in 2015. Lower-middle-income economies are those with an income per capita of between $1026 and $4035. For example, income per capita in Burundi and Cambodia is $800 and $4000 respectively (2017 est.).

- **Low literacy rate.** In some developing countries there are not enough resources to educate the entire population. This means it is possible that only a small proportion of the population are able to read and write effectively.

- **Low life expectancy.** People in developing countries are not expected to live as long as those in the developed world. For example, life expectancy is 64.9 years in Cambodia, 65.1 years in The Gambia and 50.6 years in Chad.

- **Poor infrastructure.** Developing countries have a lack of roads, railway networks, schools, hospitals and production facilities, such as factories.

- **Reliance on the primary sector.** Many developing countries rely on the primary sector for **employment**, exports and income. For example, a large proportion of the population is likely to be employed in agriculture or mining.

- **High unemployment.** There tend to be few employment opportunities in developing countries. This means that levels of unemployment are often very high. For example, unemployment rates were 28.1 per cent in Namibia (2016 est.), 34.8 per cent in Kosovo (2016 est.) and 95 per cent in Zimbabwe (2002–14 est.).

- **High population growth.** Many developing nations have high rates of population growth. For example, the rate of population growth in Canada (a developed country) is just 0.73 per cent. However, in the Democratic Republic of Congo (a developing country) the population growth is more than three times higher at 2.37 per cent.

Emerging economies: An emerging economy could be defined as one with rapid **economic growth** (the increase in a country's productive capacity – usually measured using Gross Domestic Product [GDP]). Some of the important indicators used to reflect levels of economic growth are discussed later in this chapter. However, there is a lot of risk. Investors like emerging markets since they are likely to grow more quickly than more mature markets. Therefore, a business should be able to increase profits and dividends. Economists sometimes group emerging economies together, e.g. BRICS: Brazil, Russia, India, China and South Africa, and MINT: Mexico, Indonesia, Nigeria and Turkey.

Where an emerging market is experiencing an increase in average incomes, it is likely that the middle classes are expanding (i.e. growing larger). Increasing income allows consumers to spend more, on both imports and domestically produced goods and services. Buying more domestic goods encourages the growth of domestic firms. This gives them increased market power and allows them to compete internationally. Consumers may also buy more imported goods and services from businesses in more developed economies. This increases how much profit they make and makes the emerging market more attractive to new businesses in the market. Therefore, many economists assume that the growth rates of emerging market economies will exceed those of the more developed economies.

Figure 1 shows a comparison of growth rates between some developed economies and a selection of emerging economies. The graph shows that the rate of growth in emerging economies outperforms those of the developed economies. However, you must remember that this is a trend and not a certainty. Emerging markets will continue to face many risks that might affect overall economic performance. Also, countries differ in how vulnerable they are to certain risks. They would be able to cope differently if the risks became real.

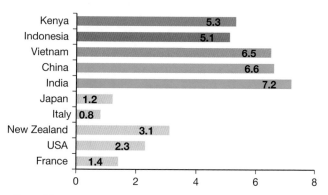

▲ Figure 1 A comparison of growth rates between emerging economies and developed economies (2017)

ACTIVITY 1

SKILLS CRITICAL THINKING, ANALYSIS, REASONING

CASE STUDY: ITALY AND THE DEMOCRATIC REPUBLIC OF CONGO (DRC)

Italy: Italy is one of the original members of the EU and currently has the third largest economy in the EU. It has a diversified industrial economy. This is divided into an industrial north with lots of private companies, and an agricultural south with higher levels of unemployment. The Italian manufacturing sector is driven mainly by the production of high-quality consumer goods. The goods are made by small and medium-sized enterprises.

DRC: The Democratic Republic of Congo, Central Africa, has a tropical climate and lots of natural resources such as diamonds, gold, copper and zinc. However, the economy is under performing. This is due to corruption (i.e. dishonest behaviour by people with power), political instability and wars. Most of the country's export earnings are made from mining. However, low commodity prices in recent years have contributed to slow economic growth, volatile inflation, a weak exchange rate and a growing government deficit.

	Italy	DRC
Population	62m	83m
Population growth rate	0.19%	2.37%
Life expectancy	82.3 yrs	57.7 yrs
GDP per capita	$38 000	$800
Literacy	99.20%	77%

▲ Table 2 Italy and the DRC – data comparison (2017 est.)

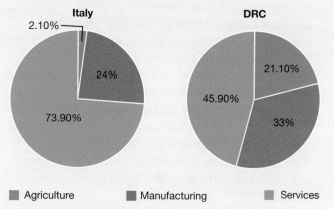

▲ Figure 2 Italy and the DRC GDP composition by sector (2017 est.)

1 Which of these two nations is the most developed? Explain your answer.
2 Explain why there are differences in the size of the economic sectors in each of these two countries.
3 Explain why a business might prefer to market its goods in an emerging economy rather than a developed economy.

GROWING ECONOMIC POWER OF ASIA, AFRICA AND OTHER PARTS OF THE WORLD

Most of the BRICS and MINT countries have experienced strong growth over the past few years. This growth is increasing the overall economic power of many of the countries in Asia, Africa and other parts of the world. For example, in 2018 and 2019, both China and India are predicted to be among the largest five economies in the world. According to Figure 3, in 2018, China's economy is predicted to be worth US$13.093 trillion, while India's will be worth US$2.876 trillion. China has been the second-largest economy in the world for several years now. It frequently comes at, or near, the top of the rankings as an exporter and as a destination for foreign investment. Its growing economic power means that it is also one of the world's biggest investors in other countries.

In 1990, China produced less than 3 per cent of global manufacturing output by value. By early 2015 this had risen to nearly a quarter. China's industrial might impacts all across South East Asia, through supply chains and outsourcing. In fact, China drives what has come to be known as 'Factory Asia' for its dominance of global manufacturing. The strength of manufacturing in Asia looks set to continue in the near future. First, China has very efficient suppliers and excellent infrastructure, allowing for further cost-effective growth. Second, it has access to lower-cost labour throughout South East Asia, including Myanmar and the Philippines. Finally, Chinese and other Asian consumers are spending more each year. This increases demand and reinforces local production and distribution.

Other emerging markets, such as Central and South America and Africa, are creating big international companies that, increasingly, are challenging the dominance of firms from the developed regions. However, because of China's dominance in manufacturing, these other regions may be less likely to follow this route to development. They may have to find new ways to grow and develop in the future.

According to the World Bank, the largest economies in the world include the USA, Japan, Germany and the UK. However, the order of leading economies may change repeatedly in the future. Around 70 per cent of world GDP growth is likely to come from emerging market economies. China and India will account for around 50 per cent of this figure. So, 20–30 per cent of future global growth may come from the rest.

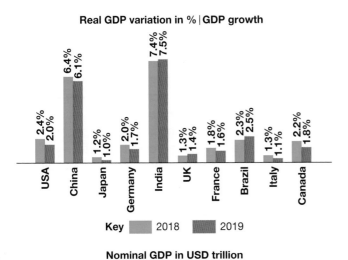

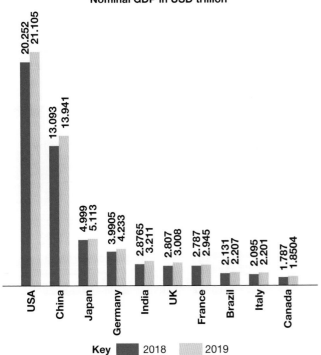

▲ Figure 3 The world's biggest economies for 2018 and 2019

IMPLICATIONS OF ECONOMIC GROWTH FOR INDIVIDUALS AND BUSINESSES

Consumers in emerging markets may be buying more goods and services, both from domestic companies and from those in more developed economies. This may make the emerging markets even more attractive to new businesses in the market. It may create trade opportunities and change existing employment patterns.

Trade opportunities: As an economy grows, consumption (i.e. people buying and using products) may also be growing. This is good for firms looking to invest or sell their products and services. So, with growth it is likely that **disposable income** is also rising. Individuals may have more money to spend, increasing the overall demand for goods and services. Demand is likely to become **income elastic** (see Student Book 1, Chapter 8), providing greater opportunities for increased revenues and profit. These goods and services can be produced domestically or imported from abroad. This creates many opportunities for trade. A number of western businesses, such as KFC®, McDonald's, Pizza Hut®, Costa Coffee® and Starbucks have started to market their goods and services in countries such as China, India and Vietnam, for example.

Individuals will benefit from increased international trade. They may be able to buy cheaper goods from overseas where production costs are lower. For example, cheaper manufactured goods from China, Bangladesh and Vietnam have entered markets in many Western developed countries. This means that individuals in these countries can buy more goods and services with their income.

Increasing international trade also brings more choice for consumers. There is likely to be a large variety in quality, designs and product ranges. This is due to an increasing number of countries opening up their economies. Greater choice resulting from growing international trade helps to increase the standard of living for individuals.

Employment patterns: In addition to looking at growth rates, a business might want to assess the employment patterns across an economy. Employment is one of the most important indicators of the health of an economy. A firm might want information on unemployment rates and trends, labour costs and productivity. They may also want to know more about the educational qualifications of potential employees.

The employment rate gives an idea of the jobs that are being gained or lost across an economy. The level of unemployment can reveal a lot about an economy, but not all of it is straightforward. As noted above, the amount of money that consumers have (disposable income) shows whether or not they can buy goods in the future. If people are out of work, they may not have much money to spend or save. If there is a high level of unemployment in a country, it may not be a good time to consider exporting there. However, unemployed individuals may be looking for jobs, so a firm could find labour to make goods that it could then export elsewhere. In this case, directly investing in a country by building a factory might be a good idea.

Unemployment rates tend to vary considerably around the world. Developed countries tend to have lower levels of unemployment. Developing countries suffer from much higher levels. Emerging economies are seeing unemployment rates fall as jobs are created quite quickly. This is because business activity in these countries is growing. However, even in some developed countries, unemployment rates have been a problem, especially since the financial crisis of 2008. Figure 4 shows that unemployment in the EU rose between 2008 and 2013/14. However, since then it has fallen to around 7 per cent in 2018.

Future employment trends are also important. For example, new technology may mean that fewer workers are required to manufacture goods.

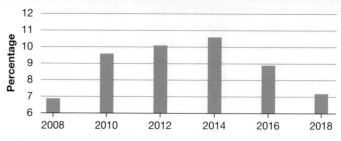

▲ Figure 4 EU unemployment levels 2008–18

ACTIVITY 2 — SKILLS ▶ CRITICAL THINKING, ANALYSIS, REASONING

CASE STUDY: GROWTH IN CHINA

The Chinese economy has experienced some of the highest growth rates in the world in the last decade. According to Figure 5, in the first quarter of 2018, the Chinese economy grew by 6.8 per cent year on year. This was the same pace as in the previous two quarters. Growth was driven by strong consumption, property investment and exports. The annual figure for 2017 exceeded the government's full-year target of 'around 6.5 per cent'. Some economists were a little surprised that China achieved this goal since policymakers (i.e. people responsible for or involved in making policies) also reduced credit growth. Economists had warned China about the risks building from years of easy credit (i.e. loans and other forms of borrowing were cheap and quite easy to obtain).

While the industrial sector grew by 6.8 per cent in the first quarter of 2018, it was retail sales that experienced significant growth. For example, in March alone, retail sales increased by 10.1 per cent. The growth was driven by sectors such as building materials (10.2 per cent), furniture (10.9 per cent), home appliances (15.4 per cent), jewellery (20.4 per cent), cosmetics (22.7 per cent) and items of clothing (14.8 per cent).

1 What are the key factors that are likely to have led to the growth in GDP in China?
2 Discuss the advantages and disadvantages of high growth rates for China.

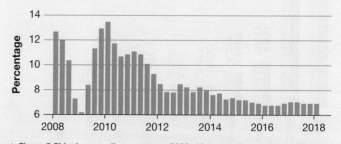

▲ Figure 5 China's expanding economy, 2008–18 (quarterly growth rate %)

INDICATORS OF GROWTH

A business needs to be able to recognise where an economy is likely to grow to find trade opportunities or investments. There are many indicators of economic growth, including GDP per capita and the **Human Development Index (HDI)**.

Gross Domestic Product (GDP) per capita: This is a measure of economic activity. It includes all of the goods and services produced in a year, divided by the number of people in the country. However, a business is interested in the trend or direction in GDP per capita. For example, China reported a very high growth rate of 6.8 per cent in 2018, but this was actually down from the figures of around 12 per cent and 10 per cent in 2010 and 2011.

Government departments collect figures for rates of economic growth in most countries. They are assessed thoroughly and adjusted for errors. A number of international organisations, such as the World Bank or the International Monetary Fund, gather economic data including growth rates from all over the world. This data is collected into useful tables and charts, published and made available free of charge. However, data may not always be consistent, comparable or easy to verify (i.e. proven to be true).

Human Development Index: The Human Development Index (HDI) combines statistics on life expectancy, education and income for any particular country into a single rankable (i.e. arranged into a particular order) value. Published by the United Nations Development Programme (www.hdr.undp.org), the index assesses a country's people and their skills, rather than just the economic conditions.

- **Life expectancy.** This is the average number of years a person can expect to live. It is an important indicator of the health of a nation as well as the quality of its healthcare and social systems. Countries with long life expectancies in 2017 included Japan (85.3 years) and Italy (82.3 years). At the other end of the scale, countries with very low life expectancies included Swaziland (52.1 years) and Sierra Leone (58.6 years).
- **Mean years of schooling.** These help to assess the average amount of education a 25-year-old person might have had. However, it does not consider the nature or quality of that education. Countries with the high scores for the average number of years of study include the USA, Australia and Germany (13.2 years), Israel (12.8 years) and Lithuania (12.7 years). A sample of countries with low scores include Burkina Faso (1.4 years), Niger (1.7 years) and Chad (2.3 years).

- **Gross National Income per capita (GNI).** This calculation illustrates the relative wealth of the population (as measured in **PPP$**). Countries with a wealthy population in 2016 include Singapore (85 020), UAE (72 830) and Luxembourg (69 640). In contrast, the poorest populations in 2016 included the Central African Republic (700), Burundi (770) and the Democratic Republic of Congo (780).

THINKING BIGGER

It is important for businesses to watch developments in world affairs carefully. These can have a dramatic impact on the economic development of a country. For example, a few years ago Russia was experiencing a period of significant growth. However, due to the country's military activities around the world, a number of economic sanctions (official rules that limit trade with a particular country in order to make it do something) have been imposed on Russia by the USA and the EU. These sanctions have restricted the performance of the economy. Growth rates have fallen from around 5 per cent in 2010 to around zero in 2018.

On a positive note, relations between North and South Korea improved in 2018 when Kim Jong-un (North Korea's Head of State) visited South Korea. There were also talks between North Korea and the USA. If the talks are successful, and North Korea abandons all nuclear development, it is possible that the North Korean economy will open up (i.e. there may be economic activity between North Korea and world), providing brand-new opportunities for a very wide range of businesses.

By keeping up to date with world affairs, businesses can identify new opportunities and reduce the impact of threats.

LINKS

The growth rates of certain countries, in areas such as Africa and Asia, for example, can affect other parts of the world. They may contribute to the growth of globalisation (Chapter 24). They are also an important factor in influencing the assessment of a country as a market (Chapter 28) and as a location for production (Chapter 29). Further rapid growth may be a contribution to the growth of international trade (Chapter 23) and an influence on mergers and joint ventures (Chapter 30).

CHECKPOINT

1 List the countries associated with the acronyms, BRICS and MINT.

2 Why are employment patterns one of the most important indicators of the health of an economy?

3 Why have many Asian economies experienced high levels of growth?

4 Suggest two opportunities that an African silver mine might experience as a result of rising economic growth.

5 How is GDP per capita calculated?

6 What are the key factors that affect external investment in an economy?

7 What does the Human Development Index (HDI) indicate about an economy?

SUBJECT VOCABULARY

disposable income the amount of money a household has available to spend and save after paying taxes

economic growth an increase in a country's productive capacity

emerging economies the economies of developing countries where there is rapid growth, but also significant risk

employment people in paid work

Human Development Index (HDI) a collection of statistics that are combined into an index, ranking countries according to their human development

income elastic the percentage change in demand for a product is proportionately greater than the percentage change in income

literacy rate the percentage of adults (over 15) who can read and write

per capita for each person; in relation to people taken individually

PPP$ are the rates of currency conversion that adjust the purchasing power of different currencies by excluding the differences in price levels between countries

primary sector the area of production involving the extraction of raw materials from the earth

tertiary sector the production of services in the economy

unemployment the number of people who are not in work but are actively seeking a job

EXAM PRACTICE

CASE STUDY: INDIAN ECONOMY

SKILLS   CRITICAL THINKING, ANALYSIS, INTERPRETATION, REASONING, DECISION MAKING

India is expected to have the world's fifth-largest economy in 2019 at US$3.211 trillion. It is one of the world's fastest emerging economies and has experienced some rapid economic growth in the last 10 years. Figure 6 shows India's economic growth rates between 2008 and 2018. In most years during this period, economic growth exceeded 6 per cent. India's GDP grew 7.2 per cent in the third quarter of 2017. This exceeded expectations and made India the fastest growing economy in world. Growth in industrial activity, especially manufacturing and construction and an expansion in agriculture, contributed significantly to the improving performance.

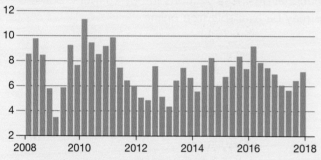

▲ Figure 6 India's growth rates (%) 2008–18

In recent years, India's economy has become a little more open. This has resulted in many overseas businesses experiencing significant success in the Indian market. Figure 7 shows that India's imports rose sharply between 2008 and 2018 from around US$22 000 to over US$40 000. India imports a wide range of goods and services including crude oil, precious stones, machinery, chemicals, fertiliser, plastics, iron and steel. Its main trading partners are China, the USA and the Middle East. However, although exports have risen over the same time period, imports have exceeded exports. Many would say that this is quite common for fast-growing economies. When an economy grows rapidly, it is usual for consumers to buy increasing amounts of imports.

Finally, many analysts expect the Indian economy to carry on performing well. It is an emerging economy with a

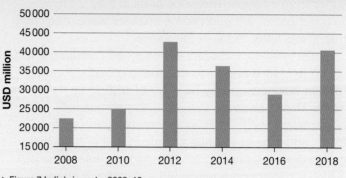

▲ Figure 7 India's imports, 2008–18

growing employment rate and people experiencing better living standards. However, there may be a number of threats. For example, poverty is still a problem. The World Bank said that around 270 million people in India live below the poverty line (i.e. the minimum level of income needed to supply basic needs, according to governmental standards). This is over 20 per cent of the population. Also, India ranked 131st out of 188 countries in the human development index in 2015. Regional differences in education, health and living standards within India – or inequality in human development – are a problem for India.

India also still relies heavily on the agricultural sector for employment and income. Figure 8 shows that the proportion of the workforce employed in agriculture in 2016 was still over 40 per cent. In many developed countries, only around 2 or 3 per cent of people are employed in this sector. In many rural areas of India, farming is undertaken on a small scale by families, which is not the most productive approach to farming.

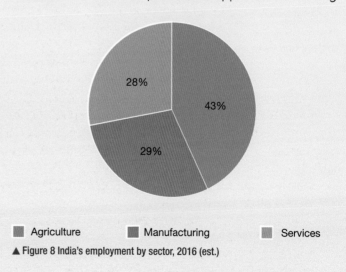

▲ Figure 8 India's employment by sector, 2016 (est.)

Another threat to the Indian economy is the price of oil. India is a huge importer of oil and some experts believe that if the price rises above $70 per barrel it could suffer from inflation. The price of oil in May 2018 was $76 per barrel, although some analysts were predicting that it was likely to fall in the future.

Unfortunately, India has experienced corruption, which acts as a barrier to economic growth because foreign businesses may be wary of setting up operations there. This is because there is a sometimes lack of transparency (i.e. allowing somebody to see the truth) and a need to bribe people in authority to 'get things done'. According to Transparency International, a global corruption agency, India was the 40th most corrupt country in the world. The Indian government did take some measures in 2016 to reduce the level of corruption. It introduced a national Goods and Service Tax (GST) to replace regional sales taxes. It forced people and businesses to open bank accounts by withdrawing Rs1000 and the Rs500 notes from circulation. People and businesses with these notes could only cash them in by depositing them in a bank account. These measures were intended to fight corruption, promote transparency, and encourage good governance (i.e. the system of rules, practices and processes by which a firm is directed and controlled).

1 Explain one reason why the human development index may be important to an economy such as India.
(4 marks)

2 Discuss the possible benefits to individuals in India of rising international trade. **(8 marks)**

3 Discuss the benefits to Indian businesses of the recent patterns of economic growth in India. **(8 marks)**

4 Assess possible threats to the Indian economy and how they might affect future economic growth. **(12 marks)**

EXAM HINT

Economies all over the world are changing over time. For example, although manufacturing is very important in China, its service sector is also beginning to expand. It is important to keep up to date with key economic changes. One way of doing this is to read the international business sections in newspapers. Some of these may be available free online.

23 INTERNATIONAL TRADE AND BUSINESS GROWTH

LEARNING OBJECTIVES

By the end of this chapter you should be able to understand:
- exports and imports
- the implications of increasing specialisation by countries and businesses
- foreign direct investment (FDI) and the link to business growth.

GETTING STARTED

France has a well-established reputation for producing high-quality cheese. Bon Fromage, a cheese producer owned by a large French food company, has been in business since 1890. The company has used its knowledge of the cheese market to sell its products overseas and has seen sales grow by 80–90 per cent in the last five years. It saw a demand for high-quality cheese in a number of European countries and other international markets and capitalised on (i.e. took advantage of) this.

Bon Fromage has been very successful in its chosen export markets in Sri Lanka, Europe and the Caribbean because it adapted its products to different markets. It used its existing relationships with upmarket hotels and restaurants to reach the same markets overseas. It also used its knowledge of air transport to expand into those markets.

Why do you think Bon Fromage decided to start exporting? How do you think it chose which countries to export to? What was the advantage to Bon Fromage of using its existing relationships with upmarket hotels and restaurants?

WHAT IS INTERNATIONAL TRADE?

International trade benefits the world. It creates opportunities for business growth, increases competition and provides more consumer choice. In more detail, international trade:
- allows countries to obtain goods that cannot be produced domestically
- allows countries to obtain goods that can be bought more cheaply from overseas
- helps to improve consumer choice
- provides opportunities for countries to sell off surplus commodities.

There is a clear difference between **visible trade** and **invisible trade**.
- **Visible trade** involves trade in physical goods. For example, India sells textiles, leather goods, gems and jewellery overseas. These are visible **exports** for India. On the other hand, India buys oil, fertiliser and chemicals from overseas. These are examples of visible **imports** for India. The difference between total visible exports and imports is called the **visible balance or the balance of trade**.
- **Invisible trade** involves trade in services. For example, the money India gets from tourists is recorded as an invisible export. On the other hand, India pays foreign carriers to transport goods to other countries. Payments for this service are recorded as invisible imports.

EXPORTS AND IMPORTS

Businesses that trade internationally export and import goods and services. Exports and imports generate revenue for businesses in different countries. This contributes to business growth.

Exports: The easiest mode of entry into the international market is through exporting. A firm continues to produce in its home market but exports some of what it makes to a foreign market. Exporting has become easier due to trade liberalisation (see Chapter 25). This has reduced **tariffs** and quotas that may otherwise have limited overseas sales.

Exporting often involves physical goods but may also include services or invisible exports. These include anything other than manufacturing, mining and agriculture. Most developed economies in the world rely on the sale of invisible items to generate export earnings. This is because in most developed countries, production is dominated by the tertiary sector. Examples include financial services, tourism, education services, advertising, media services and engineering consultancy (i.e. providing expert knowledge to a third party for a fee).

Imports: Imports are the goods and services that are brought into one country from another. For example, a Brazilian firm exports its cars and South Africa imports them. To do so, Brazil imports the transportation services of a Liberian shipping firm to collect the cars and deliver them to South Africa.

Many countries try to limit the importation of goods by placing trade barriers in the way. These barriers often involve tariffs, which are taxes that are imposed on imports. Trade liberalisation, through hundreds of treaties (i.e. written agreements between countries) and monitoring by the World Trade Organization, has reduced the use of tariffs or limited the levels of tariffs that can be levied (i.e. when official authority is used to demand payment). However, non-tariff barriers (NTBs), are proving harder to manage. These include practices such as giving subsidies (i.e. money given by governments or organisations to help keep prices low) to local firms, putting limits on the number of imports (known as quotas) and creating rules about how much of a product must be made in the country or in what way.

A firm can export or import directly. It can distribute and sell its own products, usually by hiring someone to be its local agent. However, it can also operate indirectly. It can get another person or firm to prepare the documents and take on all of the responsibility for selling and distributing the products for them. Exporting is not only the easiest way for a firm to enter the international market, it is also the least risky. A firm can limit the amount of money it spends and see if there is a good level of demand for its products.

However, this does not mean that exporting and importing are totally risk free. For example, if the South African rand was to appreciate, South African exporters would suffer. This is because the price of South African exports would rise. Therefore, demand would fall. Also,

governments can impose barriers to imports that limit a firm's access to the market. There may be conflicts with agents or distributors that are difficult to resolve from outside the country.

International trade involves exporting (selling abroad) and importing (buying from abroad). Firms benefit from trading within and between countries, even if it is sometimes difficult for them. Additionally, countries usually benefit from trade and see it as a good thing. But these benefits are sometimes indirect, complex or controversial. This will be covered in the chapters that follow.

ACTIVITY 1 SKILLS CRITICAL THINKING, ANALYSIS, INTERPRETATION

CASE STUDY: ESTONIA

Estonia is the smallest and most prosperous (i.e. financially successful) of all the former Soviet republics. The Baltic state became an open economy and developed a market system after the break-up of the Soviet Union in 1991. Estonia's economy has done very well since then. It is driven by its highly successful telecoms and electronics industries. By 2013, Estonia had become a world leader in information technology (IT). Estonian IT engineers developed the code behind Skype® and Kazaa® (an early file-sharing network). Estonia has one of the world's fastest broadband speeds and it only takes five minutes to register a firm there. Entrepreneurs wishing to start a firm log in with their national electronic identity card and then the confirmation arrives by e-mail.

Estonia's major export goods are textiles and clothes, machinery and equipment, food, wood and wood products, and chemicals. Exports from Estonia increased by 15 per cent year on year to €1.12 billion in February 2018. This was mainly driven by higher sales of mineral products, metals and articles of base metal, mechanical appliances and electrical equipment.

The major imports include machinery and equipment, minerals, vehicles, textiles and clothes, and food. Estonia has an open economy with few import barriers. Duties are levied only on certain products, such as luxury items. Export licences are only required for a handful of natural resources, such as oil shale. The lack of trade barriers, the favourable exchange rate and Estonia's positive attitude toward free trade contribute to the country's reputation as a respected trading nation.

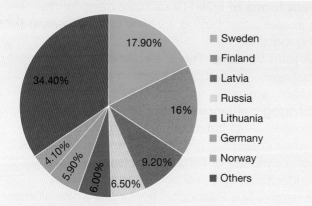

▲ Figure 1 Estonia's exports by destination (%), 2016

Legend:
- Sweden
- Finland
- Latvia
- Russia
- Lithuania
- Germany
- Norway
- Others

Values shown: 17.90%, 34.40%, 16%, 4.10%, 5.90%, 6.00%, 6.50%, 9.20%

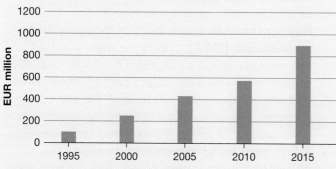

▲ Figure 2 Estonia's exports, 1992–2015

1 Look at Figure 2.
(a) Describe the pattern of exports in Estonia over the time period shown.
(b) Consider what might account for the pattern identified in (a).
2 Before 1991 most of Estonia's exports were to Russia and other Soviet partners.
(a) Outline why you think Estonia has redirected its exports since then.
(b) Why has Estonia developed a reputation for being a respected trading nation?

IMPLICATIONS OF INCREASING SPECIALISATION BY COUNTRIES AND BUSINESSES

At the core of the modern exchange economy (and international trade) is the concept of the **division of labour**. This is where workers specialise in a productive activity. Output could be increased if each worker focuses on a particular operation. Many more products could be produced than if each worker made the entire product alone. **Specialisation** increases the speed and skill with which a task can be done. This saves time, and so improves efficiency. As the market becomes larger, opportunities for specialisation increase.

Specialisation by countries: It is not unusual for countries to specialise in the production of certain goods or services. Countries are likely to specialise if they have developed more efficient production methods than those of their rivals. A country may be more efficient because it has access to cheaper resources such as labour, for example. Generally, if countries around the world specialise in this way, global output and prosperity will increase. Examples of such specialisation include China in the production of manufactured goods, Australia in mining and Bangladesh in the production of textiles.

Specialisation by businesses: The principle of specialisation can be applied to businesses. Generally, businesses will gain a competitive advantage if they specialise in the production of those products in which they are most efficient. Businesses may enjoy such a competitive advantage for a number of reasons. For example:

- A business may have particular resources that it can use wherever it goes, such as a business model, highly trained and specialised staff, or intellectual property.
- It may have acquired access to local markets, local resources and materials.
- It may be able to better organise and replace separate, cross-border trading enterprises (exporting and importing) with one firm that does it all – organises, manages and controls all trading activities.

Specialisation in production results in greater efficiency. This allows for goods and services to be produced at a lower cost per unit. This enables businesses to reduce prices or to increase profit margins, both of which can lead to business growth.

Firms may expand abroad in stages, beginning with exporting and gradually increasing their involvement in foreign markets as they gain knowledge and experience. However, exporting has its limitations. Many companies need to find other ways to expand. For example, producing abroad can be less expensive. This makes the idea of moving manufacturing to a lower-cost country attractive. Or it may be that transporting the goods or services is too expensive. This means the firm needs to move closer to where it sells or hopes to sell in the future. Additionally, governments may limit the importation of products and services. This potentially makes exporting unsuccessful, so the firm may have to find other ways to get its products to markets in other countries. Increasingly, firms are skipping these stages and taking quicker routes to the international market. For example, firms can enter a market by buying or merging with a firm that is already operating there. Some firms, especially those trading through the Internet, may even be 'born global'.

FOREIGN DIRECT INVESTMENT (FDI) AND LINK TO BUSINESS GROWTH

Many businesses outgrow their home markets and, in order to grow, they need to expand into other markets. Others become aware of opportunities for growth in new markets. When the potential competitive advantages listed above (ownership of resources, locations and internal organisation) combine, a firm can benefit from becoming a multinational company (MNC) and investing directly in other countries. Firms may choose to invest directly because the business:

- has a high potential for making a profit if it invests in a new location
- needs to maintain control over its subsidiaries in the new market
- is trying to acquire direct knowledge of the local market
- is attempting to avoid barriers to the market.

Foreign direct investment (FDI) is investing by setting up operations or buying assets in businesses in another country. The United Nations considers FDI to occur where a firm takes an equity stake of more than 10 per cent in a foreign enterprise. It is not the same as a foreign portfolio investment (i.e. investment in a range of securities to spread the risk of loss), which refers to holding stocks or bonds but not tangible assets such as buildings or machinery. However, the main characteristic of FDI is control. So, a firm might prefer FDI over exporting or licensing for many reasons, including the following.

- Managers want to keep tight control over operations in the other country or countries. The businesses may need to share a common culture or communications systems, or they may want to ensure that agreements are enforced.
- A firm wants to protect its intellectual property (such as patents, copyrights, trademarks and management know-how).
- It needs to be close to its customers.
- Its products have high transportation and logistics costs.
- It faces trade barriers or political opposition.

Different forms of FDI: FDI can take many forms, which involve either buying, building or collaborating (i.e. working together).

- **A joint venture.** This is a collaborative agreement between two parties to invest in a business and share ownership and control (see Chapter 30).
- **Strategic alliances.** These are collaborations created when firms contract to share resources (often intellectual property in the form of patents or copyrights) or certain skills (such as cultural understanding or managerial expertise). For example, Star Alliance® – the largest airline alliance in the world – operates by codeshare (i.e. where two or more airlines share the same flight). This means that a connecting point based in Frankfurt organises its member airlines' operations and bookings.
- **Buying through cross-border mergers and acquisitions (M&A).** This is the main way that businesses carry out FDI. Most M&As are actually acquisitions, with over 90 per cent of cross-border ventures involving the purchase of the entire target business. There are many reasons for buying other firms, several of which are explored in Chapter 30.
- **A firm may build 'greenfield' facilities** (i.e. on a site where business activity has not existed before, often in a rural location) if they cannot collaborate, find another firm to buy, or if it is too expensive for one reason or another. Also, many local governments may prevent certain acquisitions in order to protect competition.

Horizontal or vertical FDI: FDI can be horizontal or vertical.

- **Horizontal FDI.** Horizontal FDI refers to producing the same products or services as is done at home. For example, the takeover of the German shipping company, Hamburg Süd in 2017 by Danish conglomerate Maersk®, the largest shipping company in the world, was a horizontal merger of two firms in the same industry.
- **Vertical FDI.** This is where one firm wants to acquire materials or support for its own products or services. Basically, the firm is moving into another part of the value chain – for example, if a firm opens a call centre in another country to deliver customer or staffing support. This should help lower its costs, allowing growth in revenue or profit.

Firms engaged in FDI used to come mainly from developed countries, however, the number and size of multinational corporations coming from emerging market countries, such as China, Brazil, Mexico and South Africa, is increasing.

ACTIVITY 2   SKILLS   CRITICAL THINKING, ANALYSIS, INTERPRETATION, CREATIVITY

CASE STUDY: FDI IN INDIA

India wants to encourage foreign firms to set up operations. It started in the 1990s, when the government began to encourage globalisation. It ended regulation at home and lowered barriers to foreign investment. The government deliberately targeted the IT services sector for growth, giving it special subsidies. As a result, many foreign multinationals came to India. They were eager to take advantage of the cheap labour and the opening up of one of the world's biggest markets.

In 2016–17 foreign investment in India reached $60.1 billion. One reason for the increase was the government's decision to relax controls in industries such as civil aviation. The government considers foreign investment a key part of future economic growth. It needs around $1 trillion of investment to improve its infrastructure, which includes ports, airports and road networks.

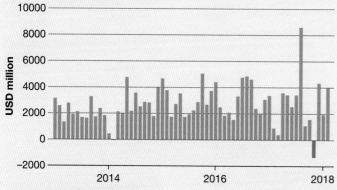

▲ Figure 3 India's FDI levels, 2013–18

In 2018, India relaxed foreign direct investment (FDI) rules. The changes were directed at the retail sector. However, rule changes also allowed overseas investors to acquire as much as 49 per cent of Air India. This was in order to speed up its divestment. Overseas retailers can now delay having to meet the 30 per cent local sourcing norm by five years. This removes a key barrier to FDI in this sector. Approvals for such investments have also been made automatic. Examples of recent FDI in India include the following.

- IKEA® plans to invest $612 million in Maharashtra to set up multi-format stores and experience centres in 2018.

- Singapore's Temasek has acquired a 16 per cent stake worth $156.16 million in Bengaluru-based Manipal Hospitals, which runs a hospital chain of around 5000 beds.
- US footwear company, Skechers®, plans to add 400–500 more stores in India over the next five years. It also plans to launch its apparel and accessories collection in India.

1 Explain what is meant by foreign direct investment (FDI).
2 How is the Indian government encouraging FDI?
3 How might India benefit from rising FDI?

EXAM HINT

You should recognise that a country can export and import both goods and services. A useful tip to help you identify whether there has been an export or import is to think about the way the money moves when it is paid. This is useful in identifying exports and imports of services. Let's look at Spain.

- Exports – goods or services are sold abroad and money comes into Spain.
- Imports – goods or services are bought from abroad and money leaves Spain.

Some examples help to illustrate this:

- **Exports of goods.** A Spanish manufacturer sells some machinery to Italy. This is an **export** of **goods** from Spain and money **comes into** the country. The Spanish business sells its products to Italian customers or businesses.
- **Exports of services.** A German company uses the financial services of a Spanish bank. This is the **export** of a **service** to a German business and money **comes into** Spain. The German business pays the Spanish bank.
- **Imports of goods.** A Spanish manufacturer of pharmaceuticals buys some chemicals from the USA. This is an **import** of **goods** to Spain and money **leaves** Spain. The Spanish business pays the USA business for the chemicals.
- **Imports of services.** Spanish tourists visit Argentina for a holiday and book with an Argentinian travel agent. This is the **import** of a **service** to Spain and money **leaves** Spain. Spanish tourists are spending their money abroad.

LINKS

One factor influencing the exports and imports of goods and services is the rate of exchange between countries. The exchange rate between two currencies is explained in Chapter 28. The role that FDI plays in business growth can be discussed when considering growing economies (Chapter 22). Further, any question considering the role that MNCs play in world trade and generating FDI (Chapter 35) can be supported by information in this chapter.

CHECKPOINT

1 Give two examples of visible trade.

2 Give two examples of invisible trade.

3 Why do some countries try to limit imports?

4 What are the risks of being involved in exporting and importing?

5 Give two advantages of specialisation by a country.

6 How does specialisation lead to greater efficiency?

7 What is meant by foreign direct investment (FDI)?

8 What are the different forms of foreign direct investment?

9 What impact might a €5 billion investment by a European business in Kenya have on economic growth in Kenya?

SUBJECT VOCABULARY

division of labour different workers specialising in different productive activities
exports goods or services that a firm produces in its home market but sells in a foreign market
foreign direct investment (FDI) investing by setting up operations or buying assets in businesses in another country
imports goods and services that are bought into one country from another
international trade exporting (selling abroad) and importing (buying from abroad)
invisible trade trade in services rather than physical products
specialisation a production strategy where a business or country focuses on a limited number of products or services This results in greater efficiency, allowing for goods and services to be produced at a lower cost per unit
tariffs taxes that are imposed on imports
visible trade trade in physical goods

EXAM PRACTICE

CASE STUDY: INTERNATIONAL TRADE IN AUSTRALIA

SKILLS CRITICAL THINKING, ANALYSIS, INTERPRETATION, PROBLEM SOLVING

Australia is an established trader in international markets. It has many natural resources and specialises in the export of commodities including iron ore, coal, natural gas, beef, wheat and wool. The main invisible export for Australia is tourism. Visitors are attracted by its lively cities, its developing cuisine, areas of outstanding natural beauty (including the Great Barrier Reef) and its unique wildlife. Figure 4 shows that Australia's exports have grown significantly in the last 10 years.

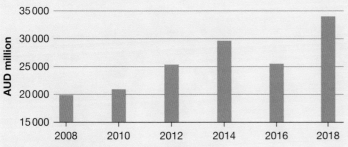

▲ Figure 4 Australia's exports, 2008–18 (AUD million)

Australia imports quite a lot of manufactured goods. The country does not produce cars and relies on imports to meet growing demand. Australia's key imports include motor cars, goods vehicles, telecommunications equipment and parts, consumer goods, machinery and industrial equipment, computers and medical products. Figure 5 shows Australia's imports between 2008 and 2018. Figure 6 shows which countries are the main sources of Australia's imports.

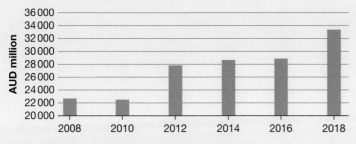

▲ Figure 5 Australia's imports, 2008–18 (AUD million)

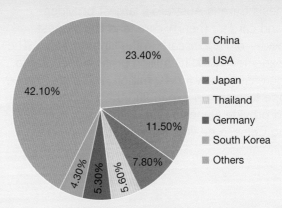

▲ Figure 6 Sources of Australia's imports, 2016

In addition to the trade in goods and services with foreign countries, Australia also attracts a significant amount of FDI. In 2016, Australia was the seventh most popular destination in the world for FDI. Figure 7 shows that in 2016, FDI in Australia was AUD64 825 million.

China is Australia's biggest source of FDI. In 2016, Chinese businesses invested a total of AUD15 400 million in Australia. This included a record 103 deals between Australian and Chinese businesses. Most of this investment was directed into commercial property, infrastructure development and healthcare. More than a third of all Chinese FDI found its way into commercial property. However, investors were moving funds away from office investment. They were moving it towards residential construction, looking beyond inner-city developments such as high-rise apartments, to medium-density greenfield (i.e. land that has not yet been built on) projects. Chinese investors also spent AUD1.7 billion on hotel assets.

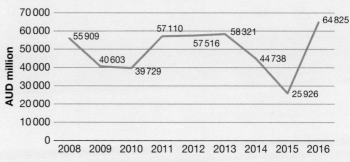

▲ Figure 7 FDI in Australia between 2008 and 2016

Adapted from https://tradingeconomics.com/australia/imports and https://www.cia.gov/library/publications/the-world-factbook/geos/as.html and http://www.abc.net.au/news/2017-05-01/chinese-investment-in-australia-at-highest-point-since-gfc/8485828 and http://overseas.ccpit.org/Contents/Channel_1619/2016/0728/676445/content_676445.htm

One Chinese business making a significant investment in Australia was Macquarie-backed China Resources. In 2016, the company bought Genesis Care® for AUD1.7 billion. Genesis Care is Australia's largest provider of cancer and cardiac (heart) care, and the biggest private provider of cancer care in the UK and Spain. The company expected AUD110 million profit in the year to 30 June, increasing to AUD140 million next year. The new owners hope to carry on expanding the business into Europe and provide Genesis Care with easier access to the growing Chinese healthcare market.

1 Calculate the proportion of Australian FDI contributed by China in 2016. **(4 marks)**
2 Explain one reason why invisible exports may be important for the Australian economy. **(4 marks)**
3 Explain one reason a country like Australia may be increasing specialisation. **(4 marks)**
4 Discuss the potential reasons for a changing pattern of international trade in Australia between 2008 and 2018. **(8 marks)**
5 Discuss the benefits of China Resources investing in the Australian economy. **(8 marks)**

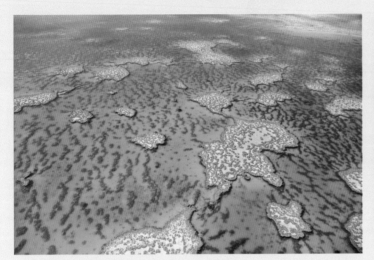

24 FACTORS CONTRIBUTING TO INCREASED GLOBALISATION

UNIT 4
4.3.1

LEARNING OBJECTIVES

By the end of this chapter you should be able to understand:

■ trade liberalisation, the reduction of trade barriers and the role of the WTO
■ political change
■ the reduced cost of transport and communication
■ the increased significance of global (multinational) corporations (MNCs)
■ increased investment flows (FDI)
■ migration within and between economies
■ the growth of the global labour force
■ structural change
■ the impact on businesses of increased globalisation.

GETTING STARTED

Over the past 20 years, economies all over the world have become more open (i.e. having no barriers to free market activity with other countries). For example, since the break-up of the Soviet Union, many countries such as Estonia, Poland, Ukraine and Latvia have started to trade with other nations. This has led to more trade, co-operation, communication between countries and movement of resources such as labour and capital.

In 1991, Latvia gained independence from the Soviet Union. Since then, it has developed strong political and economic links with other countries. For example, it joined the World Trade Organization in 1999, the North Atlantic Treaty Organization (NATO) in 2004, the European Union (EU) in 2014 and the Organisation for Economic Co-operation and Development (OECD) in 2016.

Since independence, Latvia has accepted the market mechanism. For example, it has privatised most of its state industries. This means that it has transferred most of the Latvian state-owned business organisations to the private sector. It has also reduced and removed some laws and regulations that affect free competition in the supply of goods and services in a number of markets. Finally, it has opened up its economy by allowing free trade between Latvia and the rest of the world.

Latvia has accepted globalisation. According to the **Economic Globalisation Index**, Latvia was ranked 29th in the world in 2014. This was higher than Germany (58th), the UK (45th) and Japan (125th). Figure 1 shows the pace at which Latvia has engaged in world trade since 1994 (shortly after the Soviet break-up).

Unfortunately, Latvia suffered after the financial crisis in 2008. The economy struggled due to an unsustainable (i.e. unable to continue) current account deficit and large debt. Latvia's second largest bank collapsed, and GDP fell by more than 14 per cent in 2009. Another problem was that Latvia's population fell by 13 per cent over a 10-year period. This caused concern that there would be a **'brain drain'**.

More recently, Latvia has reinvented itself as a centre for financial services. This means that it is able to organise the transfer of capital from Russia and other former Soviet republics. However, some Latvian banks have faced international criticism and have been accused of money laundering (i.e. moving illegally obtained money into legal businesses so that it is difficult to know where the money originally came from).

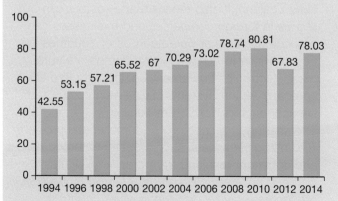

▲ Figure 1 Latvia – economic globalisation

How has political change influenced the development of business in Latvia? What evidence is there to suggest that Latvia has accepted globalisation? Why has Latvia failed to benefit from globalisation as much as its neighbours? How has globalisation had an impact on Latvia's population size? Explain your answer.

WHAT IS GLOBALISATION?

Many markets today are global. This means that some firms expect to sell their products anywhere in the world. A firm could have a head office in London, borrow money from a bank in Japan, manufacture products in China, deal with customers from a call centre in India and sell goods to countries all over the world. Firms and people are behaving as though there is just one market or one economy in the whole world. This development is called **globalisation**. It is often defined as the growing integration (i.e. combining things so that they work together) of the world's economies.

Some of the key features of globalisation are outlined below.

- Goods and services are traded throughout the world. This means that firms like Toyota, the Japanese car giant, can sell their products as easily in Australia as in India.
- Many people are able to live and work in a country of their choice. This has resulted in more multicultural societies. People from many different nations live and work together, for example in the same city.
- There is a high level of interdependence between countries. This means that events in one economy are likely to affect other economies. For example, the financial crisis in the USA in 2008 had an impact on many economies all over the world.
- Capital flows freely between different countries. For example, this means that a business or consumer in Sweden can put their savings in a bank in New Zealand. It also means that investors can buy shares in foreign companies and businesses can buy companies that operate in other countries. For example, in 2018, Chinese company Naura Microelectronics Equipment Co. Ltd acquired US company Akrion Systems LLC, a manufacturer of semiconductors, for $15 million.
- The sharing of technology and intellectual property (i.e. intangible assets, such as patents, brand names and copyright resulting from creativity) across borders. For example, patents granted in the USA are increasingly recognised in other countries.

However, restrictions to globalisation still exist. For example, countries such as Australia and the USA restrict the number of immigrants entering the country and impose trade barriers, such as quotas and tariffs. This makes it more difficult to sell goods in certain countries. Trade barriers are discussed in Chapter 25.

TRADE LIBERALISATION, THE REDUCTION OF TRADE BARRIERS AND THE ROLE OF THE WORLD TRADE ORGANIZATION

An increasing number of countries have opened up their economies and allowed trade to flow without any barriers. This is what is meant by **trade liberalisation**. Free trade agreements help to encourage trade between nations. As a result, the volume of international trade increases. Businesses can sell goods and services in new foreign markets without penalties. This increase in international trade maintains the process of globalisation.

However, there are disadvantages to globalisation, such as exploitation by businesses, and so some governments have resisted getting involved. In 2018, a number of countries, including the USA and China, also introduced fresh trade barriers. Evidence of increasing trade liberalisation is provided by recent trade agreements. Some examples of which are outlined below.

- In 2018, Mexico and the EU agreed on a wide-reaching deal to simplify the customs process. They eliminated tariffs for 'practically all' goods traded between EU member nations and Mexico. It was reported that the agreement allows companies in the EU or Mexico to bid for government contracts abroad. It also makes labour, safety and environmental safety standards clearer.
- In 2018, the USA and South Korea reached agreement over a trade deal. South Korea said it would limit its steel exports to the USA and open its markets to more US-made cars and trucks under a preliminary agreement. This was a change to the 2012 bilateral trade agreement, which involves a deal between the two countries to allow **free trade**. According to the agreement, South Korea would allow US car makers to double their vehicle exports to 50 000 a year and South Korea would not have to pay the 25 per cent tariffs on steel imports imposed by the USA in March 2018.

One reason for the growing level of trade liberalisation is the influence of the **World Trade Organization (WTO)**. The WTO was established in 1995, replacing a similar body called GATT (General Agreement on Trade and Tariffs). The WTO has 164 members and employs over 600 people, including lawyers, economists, statisticians and communications experts. The WTO promotes free trade by persuading countries to abolish tariffs and other trade barriers. It has become closely associated with globalisation.

The WTO is the only international agency overseeing the rules of international trade. It makes sure people follow the rules of free trade agreements, settles trade disputes between governments and organises trade negotiations. WTO decisions are final, and every member must follow its rules. When countries have a dispute, the WTO will analyse the case and pass its judgement. WTO members have the power to enforce WTO decisions by disciplining countries that have broken the rules. The main activities of the WTO are outlined below.

Trade negotiations: The WTO aims to reduce or eliminate trade barriers through negotiation. It does this by encouraging countries to draw up trading agreements covering matters such as anti-dumping (i.e. where foreign producers sell goods below cost in a domestic market), subsidies (money given by governments or organisations to help keep prices low) and product standards. The WTO aims to bring about trade liberalisation and lays down procedures for settling arguments. The agreements reached between countries may change over time. Changes are needed because businesses operate in a world with new products and technologies being developed all the time.

Implementation and monitoring: The WTO employs various councils and committees. They manage and monitor the application of the WTO's rules for trade in goods, services and intellectual property rights. For example, the WTO may examine trade policies to ensure that trade agreements are clear and well documented. All WTO members must carry out regular reviews of their trade policies and practices.

Settling trade disputes: Trade disputes between members are not unusual. The WTO's procedure for resolving trade disputes is vital for enforcing the rules and making sure that trade flows smoothly. Countries bring disputes to the WTO if they think their rights under their agreements have been broken. The WTO appoints independent experts to make judgements about disputes after the arguments from both sides have been presented.

Building membership: There are around 20 countries which are yet to join. The WTO encourages new members to sign up.

ACTIVITY 1　　SKILLS　CRITICAL THINKING, ANALYSIS

CASE STUDY: BRAZIL VS THAILAND TRADE DISPUTE

In 2016, Brazil filed a complaint to the World Trade Organization (WTO) claiming that Thailand had given subsidies to sugar cane producers and sugar mills. The effect of these subsidies was to reduce the global price of sugar and reduce Brazil's share of the market from 50 per cent to 44.7 per cent in four years. Brazil and Thailand are two of the world's largest sugar producers, so the market is very important to both countries.

Brazilian sugar producers gathered evidence which showed that they were losing $1.2 billion per year in revenue as a result of subsidies paid to Thailand and India. They also argued that Thailand's share of the global market had risen from 12.1 per cent to 15.8 per cent in the past four years.

Thailand said there was no evidence to support Brazil's claim. An official from Thailand's Industry Ministry said that there were no subsidies and trade had been carried out within the agreed conditions. The official said that the money had come from the country's Cane and Sugar Fund, which raised the money itself.

In 2004, Brazil challenged the EU over sugar subsidies and won. This led to the EU changing its policies for sugar production, which had an impact on the global sugar market.

The WTO will have to look at the claims made by Brazil. It will have to analyse the information which Brazil presents and also consider any defence provided by Thailand. The WTO will then have to make a judgement and decide on a course of action. This might involve imposing penalties on Thailand if the case is allowed to continue.

1 What is this dispute about?
2 Explain the role played by the WTO in settling this dispute.
3 What is meant by a free trade agreement?
4 What might be the consequences if trade agreements did not exist?

POLITICAL CHANGE

Some radical changes in the political regimes (i.e. a system of government, usually not elected in a fair way) of certain nations have helped to increase globalisation. Some examples of these are outlined below.

- In 1991, Communist rule ended in the Soviet Union and the old Soviet bloc no longer existed. Old Soviet bloc countries, such as Latvia, Georgia, Lithuania, Belarus, Estonia and Moldova, were given independence. As a result, these countries began to open up their economies and develop trading agreements with the world. Some of them joined the EU and Russia also began to allow a greater movement of goods, services and capital. In the whole region, the introduction of market forces helped to liberalise trade.
- A number of other countries in Eastern Europe wanted political and economic reform as their relationships with the old Soviet bloc were gone. For example, the Berlin Wall was removed which brought together West Germany and East Germany as a single nation. In Romania, Communist leader Nicolae Ceausescu was removed from power in 1989.
- Economic changes in China first began in the 1970s with economic reforms in the agricultural sector, where efficiency was improved by handing over plots of land to farmers. They were allowed to keep the output after paying a share to the state. Then, between the mid-1990s and 2005, a large-scale privatisation programme was organised by the government. Trade was gradually opened up and China became a member of the WTO. China is now a successful economy with a well-established manufacturing sector. They have heavy state expenditure on infrastructure and rising prosperity among the Chinese 'middle classes'. However, China is seen as an economy that is at a stage of newly advanced economic development, not yet completely 'open for business'.

REDUCED COST OF TRANSPORT AND COMMUNICATION

International transport networks have improved in recent years. The cost of flying has fallen, and the number of flights and destinations has increased. This means that people can travel to business meetings more easily and goods can be transported more cheaply. For example, a number of low-cost airlines have entered the market and brought air travel to the masses. In the EU, WOW Air®, easyJet, Jet2®, WizzAir®, Ryanair and Flybe® offer flights to a wide range of European destinations. They are affordable to the majority of the population.

India has also begun to experience low-cost air travel. Airlines such as SpiceJet®, GoAir® and Jet Airways® offer cheap internal flights and some provide international services.

Modern technology allows firms to transfer complex data instantly to any part of the world. It also means that more people can work at home, or any other location that they choose. Many people do not have to be office-based to do their jobs. This makes it easier for firms to have operations all over the world. The Internet also allows consumers to gather information and they can buy goods online from businesses located in different parts of the world. Both large and small businesses can connect with global markets by promoting their activities and products using the Internet.

Containerisation has also made a significant contribution to globalisation. Containers are identical metal boxes that can be loaded and unloaded easily from ships, lorries and trains. They provide a flexible means of transporting goods, but most importantly their use has reduced the cost of transportation significantly.

- Before the use of containers it cost $5.83 per tonne to load a ship manually. The use of containers has reduced this to just $0.16 per tonne.
- There has been a 50 per cent reduction in the amount of capital tied up in a tonne of stock in a journey from Hamburg to Sydney.
- The loss to theft has fallen because containers are locked. This has reduced insurance costs.
- The speed of loading has increased drastically, which cuts costs. Before containerisation, labour could only load 1.7 tonnes per hour onto a ship. This has risen to 30 tonnes per hour with containers. As a result, ships have got bigger and spend less time in ports.

Containerisation transformed the transportation of goods. Since it is so easy to distribute goods by lorry, due to the flexibility of containers, the number of loading ports used in Europe has fallen from 11 to just three.

ACTIVITY 2   SKILLS   CRITICAL THINKING, ANALYSIS

CASE STUDY: THE SCOURIE BAY GUEST HOUSE

Carol and Martin McDonald have run the Scourie Bay Guest House in Scotland for 30 years. However, in 2012 they expanded by buying the property next door. This increased the number of rooms to let from six to 14. This decision was taken after they advertised the guest house on their own website. They started to attract visitors from Europe, Japan and Australia.

The expansion cost a total of £300 000 and they were worried that they might struggle to fill the rooms during the quiet winter period. However, due to the global exposure of their business through the website and social media, and the growing popularity of low-cost flights, business has been very successful. In 2018 the business made a record profit of £105 000 and more than 55 per cent of guests during 2018 were from overseas.

1 What is meant by globalisation?
2 Assess the factors that have contributed to globalisation in this case.

INCREASED SIGNIFICANCE OF GLOBAL (MULTINATIONAL) CORPORATIONS

One of the reasons why globalisation has thrived in recent years is because a growing number of large firms have developed significant business interests overseas. Some of these firms are very powerful. They sell goods and services into global markets and have production plants and other operating facilities all over the world. They are called transnational or **multinational companies (MNCs)**. Multinational companies play a large and growing role in the world economy. They make significant contributions to world GDP and represent about two-thirds of global exports. They also make huge global investments in research and development.

Figure 2 shows the changes in the world's largest ten MNCs between 2006 and 2016.

The contribution made by MNCs to globalisation is likely to continue growing. This is because these corporations are under pressure to increase returns to their owners. Consequently, they will expand their current activities. They will search for new cost-effective business opportunities anywhere in the world. The role played by MNCs is discussed in more detail in Chapter 35.

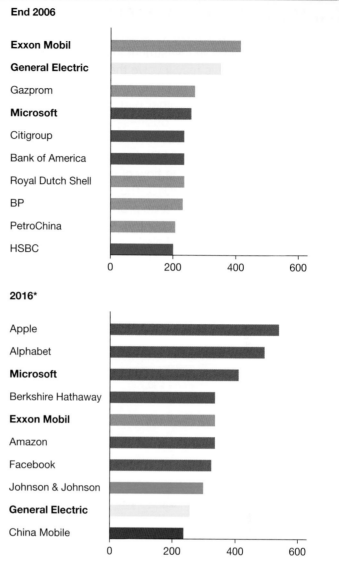

End 2006

2016*

Sector: Energy Financials Healthcare
         Industrials IT Telecoms

▲ Figure 2 Changes in the Top 10 world's biggest MNCs between 2006 and 2016 by market capitalisation ($billion)

EXAM HINT

You need to remember that it is not just large MNCs that contribute to, and benefit from, globalisation. Small businesses also play their role. The Scottish guest house in Activity 2 is one example. Also, many small businesses play a role as suppliers to the multinationals.

INCREASED INVESTMENT FLOWS

Foreign direct investment (FDI) (see Chapter 23) occurs when a company makes an investment in a foreign country. For example, this may involve the construction of a factory, distribution centre or store, or the development of a mine or tea plantation. Another part of FDI is the purchase of shares in a foreign business (10 per cent or more). Most FDI is carried out by multinational companies.

The USA has attracted more FDI than any other country in the world. Figure 3 shows the flow of inward investment for the top 10 destinations in 2016. The USA, the UK and China alone account for a very large proportion of global inward FDI (flows of FDI into a country). According to preliminary data from the United Nations Conference on Trade and Development, global FDI flows were forecast to decline in 2017 – from $1.81 trillion in 2016 to $1.52 trillion in 2017. However, FDI inflows to developing economies were expected to stabilise in 2017, reaching about $653 billion, an increase of 2 per cent over 2016.

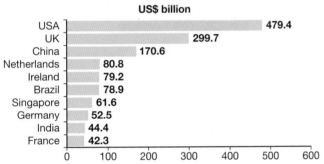

US$ billion

USA	479.4
UK	299.7
China	170.6
Netherlands	80.8
Ireland	79.2
Brazil	78.9
Singapore	61.6
Germany	52.5
India	44.4
France	42.3

▲ Figure 3 Flows of inward investment – 2016

Some specific examples of FDI around the world are outlined below.

- During a tour of Asia in 2018, the King of Saudi Arabia promised to invest around $10 billion in the Maldives tourism industry and $7 billion in the oil sector in Malaysia.
- Spain attracted 385 greenfield FDI projects in 2017, 61 more than the year before and 133 more than in 2015. Greenfield capital investment hit US$13.9 billion in 2017.
- In 2017, the UAE attracted about US$11 billion in FDI. This was about 22 per cent of the total for the whole of the Middle East and North Africa.

FDI spreads business activity, job creation and wealth all over the world. It makes a huge contribution to globalisation. FDI also allows businesses to enter markets where trade barriers exist. Countries are more likely to welcome a foreign business building a factory than one that just wants to sell products. Many governments around the world offer incentives to business to attract FDI.

MIGRATION

Migration is the movement of people who aim to live (permanently or temporarily) in a new location. It is commonly associated with the movement of people between different countries. For example, between 2018 and 2021 Canada plans to welcome 980 000 new residents to the country. It is argued that 3 per cent of the world's population live outside their country of birth. However, in some countries, such as Australia and Switzerland, migrants make up around 23 per cent of the population. How does migration contribute to globalisation?

- Migrants often import their cultures into their new environment. Often, this includes the importation of goods from their home countries. For example, in the UK there are many shops that sell products especially for Eastern European immigrants. Much of the produce sold in these stores is imported from different countries in Eastern Europe.
- Migrants often provide a supply of low-cost labour to a nation. As a result, businesses can lower their costs and gain a competitive advantage in overseas markets. This helps them to sell more overseas.
- A significant proportion of the money earned by migrants is sent back to their place of birth. This money is usually spent by families and helps to generate demand in these countries. Transnationals are likely to benefit from this increase in demand. So, economic activity is spread around the world by the migrants.
- Some migrants, such as lawyers, doctors, teachers, musicians, writers, academics and Premier League footballers, are highly skilled people. They can help to fill 'skills gaps'. Therefore, they make big contributions to businesses and national income.

Migration can also take place within a country, where people move from one region to another. This has happened on a large scale in China. During the past 30 years, workers have moved from inland regions to coastal cities within China. These people have moved in search of jobs and new opportunities that are not available in rural areas. Approximately one-third of all domestic migrants worldwide are domestic Chinese migrants. This movement of people in China has been the result of international investment and the development of the manufacturing sector. A lot of overseas businesses have invested in these manufacturing areas because land and labour are cheap. As a result, globalisation has been given a boost.

Although migration is helping to boost global wealth, some countries are worried that migration might lead to social instability. Sectors of the population might blame immigration for a range of domestic problems, such as overcrowding and unemployment. As a result, some governments are under pressure to reduce flows of migrants into their country.

GROWTH OF THE GLOBAL LABOUR FORCE

The global labour force has grown substantially. In 1980, the total number of people employed in the world was 1.7 billion. By 2017 this had grown to 3.451 billion. Growth in the global labour market might also be due to an increase in the global population from 4.45 billion in 1980 to 7.6 billion in 2017. It also might be due to more women entering the market, people living longer and working longer, and the effects of migration.

This growth in the size of the global labour market has contributed to globalisation for the following reasons.

- A bigger global labour market helps to influence global demand. This is because people in employment earn money which can be spent on goods and services. Some of this extra demand will be directed at imports sold by MNCs and other exporters. In countries like China and India, where much larger numbers of people have moved into employment, millions of people are no longer in poverty. They are making significant contributions to global demand.
- The increasing number of people making themselves available for work has negatively affected labour costs, especially in developed countries. This is because the rising supply of labour forces wages down. This has helped to keep costs down and encouraged businesses to expand their activities more widely.
- Some people moving into the labour market will set up their own businesses once they have gained work experience. This will boost the number of businesses globally. Some of the businesses might grow and develop their activities around the world adding another lift to globalisation.

STRUCTURAL CHANGE

Over time, the structure of economies (i.e. the way they are arranged) is likely to change. For example, in most Western economies the contribution made to national income by the primary and secondary sectors has fallen. In these economies, it is the huge growth in services that has provided most of the income, employment and wealth. It could also be argued that it is the movement away from these traditional sectors and into services that allows businesses and economies to thrive. This is because the returns on capital invested in many service industries are often higher. The development of knowledge-based industries, such as biotechnology (technology involving the use of living organisms), information technology, research and development, education, software development, pharmaceuticals (medicinal drugs), care,

finance, aerospace (industry concerned with aircraft and space flight) and security help countries to improve the standard of living for their people.

These structural changes have contributed to globalisation. This is because most of the industries mentioned above are export orientated. As a result, these industries are likely to set up operations in a range of countries, recruit high-quality staff from anywhere in the world and try to establish a global presence. It might also be argued that the Internet and social media have helped to deliver services to global markets. Both large and small businesses can use the Internet and social media to raise their profiles. This also helps them to communicate with potential customers and sell products.

Finally, many industries in the tertiary sector can operate anywhere, provided there is a market. They are not required to be in specific geographical locations or influenced by other locational factors. For example, a chain store like Walmart can operate anywhere in the world, provided there are people nearby who want to go shopping.

IMPACT ON BUSINESSES OF GLOBALISATION

Many would argue that the main winners from globalisation are the global companies that develop business interests overseas. Some specific benefits include the following.

- **Access to huge markets.** Global markets are much bigger than domestic markets. For example, if businesses have access to several billion customers rather than 40 million, this provides huge opportunities to increase sales. This should result in higher sales revenue and increased profit for businesses.
- **Lower costs.** If businesses are able to grow by selling more output to larger markets, they may be able to lower their costs. This is because as firms grow they can exploit economies of scale.
- **Access to labour.** One of the benefits of globalisation is the free movement of labour. This means that people are free to move around the world and find employment in other countries (subject to the border controls that still exist in most countries). As a result, businesses will have access to a larger pool of labour. This is important because if a business is growing fast there may be a shortage of domestic labour. Globalisation means that workers from overseas can help to boost the labour supply. Also, an increasing labour supply might help to prevent wages from rising, as the arrival of larger numbers of foreign workers can hold wages down – this is true in markets where unskilled labour is needed. Lower wages will help businesses to lower their costs.

- **Reduced taxation.** Global businesses can reduce the amount of tax they pay. They can do this by locating their head offices in countries where business taxes are low. Ireland has proved a popular destination for businesses, since its rate of corporation tax is just 12.5 per cent (on trading income). This is well below other rates in the world which are often higher than 20 per cent.

However, some businesses may be threatened by globalisation. There may be a number of reasons for this.

- **Competition.** Many businesses may face strong competition from overseas companies attempting to enter their markets. For example, many manufacturers in developed economies have closed down due to competition from countries like China, Vietnam, South Korea and Japan.
- **The power of MNCs Globalisation.** allows large MNCs to become very powerful. They can produce very cheaply and start to dominate global markets. This will make it difficult for firms in some markets to survive. MNCs also have huge resources which often allow them to manipulate markets and governments.
- **Interdependence.** Growing globalisation results in economies becoming more interdependent. This means that an event in one country could have an impact on businesses based in another country. For example, Brexit might have a negative impact on many businesses throughout Europe if new tariffs are introduced.
- **Exploitation.** Growing globalisation often results in businesses moving operations to countries where the legal system is under-developed. For example, they might operate in countries where child labour is acceptable. This might give these companies a competitive edge, but it also might result in more exploitation.

LINKS

Globalisation is an important business development. You may get the opportunity to make links to the topic of globalisation in a wide variety of answers. For example, when discussing the importance of exporting, importing, exchange rates, overseas marketing or outsourcing to a business, globalisation is clearly a related issue. Globalisation may be linked to many chapters, but some obvious examples include Impact of external influences (Chapter 4), Key factors in change (Chapter 25), Contingency planning (Chapter 21), Trading blocs (Chapter 26), Assessment of a country as a market (Chapter 28), The impact of MNCs (Chapter 35) and other chapters in Unit 4.

CHECKPOINT

1 State three features of globalisation.

2 Describe briefly the role played by the WTO in globalisation.

3 What is meant by a free trade agreement?

4 How do free trade agreements help to foster globalisation?

5 How might political change contribute to globalisation?

6 Describe briefly the role played by lower transport costs in the spread of globalisation.

7 How has containerisation had an impact on globalisation?

8 Outline one way in which multinational companies contribute to globalisation.

9 How has migration had an impact on globalisation?

10 How has the growth in the global labour force contributed to globalisation?

SUBJECT VOCABULARY

brain drain when highly educated and talented people find jobs overseas

Economic Globalisation Index first measures the economic flows between a country and the rest of the world in terms of international trade and international investment. This shows whether a country exchanges a lot of goods, services and investments with other countries. Second, it measures the restrictions to trade and investment, such as tariffs and capital controls on international investment. Each dimension is based on several variables that are combined in one overall index that ranges from 0 to 100

free trade trade between nations without restrictions from barriers

globalisation the growing integration of the world's economies

multinational companies (MNCs) companies that own or control production or service facilities outside the country in which they are based

remittances the money sent back to their country of origin by overseas workers

trade liberalisation the removal of rules and regulations that restrict free trade

World Trade Organization (WTO) an international organisation that promotes free trade by persuading countries to abolish tariffs and other barriers. It polices free trade agreements, settles trade disputes between governments and organises trade negotiations

EXAM PRACTICE

CASE STUDY: BANGLADESH AND GLOBALISATION

SKILLS   CRITICAL THINKING, ANALYSIS, INTERPRETATION, REASONING

Bangladesh

In recent years, the Bangladesh economy has begun to grow quite rapidly. It coped well during the financial crisis in 2008 and is now benefiting from strengthening investment and a recovery of exports. Growth will be sustained at 6.8 per cent in 2017. This is compared with the officially reported 7.1 per cent in 2016. Figure 4 shows that FDI in Bangladesh has grown steadily since 2008.

The government has taken measures to provide businesses with incentives to invest. For example, the Bangladesh Investment Development Authority (BIDA), a new authority, was making rules and regulations for investment much easier. The country is experiencing a period of political stability and the government is establishing technical schools in every upazila (administrative region) across the country. This is to provide people with a range of work-related skills.

However, there are problems such as significant infrastructure gaps and an inadequate energy supply. Bangladesh is also a country where the cost of doing business is relatively high.

One business about to invest in Bangladesh is Vietnam-based leather goods manufacturer, TBS. The company plans to spend $100 million building a factory in either Dhaka or Chittagong. It wanted to produce leather footwear and footwear components for overseas markets. TBS is one of the top five leather goods manufacturers in Vietnam and exports about $500 million each year.

The planned investment is expected to create 10 000 new jobs in Bangladesh. This will introduce the nation to new technologies in the leather industry. The leather industry is important to Bangladesh. It has 3000 tanneries and leather goods factories which employ over 200 000 workers. TBS said that it was attracted to Bangladesh's business-friendly environment, cheap workforce, the availability of raw materials and the low duties that Vietnam experiences.

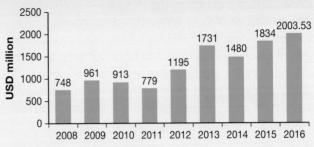

▲ Figure 4 FDI in Bangladesh 2008–16

Bangladesh has begun to benefit from globalisation, as the growth in FDI shows in Figure 4. The nation has benefited from trade liberalisation, especially the free movement of labour around most of the world. Bangladeshi overseas workers send money back to Bangladesh. These **remittances** are significant, as shown by Figure 5. In 2017, a total of US$13.53 billion was sent back to Bangladesh by people working in places like India, the UK, Saudi Arabia, Kuwait, Oman and the UAE.

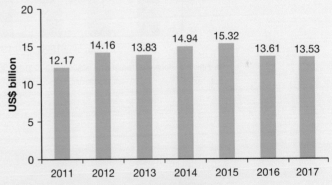

▲ Figure 5 Remittance inflows to Bangladesh 2011–17

Global air travel

Globalisation has been aided by radical improvements in transport and communication networks around the world. For example, the cost of flying between countries has fallen to the level where very large numbers of people find it affordable. In 2016, the number of people taking a flight rose to 3.696 billion. Figure 6 shows growth in airline passenger traffic between 1980 and 2015. This growth has been influenced by:

- a sharp fall in the global oil price in 2014 has helped to keep fuel costs down since then

- improvements in aviation technology which have helped to lower operating costs and improve the efficiency of aircraft
- increased competition in the industry – particularly from a number of new entrants operating as 'budget' airlines
- ease of booking – people can book airfares to anywhere in the world online very conveniently and there are also a number of online price comparison sites which can be used to find the lowest possible airfares for a particular destination.

1 Explain one benefit of globalisation to a business like TBS. **(4 marks)**
2 Discuss the World Trade Organization's role in globalisation. **(8 marks)**
3 Discuss how lower transport costs might contribute to further globalisation. **(8 marks)**
4 Assess the likely impact of globalisation on an emerging economy such as Bangladesh. **(12 marks)**

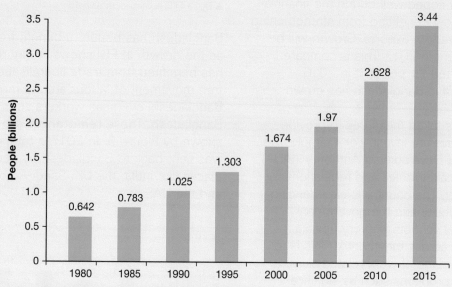

▲ Figure 6 Global air transport – passengers carried 1980–2015
Data from Air transport, passengers carried, The World Bank.

25 PROTECTIONISM

LEARNING OBJECTIVES

By the end of this chapter you should be able to understand:
- the reasons for protectionism
- tariffs
- import quotas
- other trade barriers: government legislation and domestic subsidies
- the impact on businesses of protectionism.

GETTING STARTED

Australia produces some of the cheapest sugar in the world. However, Australian sugar producers face difficulties when it comes to selling to many other countries because of trade barriers. For example, sugar farmers are heavily subsidised in the USA and there are also quotas and tariffs (import controls) imposed on imports. Farmers in Europe are also heavily supported and trade with the EU is challenging.

Australian Greg Beashel, chairman of the Global Sugar Alliance, suggested that Australia is one of the lowest-cost producers of sugar in the world. However, they cannot make more money because of the government subsidies used by some countries in the global market.

Why is it hard for Australian sugar producers to sell in overseas markets? Why do you think countries impose trade barriers like those in the case above? What might be the benefits of lifting all trade barriers?

WHAT IS PROTECTIONISM?

Many governments and businesses might argue that free trade could benefit the global economy. However, sometimes countries believe that it is in their interests to restrict trade. For example, governments may think it is necessary to protect their domestic producers from overseas competition, or they may give financial help to exporters. This approach is called **protectionism**. There are several reasons why some governments have opted to use **trade barriers**.

Preventing dumping: A government may use trade barriers if it feels that an overseas firm is **dumping** goods. Dumping is where foreign producers sell goods below cost in a domestic market. This is considered to be unfair competition for domestic producers. If very cheap imports are being sold below cost in a country, domestic producers will find it very difficult to survive in the long term. One example of dumping was reported in 2016 by the US authorities. The US Commerce Department said that truck and bus tyres were being dumped in the USA at below market prices. The department said the tyres were being dumped by Chinese manufacturers at margins ranging from 20.87 per cent to 22.57 per cent. It was claimed that 9 million tyres had entered the US market – worth about $1 billion.

Protecting employment: Trade barriers may be used if domestic industries need protection from overseas competitors to save jobs. Unemployment is undesirable (i.e. not wanted). A government may be criticised if jobs are being lost because of cheap imports.

Protecting infant industries: It is often argued that **infant industries** need protection. Infant industries are new industries that are not established yet. Many argue that infant industries should be protected from strong overseas rivals until they can grow, become established and exploit economies of scale. However, this approach may not be successful because governments have a poor record when identifying infant industries with potential.

To gain tariff revenue: A government can raise revenue if it imposes tariffs on imports. This money can be spent on government services to improve living standards. For example, in July 2018 the Indian government raised tariffs on 29 different products from the USA in response to the tariffs imposed by the USA on Indian steel and aluminium. The new tariffs were expected to raise an additional $240 million in revenue for the Indian government.

Preventing the entry of harmful or undesirable goods: A government might be justified in protectionism if overseas producers are trying to sell goods that are harmful or undesirable. For example, the EU banned all beef from cows who were given growth hormones. They thought it was not safe for humans to eat. **Administrative barriers** might be used to prevent this type of international trade.

Reduce current account deficits: A country might need to use trade barriers because it has a very large current account deficit on the balance of payments. A country has to pay its way in the world. If a current account deficit gets out of control, action may be needed. A government might try to reduce imports and increase exports at the same time to reduce the deficit. In 2018, the USA said it might impose some trade barriers on India to help reduce a US$24 billion trade deficit with the country. Steel, textiles, gems and jewellery, automobile components, food and leather could all be potential targets for the barriers.

Retaliation: One motive for imposing trade barriers is to retaliate (fight back) against dumping. If a foreign business dumps a large quantity of goods below cost, a government may impose heavy taxes on those goods when they come into the country. Retaliation may also occur if a country imposes trade barriers on exporters. That country may retaliate by imposing trade barriers on that nation's imports. This can result in a **trade war**. This may reduce trade between two nations and have a negative impact on the both of them. In 2018, the USA imposed tariffs of 25 per cent on imports of steel and 10 per cent on imports of aluminium (although Canada and Mexico did not have to follow this). China retaliated almost immediately, with US$3 billion of tariffs on US imports.

National security: Some governments have used trade barriers to protect national security. This argument recognises the threat to a nation if it becomes over-dependent on trade with other countries for its economic sustainability. For example, if a country relied heavily on imports for its energy supply, it might suffer considerably if that supply was restricted or broken. In 2018, the USA imposed tariffs on steel and aluminium using national security as a reason. According to White House National Trade Council Director, Peter Navarro, national security is the primary reason behind US steel and aluminium tariffs for Europe, Canada and Mexico.

ACTIVITY 1 SKILLS CRITICAL THINKING, ANALYSIS

CASE STUDY: RAINBOW CHICKEN LTD FOODS

In 2016, Rainbow Chicken Limited Foods (RCL Foods), a South African company, said it was cutting about 1200 jobs in Hammarsdale. It said that there may be more job cuts as the company struggled to compete with cheap imports from the USA, Brazil and EU countries.

Job cuts caused by cheap imports have occurred in the region before. Historically, the industrial area had a big textile industry. However, as a result of the new democracy, and the relaxation of trade barriers between South Africa and other countries, the Hammarsdale area lost more than 40 000 textile jobs, mainly because of cheaper imports from China.

These new job losses had a very negative impact on the Mpumalanga township in Hammarsdale. It left thousands of households without a livelihood. A spokesperson for RCL Foods said that tens of thousands of tonnes of surplus chicken arrive in the South African market monthly, and the EU is one of the main sources of this meat. It was also pointed out that smaller abattoirs and poultry farmers would have to close. This was because costs were rising, and they could not charge enough to recover their costs. Surplus chickens from overseas markets were driving down prices.

1 Explain what is meant by dumping.
2 Analyse the impact imports have had on employment in South Africa.
3 A government might respond to dumping by using protectionism. Explain one other reason why a government might use protectionism.

TARIFFS

Governments can use a number of trade barriers to restrict trade. One approach is to make imports more expensive. This will reduce demand for imports and increase demand for goods produced at home. Imports can be made more expensive if the government imposes a special tax on them. For example, if a government adds $50 to the price of an imported camera, demand should switch from foreign cameras to home-produced cameras. Taxes on imports are called tariffs or customs duties. In addition to reducing imports, tariffs also raise revenue for the government. However, the imposition of a tariff may only have limited impact if demand for the import is price inelastic. This is because demand will not fall in relation to the price increase. The fall in demand will be less in relation to the increase in price.

Globalisation is accelerating, and an increasing number of countries are allowing foreign business to enter their economies. But, there are many examples of countries imposing tariffs on imports. Here is a selection.

- In 2015, Ecuador imposed tariffs of 21 per cent on imports from Colombia and 7 per cent on imports from Peru. The main purpose of these tariffs was to reduce the negative impact of a stronger US dollar. Colombian and Peruvian officials claimed that the tariffs were a protectionist move and that they were against the principles of the Andean Community (CAN), a customs union formed by Bolivia, Ecuador, Colombia and Peru.
- In 2018, the Indian government raised tariffs on almost 50 product groups, from clocks and kites to television and auto components. The measures follow new duties imposed in December 2017 on electronic goods such as mobile phones and microwave ovens. The highest tariffs were those on fruit and vegetable juices – up to 50 per cent.
- The EU imposes tariffs on imports from a number of countries. Some examples of tariffs imposed on goods from Nigeria in 2018 included those on live animals (15 per cent), meat products (26 per cent), dairy produce (31 per cent) and sugars and sugar confectionery (28 per cent).

IMPORT QUOTAS

Another way of reducing imports is to place a physical limit on the amount allowed into the country. This is called an **import quota**. By restricting the quantity of imports, domestic producers face less of a threat. They will have more of the market for themselves. However, quotas will raise prices because fewer of the cheaper imports are available. An extreme form of quota is an **embargo**. This is where imports are completely banned from a country. Most embargos are imposed for political reasons.

In September 2017, Canada enforced an asset freeze and dealings ban on Venezuela. The sanctions are based upon a USA–Canada agreement in response to human rights violations in Venezuela (for example, the Venezuelan government arrested thousands of protestors in April 2017).

Placing physical limits on the flow of imports means that some demand for those goods will be met by domestic producers. This will help to protect or increase domestic employment. At the same time, quotas help to prevent domestic or imported goods from overpowering the market. This improves consumer choice. Some examples of countries using import quotas are given below.

- Japan has made use of use of quotas in recent years. For example, in 2018 it planned to double its quota for non-fat dried milk imports from 14 000 metric tons to 27 000 metric tons. Japan's consumers want to enjoy healthier products, such as yogurt, which use the dairy ingredient.
- In 2018, India imposed a quota of 5 million tonnes on pulses. This was to protect the prices of pulses in India, which had fallen so low that it threatened the survival of many businesses.
- Vietnam uses quotas to control the quantity of sugar coming into the country. In 2017, Vietnam's WTO import quota was 89 500 tonnes (44 000 tonnes of raw sugar and 45 500 of refined sugar).

ACTIVITY 2 | SKILLS | CRITICAL THINKING, PROBLEM SOLVING

CASE STUDY: MALAYSIAN TARIFFS

In 2018, Malaysia imposed anti-dumping tariffs on a range of steel imports from China, South Korea and Thailand. It was claimed that these countries were selling their products at unfairly low prices in Malaysia. Tariffs of 111.16 per cent were placed on cold-rolled stainless steel (CRSS) for five years by Malaysia's Ministry of International Trade and Industry (MITI). The ministry said that an investigation would be carried out over this time period to make the pricing policies used by businesses in these countries clearer.

Two companies based in Taiwan, Tang Eng Iron Works Co. Ltd and Walsin Lihwa Corp. are the largest suppliers of CRSS to Malaysia. They will have to pay 7.78 per cent and 2.79 per cent anti-dumping tariffs respectively. Other exporters in China will have to pay tariffs ranging between 2.68 per cent and 23.95 per cent. South Korean firms will pay between zero and 7.27 per cent. Finally, Thai exporters will have to pay the highest tariffs – ranging from 22.86 per cent to 111.61 per cent.

1 Explain the difference between a tariff and a quota.
2 An exporter based in Taiwan sells a MYR50 000 consignment of CRSS to a Malaysian importer. Calculate the amount the Malaysian importer would have to pay for this consignment including a tariff of 111.61 per cent.
3 Why has Malaysia imposed tariffs on imports of CRSS?

THINKING BIGGER

Although there are several motives for restricting trade, some barriers may not be effective. One problem is that countries may retaliate when barriers are imposed. For example, if one country imposes a tariff on another country's goods, that country may well impose tariffs of its own to block goods coming in. This behaviour could escalate into a trade war where trade between countries eventually stops.

Tariffs might also be ineffective if demand for imports is inelastic. For example, if tariffs increase the price of an import by 20 per cent, demand will only fall by 2 per cent if price elasticity of demand is −0.1. Therefore, the imposition of the tariff will only have a very limited impact.

Finally, when considering trade barriers, countries seem to favour the use of tariffs rather than import quotas. Typically, the tariff is seen as a more efficient way to place limits on the inflow of international goods without making things more difficult for producers who import goods. For many, tariffs represent the best approach to supporting the domestic economy. They provide consumers with a wider choice and promote genuine competition between businesses.

GOVERNMENT LEGISLATION

Some countries avoid the use of tariffs and quotas, but still manage to reduce the amount of imports coming in. They do this by insisting that imported goods meet strict regulations and specifications. In some cases, legislation can be passed to prevent entry. For example, a shipment of toys might be returned if they fail to meet strict safety regulations that are imposed by legislation.

Goods that fail to reach cultural or environmental standards may also face administrative barriers. For example, certain products cannot be imported into the EU. In the case of food products, the Food Standards Agency sometimes issues advice saying that particular food products should not be eaten. The most common examples of legal import bans aim to protect consumers from potentially harmful goods. For example, Australia has a wide range of import controls for some food and animal products. Many of these controls are to protect the environment, wildlife and domestic animals from infection.

DOMESTIC SUBSIDIES

Quotas and tariffs aim to reduce imports. Another approach to protectionism is to give a subsidy to domestic producers. This involves giving financial support, such as grants, interest-free loans or tax breaks, to exporters or domestic producers who face strong competition from imports. If subsidies are given to domestic producers, this will lower prices for consumers. This is because subsidies reduce production costs and increase supply. This forces equilibrium prices down. If subsidies are given to exporters, it becomes easier for home businesses to break into foreign markets.

Government subsidies to either domestic producers or exporters may break free trade agreements. However, there are many examples of governments using subsidies to influence the flow of exports and imports. A small sample is given below.

- To reduce how much a nation relies on rare-earth (i.e. rare metallic elements, such as minerals, that are found naturally) imports from China, the Japanese government promised $65 million in subsidies in 2012 to domestic businesses. The money was given to businesses that supported projects aiming to reduce the use of rare-earths.
- In the UK, a number of businesses received subsidies from the government to support the development of fossil-fuel projects overseas. For example, businesses involved in oil exploration projects with Petrobras® in Brazil were handed £528 million. Also, Rolls-Royce® was loaned £330 million to work with Russia's Gazprom® on gas-power initiatives.

IMPACT OF PROTECTIONISM ON BUSINESSES

It might be argued that, in the short term, the use of trade barriers to reduce competition from overseas will benefit domestic businesses. This is because competition is reduced. Sometimes that competition may be unfair – for example, if foreign businesses are dumping goods. If tariffs are imposed on imports, domestic producers can compete more easily in the market because the prices of imports are now higher. This will increase their sales volumes, revenues and profits. Some of the extra profits may be used to develop new products and/or improve production techniques. This will help to improve the efficiency and competitiveness of domestic businesses. In a similar way, the quantity of imports is reduced if quotas are imposed. This means that domestic producers can fill the gap in demand.

However, in the long term, businesses are likely to benefit more from free trade. Therefore, protectionist policies will harm businesses. Free trade encourages competition which can motivate domestic businesses to improve efficiency. If they become more efficient, they will win a bigger market share and become more prosperous. Free trade also leads to increased specialisation, where a country only produces goods that they are efficient at and in which they have a lower opportunity cost. Specialisation raises levels of output which means that businesses experience higher sales levels and more profit. There is general agreement among economists that countries, businesses and consumers will all benefit in the long term if trade barriers are eliminated.

One of the problems of protectionism is that it is likely to attract retaliation from overseas governments. If one country imposes tariffs on the goods from another, the other country is likely to impose tariffs in return. For example, in March 2018, the USA imposed tariffs of 25 per cent on imports of steel and 10 per cent on imports of aluminium. Consequently, in April 2018, Beijing imposed $3 billion tariffs on US imports. This included a 15 per cent duty on 120 American products including fruits, nuts and steel pipes and a 25 per cent tax on eight others, like recycled aluminium and some meat products. When countries start to behave in this way, a trade war might develop which will have a negative impact on businesses in both countries.

LINKS

You can demonstrate your synoptic skills by linking this topic to answers relating to global competitiveness, assessing overseas markets and assessing a country as a suitable production location. For example, businesses often choose a particular international location for a factory to avoid trade barriers. This is because if an overseas business produces goods in another country, the output is not classified as an import for that country. Links might be made to other chapters, such as SWOT analysis (Chapter 3), Impact of external influences (Chapter 4), International trade and business growth (Chapter 23) and Trading blocs (Chapter 26).

CHECKPOINT

1. State three reasons why a country might impose trade barriers.

2. Describe the impact of tariffs on domestic producers.

3. What is the aim of dumping by businesses?

4. How do import quotas reduce imports?

5. Which type of trade restriction will help to raise revenue for a government?

6. What is meant by administrative barriers to trade?

7. How might subsidies be used as a form of protectionism?

8. What might be the impact on a domestic meat processor if high tariffs are placed on imports of fresh meat?

SUBJECT VOCABULARY

administrative barriers rules and regulations (such as trading standards and strict specifications) that make it difficult for importers to enter an overseas market
dumping where an overseas firm sells large quantities of a product below cost in the domestic market
embargo a complete ban on international trade – usually for political reasons
import quota a physical limit on the quantity of imports allowed into a country
infant industries new industries that are not established yet
protectionism an approach used by a government to protect domestic producers
subsidy financial support given to a domestic producer to help compete with overseas firms
tax break a tax advantage designed to help businesses
trade barriers measures designed to restrict trade
trade war where two or more countries try to damage each other's international trade by imposing trade barriers

EXAM PRACTICE

CASE STUDY: US TARIFFS

SKILLS ▶ CRITICAL THINKING, ANALYSIS, INTERPRETATION, REASONING

During the 2016 US election campaign, Donald Trump said that he would 'put America first' in trade deals. He felt that a number of historic trade deals made on behalf of the USA were not good for the country. He said he would protect US jobs by imposing trade restrictions if elected. In January 2018, the US government announced that it would impose tariffs on solar panels and washing machines. Trump imposed a 20 per cent tariff on the first 1.2 million imported large residential washers, and a 50 per cent tariff on machines above that number. A 30 per cent tariff was to be imposed on imported solar cells and modules. Whirlpool®, the US business which campaigned for protection against rivals Samsung® and LG Electronics® after years of anti-dumping cases, was one of the businesses relieved at the action. Whirlpool's share price rose 1.8 per cent immediately after the announcement.

In March 2018, Trump imposed tariffs of 25 per cent and 10 per cent on imports of steel and aluminium respectively. This was in response to a government report which concluded that foreign shipments of metals were threatening national security interests. However, Trump said that tariffs on the EU, Mexico and Canada would be delayed until 1 June so that they could protect some countries from this. The EU said that the tariffs broke international trading rules and promised to retaliate if imposed. For example, they would impose restrictions on imports of Harley Davidson® motorbikes and certain drinks products. China also said it would retaliate with around $3 billion of tariffs. It promised to suspend tariff concessions on 120 US food products. Fresh and dried fruits, almonds and pistachios would be subject to an additional 15 per cent tariff and eight other items, including some frozen meat products, would be subject to a 25 per cent tariff.

The Trump administration says the ultimate goal of its tariffs on imports from China is to bring back manufacturing jobs in the USA. However, Jason Andringa, who runs an agricultural and construction equipment maker called Vermeer in Iowa, says they could have exactly the opposite effect. This is because international supply chains are complex, and the new tariffs could have damaging unintended consequences. For example, Vermeer imports cabs which are assembled in its Chinese plant and used for its drilling vehicle made in Iowa. This helps the company to keep costs down so that it can compete with international rivals. However, these components would be affected by the new tariffs. This would raise costs, reduce competitiveness and threaten jobs. 'We have 600 jobs at our Iowa factory as a result of being able to import products, and we have American production sold into global markets,' said Mr Andringa.

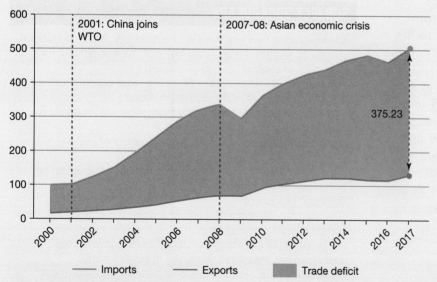

▲ Figure 1 US trade with China, 2000–17

Trade in Goods with China, 2017, https://www.census.gov/foreign-trade/balance/c5700.html, U.S Census Bureau

The US government targeted its tariffs on Chinese components and other intermediate goods. This was to avoid tariffs on consumer goods such as phones and clothes. However, if the production of these imported items were to be carried out in the USA, costs would rise and jobs would be ultimately lost. The pressures on US manufacturers caused by the proposed tariffs are made worse by the threatened retaliation by China against US exports, including soya beans and aircraft.

One of the dangers of imposing trade barriers is that a trade war can break out between countries. This is where one country retaliates to the imposition of trade barriers by taking action of its own. In the long term, trade between nations stops completely, negatively affecting both of them. Many economists would argue that no one can win a trade war. The only outcome will be lower income and employment for every country involved.

In May 2018, China and the USA said they would delay the imposition of many of the tariffs described above. The decision to 'hold' was taken after negotiations between the two nations took place. The USA tried to persuade China to buy around $200 billion more goods and services from the USA. This was to reduce the massive $335 billion trade imbalance between the two countries. Figure 1 shows the trade between China and the USA between 2000 and 2017.

1 Explain how a government might use legislation rather than tariffs to control imports. **(4 marks)**
2 Discuss one impact that US protectionism might have on the US trade balance. **(8 marks)**
3 Evaluate whether or not US tariffs will benefit US businesses, such as Whirlpool and Harley Davidson. **(20marks)**

Potentially most affected states (number of jobs, '000)

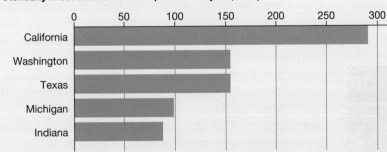

Largest industries potentially affected (number of jobs, '000)

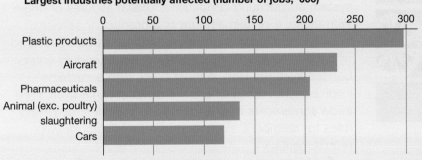

▲ Figure 2 Threat to jobs caused by China's tariffs

26 TRADING BLOCS

LEARNING OBJECTIVES

By the end of this chapter you should be able to understand:

- the expansion of trading blocs: the EU and the single market, ASEAN and NAFTA
- the impact of trading blocs on businesses.

GETTING STARTED

Ludvik Andel owns a large motor-parts firm in the Czech Republic that produces alloy wheels. His business has been operating for 20 years. He has always exported his goods and works quite closely with automobile companies based in Germany.

Between 2004 and 2014, 13 countries joined the European Union (EU), including the Czech Republic, Estonia, Poland and Croatia. By joining the EU, these countries were able to participate in the EU's single market. This meant they could enjoy completely free trade between member countries. By co-ordinating product regulations, trade between countries is easier. Additionally, because of the EU having a strong presence globally, trade to other countries outside the EU is also easier.

How do you think the Czech Republic joining the EU affected Ludvik's company? What do you think the benefits are for him now of doing business with companies in Germany? Do you think there are any benefits for the companies in Germany as well?

THE EXPANSION OF TRADING BLOCS

Just as people often prefer to shop close to where they live, businesses also prefer to trade within their geographical region. It is cheaper to transport goods shorter distances, so logistics costs will be lower. Also, being similar to and familiar with nearby markets makes regional trading preferences stronger. The World Trade Organization (WTO) has promoted global free trade, but governments are more likely to sign regional trade agreements (RTAs). There are now over 300 RTAs, involving countries all over the world.

RTAs are made between two or more countries within a geographical region. They are designed to facilitate trade by bringing down barriers. These arrangements include several varieties of agreement as the level of integration (i.e. joining two or more things together) increases.

RTAs create **trading blocs**. A trading bloc is a group of countries that have signed a regional trade agreement to reduce or eliminate tariffs, quotas and other protectionist barriers between themselves. These countries play a very big role in shaping the patterns of business expansion. Trading blocs can take a number of different forms.

Free trade areas: A free trade area (FTA) exists where member states remove all trade barriers, such as tariffs and import quotas, between themselves, but each member state keeps different barriers against non-member states. However, within FTAs, taxes and excise duties (i.e. a percentage tax on the manufacture, sale or use of locally produced goods) may be different. The North American Free Trade Agreement (NAFTA) is an example of an FTA. It is essentially an RTA, but with much greater depth and scope in its tariff reductions.

In order to protect the region, countries may use a system of allocating certificates, known as rules of origin. With these, a certain amount of a product or service must be certified (i.e. proven in writing) as being created within that region. Consequently, when a product enters Canada from the USA, it must come with a customs invoice that certifies where the product came from. Free trade agreements may also impose additional qualifying rules for members, such as minimum content or value requirements.

Customs unions: A customs union is similar to a free trade area, except that the members adopt a common set of barriers against non-members. This means only one set of rules regarding customs duties and rules of origin will apply when a product is shipped from outside the union to any of the member states. Moreover, the product can then be moved freely throughout the countries within the union.

An example of a customs union is CARICOM, or the 'Caribbean Community', which includes 15 nations and dependencies (colonies). It was created to co-ordinate economic policies and promote integration to encourage development. It is trying to copy the stages through which the EU developed.

Common markets: A **common market** is much more integrated than free trade arrangements or customs unions. This is because goods, labour and capital can move freely across the member states. Tariffs are usually removed, and non-tariff barriers eliminated, or at least reduced. Workers can relocate from one country to another without being stopped. All of this integration means that the members of a common market must work together on economic and political policies that affect the market. Examples of common markets include ASEAN and the Southern Common Market (Mercosur) in South America.

Single market: A common market is considered to be the starting point for the creation of a **single market**.

Here, most of the trade barriers between members have been removed. Common laws or policies work to make the movement of goods, services, labour and capital between countries as easy as the movement within each country. Borders, standards and taxes are made to be used together if possible, so as not to interfere with the commerce between members. The EU is a single market, but it is also an **economic and monetary union** (see below).

Economic unions: An **economic union** is a type of trade bloc involving both a customs union and a common market. Its aim is normally closer economic, political and cultural ties between member states. Where an economic union involves a common currency, it is called an economic and monetary union. The EU is one of the few fully operating economic and monetary unions, but there are ongoing attempts to create others, such as Mercosur and the Economic Community of West African States (ECOWAS). Table 1 shows the differences between the various forms of integration involved in the formation of trade blocs.

This chapter focuses on the impact of three main trading blocs – the EU, ASEAN and NAFTA – on businesses. Some information on each of these is shown in Table 2 and Figure 1.

Integration	Common external tariff	No internal trade barriers	Free movement of goods, labour and capital	Common currency
Free trade area		✓		
Customs union	✓	✓		
Common or single market	✓	✓	✓	
Economic and monetary union	✓	✓	✓	✓

▲ Table 1 Integration and trading blocs

Region	Group	Member countries	Date of formation	Type of agreement
Europe	EU	Austria, Belgium, Bulgaria, Croatia, Denmark, France, Finland, Germany, Greece, Ireland, Italy, Luxembourg, Netherlands, Portugal, Spain, Sweden, the UK, the Czech Republic, Poland, Romania, Hungary, Slovenia, Slovakia, Estonia, Lithuania, Latvia, Cyprus, Malta	1993	Economic union
South East Asia	ASEAN	Indonesia, Malaysia, the Philippines, Singapore, Thailand, Brunei, Cambodia, Laos, Myanmar, Vietnam	1967	Free trade area
North and Central America	NAFTA	Canada, Mexico, USA	1994	Free trade area

▲ Table 2 Trading bloc data for the EU, ASEAN and NAFTA, 2015*

*Students are not required to memorise all of the member countries

▲ Figure 1 A map showing the EU, NAFTA and ASEAN trading blocs

THE EUROPEAN UNION AND THE SINGLE MARKET

The European Union is the most powerful trading bloc in the world. Its first foundations date from 1993, and the trading bloc has expanded from the six founding members to 28 countries in 2018. The Single European Act of 1987 supported internal liberalisation, but barriers to cross-border trade continued to exist, and deeply rooted national cultures slowed the process.

After gradual integration and consolidation (i.e. joining into one), the EU emerged with the Maastricht Treaty in 1992 (also called the Treaty of the EU). This treaty marked the change from the European Economic Community (EEC) to the EU. Some of the key changes brought about by this treaty included:

- economic and monetary union
- a common foreign and security policy
- more power to the European Parliament
- a system for developing co-operation between members on justice and home affairs issues
- pressure on members to become a 'citizen of the Union'.

The EU developed a single market. The single market guarantees the free movement of people, goods, services and capital throughout the member states,

as well as making laws, policies and regulations work together in key areas. A monetary union was completed in 2002, further integrating most of the European economies.

Consequently, businesses operating in most European countries are able to move and compete equally in all other countries in the EU. They can operate to similar standards and processes and pay using a common currency (the euro). Once goods enter anywhere at an EU border, they cannot be subject to customs duties, taxes or import quotas as they are transported throughout the bloc. The same general principle applies to the movement of people and the purchasing of property (including shares in companies).

However, this process has not been straightforward and is not yet fully complete. In 2018, not all European countries belong to the union, including Iceland, Norway, Liechtenstein and Switzerland (see Figure 1). Nor did all of them sign up to a single currency: the UK, Denmark and Sweden decided not to join the euro and have kept their own separate currencies. Moreover, most European countries remain culturally distinct (i.e. different and separate), having separate languages, customs and religions. Integration into the EU does not appear to be changing this over time. Finally, in June 2016, the UK voted to leave the EU.

ACTIVITY 1   SKILLS   CRITICAL THINKING, REASONING

CASE STUDY: CROATIA AND THE EU

The EU traces its origins to the European Coal and Steel Community (ECSC) and the European Economic Community (EEC) that were formed just after the Second World War with the aim of developing economic co-operation. However, since then, the membership has grown from six countries to 28. The EU has common policies in a wide range of areas, in addition to trade agreements. The EU has developed common policies on issues such as climate, the environment, health, migration, justice and security. Since it was formed, the EU has delivered more than half a century of peace, and relative stability and prosperity. It has helped to drive economic growth in the region and raised living standards for its members.

The last country to join the EU was Croatia in 2013. Croatia first applied for membership of the EU in 2003. However, it had to gain approval over a 10-year period to ensure that it could meet the conditions of membership. After 12 months of membership, Croatia was still in **recession** and awaiting access to EU structural funds. The €1 billion per year promised by the EU would be used to help small and medium-sized enterprises (SMEs) develop new products.

A government official said that people in Croatia had low expectations regarding the benefits of joining the EU. However, exports to the EU rose by 15 per cent. Business owners reported that it was now much easier doing business with EU countries. One business owner, an olive oil producer in the north of the country, said that the EU was working in their favour (i.e. to their advantage). It was now easier to sell larger quantities to the EU, i.e. there was less paperwork. The owner also said that the outlook for the younger generation is much better. For example, they realise that investment and support for rural products is beginning to emerge.

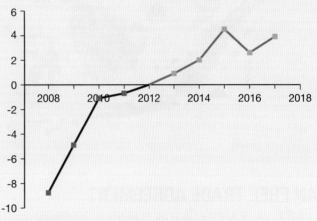

▲ Figure 2 Croatia current account balance 2008–18 (% GDP)

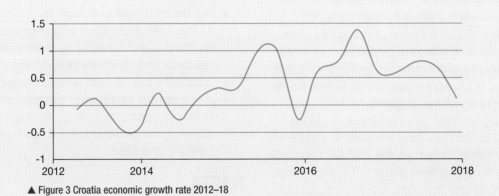

▲ Figure 3 Croatia economic growth rate 2012–18

1 What is the purpose of the EU?
2 How will businesses in Croatia benefit from EU membership?

3 What are the possible impacts of Croatia joining the EU?

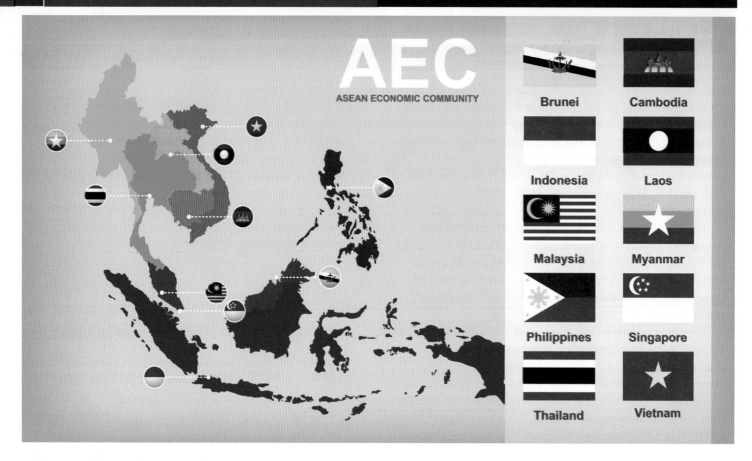

ASEAN FREE TRADE AGREEMENT

South East Asia is a very diverse region: economically, politically and culturally. According to its charter, the Association of South East Asian Nations (ASEAN) was established in 1967 to promote growth, social progress and sociocultural evolution among its members. It also aims to promote regional peace and stability. The associated free trade area covers a population of more than 600 million people and continues to expand. It has also completed free trade agreements with China, Korea, Japan, Australia, India and New Zealand.

ASEAN has an agreement covering trade in goods and one relating to customs, which are part of a drive to create a common market known as the ASEAN Economic Community (AEC). As a common market, it will promote the free flow of goods and services, investment, labour and capital. Areas of co-operation include:

- macroeconomic and financial policy
- labour policies, including education and professional qualifications
- infrastructure and communications
- e-commerce
- regional sourcing (businesses buying more resources from within the trade bloc).

The AEC is a very ambitious plan. In early 2015 some countries appeared ready to move to a fully integrated system, including Singapore, Thailand, the Philippines, Malaysia, Indonesia and Brunei. Others were a little

behind in eliminating tariffs, such as Cambodia, Vietnam, Laos and Myanmar.

In 2017, the Philippines took over the chairmanship of ASEAN and made a number of proposals. Examples of these included:

- the development of a trade facilitation index (a measure of the costs associated with overseas trading, such as checks and controls) to assess member countries' customs and clearance procedures
- establishing an e-commerce framework across the bloc
- a system for companies to self-certify (i.e. provide their own proof in writing) for their products' origin, allowing for preferential (i.e. giving an advantage) tariffs in the bloc.

NAFTA

The North American Free Trade Agreement (NAFTA) – see Figure 1 – dates back to 1994 and pulls together Canada, Mexico and the USA in a free trade zone. The agreement covers trade and investment, labour, financial dealings and intellectual property, including common environmental issues. Members agree to eliminate tariffs on most manufactured goods and to treat investors from the other two countries as if they were domestic investors.

However, the members do not share a common external trade policy, nor do they have any provision for co-ordinating exchange rates. This is normal with a free trade agreement. So, the USA, Mexico and Canada still negotiate (i.e. to try to reach an agreement by discussion) independently with non-NAFTA countries, organisations and trading blocs over the rules that govern their trading relationships.

As a free trade area, NAFTA does not aspire to the level of integration of the EU. Yet, its operation raises concerns over sovereignty. The USA, with a GDP ten times that of the other members, is clearly the dominant power, raising issues of dependency for Canada and Mexico. To address this, the members signed up to a dispute resolution system designed to balance out the rights and obligations of each member. However, this system has been criticised for being weakly enforced.

NAFTA has been beneficial to US and Canadian consumers through the lowering of prices for agricultural products. Sellers in each country have benefited from the larger and more diverse markets on offer, and producers from the lower-cost locations closer to home.

However, some believe that the agreement has been bad for Mexico, especially its farmers. Since joining NAFTA, overall economic growth has not increased significantly, real wages (i.e. wages in relation to the cost of things) have declined and unemployment has increased. Although this economic weakness may be due to many factors beyond NAFTA's influence, the arrival of heavily subsidised corn from the USA clearly caused problems for Mexican farmers. When cheap corn first entered the market, Mexico's consumers were pleased. They could buy cheaper flour for their staple food, tortillas. However, the competition forced many poor, small farms out of business. The US government then began to encourage the manufacturing of ethanol, a 'green' fuel, and corn was used for this instead. The supplies of corn to Mexico began to stop, but the farms that used to grow it no longer existed. There was nothing to fill the resulting shortage. Consequently, the price of corn rose, and Mexican consumers suffered.

FACTORS TO CONSIDER IN TRADING BLOCS

There are four key factors to consider in trading blocs.

Where to produce: A company may be able to move to a neighbouring country where the costs of land, labour or capital are most favourable (i.e. give an advantage) to it. They can then ship goods and services to other members.

Where to sell: Companies may view a trading bloc as one big market for their goods and services. This can present opportunities, but also threats. For example, with the creation of NAFTA, many Mexican retailers were driven out of business by big American and Canadian firms.

How to enter a market: The market entry strategy may be adapted according to the opportunities presented by the free trade areas or common market. It can range from new investments through to joint ventures and mergers.

Business strategy: A business may not have been able to export to a neighbouring country because of the existence of trade barriers. Once these barriers are negotiated away as part of a trade agreement, they may be able to do so. For example, once fully operating, the AEC should encourage firms from Vietnam to increase trade with Malaysia.

IMPACT OF TRADING BLOCS ON BUSINESSES

Trading blocs are likely to create both opportunities and drawbacks for businesses.

Opportunities for businesses: Businesses may be able to benefit in a number of ways. There might be certain opportunities that result from operating within a trading bloc.

- Freeing regional trade may allow individual members to specialise in the areas their country already has advantages in.
- The market for firms' goods and services should increase. Trading blocs often do more than reduce tariffs – they may also improve capital flows, make regulations more efficient and improve competition. They may actually improve the market for non-members as well, even if not by as much as for members.
- As the volume of trade increases within the region, producers are able to benefit from economies of scale. This leads to lower costs for them and usually lower prices for consumers.
- Resources may be easier to source and labour easier to recruit, while production and transport costs may continue to fall.
- As trade increases, it may result in greater competition. Therefore, there will be more efficiency in the market.
- Trading blocs may also provide a counterbalance (i.e. to have an equal but opposite effect) against globalisation, protecting industries in an area against predatory (i.e. taking advantage of weaker people or organisations) competitors from more economically powerful regions. Moreover, being part of an RTA may give regions the power to negotiate for better deals in the global market.

Therefore, for large, well-placed firms, trading blocs offer new potential markets including the prospect of higher efficiency and productivity through larger factories, lower overheads, and faster and possibly less costly logistics. For example, from a firm's point of view, NAFTA allows it to conduct business in the USA, Mexico and Canada, as long as it meets certain rules relating to content, labour standards, safety requirements and environmental regulation. Prior to NAFTA's formation, many US and Canadian producers looked to South East Asia or China for lower-cost production sites for building a new factory. With the free trade agreement, Mexico's lower-cost labour force and proximity made it a practical alternative. Firms such as IBM® and Gap® moved their production to Mexico, where manufacturing costs were competitive and delivery faster.

Drawbacks for businesses: On the other hand, existing businesses within a trading bloc, or those seeking to move to a country within the trading bloc, could face drawbacks and problems.

- Trading blocs may actually harm overall trade. This is because countries outside the region may be better placed to specialise or develop a competitive advantage in a product or service, and yet they are closed out of the market. Thus, blocs may lead to trade diversion (i.e. being moved somewhere else) rather than trade creation. For example, Indonesia may produce a crop more cheaply than countries in the EU. However, the EU's agricultural subsidies and abolition of tariffs may make the price of a crop produced in Europe artificially low.

- Inefficient producers may be protected from competition. This may divert trade away from more efficient producers and potentially harm consumers. For example, less efficient producers within regions may lobby for protection, so that they do not have to reform and compete.

- The overall benefits may turn out to be small if an agreement limits the goods/services that are traded.

- Locally, some of the benefits may be distributed unequally, causing political and social tensions within the region.

- Globally, the benefits accrued inside the trading bloc may lead to tensions with other regions, leading to possible retaliation. This would cause further harm to global trade.

- Members of RTAs, especially those in free trade agreements, may have different levels of economic power. This can cause long-term economic and political imbalance and potential conflict.

- For smaller organisations, opening up competition and a larger market may result in more competitors. This can put pressure on their pricing strategies, since larger producers may be able to produce at a lower cost and in a better location. Small firms often fear the consolidation of a trading bloc and the competitive changes in the marketplace that it brings.

EXAM HINT

Although you should be aware of the three main trading blocs (the EU, ASEAN and NAFTA), a detailed in-depth knowledge of each is not required. However, you could be asked to explain and assess the opportunities and problems for (a) a business located within a trading bloc member country or (b) a business that aims to sell into a trading bloc from a country that is not a member. The Eurasian Economic Union, featured in 'Thinking bigger', suggests certain benefits (free movement, co-ordinated policy and improved ties and relations), but also possible drawbacks (trade diversion from other countries) for businesses operating in the bloc.

ACTIVITY 2   SKILLS   REASONING, CREATIVITY

CASE STUDY: BWD ENTERTAINMENT

BWD Entertainment is a German-based media company. Originally a magazine company, it has diversified into radio and trade newspapers. It also runs a book publishing business. In the 2000s, it acquired stakes in magazine publishing companies in Spain, the Netherlands and Italy, and owns radio companies in both Germany and France.

The directors of the company recently completed a strategic review and decided to target Croatia as an entrant to the EU in 2013. The directors felt the Croatian economy was likely to grow at a faster rate than the EU average over the next 10–20 years. This should give scope for increasing sales over time. Three specific strategies were identified:

- buy an established Croatian magazine company, then use its editorial expertise and distribution system to push a number of new magazines based on ones which are already popular in Germany, Spain and Italy

- buy a Croatian magazine company which already has strong market share. By giving new finance, BWD would allow the existing Croatian management greater opportunities to launch new magazines aimed at the local market

- set up a new company, recruiting editors and other workers from established Croatian magazine companies, but also putting in staff from existing BWD operations in other European countries. This would probably be the highest-risk strategy.

1 Explain why there might be greater scope for marketing magazines in Croatia than in Germany or Italy over the next 10 years.

2 By considering the possible advantages and disadvantages of each of the three strategic options, discuss which is likely to be the most successful for BWD. In your answer, identify what other information would be needed to make an informed choice.

THINKING BIGGER

On 1 January 2015 a new trading bloc emerged. Russia, Belarus and Kazakhstan signed a treaty in 2014, formally creating the Eurasian Economic Union. Armenia and Kyrgyzstan followed, officially becoming part of the bloc in early 2015.

Whether this will last is a key question, especially as a trade war seemed to emerge in April 2015 between Russia and Kazakhstan. Political experts have stated that the signing of the treaty was part of a continuing effort by the Russian President Vladimir Putin to create an independent economic force led by Russia.

The creation of the bloc, which has a combined economy of $2.7 trillion and vast energy resources, deepens ties among the countries which began with the creation of a customs union in 2010. It guarantees the free movement of goods, services, capital and workforce. It will result in a co-ordinated policy for key economic sectors. The trading bloc was created as the basis of what will become the Eurasian Union and will eventually include more former Soviet states.

LINKS

Trading blocs can have a great effect on the selling and trade patterns of businesses that sell within countries that are members, and also on businesses selling from a country that is not a member. You could use this to consider why businesses have chosen to relocate operations globally (Chapter 29) or enter into mergers (Chapter 30) and the effect on globalisation (Chapter 24). You could also consider how selling into countries that are part of a trading bloc could affect a business's view of that country as a market (Chapter 28).

CHECKPOINT

1 Name three trading blocs.

2 Briefly explain why there has been an expansion in trading blocs.

3 What impact do trading blocs have on business?

4 What are the drawbacks of trading blocs on business?

5 What impact might EU enlargement have on (a) a farmer in Spain (b) a shoe manufacturer in Italy?

6 How might a Swedish manufacturer be at a competitive disadvantage because Sweden does not use the single currency?

SUBJECT VOCABULARY

common market a market where goods, labour and capital can move freely across the member states; tariffs are generally removed and non-tariff barriers eliminated, or at least reduced
customs union a union where member states remove all trade barriers between themselves and members adopt a common set of barriers against non-members
economic and monetary union an economic union that uses a common currency
economic union a type of trading bloc involving both a customs union and a common market
free trade area (FTA) a region where member states remove all trade barriers between themselves, but each member state nevertheless keeps different barriers against non-member states
recession a less severe form of economic depression
single market a market where most trade barriers between members have been removed and common laws or policies aim to make the movement of goods and services, labour and capital between countries as easy as the movement within each country
trading bloc a group of countries that has signed a regional trade agreement to reduce or eliminate tariffs, quotas and other protectionist barriers between themselves

EXAM PRACTICE

CASE STUDY: ASEAN AND BEMYGUEST®

SKILLS CRITICAL THINKING, ANALYSIS, INTERPRETATION, REASONING

Despite rising concerns about free trade and financial conditions in the ASEAN region, economic growth has been robust. It was estimated that GDP rose by 5.2 per cent (on an annual basis) in the second quarter of 2018. Strong labour markets in the region's countries and large infrastructure projects in key economies such as Indonesia and the Philippines have led to growth. In the future, there are concerns that growth might be hindered by rising oil prices, a possible trade war between the USA and China and tighter financial conditions.

In 2016, Mr S. Iswaran, the Minister for Trade and Industry in Singapore, said that ASEAN would benefit from increased digital connectivity in the future. ASEAN is already the fastest growing region in the world in terms of Internet adoption, with 3.8 million new users per month gaining access to the Internet. He said that the region would prosper if all countries in the region supported digital connectivity and businesses kept pace with technological developments in digitalisation. He suggested that the digital economy in ASEAN could grow to US$200 billion by 2025 with around US$88 billion going to e-commerce. He also said that SMEs (small to medium-sized enterprises) would benefit as they gained access to a larger consumer market.

One company that is already benefiting from increasing digitalisation is Singapore-based BeMyGuest®. This company is the leading provider of tours and travel activities in Asia. It is a fast-growing business and has won a number of industry awards such as the Best Business Innovation at the 2016 Singapore Tourism Awards and the Best Strategic Partner for Internationalisation in 2017. BeMyGuest was also named one of the Top 5 in the Travel category of Fast Company's World's Most Innovative Companies 2016 alongside Uber® and Airbnb®. The company generates much of its revenue by taking a commission (a percentage of the fee) when users book the activities listed on the site. BeMyGuest provides access to thousands of small to medium-sized travel businesses in Asia. It verifies (i.e. shows that they are genuine) them and lists their products on the bemyguest.com platform. The online platform helps travellers to discover and book quality experiences in Asia.

In 2017, the company raised SG$11.5 million to help accelerate business growth. At the same time, it also launched BeMyGuest Labs. This is a business-to-business (B2B) platform where suppliers and resellers use BeMyGuest's distribution network through a range of travel technology solutions, such as B2B agent's marketplace, e-tickets and revenue management systems.

	Population (million)	GDP per capita (US$)
Brunei	0.4	26958
Cambodia	16	1269*
Indonesia	262	3878
Laos	6.7	2400*
Malaysia	32.1	9896
Myanmar	52.6	1264
Philippines	105	2978
Singapore	5.6	57495
Thailand	69.1	6591
Vietnam	93.6	2355

*2016 figures

▲ Table 3 Population and GDP per capita for each ASEAN member, 2017

1 Calculate the total GDP for Vietnam and the Philippines to determine which has the highest. **(4 marks)**
2 Discuss the possible benefits to BeMyGuest of a more integrated digital economy in the ASEAN region. **(8 marks)**
3 Assess the impact on companies like BeMyGuest of operating within the ASEAN trading bloc. **(12 marks)**

GLOBAL MARKETS AND BUSINESS EXPANSION

This section looks at how businesses might cope with operating in global markets. It starts by exploring the conditions that prompt trade. For example, it explains the impact of push and pull factors on businesses and how offshoring and outsourcing might be used to improve competitiveness. It also investigates the factors that might be considered when a business assesses a country as a market such as disposable income, ease of doing business, infrastructure, exchange rates and political stability. This includes looking at how Porter's Five Forces might be used to assess a market. The section covers how a business might assess a country as a potential production location by considering factors such as costs, the skills and availability of labour, infrastructure and government incentives. The reasons for global mergers, takeovers and joint ventures are also explained. The section concludes with a look at how uncertainty in global markets, such as movements in exchange rates and skills shortages, might impact on expansion.

27 CONDITIONS THAT PROMPT TRADE

LEARNING OBJECTIVES

By the end of this chapter you should be able understand:

- push factors: saturated markets and competition
- pull factors: increased sales and profitability, risk spreading and economies of scale
- the cost competitiveness of offshoring and outsourcing
- extending the product life cycle.

GETTING STARTED

Spain is the largest producer of olive oil in the world. The nation has more than 300 million olive trees, covering an area of 500 million acres. One producer, Carvajal Oils, is based in Andalusia, near the town of Olvera. It began as a small family business in 1972. The Carvajal family owned a plot of land and produced oil from the olive trees growing there. They supplied shops, hotels and restaurants in local villages such as El Gastor, Algodonales, Zahara and Montecorto.

For 30 years the family made a fairly comfortable living, but in 2002 the two Carvajal brothers decided to expand the business. They thought the best way to do this was to start exporting because in Spain the market was fairly saturated (i.e. there was more of the product than there were buyers for it). They decided to specialise in the processing of extra virgin olive oil and supply France and the UK. They invested in some modern processing machinery and bought in olives from a wider area – including Cordoba and Jean.

The Carvajal brand sold well in these new markets. Health advice, which recognised the benefits of eating olive oil instead of butter and other types of fat, also assisted sales. Profits rose for a few years but then flattened as an increasing number of businesses began to specialise in extra virgin olive oil. Competitive pressure prompted Carvajal Oils to develop new products and find new markets. The business began developing a range of flavoured olive oils (such as chilli or rosemary, for example) and started to market their products in other countries, such as Sweden, Norway and Finland. These new products were very popular in foreign markets.

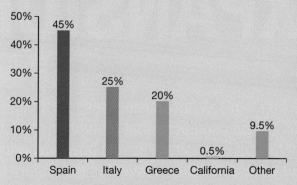

▲ Figure 1 World olive oil production by country

Why did Carvajal Oils start to export their goods? Outline two benefits of selling goods abroad. What might be the risks to a business like Carvajal Oils of exporting?

INTRODUCTION TO THE CONDITIONS THAT PROMPT TRADE

International trade is vital for many economies around the world. It helps to raise living standards and results in higher levels of output, income and employment. However, there are some specific reasons why countries trade with each other.

- **Obtaining goods that cannot be produced domestically.** Many countries are unable to produce certain goods. This is because they lack the natural resources that enable such production. For example, Iceland cannot produce certain types of food because it does not have the right climate and France cannot produce gold or diamonds because the country does not have any deposits. Many countries are prompted to trade in order to obtain goods that cannot be produced domestically.

- **Obtaining goods that can be bought more cheaply from overseas.** Some countries can produce certain goods more efficiently than others. This may be because they have cheaper or more abundant resources or because they have become experts through specialisation. For example, China can produce manufactured goods more cheaply than many countries because it has a cheap labour force. It makes economic sense to buy goods from other countries if they are cheaper.
- **Excess supplies.** Some countries have surplus commodities. In some cases, countries have so much of a resource that they could never use it all themselves. For example, the UAE has huge reserves of oil. Much of the oil produced is sold abroad and the UAE uses just a fraction of its oil output each year; 40 per cent of its exports are oil and gas.

There are many conditions that encourage trade. On one level, there are economic factors, such as the impact of being a member of the European Union. But there are also creative and entrepreneurial ambitions to seek new markets that dominate the desire for trade. These are enabled by a skilled workforce that contributes by providing high-quality goods and services which are in demand.

Although the politics and economics of free trade will never be simple, trade has continued to expand and many consider that we have a 'global consumer culture' stretching across the world. Regardless, businesses see expanding into international markets as an opportunity to find new resources and markets for their goods, as well as producing their goods and services at a lower cost. This may make more money or extend the life of their products or services.

Firms may be motivated to go abroad for many reasons. One way this can be categorised is to divide them into 'push' factors (where firms are seeking opportunities) or 'pull' factors, where a market overseas holds a particular attraction for a business.

PUSH FACTORS

Push factors are negative factors in the existing market that encourage an organisation to seek international opportunities. They force a business to seek overseas markets in which to sell its products. A firm may be attempting to overcome weaknesses in its existing markets, or it may be looking to lower its costs.

Push factors include saturated markets and competition. Competition may drive prices down due to lowered costs, or there may be declining demand for a product, due to changes in tastes, availability of substitutes or new technologies.

Saturated market: A saturated market is one where most of the customers who would buy a particular product already have it, so there is limited remaining opportunity for growth in sales. For example, a cycle manufacturer may have limited opportunities to sell in countries where cycling is very popular. However, it may be able to find a new market in a country where the sport is only just becoming popular. Most people in the USA own mobile phones with the same basic functions. In order to increase sales, the firms in this saturated market could make their products different to what is already on the home market. Alternatively, they could look elsewhere to sell their product in a market where there is still a demand for it.

Competition: A rise in competitors or a high level of competition in the domestic market may force a business to sell abroad. Competitors could be selling similar products at a lower price or a higher quality. This may make selling the original product difficult or unprofitable. Taking the same example as above, the market for mobile phones is highly competitive: Apple, Samsung, Nokia®, HTC®, Blackberry® and Sony® are just a few of the many providers. Where all of the brands are able to compete in a market, the businesses will be forced to make their products different or move to a market where the competition is less fierce for reasons of price, quality or product age.

Faced with competition in its domestic market, a business may be forced to look at markets abroad. This may involve changing the product to meet the tastes of those consumers. For example, in 'Getting started', the competitive pressure prompted Carvajal Oils to find new markets in Sweden, Norway and Finland. The business also developed a new range of products by adding chilli and rosemary flavours to olive oil. These new products appealed to customers in foreign markets.

ACTIVITY 1   SKILLS   CRITICAL THINKING

CASE STUDY: PREMIUM FRESH TASMANIA

The Australian state of Tasmania saw its exports of goods rise by 33 per cent in 2017. The total value of exports rose from AUS$2.583 billion to AUS$3.436 billion. Tasmania's most popular exports include non-ferrous metals, fresh produce, tourism and education. The majority of sales were in Asian markets – government figures showed that 13 of Tasmania's 14 biggest overseas export markets were in Asia.

One Tasmanian business that has benefited from rising exports is Premium Fresh Tasmania. The privately owned business has grown from a small farming enterprise to one of the largest growing, washing, grading and packing operations in the country. Premium Fresh Tasmania owns a 10000-square-metre factory and uses the latest technology to pack over 30000 tonnes of carrots, onions, swedes, turnips, shallots, leeks and broccoli every year.

Australia produces most of its own food and it exports an increasing amount. Premium Fresh Tasmania takes advantage of Australia's counter-seasonality (when it is summer in Australia, it is winter in Europe) to export produce to Europe, the Middle East and Asia. This means that during the Australian harvesting season, when there is an abundance of fresh produce, Premium Fresh Tasmania sells to countries where there is less availability of fresh produce due to the climate.

In 2016–17, Premium Fresh Tasmania increased export sales by nearly 20 per cent. It exported asparagus to Japan for the first time, making it the only Australian asparagus available in the Japanese market in December and January. Premium Fresh Tasmania is committed to exporting and, as a result, won an Australian regional export award in 2017. The award recognised the business's commitment to its export activities and to customers in the provision of value-added goods and services. Diversification of its product range to take advantage of seasonality has also been an advantageous strategy.

1 Explain two reasons why nations trade.
2 How important are push factors in Premium Fresh Tasmania's decision to increase exports?

PULL FACTORS

Pull factors entice firms into new markets. They are the opportunities that businesses can take advantage of when selling into overseas markets. There are many pull factors, and those that are the most important to a firm

depend upon the nature of the business and the current state of its home market. However, the following lists many common attractions:

- new or bigger markets
- lower-cost or more secure resources, such as minerals, land or labour
- lower cost of transportation
- technological expertise, including research facilities
- managerial or financial expertise
- organisational skills
- assets, such as brands, patents or other intellectual property.

A firm may be enticed by these factors since they may help it to achieve economies of scale or to spread its **risks**.

Increased sales and profitability: Many businesses want to grow by selling more to existing and new customers. Firms can usually grow sales by exploiting overseas markets. An increasing number of businesses have become multinational corporations. They sell goods and services to many countries all over the world. This allows them to increase sales revenue and raise profits. Many public limited companies are under pressure from their institutional owners (pension funds, insurance companies and investment trusts, for example) to grow and deliver higher profits and higher dividends. This means they are looking to find new markets.

In some of the emerging economies there are new markets that haven't been developed yet. Some of these are attractive to a wide range of businesses. For example, US companies Walmart and Starbucks have been developing their interests in the Indian market. Walmart India owns and operates 21 B2B modern wholesale stores under the brand name of 'Best Price'. The coffee chain Starbucks has 28000 coffee shops in 75 different countries. However, it hopes to make India, where it has over 100 shops, one of its top 5 global markets.

Economies of scale: Economies of scale occur where increasing the scale of production leads to a lower cost per unit of output. Put simply, increasing size or speed increases efficiency and lowers costs. If a factory were to increase its size, average costs would fall as output rises. The firm could buy supplies in large amounts, usually at a discount. It could use more expensive technology to run its processes with machines and train its workers in increasingly specialist tasks. However, bigger is not always better. Above a certain size, unit costs can rise and resources can be spread too thinly. This is called diseconomies of scale.

Risk spreading: Chapter 21 discussed risk and how to reduce it in the context of contingency planning. One way of defining risk is the probability of a bad event happening multiplied by its negative impact. This can range across financial, strategic, operational and hazard-related risks. Where they can be recognised and quantified, risks can usually be insured against. Where they cannot, they pose a threat to a firm's strategy and need to be addressed.

By expanding into other countries and markets, a firm may be able to limit the various risks that it faces. For example, over-dependence upon one market may leave a firm vulnerable in the short term if that market faces an economic challenge, such as a recession, where growth slows and people lose their jobs. Or, in the long term, a region characterised by a rapidly ageing population may not be a worthwhile place for a business that sells mainly to the under-30s. Expanding abroad may help a firm to minimise the impact of such risks upon its overall profitability.

IMPROVING COST COMPETITIVENESS BY OFFSHORING AND OUTSOURCING

Offshoring: Offshoring involves moving manufacturing or service industries to a location with lower costs. A classic example is the relocation in the 1980s of many call centres from the UK to India, where well-educated workers speaking good English were employed on a lower wage and for longer hours than British workers. Therefore, a firm may offshore in order to:

- reduce costs
- hire workers with particular skills.

Many people disagree with moving jobs to other countries, especially where a lot of jobs are lost in the home country. This could potentially damage a firm's reputation. Other risks may also emerge, such as complications caused by language or cultural differences. There may be political, economic, technological or intellectual property (i.e. an idea that is protected from being used by someone else by the law) risks associated with the host country.

Some firms that are focused on reducing costs don't realise that offshoring can actually fail. The process may increase management costs, reduce efficiency or quality, expose firms to corruption and the loss of intellectual property. It could be too expensive to continue.

Outsourcing: Outsourcing involves moving an entire business function or project to a specialist external provider. For example, many large firms have outsourced their information technology and payroll functions. Others have moved human resources, accounting, supply and logistics, and transportation. In general, a firm might outsource for similar reasons to offshoring:

- to reduce costs
- in order to specialise areas of the business
- to focus on the core competences of the business rather than the support functions

- in order to improve speed, flexibility or quality
- to comply with rules or regulations.

Moving jobs to other organisations does have risks, but fewer people disagree with this than with offshoring. A firm can become vulnerable through loss of expertise or knowledge if it relies too much on others. In addition, others' interests may not remain in agreement, so moving jobs isn't as efficient as expected. Poor communication issues can cause problems and be expensive to the business.

Labour productivity: Firms often want to move operations to where labour is cheap. However, the amount that workers can produce in relation to their cost is more important. This is known as labour productivity (see Chapter 19). It is defined as the amount of goods and services produced by one hour of labour. Many factors may affect the productivity of a worker. These include skills and qualifications, working conditions and technological support, as well as rules and regulations.

ACTIVITY 2 **SKILLS** CRITICAL THINKING, PROBLEM SOLVING

CASE STUDY: OFFSHORING IN CHARLOTTE, USA

Charlotte is a major city and commercial centre in North Carolina, USA. In 2017, a number of businesses in the city announced plans to move jobs to new overseas locations. Such offshoring has been used by US businesses for many years and is showing no sign of slowing down, especially in businesses that are under pressure to increase profits.

In 2017, the following moves were announced.

- A home improvement chain called Lowe's® (based in Mooresville, North Carolina) removed 125 tech workers in June. Most of these jobs were moved to Bangalore, in India. People who work in IT are particularly vulnerable to offshoring. It has been suggested that a computer programmer in Charlotte would cost between $60 000 and $80 000 a year, while in India the cost might be only $60 a month.
- A bank called Wells Fargo® (based in San Francisco) said it was looking at moving some work offshore. However, the bank did not say how many jobs would be affected or where they would be sent.
- Retailer Ralph Lauren® cut 107 jobs in Kernersville, Greensboro and High Point. The company did not say whether the IT jobs were moved offshore, but it did say that some of the eliminated jobs were outsourced to another business with offices all over the world, including in India.

- The Bank of America has advertised for more than 140 jobs in Indian cities like Mumbai, Hyderabad and Gurugram. The vacant jobs range from software engineer to human resources consultant.

These companies say that offshoring is a way to cut costs, stay competitive and meet customers' needs.

Businesses are moving work overseas in different ways. For example, when Lowe's moves IT work to its offices in Bangalore, the workers there are still Lowe's employees. In other cases, companies move the work done by their own employees to different vendors overseas, who take over IT and other functions.

1 Calculate the amount that Lowe's can potentially save by offshoring 125 IT jobs to India (assume that IT workers cost $80 000 p.a. in the USA).
2 What is the difference between outsourcing and offshoring?
3 What might be the possible impact on companies like those described above in the case of continual offshoring and outsourcing?

EXTENDING THE PRODUCT LIFE CYCLE

The concept of the product life cycle was developed in the 1960s to describe the stages in the life of a product, as explained in Chapter 9 in Student Book 1.

These stages again in brief are as follows:
- **Development.** The product is researched and designed, and a decision made about whether to launch the product.
- **Introduction.** From the development of an original idea to the launch of the product on the market.
- **Growth.** When the product takes off and sales increase.
- **Maturity.** When sales are near their highest but are slowing down.
- **Decline.** When sales begin to fall.

When a product has reached the decline stage, with falling sales, market saturation and a decline in profits, a firm has to decide what to do. They can get that product out of the market altogether or attempt to extend the product life cycle. The firm could choose to move production to new markets in order to reduce costs. This allows the firm to increase margins. Or it could explore selling to new markets. A product that is in a mature stage in one market may be at an introductory stage elsewhere. Therefore, a firm can sell a product in the new market and extend its life cycle.

For example, the Apple iPod® was launched in 2001 and went through many changes to remain competitive, with new technologies, music streaming, fashion and changing tastes. By 2009 sales had begun to decline. By outsourcing production, and adding new uses and variations, Apple extended the life cycle of the iPod (although in 2013 it ceased introducing new models).

When extending the product life cycle into international markets, a firm has to make a decision as to whether to change the product in order to improve it for the new markets, or standardise the product for global use. Also, the life cycles of products can vary a lot. For example, fashion items or new technologies may have very short life cycles, while luxury goods and precision watches may have very long ones.

THINKING BIGGER

The product life cycle has been used by firms as an instrument of competitive power and it remains at the centre of the marketing strategy of many firms as they maximise product lines along the commonly shaped product life cycle curves such as those shown in figures 2, 3 and 4 in Student Book 1, Chapter 9.

Why, then, do some products 'defeat' the curve? Business writers talk about repositioning products so that they are 'rescued'. They add new features, sell in multiple markets and can convince customers that a new offering is different.

It is useful to think about why a brand such as KitKat® (introduced by Rowntree's in York, UK in 1911 and relaunched in 1935) is still the number one selling chocolate bar in many countries, including Japan. Also, think about *The Simpsons* (the animated show created by Matt Groening as a brand that is unique in TV history). The 27th season has started production. *The Simpsons'* positioning has had an important impact on its progress along the life cycle. Most live-action sitcoms have a compressed life cycle, in part because actors age. *Friends* exited after a 10-year run when its stars, originally cast as 20-somethings, started approaching 40. But cartoon characters are ageless (Bart Simpson has been 10 years old for a decade and a half). Just as Bugs Bunny exploited the cartoon medium to stay fresh for 65 years, *The Simpsons* has allowed the series to pause on the life cycle curve at a point at which live-action sitcoms usually head into decline. *The Simpsons* is just as much a brand as KitKat. Why do they last?

You could use this information in a variety of ways. Obviously, it can be used if answering questions on product life cycles and selling in multiple markets. It is also useful to think through why some products last for so long and whether others can adopt their techniques.

LINKS

As we have mentioned in this chapter, extending the product life cycle of a business can be one factor that prompts a business to trade. Chapter 9 in Student Book 1 explains the stages of a product life cycle, and information there can be used to help answer questions relating to this as an appropriate reason for trade. Other factors that might be important are push factors such as competition (this book, Chapter 31) and pull factors such as economies of scale (this book, Chapter 5).

CHECKPOINT

1 Outline the factors that can prompt trade.

2 What are push factors?

3 How does a market become saturated?

4 What impact might competition in domestic markets have on business strategy?

5 How do pull factors entice businesses into a market?

6 How might trading in global markets impact on a company's sales and profitability?

7 Outline how exporting could limit risks.

8 Describe how the product life cycle can be extended by selling in multiple markets.

SUBJECT VOCABULARY

global consumer culture a global culture where social status, values, and activities are centred on the consumption of goods and services
offshoring moving jobs to other countries
outsourcing moving jobs to other organisations
pull factors factors that entice firms into new markets and the opportunities that businesses can take advantage of when selling into overseas markets
push factors factors in the existing market that encourage an organisation to seek international opportunities
risk the probability of a (bad) event happening multiplied by its (negative) impact
saturation (saturated market) the point when most of the customers who want to buy a product already have it, or there is limited remaining opportunity for growth in sales

EXAM PRACTICE

CASE STUDY: ZARA®

SKILLS CRITICAL THINKING, PROBLEM SOLVING, REASONING

Zara® has become one of the largest clothing retailers in the world. It was founded in 1975 with its first store in La Coruña in north-west Spain. Zara is the successful brand of the multinational clothing company, Inditex. Inditex's other brands include Pull & Bear®, Massimo Dutti® and Bershka®. Founder Amancio Ortega, one of the wealthiest men in the world, has established over 7000 stores since 1988 and profits exceed €2 billion a year. It is unique in that it is a fashion house as well as producer of most of the clothes sold in its shops.

Between 1975 and 1988, Zara concentrated on developing its home market. By 1988, facing a saturated market and limited growth in Spain, Zara decided that it had to expand internationally if it was to continue to grow. Spain joined the EU in 1986, and so gained barrier-free access to the huge European consumer market. Moreover, the 1980s were also a time of rapid globalisation and converging fashion tastes, so Zara saw many market opportunities, as well as a chance to gain economies of scale and spread its risks.

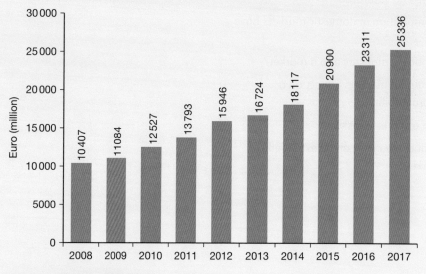

▲ Figure 2 Inditex sales 2008–17

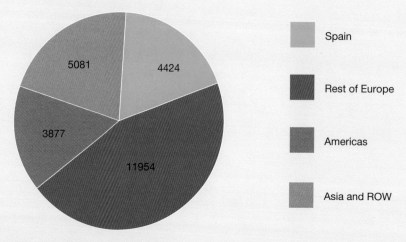

▲ Figure 3 Inditex sales by region, 2017

Zara's first big move was to Portugal which had a similar cultural environment to Spain. Between 1989 and 1996, Zara opened stores in several European countries and Mexico, as well as the key fashion centre of New York in 1989. The New York expansion held risk, but also provided insight into competitor business models, such as Gap. After 1997, Zara began a rapid phase of international expansion that has made it into a globally recognised brand. Inditex, Zara's parent company, saw growth and then share prices soar, partly as a result of these strategies. Figure 2 shows the rise in sales from 2008 to 2017. In 2017, Zara was responsible for around 66 per cent of total sales and 61 per cent of total selling space for the Inditex group.

Zara has also moved into online trading as a new route to growth. For example, opening e-commerce operations in Russia and Canada, and more recently in India, New Zealand and Australia. In 2017, Zara was ranked 24th on global brand consultancy Interbrand's list of best global brands. Its core values are: beauty, clarity, functionality and sustainability.

Zara's rapid growth is showing no signs of stopping after Inditex reported a 14 per cent jump in sales to €5.6 billion in the first quarter of the year. Inditex has repeatedly outperformed its retail rivals, including H&M®. This is because its fast-fashion model allows it to quickly respond to catwalk trends and copy popular, best-selling products in new colours and styles. Inditex also continues to generate growth from store sales, even though many of its rivals are facing difficulties in this market. For example, in 2017 it opened its largest Indian store in Mumbai. India's clothing market is expected to grow at 12 per cent to $67 billion in 2017 from $60 billion in 2016. This growing Indian market will clearly be important to Zara and Inditex going forward. Zara's success is partly due to Zara's commitment to multichannel and online strategies. You can see this as the firm expanded its online operations in Asia in the last quarter of 2017.

Zara relies heavily on its European supply chains, which allow the company to deliver new products to its shops faster than its rivals. In contrast, many of its competitors buy their clothes from factories in China, Indonesia and Bangladesh. Around 55 per cent of Zara's products are made in Spain, Portugal, Turkey and Morocco.

Finally, Zara has also looked at click-and-collect operations (i.e. ordering online and collecting in store). For example, in 2018 it opened a new temporary click-and-collect store at Westfield Stratford in east London, UK. The temporary concept store was opened while Zara's main store was being improved. The new store has been adapted to cope with the growing number of click-and-collect orders. It will help customers with their online transactions – dealing with returns and exchanges, for example.

1 Calculate the proportion of sales Inditex generates in exports in 2017. You are advised to show your working. **(4 marks)**

2 Explain one reason why exports are important to Zara and Inditex. **(4 marks)**

3 Assess the importance of push and pull factors in Zara's decision to expand in the EU. **(12 marks)**

4 Evaluate whether or not the success of Zara results from its reliance on international trade. **(20 marks)**

EXAM HINT

Remember the importance of application when answering questions. You must write answers which relate to the specific business in the question. You should avoid writing 'generic' answers. These are answers that can be applied to any business. For example, when answering question 3 in 'Exam practice', you should avoid writing generally about push and pull factors. You need to write about the specific push and pull factors that have influenced Zara.

28 ASSESSMENT OF A COUNTRY AS A MARKET

LEARNING OBJECTIVES

By the end of this chapter you should be able to understand the important factors when assessing a country as a market, including:
- levels and growth of disposable income, ease of doing business, infrastructure, political stability and exchange rates
- the application of Porter's Five Forces in assessing potential markets.

GETTING STARTED

With its large population, India (like its neighbour, China) has looked like an attractive market for business for a long time. With 1.2 billion people and growth in GDP (as shown in Figure 1), this economy presents many opportunities for businesses wishing to invest.

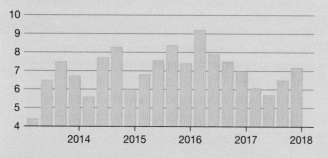

▲ Figure 1 India: growth in GDP as an annual percentage, 2014–18

However, unlike China, India is still convincing international investors that they can improve in certain areas. These are still being developed and are required for a good environment when carrying out business. Narendra Modi (India's prime minister from 2014) has promised that his government will improve the environment for doing business. In a World Bank list for 'Ease of doing business', India was ranked no. 142 (i.e. there are 141 countries that are easier to do business with). This is because of high levels of corruption, bureaucracy and regulation that slow down investment.

In recent years, the Indian government has introduced policies designed to make India's business environment more attractive to entrepreneurs and investors. Policies included making regulations simpler, improving infrastructure, speeding up procedures to resolve disputes, and introducing a single national goods and services tax to raise more revenue and help create an internal market for India. Companies wishing to start a new business should be able to gain land for development more easily. They can obtain all the permits for that development through a single place, giving access to all of the government departments. In 2016, the government also took a dramatic measure to reduce corruption in the country. The process used was called 'demonetisation'. On 9 November 2016, all Rs500 and Rs1000 bank notes stopped being legal tender. Everyone with these notes had to pay them into an Indian bank account. The main purpose of this action was to improve financial transparency. The government believed that the proportion of transactions using cash in India was far too high. If everybody used a bank account, all transactions could be traced and more taxes would be collected.

By 2017, India had moved up in the world under the World Bank's 'Ease of doing business' rankings to no. 100.

Suggest three things that a business might consider before selling goods and services into a new country. Do you think the reforms mentioned above, and their impact, might make the market more attractive to businesses looking to invest or sell goods or services in India? What benefits to India do you think there would be of more businesses moving into their market?

FACTORS TO CONSIDER

Assessing a country as a market is never easy. You must carry out a huge amount of research to decide whether a place is good for investment. You need a full understanding of the company's competitive advantages and whether the investment, if successful, will improve these. Even then, many companies make a wrong decision. There are some key factors to consider, such as the levels and growth of **disposable income**, ease of doing business, infrastructure, political stability and exchange rates. These are covered in detail below.

LEVELS AND GROWTH OF DISPOSABLE INCOME

There may be many reasons why a business might want to sell its goods and services in other countries, as explored in Chapter 27. However, if an enterprise wants to sell to a customer, the customer must have the money with which to buy that good or service. Therefore, it is important for a business to think carefully about whether the consumers in a particular country currently have – and will have in the future – sufficient disposable income.

Disposable income: Disposable income, as briefly introduced in Student Book 1, Chapter 4, is the amount of money that a person has left over after they have paid their taxes and other deductions. This remaining, or disposable, income can then be used for consumption or for saving.

When thinking about international trade, it is important to understand the average level of household disposable income compared to other countries. A business can find out about the level of disposable income in a particular country by carrying out online research. Data for other countries may be found through sources such as the OECD, Euromonitor, the World Bank or the UN.

A falling level of disposable income may mean that people with low incomes are struggling to pay for what they consider to be a minimum standard of living. Those on higher incomes may be reducing expenditure on luxuries or unnecessary items. As a result, people will be consuming less, total expenditure in markets may be falling and there are likely to be reduced savings. For example, Figure 2 shows how the Greek consumer has suffered significant falls in average monthly income every year between 2013 and 2018. This is due to Greece's difficult financial situation. The Greek consumer now has less money to spend on a wide range of goods and services.

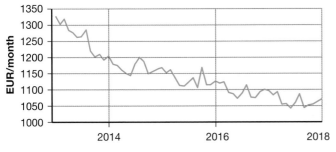

▲ Figure 2 Greece's average monthly salary 2013–18

By contrast, Figure 3 shows similar data for Germany over the same time period. The disposable income of German consumers rose throughout this period. This meant that many German consumers had more money to buy goods and services or to add to their savings. (Note that in Figure 2, income patterns in Greece are represented by average monthly incomes but in Figure 3 income patterns in Germany are measured by total disposable income).

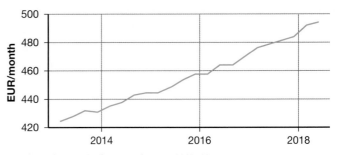

▲ Figure 3 Germany's disposable income, 2013–18

A business looking to expand into a market wants to ensure that consumers have sufficient disposable income to purchase its goods and services. It also wants to ensure that the country's level of disposable income is at least steady and hopefully growing over time. If disposable income is steady or rising, and has been so for several years, it may mean that the consumers will be able to buy products both now and in the future. This makes the market an attractive one to expand into.

For example, because of the rising disposable incomes of the growing young professional class, India's luxury goods market has been on the increase. This is due to fashion, but also because items such as jewellery and watches are purchased as investments. According to Euromonitor, up to 2030 the number of Indian households with a disposable income of between $10 000 and $25 000 will continue to increase significantly. This makes India a growth market for the makers of many products.

EASE OF DOING BUSINESS

An important factor to consider when evaluating a country as a potential market is how easily it can do business. If a business faces problems with its goods entering a country, setting up premises or dealing with everyday trading activities in a particular country, it is likely to look at alternative markets. Such problems with the ease of doing business are likely to cause delays in sales, increased costs and may potentially affect other parts of the business in the distribution chain.

Every year, the World Bank Group publishes a report summarising its research into how difficult the regulations of each country are for its business. The higher the ranking, the easier it is to start and operate a business in a country.

Table 1 in Activity 1 shows that New Zealand and Singapore are at the top of the rankings, indicating that they are good locations for a company to consider with respect to the ease of doing business. The five countries right at the bottom of the rankings (not shown in the chart) are Somalia, Eritrea, Venezuela, South Sudan and Yemen. These countries are not considered to be good locations for marketing goods and services.

Countries at the lower end of the rankings may have some features in common. For example, low GDP, political instability and high crime rates. However, all of these things can be improved on. As noted in the 'Getting started' activity, India rose in the World Bank's Ease of doing business rankings from no. 142 in 2014 to no. 100 in 2017.

There are ten indicators produced by the World Bank that track the life cycle of a business from its creation to its end. At each stage, the potential problems are indicated:

1. starting a business (number of procedures, time it takes, cost and minimal capital requirements)
2. dealing with construction permits (number of procedures, time it takes, days and cost)
3. getting electricity (number of procedures, time it takes, days and cost)
4. registering property (number of procedures, time it takes, days and cost)
5. getting credit (strength of legal rights, information required)
6. protecting minority investors
7. paying taxes (payments per year, time, percentage of profit)
8. trading across borders (documents required, time to export/import, cost to export/import)
9. enforcing contracts (number of procedures, time, cost as percentage of claim)
10. resolving insolvency.

ACTIVITY 1   SKILLS ▷ INTERPRETATION, REASONING

CASE STUDY: EASE OF DOING BUSINESS

	New Zealand	Singapore	South Korea	Malaysia	Cyprus	China	Kenya	India	Pakistan
Ease of doing business ranking	1	2	4	24	53	78	80	100	147
Starting a business	1	6	9	111	50	93	117	156	142
Dealing with construction permits	3	16	28	11	120	172	124	181	141
Getting electricity	37	12	2	8	67	98	71	29	167
Registering property	1	19	39	42	92	41	125	154	170
Getting credit	1	29	55	20	68	68	29	29	105
Protecting minority investors	2	4	20	4	43	119	62	4	20
Paying taxes	9	7	24	73	44	130	92	119	172
Trading across borders	56	42	33	61	45	97	106	146	171
Enforcing contracts	21	2	1	44	138	5	90	164	156
Resolving insolvency	32	27	5	46	21	56	95	103	82

▲ Table 1 Ease of doing business rankings 2017 (countries are ranked from 1 to 190)

Table 1 shows a selection of countries ranked according to how 'business friendly' they are. It is a lot easier to sell goods and services in some countries than others. The countries at the top of the rankings such as New Zealand, Singapore and South Korea have maintained their high rankings for a number of years. These are the easiest places to do business. They usually have these features in common:

- a well-developed infrastructure
- proper legal protection
- minimal bureaucracy
- a good record for collecting taxes and offering credit.

1 How useful might Table 1 be to a construction business considering the export of its services for the very first time?
2 Discuss the reasons why countries at the bottom of the World Bank's rankings are unattractive to businesses as markets.

INFRASTRUCTURE

The quality of a country's infrastructure is an important factor in any decision to move into a new market. Customers may have sufficient disposable income to purchase a business's goods and services. However, those goods and services must still be made and delivered to the buyer. This requires a certain level of communication and adequate transportation links. Many developing countries have underdeveloped and unreliable transportation infrastructure. This can add significantly to a company's production and operating costs. For example, there may be awkward entry points (airports, sea ports, etc.), few or unreliable trains or shipping lanes, incomplete road networks or limited warehousing facilities. A delay or failure to deliver due to poor infrastructure can lead to lost sales and increased costs. This can make a market less attractive to a business.

Communication infrastructure is equally important. Many companies want to co-ordinate production, sales and distribution, and this is best done electronically. However, electricity shortages and limited Internet coverage may mean that such efficiencies are not possible.

For example, the Emirate of Dubai has huge oil reserves and a good location. It has used the proceeds from the sale of its oil to further develop its infrastructure, including the following:

- an artificial harbour for ships
- the Jebel Ali Free Trade Zone
- an information technology hub called Dubai Internet City, where businesses such as IBM® pay no tax, and have few currency restrictions and limited regulation
- the Dubai Ideas Oasis to encourage venture capital and new business start-ups
- the Dubai Knowledge Village to improve educational opportunities
- many hotels, tourist attractions and residential complexes to make Dubai an attractive destination for visitors.

This infrastructure investment appears to be getting results. Dubai is one of the seven monarchies of the United Arab Emirates (UAE), so it is difficult to separate out its growth rate from the others using the World Bank statistics. Nevertheless, according to Dubai government statistics, foreign direct investment has significantly risen year on year since 2012.

POLITICAL STABILITY

Political decisions and events can have a significant effect on a country's business environment. They can cost investors some or all of the value of their investment. A country with a calm political situation can reduce uncertainty. This might make that country attractive as a potential market to businesses.

Therefore, it is important to think carefully about the political situation in a country before investing and to critically assess the potential risks. There are a few obvious issues to check for in the target market:

- the nature of the government and its relationship with business
- the nature of the government and its relationship with major international institutions, such as the United Nations, the World Trade Organization, the International Monetary Fund and the World Bank
- the government's legal orientation and approach to regulation and taxation
- the possible political risks that may emerge in the near future, such as elections, political vacuums, coups, terrorism, human rights issues or protests.

There are also many risks that a business might need to be aware of:

- instability during an election
- increasing authoritarianism
- factions in government, such as when political parties split
- increasing levels of corruption
- external threats (border conflicts, trade disputes, invasion) that may cause internal power changes.

It is often difficult for a business to measure the level of corruption that it might face when entering a market. Transparency International is a non-governmental organisation established to fight corruption. Every year, it publishes the global Corruption Perceptions Index, which measures the perceived (i.e. how something is seen by others) levels of public sector corruption in countries and territories around the world. It is a useful starting point for understanding whether a country is perceived to be corrupt. The index, which ranks 180 countries by their perceived levels of public sector corruption according to experts and business people, uses a scale of 0–100. The worst score is 0, showing that a country is perceived to be highly corrupt. A country with scores approaching 100 are thought to be 'clean' (i.e. free of corruption). In 2017, the index found that more than two-thirds of countries scored below 50, with an average score of 43. Some examples are shown in Table 2.

Country	Rank	Score
New Zealand	1	89
Demark	2	88
Finland, Norway & Switzerland	3	85
Singapore & Sweden	6	84
Cyprus	42	57
China	77	41
India	81	40
Sri Lanka	91	38
The Maldives	112	33
Egypt and Pakistan	117	32
Kenya and Bangladesh	143	28
Somalia	180	9

▲ Table 2 Selected ranks from Transparency International's Corruption Perceptions Index, 2017

EXCHANGE RATES

The exchange rate is the price of one currency against another. A currency can rise in value, or 'appreciate' against other currencies. For example, when the pound appreciates against the euro, £1 will buy more euros. Likewise, a currency can fall in value, or 'depreciate' against other currencies. In this case, if the pound was to depreciate against the euro, it would be able to buy fewer euros. Appreciation and depreciation of currencies is explored further in Student Book 1, Chapter 41.

Changes in exchange rates can have a very large impact on a business that is operating internationally. For example, if a small business from Spain was planning to export its goods to Japan, it would want those goods to be purchased in euros. However, if the euro was to appreciate against the yen, this would make the business's goods more expensive to Japanese consumers. It might reduce its sales and profits. Or, if a large Spanish business was considering buying a Japanese business, it would want to buy yen to pay the Japanese shareholders for their shares. A strong euro would lower the price that the Spanish business had to pay because it would take fewer euros to buy the required amount of yen. This means a business looking to expand abroad would want to think about the relationship between its home currency and the currency of the country or countries with which it is trading. Also, it would want to consider this relationship over time, since currencies can fluctuate (change in value, often from one extreme to the other; a fluctuation refers to one of these values or to the act

of changing). For example, the euro might appreciate one week yet fall the next. A business may not be very concerned unless the overall trend was for the euro to get stronger.

WORKED EXAMPLE

Assume that a car made in France costs €10 000 to produce and sells for €12 000 in the French market. The exact same car, exported and sold to the UK, would be more expensive in 2017 than it was in 2015 (assuming no change in production costs). This is because the exchange rate changed. In July 2015, €1 = £0.70, however, in July 2017, €1 = £0.90. Therefore, the difference in prices to UK customers is given by:

2015 €12 000 × 0.7 = £8400
2017 €12 000 × £0.9 = £10 800

This may lead to a decrease in demand for the car and lower profit margins for the car maker. However, this will also depend on other factors – for example, the price elasticity of demand for the model and the level of growth in the various markets where the car is sold. Also, it is very unlikely (as assumed above) that production costs would remain the same. This is because some of the components for the car are likely to come from the UK (since many car components are made in the UK). Therefore, the exchange rate will affect the cost of these components and the overall cost of making the car. In this case, it could lower production costs – and the car company could possibly afford to lower the price of the car as a result.

Fluctuating exchange rates cause problems for businesses. They create uncertainty because currency movements are unpredictable and can be quite sharp. For example, after the UK voted to leave the EU in June 2016, the value of the pound fell by about 15 per cent almost overnight. A business might want to protect itself from adverse movements in the price of currencies. It can do this in many ways, including:

- adjusting prices in the domestic currency
- taking out insurance to protect it from financial loss
- buying and selling currency when prices are favourable
- using financial instruments, such as hedging, to try and hedge against the financial risks.

ACTIVITY 2   SKILLS   CRITICAL THINKING, PROBLEM SOLVING

CASE STUDY: VORMER DIAMONDS

In May 2017, Dutch company, Vormer Diamonds, decided to organise an export drive into India, which imports around €30 billion of precious stones each year. Vormer has been pressurised by shareholders to grow more rapidly. Negotiations with an Indian agent were at an advanced stage in May 2017 and it was thought that Vormer could sell about €2 million diamonds in the first year. However, by the end of the year the exchange rate between the euro and the rupee moved against the Dutch firm. In May 2017, €1 = Rs72, however, by May 2018, €1 = Rs80. Unfortunately for Vormer, this appreciation in the euro had a negative impact on sales. After the initial export costs were taken into account, and commissions to the agent, Vormer struggled to break even on the deal in the first year.

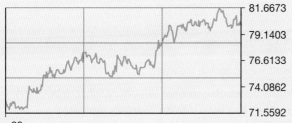

81.6673

79.1403

76.6133

74.0862

71.5592

May 23

▲ Figure 4 Exchange rate between the euro and the Indian rupee, May 2017–May 2018

1 Calculate the change in the price of the diamonds to Indian customers between May 2017 and May 2018.
2 Why might exchange rates cause difficulty for businesses engaging in international trade?
3 How might businesses protect themselves from fluctuations in the exchange rate?

APPLICATION OF PORTER'S FIVE FORCES MODEL TO ASSESS MARKETS

In Chapter 4 it was explained how Porter's Five Forces model could be used to analyse the competitiveness of an industry. The model suggests that businesses should consider five different forces when evaluating strategies.

- **The bargaining power of suppliers.** Suppliers, like any business, want to maximise the profit they make from their customers. The more power a supplier has over its customers, the higher the prices it can charge. This means it can move more profit from the customer to itself. Therefore, limiting the power of suppliers will improve the competitive position of a business.

- **The bargaining power of buyers.** Suppliers want to charge maximum prices to customers and buyers want to obtain supplies for the lowest price. If buyers or customers have considerable market power, they will be able to beat down prices offered by suppliers. For example, the major car manufacturers have succeeded in forcing down the price of components from component suppliers. This is because of their huge buying power and there are only a few major car manufacturers in the world.

- **The threat of new entrants.** If businesses can easily come into an industry and leave it again if profits are low, it becomes difficult for existing businesses in the industry to charge high prices and make high profits. Existing businesses are constantly under the threat that if their profits rise too much this will attract new suppliers into the market who will undercut their prices.

- **Substitutes.** The more substitutes there are for a product, the fiercer the competitive pressure on a business making the product. Equally, a business making a product with few or no substitutes is likely to be able to charge high prices and make high profits.

- **Rivalry among existing firms.** Rivalry among existing firms in an industry will also determine prices and profits for any single firm. If rivalry is fierce, businesses can reduce that rivalry by forming cartels or engaging in a broad range of anti-competitive practices.

Porter's model can be used to assess the potential of an overseas market. It can help businesses to look at the balance of power in a market between different types of organisations. It can determine whether entering into such a market will be profitable. Porter's model is a strategic tool designed to give a global overview, rather than a detailed business analysis technique. It helps to review the strengths of a market position, based on the five key forces outlined above. However, sometimes not all the information is available, and businesses may need to make assumptions. For example, it may be difficult to get specific market information on parts of the Middle East or China.

Consider the example of Gentry plc, a French supplier of airport ground handling services such as cabin services, catering, ramp services and passenger services. The company is considering whether to enter the Moroccan market. From experience, Gentry knows that at least 50 per cent of airlines outsource such services. Gentry used Porter's Five Forces to help assess whether the market is likely to be profitable. As a result, it concluded that the biggest threat to the company if it entered the market would be the bargaining power of the customers (the airlines that hire the services). Many of these tend to be large businesses, often funded by the state. A summary of the conclusions drawn by Gentry is shown below:

- competitive rivalry or competition **(moderate force)**
- bargaining power of buyers or customers **(strong force)**
- bargaining power of suppliers **(weak force)**
- threat of substitutes or substitution **(weak force)**
- threat of new entrants or new entry **(moderate force)**.

Based on these conclusions, Gentry will have to develop entry strategies to manage the relative size of the threats discovered by the analysis.

LINKS

Several factors can be taken into account when assessing a country as a potential market. You can demonstrate your synoptic skills by drawing on other areas of the specification to support the arguments that you put forward in answers. This could include information, for example, in Student Book 1, Chapter 4 (Demand), and in this book, Chapters 22 (Growing economies), 25 (Protectionism), 26 (Trading blocs), 31 (Global expansion and uncertainty) and 36 (International business ethics).

THINKING BIGGER

The Walt Disney® Company planned for massive success with its Shanghai, China resort in 2016. Over $5 billion were spent in constructing the largest theme park in the world. Disney expected 25 million visitors in its first full year because of its advanced technology, new attractions and a *Toy Story*-themed hotel. Shanghai is used to large crowds as the World Expo, held in 2010, attracted 73 million people and this indicated that disposable income in China was sufficient to lead to this significant investment. It also showed that Shanghai was becoming a tourist destination with all the required infrastructure in place.

In 2018, following a successful start to the Chinese project, Disney opened a new attraction. This was called Toy Story Land, an attraction in the style of the movie franchise, and is one of the fastest-paced expansions for a Disney theme park. CEO Bob Iger said the Shanghai Disney Resort will keep expanding to satisfy Chinese consumers' 'strong and growing demand for high-quality themed entertainment'.

You could use this information in a variety of ways. Obviously, it can be used if answering questions on the assessment of a country as a market. It is also useful in evaluating how that market might develop in the future.

CHECKPOINT

1 What is disposable income?

2 Why is disposable income important when a business considers breaking into an overseas market?

3 How might the ease of doing business affect the decision to enter a market in a new country?

4 Show how a country's infrastructure is an important factor when deciding whether to market products in a new country.

5 How might political stability affect the decision to market products in a new country?

6 What impact might exchange rate fluctuation have on the decision to market products in a new country?

7 How might the bargaining power of suppliers influence a firm's decision to locate in a foreign market?

SUBJECT VOCABULARY

demonetisation to remove the value of a note or coin so that it is no longer able to be used as money
disposable income the amount of money that a person has left over after they have paid their taxes, national insurance and other deductions

EXAM PRACTICE

CASE STUDY: ASSESSING UGANDA AS A POTENTIAL MARKET

SKILLS CRITICAL THINKING, ANALYSIS, INTERPRETATION, DECISION MAKING, REASONING

Uganda is located in equatorial Africa. It has a population of about 41.5 million and a literacy rate of 78.4 per cent. Since gaining independence in 1962, Uganda has had good and bad periods. Economic development was negatively affected by a military coup (i.e. a sudden, illegal change of government) and political instability in the north of the country. However, in recent years, a period of political stability has provided an environment in which businesses could develop. Policy decisions made by President Yoweri Museveni's government and relying more heavily on the private sector has helped to lift many of the nation's residents out of poverty.

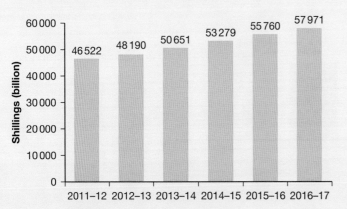

▲ Figure 5 Uganda GDP growth, 2011–12 to 2016–17

In the last three decades, Uganda has been one of Africa's fastest growing economies. Figure 5 shows GDP growth between 2011–12 and 2016–17. Other developments in the country include the following:

- Uganda has become an influential voice in Africa due to its membership of key trading blocs in the region and its role played in regional peacekeeping.
- The government has implemented a National Development Plan, which will run until 2020. It aims to improve the country's competitiveness and improve economic growth.
- The size of the population is also predicted to grow to around 214 million by 2100.
- Uganda was ranked the world's most entrepreneurial country by British B2B Marketplace Approved

Index – with 28 per cent of its adults having started their own business.

- Government help has been given to small business owners, providing them with access to easier credit and training.
- There has been some key investment in communications infrastructure such as fibre optics. This has raised Uganda's position in Internet usage in Africa to 15th.

Regarding infrastructure, Uganda has one of the poorest road networks in east Africa. The state of its roads is holding back growth, regional trade and development. Reasons for this include slow government action in obtaining supplies, in construction and with climate change. Heavy rains have started to destroy bridges and roads, cutting off rural areas at times. For example, a one-day journey from the northern Karamoja region to Kampala, the capital city, may take three days in the rainy season. Farmers and traders suffer as a result. For example, money is lost when fresh food products take too long to reach their destination.

However, a road linking Uganda with South Sudan is due to be completed soon and others too. Around 13 per cent of the recent budget was moved to infrastructure. President Yoweri Museveni said, 'When you talk about agriculture, you must not forget the roads.' Foreign investors also appreciate transport infrastructure.

One of the biggest investors to date in Uganda is China. Chinese companies, including some state-owned multinational corporations (MNCs), have been involved in a number of infrastructure projects in the country. For example, in the last 10 years, 70 per cent of the 48 road contracts in Uganda have been awarded to Chinese companies.

In 2018, Chinese company Xinlan Group announced that it was going to build a smartphone factory in Uganda. The new plant was expected to cost around US$10 million and employ about 5000 Ugandans once built. The project was also expected to improve access to the Internet in the country.

May 24

▲ Figure 6 The exchange rate between the euro and the Uganda shilling, May 2017–May 2018

	Mauritius	Kenya	Zambia	Uganda	Cameroon	Angola	Somalia
Ease of doing business – world ranking	25	80	85	122	163	175	190
Ranking in Africa	1	3	5	13	33	40	48
Starting a business	2	18	15	35	21	25	47
Dealing with construction permits	1	19	7	25	25	10	47
Getting electricity	1	3	24	34	10	30	48
Registering property	2	21	30	20	42	39	31
Getting credit	9	5	1	8	10	46	47
Protecting minority investors	4	5	10	15	23	7	48
Paying taxes	1	14	2	12	44	15	48
Trading across borders	4	19	27	18	46	48	31
Enforcing contracts	1	10	22	5	35	41	17
Resolving insolvency	1	12	9	19	25	43	39

▲ Table 3 Ease of doing business – a sample of African states

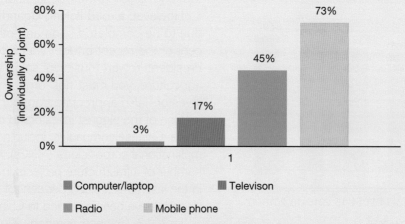

▲ Figure 7 Ownership of ICT equipment in Uganda, 2016–17

Q

1 Explain one reason why infrastructure is important to a business entering a new overseas market. **(4 marks)**
2 Explain one reason why corruption might influence the decision by a business to enter a market. **(4 marks)**
3 Discuss how a business like the Xinlan Group might use Porter's Five Forces model when assessing the potential of a market. **(8 marks)**
4 Assess the attractiveness of Uganda as a potential market for a European computer manufacturer.

(12 marks)

29 ASSESSMENT OF A COUNTRY AS A PRODUCTION LOCATION

LEARNING OBJECTIVES

By the end of this chapter you should be able to understand the important factors when assessing a country as a production location, including:

- costs of production
- skills and availability of labour force
- infrastructure
- location in a trading bloc
- government incentives
- ease of doing business
- political stability
- natural resources
- likely return on investment.

GETTING STARTED

Vietnam is an increasingly popular location for overseas businesses looking to open a new factory. By 20 December 2017 there were a total of 2591 new projects, worth US$21.27 billion in the country. This is an increase of 42.3 per cent on the previous year. Vietnam is appealing to the processing industry and manufacturing sector. The investment has come from 115 different countries. However, Japan is the biggest investor, contributing 25.4 per cent of the total. It is followed by Korea with 23.7 per cent and Singapore with 14.8 per cent.

Vietnam is an open economy with a population of almost 100 million people. Over 60 per cent of the population are under the age of 35. This means Vietnam has a huge supply of cheap, good-quality workers. According to the World Bank's ease of doing business rankings, Vietnam has risen from 91st to 82nd in the world between 2016 and 2017. Vietnam is also politically stable. It is currently focused on improving the business environment with the aim of improving competitiveness.

In 2017 Nestlé®, the Swiss multinational food and drink producer, opened a new factory in Vietnam. The factory will produce cartons of the drink Milo® and employ 200 people. The Hung Yen plant was built to supply Nestlé's market in the north of the country. The investment comes as Nestlé's plant in the south, one of six others, reaches full capacity. Nestlé now employs over 2000 people in Vietnam.

The factory is equipped with up-to-date environmental technology, including environmentally friendly refrigeration units, and heat and energy recovery facilities. It will also send zero waste to landfill sites.

Give reasons why Nestlé has located a production plant in Vietnam. Do you think that other European businesses will do the same as Nestlé? How might Vietnam benefit from businesses like Nestlé building new factories in the country?

LOCATING PRODUCTION

A new business organisation, or an existing business that is expanding its operations, will need to consider which country it wants to base its production in. For example, French car manufacturer Renault has factories in Morocco, Slovenia, Turkey, Russia, Romania and Argentina – only about 25 per cent of Renault's cars are now produced in France. There are several factors to consider when choosing a suitable foreign location. These are discussed in this chapter.

According to a report published by Deloitte in 2016, China was the most competitive nation for manufacturing. Around 29 per cent of China's GDP is generated by manufacturing, and labour costs were $3.28 per hour. Around 93 per cent of China's exports are manufactured goods. However, by 2020, China is expected to be replaced by the USA at the top (see Table 1).

The report also said that a nation's 'talent' was the most important driver of manufacturing competitiveness. This was followed by cost competitiveness, productivity and then supplier network. Figure 1 shows the rankings for the drivers of global manufacturing competitiveness and Table 1 shows the predicted ranks for 2020.

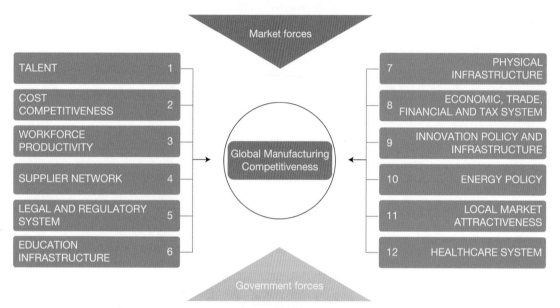

▲ Figure 1 Global CEO survey: drivers of global manufacturing competitiveness

Rank	Country	Score
1	USA	100
2	China	93.5
3	Germany	90.8
4	Japan	78
5	India	77.5
6	South Korea	77
7	Mexico	75.9
8	United Kingdom	73.8
9	Canada	68.1
10	Singapore	67.6
11	Vietnam	65.5
12	Malaysia	62.1

▲ Table 1 Global manufacturing competitiveness index, 2020 (predicted)

COSTS OF PRODUCTION

Many businesses locate factories in countries that have low production costs. By keeping costs low, a business may gain a competitive edge in the market. Some of the main production costs, such as labour, energy, raw materials and land, are a lot lower in Asia than in other parts of the world. This is illustrated in the high position of several Asian countries in Table 1.

Low wage costs are often an important factor in attracting businesses. This is particularly true for businesses that employ a large labour force. In 2017, US company, Chembio Diagnostics, said that it would move some of its production to Malaysia after a rise in the minimum wage in New York. According to Sharon Klugewicz, president of Chembio's Americas division, 'We're looking more and more toward automation and moving some of the work to the lower-cost facility in Southeast Asia.'

Labour costs in some countries that were traditionally low, such as China, have started to rise and look set to continue their upward trend. More recently, the lowest wages were to be found in Myanmar, Bangladesh and Cambodia. However, some of these locations are politically unstable and may have poor infrastructure.

The rising cost of energy and land is having an increasing impact on the location plans of some businesses. For example, energy prices in Europe were rising fast in 2013. This was beginning to have a negative impact on business location decisions. Table 2 (Activity 2) shows the hourly manufacturing wage rates in a selection of countries around the world. Switzerland is the most expensive place in the world to employ manufacturing workers, at an hourly rate of $60.36 per hour. In contrast, in India hourly wage rates were $1.66 and in Brazil they were $7.97.

ACTIVITY 1   SKILLS   PROBLEM SOLVING, REASONING

CASE STUDY: INTERNATIONAL PRODUCTION COSTS

China is now the second largest economy in the world. It has risen from 9th position in 1980 to its current position in 2010. One of the main driving forces behind this rise was its role as a low-cost manufacturer. However, China is now focusing more on medium to hi-tech manufacturing. The average wage in China has also increased. For example, between 2008 and 2017 the average yearly wage rose from CNY29 229 to CNY74 318.

This has given other nations the opportunity to fill the gap left by China as a low-cost producer. Deloitte predicts that countries like Malaysia, India, Thailand, Indonesia and Vietnam (the 'Mighty 5' or MITI-V countries) will provide lower-cost environments in the future. Some experts suggest that India will be the world's low-cost manufacturing centre very soon. It is thought that these countries will attract increasing numbers of manufacturers of labour-intensive, commodity type products like clothes, toys, textiles and basic consumer electronics.

Although cheap labour is an important factor when locating a production plant, some say that this will become less important. This is due to rapid developments in technology, especially the ability of machines to replace people in factories. Business analysts are predicting that the number of employees in manufacturing will fall significantly due to automation (i.e. work done by machines rather than people). Martin Ford's bestselling 2016 book, *The Rise of the Robots: Technology and the Threat of*

Mass Unemployment suggests that many professional sector jobs will be lost. This is in addition to those in low-cost manufacturing, since the level of automation is rising rapidly.

Country	US$ per hour
Switzerland	60.36
Germany	43.18
Netherlands	34.60
United Kingdom	28.41
South Korea	22.98
Argentina	16.77
Portugal	10.96
Poland	8.53
Brazil	7.97
Turkey	6.09
Mexico	3.91
Philippines	2.06
India	1.66

▲ Table 2 International wage rate comparison for a selection of countries – 2016 (US$ per hour)

1 A German producer is planning to shift 2400 manufacturing jobs to the Philippines. Using the information in Table 2, calculate the amount of money that could be potentially saved in manufacturing wages each year (assume that employees work 35 hours per week, 48 weeks per year on average).
2 Why is China losing its position as the lowest-cost manufacturer?
3 Explain why, in the future, cheap labour may not be such an important factor when assessing a country as a production location.

SKILLS AND AVAILABILITY OF LABOUR FORCE

A business needs to consider the cost of labour when selecting locations for its production facilities. It also must consider the quality of human capital. A business is not likely to locate a factory to another country only for cheaper labour. A business has to also consider whether the labour force in a country has the skills required to maintain quality standards. Businesses cannot afford the consequences of poor-quality work. In some countries where labour is cheaper, workers might be unskilled and poorly educated. This means that a business locating production in that country may have to invest substantial sums of money in training, unless all the work on offer is unskilled.

As stated in Activity 1, India is rapidly becoming an attractive location for manufacturing operations. India's strengths are its mixture of high- and low-skilled labour and the potential to sell to its huge market of 1.2 billion consumers. Although much of the population is poor, their incomes are rising. India also has a healthy number of university graduates. This is very important, since many businesses need manufacturing engineers, design engineers and supervisors. India compares well to other countries in the Mighty 5 (MITI-V).

Fairly recently, a number of businesses have moved production back from east Asia in a process called **reshoring**, which in some cases may be because of poor quality control in east Asian factories. For example, in 2017, reports said that reshoring and foreign job announcements increased by 170 000 in the USA. This increase was due to lower taxes and the rules and regulations becoming less strict. However, the USA has to become more competitive to bring back 10 per cent of the 5 million jobs that have gone offshore. The growth in reshoring is shown by the graph in Figure 2, and Table 3 shows some of the main reasons why many US companies are reshoring. They are divided into negative offshore factors and positive domestic factors.

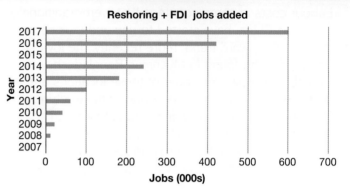

▲ Figure 2 The trend in reshoring

Any business that locates production in a particular country will have to ensure that there are enough workers near the chosen site. The business will also have to consider whether there would be enough workers in the future if the facilities needed to expand.

In 2014 it was widely reported that some businesses were beginning to find recruitment difficult in China. For example, Jenlo Apparel Manufacturing, a Canadian-owned clothing company, opened a factory in southern China in 2008. They had recruitment problems because China's 30-year one-child policy meant there was a shortage of workers. In addition, economic commentators noted that workers increasingly did not want to work in factories. They also did not want to work for exporters because the quality standards are more challenging than those for goods produced for the domestic market.

Top 10 factors, reshoring + FDI, 2010–17					
Rank	Negative offshore factor	Citings	Rank	Positive domestic factor	Citings
1	Quality/rework/warranty	292	1	Government incentives	527
2	Freight cost	196	2	Proximity to customers/market	493
3	Total cost	147	3	Skilled workforce training/availability	446
4	Delivery	100	4	Images/brand made in USA	398
5	Inventory	91	5	Eco-system synergies	336
6	Rising wages	88	6	Lead time/time to market	251
7	Supply chain interruption risk/natural disaster risk/political instability	78	7	Infrastructure	239
8	Intellectual property risk	64	8	Automation/technology	211
9	Communications	61	9	Manufacturing/engineering joint innovation (R&D)	155
10	Green considerations	53	10	Higher productivity	141

▲ Table 3 Top 10 reasons for reshoring in the USA

INFRASTRUCTURE

When considering a suitable country for a location, the quality of infrastructure is important. In some countries the infrastructure might be poor. For example, in some developing countries where labour might be cheap, the quality of infrastructure might be inadequate to support a large production facility. Any of the following factors might be encountered.

- Roads might be poorly constructed and inadequately maintained. In some countries they may be unsealed. This slows down the transportation of finished goods to customers, and raw materials and components to the site from suppliers. Some areas might be at risk of natural disasters, such as flooding, which may cause a break in the supply of vital components.
- Increasingly, access to a good broadband network is of great importance to businesses when considering locations for production. This is because businesses need rapid and reliable Internet connections to communicate with stakeholders and facilitate e-commerce. Some countries may still be developing their broadband networks, while other networks might be slow and unreliable.
- Some countries may not have modern airports and ports. This might make it difficult for business personnel to travel to and from production facilities and to ship goods out of the country.
- Railway networks may not exist or may not be sufficiently developed. This might be a problem if large or heavy goods need to be transported in large quantities.
- There may be a lack of investment in education. This can affect the quality of human capital and may discourage managers and other senior staff from locating near the site as families moving to the location would desire good-quality schools for their children.
- There may be a difference in the quality of hospitals. This may discourage senior employees from moving away from their home country. The quality of healthcare might also impact on the quality and health of human capital.
- A lack of commercial services and suppliers may discourage a business from locating in some countries. Businesses may need access to printers, IT support, bankers, insurance providers, advertising agencies, cleaners, maintenance companies and manufacturers of components. Some countries cannot guarantee such facilities.

Before locating a factory overseas, a business will need to identify its infrastructure needs and determine whether a particular country is able to meet them.

LOCATION IN A TRADING BLOC

Some businesses locate production facilities in certain countries to avoid trade barriers, such as tariffs and quotas. This can be achieved by building a plant inside a trading bloc. This is discussed in detail in Chapter 26. The output of a business located inside a trading bloc will be free from trade barriers when sold to any member of that bloc. For example, one of the reasons why Japanese car manufacturers, such as Nissan, Honda® and Toyota, have located car factories in the UK is to avoid EU trade barriers. Cars made in the UK, even though the business owners are Japanese, can be sold in France, Germany, Italy and all other EU member countries without attracting tariffs. This makes the cars cheaper when sold in these countries.

GOVERNMENT INCENTIVES

Governments may be able to influence the location of business. They are usually keen to attract foreign direct investment (FDI) because of the benefits it brings, such as income and employment. They can do this by providing incentives to businesses to locate their production facilities in their country. Governments may offer financial incentives, such as tax breaks, lower rates of company tax, interest-free loans, cheap land and better rates on business premises. For example, Bangladesh offers some of the most attractive packages of fiscal, financial and other incentives to foreign entrepreneurs in south Asia. Some examples include:

- **Tax Exemptions.** New business investments are exempt from tax for between five and seven years (15 years for investment in electric power).
- **Duty.** All import duties are removed for export-oriented business ventures.
- **Income Tax.** Double taxation can usually be avoided because Bangladesh benefits from bilateral investment agreements. Exemptions from income tax of up to three years for the expatriate (i.e. living in another country) employees in industries are specified in the relevant schedules of the income tax ordinance.
- **Remittances.** Capital, profits and dividends can be returned to the investor's own country without penalty.
- **Easy exit.** Business investors can withdraw their investment either through the decision of an annual or extraordinary general meeting and the money raised can be returned to the investor's own country with authorisation from Bangladesh Bank.

- **Ownership.** Foreign investors can set up operations independently or in joint ventures with Bangladeshi partners.
- **Other incentives.** Six-month multiple entry visas for investors; tax exemptions on royalties or technical know-how fees received by foreign investors; tax exemption on the interest on foreign loans (subject to conditions) and permanent residency (if investing $75 000).

In addition to financial incentives, governments might be able to use other methods to attract businesses. For example, they might reduce 'red tape' (bureaucracy), liberalise trading laws, invest in education and training to improve the skills of the labour force and invest in infrastructure to facilitate the free movement of goods and people.

Tax regimes are very important to businesses when considering location. According to research published by PricewaterhouseCoopers (PwC), a large financial services company, around 63 per cent of the 1344 CEOs surveyed worldwide said tax policy was an important consideration when choosing a location. Some of the lowest corporation tax rates around the world are to be found in Ireland where they are 12.5 per cent, Hungary (9 per cent) and Uzbekistan (7.5 per cent). The world average is 22.5 per cent.

Financial incentives may also be offered to businesses locating in developing countries. For example, governments in Kenya, Tanzania, Uganda and Rwanda in east Africa have offered a wide range of tax incentives. Examples include corporation tax holidays and reductions in standard taxes, such as VAT and customs duties.

EASE OF DOING BUSINESS

When choosing a suitable location, the commercial environment is a very important consideration. This is often referred to as the 'ease of doing business'. It is a lot easier to do business in some countries than others. It is important to choose a location where it is easy to do business because trading restrictions and additional costs can be frustrating and expensive for businesses. The ease of doing business may depend on factors like the following:

- the ease with which businesses can be started and closed down
- the efficiency with which contracts are enforced
- the amount of bureaucracy, e.g. the ease with which permits can be obtained for construction projects
- the availability of trade credit
- the efficiency of tax collection
- the ease of resolving insolvency.

Table 4 (Activity 2) shows the Top 10 easiest places in the world to do business in 2017. New Zealand is ranked no. 1, while many of those nations at the bottom of the

rankings are developing countries, which may have poor infrastructure and political instability. These rankings are likely to provide a very useful guide to businesses looking for a suitable overseas location. They will also provide some incentive to governments to introduce measures that might improve their ranking – that is, if the government is concerned about flows of FDI into the country.

POLITICAL STABILITY

Some countries are politically unstable. This might mean that it is too dangerous to do business there. Alternatively, the risk of possible financial loss might be far too high due to political problems. Examples of places that might be avoided by foreign businesses looking for an overseas location include, for example, Syria, Somalia and parts of Latin America.

One of the problems in some of these countries is the risk of kidnapping. It is widely reported that business people are common targets for kidnappers aiming to extract ransoms from employers and relatives. Latin America is reported as one of the most dangerous places for kidnapping. Statistics on kidnapping are not reliable, but reports estimate them to be between 5000 and 10 000 per year.

In some countries, political systems are corrupt, and bribery is commonly reported as an accepted feature of 'doing business'. In 2013, the most commonly recorded issues by the Institute of Business Ethics media monitoring were bribery, corruption and facilitation payments. In some countries, political systems mean bribery is common practice but most businesses are likely to avoid trading with countries where this is the case.

Finally, businesses may avoid locating operations in some countries due to their human rights records. One of the main reasons for this is to avoid consumer boycotts (i.e. refusal to buy a product or take part in an activity) or shareholder disapproval.

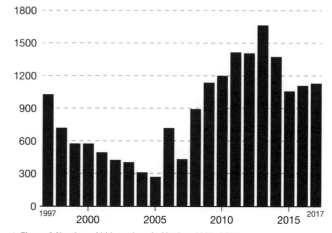

▲ Figure 3 Number of kidnappings in Mexico, 1997–2017

NATURAL RESOURCES

Some types of business activity, like mining, require large quantities of natural resources. Mines can only be sunk in locations where there are proven mineral deposits. This means mining companies can only choose locations where these deposits exist. Up until recently, when commodity prices were very high, Africa attracted a number of mining companies. For example, Rio Tinto® acquired a coal-mining project in Mozambique for $2.7 billion in 2011. However, following a fall in commodity prices, even Africa suffered a drop in foreign business interests.

Businesses that use natural resources in their production processes are also likely to set up near their sources. For example, steel producers may locate production plants near iron ore mines or coal mines. ArcelorMittal®, the Luxembourg-based multinational steel producer, has operations in more than 60 countries around the world. It is the largest steel company operating in South Africa, where it has several mines and steelworks producing long and flat steel for a range of different industries. Steel producers are keen to locate close to mines as the transportation of iron ore and coal can be very expensive because these materials are big and heavy.

ACTIVITY 2   SKILLS ▷ CRITICAL THINKING, REASONING

CASE STUDY: EASE OF DOING BUSINESS

Singapore claims to have an excellent infrastructure, transparent laws, a sound economy and convenient online portals. In 2017, it was ranked the 2nd-easiest place in the world to do business by a World Bank survey.

1 Businesses prefer to locate operations where it is 'easy to do business'. What does this mean?
2 What are the possible attractions of a business looking at Singapore as a suitable overseas location?

	New Zealand	Singapore	South Korea	Malaysia	Cyprus	China	Kenya	India	Pakistan
Ease of doing business ranking	1	2	4	24	53	78	80	100	147
Starting a business	1	6	9	111	50	93	117	156	142
Dealing with construction permits	3	16	28	11	120	172	124	181	141
Getting electricity	37	12	2	8	67	98	71	29	167
Registering property	1	19	39	42	92	41	125	154	170
Getting credit	1	29	55	20	68	68	29	29	105
Protecting minority investors	2	4	20	4	43	119	62	4	20
Paying taxes	9	7	24	73	44	130	92	119	172
Trading across borders	56	42	33	61	45	97	106	146	171
Enforcing contracts	21	2	1	44	138	5	90	164	156
Resolving insolvency	32	27	5	46	21	56	95	103	82

▲ Table 4 Ease of doing business rankings 2017

LIKELY RETURN ON INVESTMENT

Businesses looking for locations are likely to consider a number of different options before making their final decision. Many of the factors above are likely to be considered, depending on the nature of the industry in which a business operates. During the decision-making process, SWOT analysis and PESTLE analysis can help to assess the suitability of different locations. Also, quantitative techniques might be used to help make the final location decision. Quantitative techniques can help to evaluate the financial costs and benefits of investing in particular locations.

QUANTITATIVE METHODS

Chapter 10 looked in detail at how to evaluate investment projects. Table 5 shows two potential sites for a business which is considering relocating its premises. It gives the initial cost of the move and then the cost savings to be made in each year. This is compared with the existing site.

Three investment appraisal methods can be used to show which site should be chosen (if any). It is assumed that at the end of five years, the business will be relocating again, so no cost savings will be considered after the end of five years.

Payback method: The business will calculate how long it will take to get back the initial investment with the payback method. In location A, the initial cost is $12 million and with annual savings (the equivalent of increased cash flows) of $3 million, the investment will be recouped in four years. With location B, the initial cost is higher at $15 million, but the cost savings are $5 million per year. The result is that the investment will be recouped in three years. So on the payback method, location B is the preferred location.

Average rate of return (ARR): With the average rate of return method, the net return per annum is divided by the initial investment and expressed as a percentage. With location A, there will be a total cost saving (i.e. increased cash flow) over five years of $15 million. With an initial cost of $12 million, this gives a return of $3 million ($15 million − $12 million). So the ARR is [($3 million ÷ $12 million) ÷ 5 years] × 100 per cent, which is 5 per cent.

With location B, the cost saving is $25 million over five years with an initial cost of $15 million. So, the ARR is [($10 million ÷ $15 million) ÷ 5 years] × 100 per cent, which is 13.33 per cent. On the average rate of return method, location B is also the preferred location. These results are summarised in Table 6.

	Location A ($ million)	Location B ($ million)
Initial cost	12	15
Annual cost savings/increased cash flow		
Year 1	3	5
Year 2	3	5
Year 3	3	5
Year 4	3	5
Year 5	3	5

▲ Table 5 Initial costs and cost savings of locations A and B

Discounted cash flow: With discounted cash flows, the value of future cash flows must be reduced to show their present value. The important point about discounted cash flow is that, just as money invested today will grow in value because of compound interest, so the opposite is true: the value of cash available in the future is worth less today.

In Table 7, the cost savings (or net cash flows) have been discounted back assuming a discount rate of 15 per cent. The net present value of the cost savings falls the further into the future it occurs. When it is added up, the net present value of the cost savings at location A don't cover the initial investment needed. So moving to location A is unprofitable at this rate of discount.

But moving to location B shows a positive net cash flow. The cost savings outweigh the initial cost of the investment by $1.9 million. So, this would suggest that the company should move to location B. Location B would always be preferred over location A, whatever the rate of discount used. However, if the rate of discount were much higher than 15 per cent, the discounted cash flow technique would suggest that even location B would give overall negative cash flows. Therefore, moving at all would not be profitable.

	A	B
Initial cost	12	15
Increased cash flow	15	25
Net cash flow	3	10
Net cash flow per year	0.6	2
ARR (net cash flow per year ÷ initial cost × 100)	5%	13.33%

▲ Table 6 The ARR for locations A and B

	Location A ($ million)	Location B ($ million)	Discount 15%	Location A ($ million)	Location B ($ million)
Initial cost	12	15	1.00	12.0	15.0
Annual cost savings/increased cash flow					
Year 1	3	5	0.87	2.6	4.4
Year 2	3	5	0.76	2.3	3.8
Year 3	3	5	0.66	2.0	3.3
Year 4	3	5	0.57	1.7	2.9
Year 5	3	5	0.50	1.5	2.5
Total cost savings	15	25		10.1	16.9
Net cash flow	3	10		−1.9	1.9

▲ Table 7 Initial costs and cost savings of two new locations discounted at 15 per cent

LINKS

The information in this chapter may be of use when demonstrating your synoptic skills when answering questions on global competitiveness. For example, you could explain how government incentives to locate in a particular country could lower costs and give a business a competitive edge. Other chapters that link effectively to this chapter include Production (Student Book 1, Chapter 37), Economic influences (Student Book 1, Chapter 41) and, in this book, SWOT analysis (Chapter 3), Impact of external influences (Chapter 4), Investment appraisal (Chapter 10), Business ethics (Chapter 16), Protectionism (Chapter 25), Trading blocs (Chapter 26) and Impact of MNCs (Chapter 35).

CHECKPOINT

1 Why are labour costs in China starting to rise?

2 For which industries are energy costs likely to be important when looking for an overseas location?

3 Why might the quality of human capital in a potential location be important to a business looking for a new site?

4 How might the quality of a nation's infrastructure be an important factor in factory location?

5 What sort of incentives might a government offer to encourage a business to locate a site in its country?

6 What is meant by the 'ease of doing business' when looking for a suitable country to locate production?

7 Why is political stability an important issue when locating plants overseas?

8 For which type of industry is the availability of natural resources an important location factor?

9 State three quantitative methods that might be used when choosing production locations abroad.

10 What is the main advantage of using quantitative methods when making a location decision?

SUBJECT VOCABULARY

open economy where a country allows the free movement of goods, services, capital and labour into and out of the economy
reshoring bringing production back home after using foreign production facilities for a period of time

EXAM PRACTICE

CASE STUDY: LOCATING PRODUCTION IN MALAYSIA

SKILLS CRITICAL THINKING, ANALYSIS, REASONING

Malaysia has a population of 31 million and is classed as an upper-middle-income country. It became independent in 1957 after a period of British rule. However, this was followed by a period of political instability until around 1965. Afterwards, Malaysia's economy began to develop.

The country was dependent on the sale of raw materials for exports, but it diversified into manufacturing, services and tourism. Malaysia now hopes to achieve high-income status by 2020. It wants to move higher up the value-added production chain by attracting investments in high-technology, knowledge-based industries and services. Unemployment in Malaysia is very low – it was around 3.5 per cent in 2017.

Along with nine other South East Asian countries, Malaysia is a member of ASEAN, an important trading bloc in the region. It also signed the 12-nation Trans-Pacific Partnership (TPP) free trade agreement in 2016. However, the future of this agreement looks uncertain since the USA withdrew in 2018.

The government is keen to attract foreign businesses to set up operations in Malaysia. Established in 1967, the Malaysian Industrial Development Agency (MIDA) provides support and guidance for businesses wishing to invest in manufacturing and service provision in Malaysia. Some of the incentives on offer to foreign investors include the following:

- no restriction on foreign equity ownership
- a liberal employment policy for expatriates
- free movement of funds for foreign investments in Malaysia
- the protection of intellectual property rights
- a company tax rate of 25 per cent
- an individual tax rate from 0–26 per cent
- minimum conditions of employment under the Employment Act 1955
- trade unions and friendly industrial relations.

Malaysia also offers foreign businesses some attractive facilities. Examples include:

- a complete system of vocational and industrial training
- financial assistance for the training of workers
- a well-developed financial and banking sector providing credit to industry
- export credit refinancing and insurance

- an active and efficient stock exchange for raising capital
- fully developed industrial parks for industry (including high-tech parks and free zones for export industries)
- plenty of electricity and water supplied at reasonable costs
- high-quality telecommunications network and services
- well-equipped seaports and airports connected to the world
- a network of well-maintained highways and railways.

Malaysia is a business-friendly country and was ranked 24th in the World Bank's ease of doing business rankings in 2017. It scored particularly highly on protecting minority investors (4th), getting electricity (8th) and dealing with construction permits (11th). Large numbers of foreign businesses have set up operations in the country. Some examples are given below.

- **Osram®.** In 2017, Osram, the German multinational lighting manufacturer, opened a $440 million factory in Kulim. Osram plans to employ around 1500 people at Kulim, making chips using a combination of both manual labour and automation. Osram said that Malaysia is the preferred site because its legal system is effective in protecting intellectual property – unlike some other countries. Another reason is because the country offers a skilled and affordable labour force. They speak the English language, which also helps.
- **Toyota.** Japanese car maker Toyota plans to open a new factory in Malaysia in 2019. The new plant will be located on the Bukit Raja Industrial Estate, in Klang. It will cost around RM2 billion to build. It will have an initial annual capacity of 50 000 units a year, which can be expanded to meet increased demand. Combined with the current factory, Toyota's Malaysian production volume will be around 90 000 to 100 000 units per annum. The cars produced by the new plant will be for the domestic market. Toyota believes that the Malaysian car market will grow in the mid to long term.
- **Cuckoo Electronics®.** South Korea's home appliance maker, Cuckoo Electronics Co. Ltd, said that it plans to build a RM100 million factory in Malaysia in 2018. It wants to produce water purifier products. The expansion of its manufacturing to Port Klang, Selangor, will help meet rising demand in South East Asia with its huge potential market. The location of this new plant in Malaysia will also reduce transportation costs.

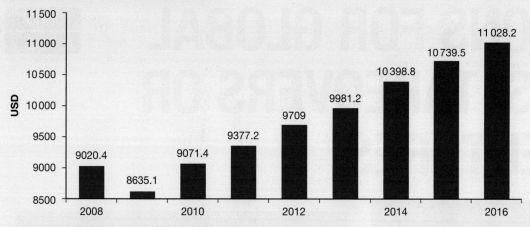

▲ Figure 4 Malaysia GDP per capita, 2008–16

Malaysia GDP per capita 2008-2016, HYPERLINK "https://tradingeconomics.com/%20malaysia/gdp-per-capita"https://tradingeconomics.com/ malaysia/gdp-per-capita, Trading Economics

Q

1 Explain one reason why a business might use quantitative decision-making methods when assessing a country as a production location.   **(4 marks)**
2 Discuss how governments can influence business location decisions.   **(8 marks)**
3 Assess the factors that might make Malaysia an attractive location for production for Toyota.   **(12 marks)**

EXAM HINT

When answering questions on assessing countries as business or production locations, you need to remember that you are not discussing assessment of a country as a market in the context of exporting, for example. This is dealt with in Chapter 28. There is quite a difference between selling in different countries and setting up factories in different countries. A huge financial commitment is necessary when setting up production plants in different countries. There can be far more at stake.

30 REASONS FOR GLOBAL MERGERS, TAKEOVERS OR JOINT VENTURES

LEARNING OBJECTIVES

By the end of this chapter you should be able to understand the key reasons for global mergers, takeovers or joint ventures, such as:

- spreading risk and economies of scale
- entering new markets/trading blocs
- acquiring national/international brand names/patents
- securing resources/supplies
- maintaining/increasing global competitiveness
- reducing competition
- making use of local knowledge
- government or legal requirements
- accessing supply chains/distribution networks
- sharing costs/risks.

GETTING STARTED

The Brazilian aircraft manufacturer, Embraer, has pursued a strategy of growth through acquisitions. It began by making military aircraft and then moved into the small private and commercial plane sector. It was privatised in 1994 and entered into a series of strategic alliances (i.e. agreements between countries or organisations) in order to gain access to technology, resources and brand recognition (i.e. how people identify a brand by its features and attributes). Next, it began to base production facilities in other countries, including China, France, the USA and Portugal. By 2012, 90 per cent of its global sales were outside of Brazil.

In 2018, Embraer entered a joint venture with giant aircraft manufacturer, Boeing®. The US company will have a controlling 51 per cent stake in the partnership. The aim of the partnership is to create a new company focused on commercial aviation (excluding Embraer's defence unit).

Why do you think acquiring or allying with other firms is important to Embraer? What benefits do you think they gain from becoming an international company? What risks do you think are involved? Why might Embraer accept Boeing's 51 per cent controlling interest in the new partnership?

REASONS WHY BUSINESSES JOIN TOGETHER

As discussed in Chapter 22, there are many reasons why a firm might wish to buy or join forces with a foreign company. For example, exporting may not make sense if countries can produce the product or service more cheaply. Arrangements such as **licensing** or **franchising** may not make commercial sense.

- **Licensing.** A firm enters into a licensing contract with another firm to use its brand, **intellectual property** or to produce its product or service in return for a fee. For example, Disney licenses its brand name for merchandise and inventors license their patents to manufacturers.
- **Franchising.** Franchising involves a long-term co-operative relationship whereby one party, the franchisor, contracts with another, the franchisee, to run its business. McDonald's is a well-known example of a franchise.

Rather than licensing or franchising, firms may select **joint ventures** or cross-border mergers and acquisitions. In fact, these two forms of investment are the main foreign investment routes for most international companies.

Figure 1 shows the number of cross-border M&A (mergers and acquisitions) deals – mergers and acquisitions involving businesses in different countries – between 2007 and 2016. M&A deals fell after 2007 quite sharply. This was due to the financial crisis and global recession which began in 2008. However, the number of deals recovered and by 2016 they were approaching the number that had been reached in 2007.

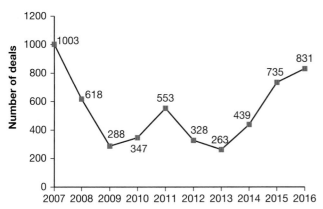

▲ Figure 1 The number of cross-border M&A deals between 2007 and 2016

There are many reasons why cross-border deals are completed and some of these are explained below. However, it is important to remember that every investment decision is specific to the firms involved and the circumstances that each firm faces. Also, in the decision-making process, the personal role that senior managers play needs to be considered. It is important to consider the factors of confidence or uncertainty.

The rest of the chapter looks at some of the reasons why acquiring another firm or arranging a joint venture might be sensible. Often these reasons are connected. For example, the need to spread risks will be linked to a desire to enter a new market or trading bloc. What is often referred to as a 'merger' is actually a takeover or acquisition. Sometimes, this is not obvious until well after an agreement is completed.

SPREADING RISK AND ECONOMIES OF SCALE

Spreading risk: During economic downturns (i.e. a fall in the amount of business), even companies with strong balance sheets can face serious difficulties, as outlined

in Student Book 1, Chapter 36. Therefore, it makes sense to try and protect the firm from the consequences of a downturn or crisis by locating in markets where these risks are less likely to occur – or at least less likely to occur at the same time as they occur in the home market.

For example, Pingo Doce®, founded in 1980, is a Portuguese supermarket chain. It began its expansion in the 1990s in order to diversify (i.e. develop to include a wider range of something in order to be more successful) away from the Portuguese market. Though its first venture in Brazil failed, its second one in Poland succeeded. Instead of building huge stores like Carrefour®, it chose to focus on small, local shops and bought the discount chain Biedronka, which is now Poland's biggest food retailer. In 2012, Pingo Doce began trying to diversify away from the struggling European market and into the growth markets of Latin America. In 2018, it also announced that it would relaunch its e-commerce operations, 15 years after the previous attempt (which lasted for five years) was closed down.

Economies of scale: One of the main motives for mergers and acquisitions is to grow rapidly to a size where costs can be reduced significantly by exploiting economies of scale. For example, in 2017 two chemical giants, the Huntsman Corporation® of the USA and Clariant® of Switzerland, merged in a $14 billion deal. The merged company was thought to generate cost savings of $400 million per year. The chemicals industry has been a major source of deals, as a number of rivals try to gain scale and reduce costs. Recent transactions have included deals between Dow Chemical® and DuPont® and Bayer® and Monsanto®.

ENTERING NEW MARKETS AND TRADING BLOCS

Instead of growing organically, businesses can take a shorter route to international growth through mergers and acquisitions. For example, Indian company Tata Motors® purchased Jaguar Land Rover® from the Ford Motor Company. This route appears increasingly popular.

Equally, firms in established industries may find that the only way that they can grow is through merging with or acquiring firms in other markets. This has been the case in telecoms in some countries where growth has been limited. For example, a number of cross-border mergers have been proposed in Europe. Orange®, France's leading operator, held talks from January 2016 to buy Bouygues® for an expected €10 billion ($11.3 billion). In the UK, CK Hutchison, which operates the brand Three®, agreed in 2015 to pay £10.25 billion ($15 billion) for O2®, owned by Spain's Telefónica. Another merger involving Hutchison was proposed in Italy. In each case, the number of operators would have fallen to just three.

Firms may want to tap into markets that are growing, but they do not always find it easy to gain access. For example, the Chinese auto firm Shanghai Automotive Industry Corporation (SAIC) operates factories with Volkswagen (VW) and General Motors (GM). This long-running joint venture began solely because of limits that the Chinese government placed upon foreign firms entering the Chinese market. In order to gain access to the billions of Chinese consumers, VW and GM had to work with SAIC through a joint-venture arrangement. VW and GM count the agreement as a success. Much of SAIC's profits come from the joint venture. Some commentators feel that SAIC would benefit from developing their own technology and capabilities further.

ACQUIRING NATIONAL AND INTERNATIONAL BRAND NAMES/PATENTS

A business may want to become a global player in the international market. However, a lack of **brand recognition** or the possession of a patent may prevent other businesses from copying its product or producing similar products. By purchasing a business or a product with a strong brand name, it could gain both quickly.

Using mergers, acquisitions and joint ventures is an effective way to gain a strong reputation or to get access to intellectual property. It can have a number of benefits for a business:

- there is likely to be strong brand recognition
- there will be brand loyalty
- it limits competition for the product
- a business will not face the high risk, cost and uncertainty of launching a new product.

It is important to realise how easily a brand can be destroyed if care is not taken post merger to ensure that employee confidence and customer satisfaction are looked after. It may be that the strongest brand is adopted over the weakest one, or some sort of portfolio of brands can be created as part of a differentiation strategy.

Developing intellectual property internally, through in-house research and development, can take a very long time and involve a lot of financial risk. Intellectual property involves an idea, such as an invention,

literary work or artwork, that the law protects from unauthorised (i.e. without official permission) use by others. This protection occurs through such legal processes as:

- patents for inventions
- **copyrights** for literary works or computer programs
- trademarks for brand names or designs.

Establishing intellectual property can be expensive. It is often easier to gain access to intellectual property by buying it in an acquisition or through a joint-venture agreement.

ACTIVITY 1　　SKILLS　CRITICAL THINKING

CASE STUDY: TAKEOVER OF MEAD JOHNSON® BY RECKITT BENCKISER®

In June 2017, the UK household goods group, Reckitt Benckiser, took over the US baby milk group, Mead Johnson, in a deal worth $17.9 billion. The deal was first announced in February 2017. However, it could not be finalised until regulators in 10 different regions allowed it to go ahead. China was the last of these regions to give approval.

Mead Johnson is an influential supplier of nutrition products for babies, children and pregnant women. It has about 14 per cent of the global baby food market and only Nestlé has a bigger market share of around 20 per cent. The baby food market is very large, valued at around $53.3 billion in 2015. It is forecast to grow to $76.5 billion by 2021.

Reckitt sells a number of high-profile brands around the world such as Dettol®, Scholl®, Harpic® and Vanish® products. It also supplies over-the-counter (OTC), non-prescription products such as Nurofen®.

One of the main reasons why Reckitt bought Mead was to develop a new market outside of its current area of expertise. However, some experts have suggested that Reckitt lacks experience in this field and might struggle to make a success of the deal. Reckitt believes that its record in brand building and innovation (i.e. introducing new products and ideas) is good and that the acquisition will help to grow sales rapidly. Also, Reckitt has experienced some difficulties in emerging markets. Sales growth in some developed countries are starting to slow. The purchase of Mead should give a much-needed boost to sales. Fifty per cent of Mead's sales are in Asia and 17 per cent in South America. Some experts suggest the deal could boost earnings per share by 10 per cent in its first year.

1 How might Reckitt's acquisition of Mead spread risk?
2 Explain one other motive for the takeover.

SECURING RESOURCES OR SUPPLIES

Firms may often choose to merge with another firm to secure resources or supplies further back in the supply chain. This is known as backward vertical integration (see Chapter 7). A firm may want, or even need, to merge with another firm because:

- the resources used in the creation of its product or service are rare or hard to get. It needs to ensure reliable sourcing
- it needs to ensure that the inputs are of a suitable quality or price.

For example, Starbucks' rapid international expansion, along with several disease threats to coffee plants, has meant that it faces strong competition for supplies of high-quality coffee beans. Consequently, it bought its own coffee farm in Costa Rica to help obtain a reliable supply of the best coffee beans.

MAINTAINING OR INCREASING GLOBAL COMPETITIVENESS

Merging or joining with another firm can provide bigger markets and provide opportunities to make cost savings, by exploiting economies of scale, for example. This could make the firm much more competitive in terms of its **pricing power** over customers and suppliers. If there is a lot of competition in the market, or if a firm is hoping to become a dominant global player, merging or acquiring another firm can be part of a successful strategy.

For example, a proposed merger between Applied Materials and Tokyo Electron is due to a need for scale. There is an increasing demand for computer chips, but the machines that make the chips are very expensive. This merger gives the two firms a quarter of the market and increases their strength against their customers (Intel®, Samsung®, Taiwan Semiconductor®). In summary, the objective of the merger is to acquire scale and cut costs. This reduces downward pressure on prices. As a result, this would allow for long-term planning (as research and development is very expensive).

Alternatively, two firms can cross-sell product ranges or services. This could increase overall sales and even lower internal costs. For example, mergers of banks or financial services firms have occurred in order to provide one contact point for customers to a range of different financial services.

Likewise, engaging in a geographically diverse collaboration can improve a firm's tax position. For example, a firm may select a merger partner that is located in a country where the overall tax take is lower. The merged firm can then relocate its headquarters to the lower tax location in order to save money. Such moves are a source of considerable political disagreement. However, a firm will want to reduce its overall taxation but as legally and ethically as possible. The money saved from lower tax bills can be used to invest and to further improve the firm's competitive position.

In 2014, Facebook spent $22 billion on buying WhatsApp®, a mobile messaging service. WhatsApp had made $10.2 million the year before and was reported as loss-making. So why would Facebook want to buy the firm and pay that much for it? It may have been to get rid of a competitor in the market, but equally important was that WhatsApp has a better form of messaging. However, another important reason for such a takeover might be defensive. If Facebook hadn't bought it, one of its competitors might have. It will be interesting to see if Facebook's purchase of WhatsApp develops commercially or whether it may have been more of a defensive purchase. A purchase might turn out to be a mistake and a waste of money, but at its worst it might severely impact on a firm's competitiveness.

REDUCING COMPETITION

An important motive for some cross-border mergers and acquisitions is to reduce competition in the market. For example, if a market is dominated by five large firms and two join together, following the merger there are only four. With less competition, a business might start to dominate the market. There may be possibilities for price increases and there will be less pressure to innovate (i.e. come up with new ideas). In 'Getting started' above, the US aircraft manufacturer Boeing took over a Brazilian rival Embraer. This transaction is likely to reduce competition in the market.

However, such acquisitions are often watched by industry regulators. A merger or acquisition could be blocked if it acts against the public's interest. Alternatively, it might continue with conditions attached. For example, sometimes a business may be required to sell off some assets before a merger or takeover can continue. In 2018, South African platinum miner, Lonmin was taken over by another South African miner, Sibanye-Stillwater. Sibanye is the largest individual producer of gold from South Africa and is one of 10 largest gold producers in the world. Sibanye is also the third-largest producer of palladium and platinum. However, competition authorities from both South Africa and the UK said that the takeover would probably be investigated. They argued this because of concerns that competition in the industry would be reduced too much following the takeover. If the deal is approved, Sibanye will become the second-largest producer of platinum in the world.

MAKING USE OF LOCAL KNOWLEDGE

Sometimes, business partnerships are formed across borders because a particular company lacks the knowledge and expertise in order to enter a new foreign market. It is very risky to set up operations in a foreign market. One approach way to reduce the risk is to form a partnership with a company inside the new country. They will already have knowledge of the market. A number of US and European companies have used this approach when setting up operations in Asian markets such as China, Vietnam and Thailand. Such markets are often unfamiliar to western businesses. They often have different business practices and cultures to those of western countries. Joint ventures, partnerships and alliances are a common feature of foreign business ventures.

In 2018, Aggreko®, the UK-based global leader in mobile, modular power and heating and cooling, formed a joint venture in China with power rental company Shanghai Yude. The new company called Shanghai Yude Aggreko Energy Equipment Rental Co. Ltd, will be managed by Shanghai Yude, in agreement with Aggreko's standards and procedures. The move is part of Aggreko's long-term strategy to grow its business in China with experienced and respected local partners.

This example helps to show the value that businesses put on local businesses when entering a new market.

GOVERNMENT OR LEGAL REQUIREMENT

Governments in some countries are concerned that foreign businesses will enter domestic markets and dominate them. This could threaten the survival of local businesses. Consequently, some governments insist that firms entering their country do so in partnership with domestic operators. This helps to ensure that some of the benefits such as income, exports and employment, are shared with domestic companies. It also helps to protect domestic companies. Even if there are no formal legal requirements to secure partnerships with domestic operators, a government is much more likely to give a foreign company the go ahead if a new venture is planned in partnership with a local company.

ACTIVITY 2 **SKILLS** CRITICAL THINKING, ANALYSIS

CASE STUDY: JOINT VENTURE BETWEEN AAR (USA) AND INDAMER (INDIA)

US company AAR®, which employs over 5500 people around the world, is a global provider of aviation services to commercial airlines. In 2018 it announced a joint venture with Indamer Aviation®, a leading Indian aviation company. The aim of the venture is to develop a new airframe maintenance, repair and overhaul (MRO) facility in Nagpur. The facility is designed to serve India's fast-growing commercial aviation market. The venture works well with the Indian government's 'Make in India' initiative. This was introduced by Prime Minister Narendra Modi to encourage businesses to manufacture goods in India. The initiative aims to raise the contribution made by manufacturing to GDP from 16 per cent to 25 per cent by 2025. 'Make in India' involves the use of several initiatives to:

- promote foreign direct investment
- implement intellectual property rights
- develop the manufacturing sector by targeting 25 sectors of the economy. These range from automobile to Information Technology (IT) and Business Process Management (BPM).

The initiative also aims to create jobs, encourage innovation, improve skill development and protect intellectual property. Consequently, the new joint venture between AAR and Indamer will employ Indian nationals. Also, a training school will allow hundreds of students to gain skill sets and employment in Nagpur. Some of the initial training will take place in the USA. AAR said that it was looking forward to expanding it's MRO expertise outside the USA with Indamer. Importantly, Indamer has the local market and cultural knowledge needed to make a success of the venture. Rajeev Gupta, Indamer Aviation's CEO, said, 'AAR is the ideal partner for us and brings the knowledge and processes needed to help establish in-country capability and jobs in aircraft heavy maintenance.'

1 Why is Indamer's involvement in the joint venture important to AAR?
2 How has India's government influenced this joint venture?

ACCESSING SUPPLY CHAINS AND DISTRIBUTION NETWORKS

Another important reason for cross-border business partnerships is for companies to access supply chains and distribution networks. The acquisition of operations in different stages of product is called vertical integration (see Chapter 5). If a business acquires a supply chain, this is called backward vertical integration. In contrast, if a business acquires a distribution network, this is called forward vertical integration.

Supply chains: One motive for taking over a business that operates in the supply chain is to guarantee supply. Businesses like to be in complete control of the supply chain if possible. It reduces levels of uncertainty and helps to maintain quality in supplies. Another motive is to get rid of the profit margin taken by suppliers. In recent years, a number of luxury brands have been buying farms to secure control. This popular global strategy helps companies to get materials that are critical to the development of their brand's success. It also helps a business to maintain higher ethical standards, by ensuring that the production of supplies meets with environmental regulations, for example. A few years ago, Ermenegildo Zegna®, the Italian luxury menswear brand, took control of Achill Farm, a giant sheep station in Armidale, Australia. This was to protect the supply of the special merino wool needed for Zegna's suits and sweaters. More recently, a number of companies have purchased suppliers of live animals. For example, Hermes® owns an alligator farm in Louisiana and two crocodile farms in Australia. Similarly, LVMH® has bought the Johnstone River crocodile farm in Queensland, Australia.

Distribution networks: The main motive for buying distribution networks is to guarantee outlets for produce. Manufacturers can reduce risk and operate more confidently if they know that they can sell output immediately using distribution channels that they own. The ownership of distribution channels also moves the profit margins to the manufacturer. This means the bottom line improves. In 2018, JAB, the German family-owned investment company, purchased the US soft drinks producer, Dr Pepper Snapple® for $19 billion. This was the largest soft drinks deal on record and created a potent competitor for Coca-Cola and Pepsi®, the two market leaders. Some experts argued that JAB had made the purchase for distribution reasons. Access to the US soft drinks market has been dominated in the past by Coca-Cola, Pepsi and the Dr Pepper® networks. The acquisition of Dr Pepper gives JAB a huge bottling and distribution network that could be used to sell a wide range of drinks. JAB would be able to add a great deal to the current network.

SHARING COSTS AND RISKS

Some cross-border partnerships happen because firms want to share the costs and risks of business ventures. Developing foreign markets is very risky because of their unfamiliar nature. This means a business is more likely to speculate in new markets if it can share the costs and risks with another. This might reduce the potential profits that a new venture might bring. More importantly, it reduces the costs and risks of the venture and any losses that are made if things go wrong.

In 2017–18, joint ventures were announced between:

- Germany's BMW® and China's Great Wall Motors® to make plug-in electric Minis® for the Chinese market in the future
- Malaysian budget airline AirAsia® and the China Everbright Group®, to set up a new low-cost carrier in China
- SSP Group plc, a leading operator of food and beverage outlets in travel locations worldwide, and Travel Food Services Private Limited (TFS®), a leading operator of food and beverage concessions in travel locations in India
- US soft drinks giant Pepsi and Japanese consumer company Suntory Beverage & Food, to expand the sale of soft drinks in South East Asia.

These cross-border joint ventures (and many more) will help the businesses to share the risks and costs of business development in new markets.

LINKS

There are a variety of reasons for mergers and joint ventures. To show your synoptic skills, you could use information from other chapters to support your arguments about the main reasons for mergers and takeovers in a global context. This could include using information about how mergers can change and improve channels of distribution (Student Book 1, Chapter 13), the reasons why businesses want to invest in other countries (this book, Chapter 24), how entering new markets through mergers can help a business overcome trading blocs (Chapter 26), how mergers might improve marketing globally (Chapter 32), global expansion and uncertainty (Chapter 31) or the effect on economies of scale (Chapter 5). The effect that mergers and joint ventures might have on globalisation could be considered when answering questions in Chapter 24 or when considering types of business growth in Chapter 5.

CHECKPOINT

1 State two reasons why firms might join together.

2 How might a merger reduce business risk?

3 Why might a business buy a company that operates inside a trading bloc?

4 State two examples of businesses that might try to acquire brand names through merging.

5 Why might it make more sense for businesses to acquire intellectual property rather than developing it themselves?

6 How can mergers lead to increasing competitiveness?

7 Some firms merge with overseas rivals to reduce competition. How is competition reduced in this case?

8 Give one reason why a large MNC supermarket chain might buy a food manufacturer in another country.

SUBJECT VOCABULARY

brand recognition how people identify a brand by its features and attributes

copyright a legal right that grants the creator of an original work the sole right to determine and decide whether, and under what conditions, this original work may be used by others

franchise a business model in which a business (the franchisor) allows another operator (the franchisee) to trade under their name

global mergers where two or more businesses from different countries join together and operate as one

intellectual property a product that is a creation of the mind, such as an invention, literary work or artwork, that the law protects from unauthorised use by others. Types include patents, copyrights and trademarks

joint venture where two or more businesses co-operate to share the costs and profits from a business venture

licensing a contract with another firm to use its intellectual property or to produce its product or service in return for a fee

pricing power the effect that a change in a firm's product price has on the quantity demanded of that product

EXAM PRACTICE

CASE STUDY: MIAOLI TOYS

SKILLS   CRITICAL THINKING, INTERPRETATION, PROBLEM SOLVING

Miaoli Toys® is an established toy manufacturer based in Taiwan. It has several factories in South East Asia and sells to markets in many parts of the world. It has a wide range of toys and includes plastic toys, electronic toys, games and learning aids for children. Miaoli Toys is owned by a large Japanese private equity company. This company has told the media that the toymaker will be sold if it does not improve its performance. Figure 2 shows that sales growth has slowed right down in the last four years.

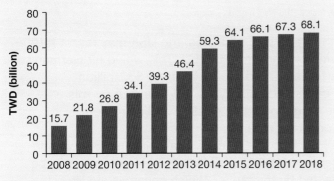

▲ Figure 2 Miaoli Toys sales revenue 2008–18

Historically, Miaoli has used both organic and inorganic growth strategies to advance company sales. In order to improve sales growth and meet the needs of the owners, some immediate deals may be required.

Two possible deals have been identified:

- **A joint venture with Twngo.com, an online Chinese retailer.** Miaoli Toys would have to pay TWD12 billion to set up the joint venture with Twngo.com. The profits from the venture would be split 50/50 and Twngo.com would meet all the IT costs. Miaoli would benefit from Twngo's online experience and have exposure to the huge, growing Chinese market for toys. The payback for this investment would be quite quick – around three years. However, in the first year Miaoli expects to make a heavy loss, which would affect the profits of the whole company. If it went ahead, the joint venture would generate TWD14.4 billion in sales in the first year. Total variable costs would be TWD4.4 billion and overheads would be TWD 2.1 billion.

- **Purchase ToyStop®, a European toy store chain.** ToyStop is a Danish-owned toy retailer with 220 stores in northern Europe. The acquisition would cost Miaoli TWD19.7 billion. However, the chain is currently profitable and Miaoli already supplies a number of toy chains in southern Europe. Extending its distribution network to northern Europe would be fairly simple. There would be some significant cost savings when transporting toys from Taiwan to Europe. Miaoli would be able to exploit some economies of scale in distribution. The deal would also fill a gap in Miaoli's European market exposure. The profits from the acquisition would not have to be shared. Also, the purchase price includes the stores themselves. Some of them are on high-street sites in top retail locations.

The main problem with this option is the high cost and the market uncertainty. In 2018, a large US toy chain called Toys "R" Us®, which had been established since 1948, collapsed. The chain had struggled to deal with debt and finally 'went under' (i.e. was unable to pay what it owed) when suppliers got scared. There is also the worry that a wider range of high street retailers have closed down in the West in recent years. However, Miaoli's financial director believes that, in the long term, much higher levels of profits could be generated from this venture. It might also be possible to sell and lease back many of the stores, which could be quite a profitable strategy.

Q

1 Calculate the loss made by Miaoli Toys from the joint venture with Twngo.com in the first year (if the venture went ahead). You are advised to show your working.

(4 marks)

2 Explain one way Miaoli Toys will benefit from economies of scale if it buys ToyStop. **(4 marks)**

3 Discuss how both of the proposed deals provide Miaoli Toys with access to cross-border distribution networks.

(8 marks)

4 Miaoli Toys could invest in a joint venture with Twingo.com or buy ToyStop. Evaluate which is the best option for Miaoli Toys. **(20 marks)**

31 GLOBAL EXPANSION AND UNCERTAINTY

LEARNING OBJECTIVES

By the end of this chapter you should be able to understand:
- the impact on businesses of movements in exchange rates
- skills shortages and their impact on international competitiveness.

GETTING STARTED

On 31 May 2018, the USA made the decision that it would extend steel and aluminium tariffs to the EU, Canada and Mexico. It said that a 25 per cent tax on steel and a 10 per cent tax on aluminium would start at midnight. The tariffs were introduced in March 2018, with the USA claiming it was for national security reasons. However, the EU, Canada and Mexico were given exemptions while discussions took place to find other solutions. For example, since the original announcement, South Korea, Argentina, Australia and Brazil have agreed limits on the volume of metals they sell to the USA. This is to avoid the tariffs. The tariffs will affect products such as plated steel, slabs, coil, rolls of aluminium and tubes. These are raw materials which are used in US key industries such as manufacturing, construction and oil.

Analysts have said the world is now closer to an all-out trade war than it was in the 1930s, with three huge trading regions potentially involved – the USA, the EU and China. The response from world leaders was critical. For example, German Chancellor Angela Merkel said the tariffs risked an 'escalation spiral' in global trade.

The USA is likely to be reported to the World Trade Organization (WTO) for its protectionist approach. Many countries have promised to respond negatively. For example, the EU has said that it would introduce tariffs on Harley Davidson motorcycles, orange juice and Levi® jeans. China has already put duties on $3 billion worth of US goods, including products such as nuts.

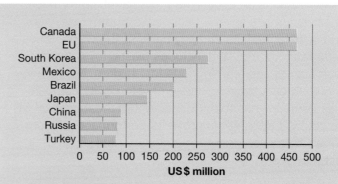

▲ Figure 1 US steel imports – sources

If the trade war escalates, the USA may target further tariffs on cars from the EU. This would hit Germany particularly hard. In 2017, about $32 billion of cars were sold by the EU to the USA. This was five times the value of steel and aluminium exports together.

How might US steel and aluminium producers be affected by the tariffs? How might US consumers be affected by the tariffs? Which countries are likely to be worst affected by the tariffs? Do you think that the US government was right to introduce tariffs on steel and aluminium? Why might new trade barriers result in global uncertainty?

GLOBAL EXPANSION

Globalisation has been increasing since the 1980s. Huge numbers of businesses and consumers have enjoyed the benefits of more trade, more jobs, higher incomes and more choice. The number of multinationals has grown significantly in this time.

The multinationals benefit most from global expansion. Being multinational can help an enterprise to develop **competitive advantages** that are not available to single-nation companies. Multinational corporations (MNCs) often benefit from the following.

- Global operations can bring much bigger economies of scale.
- Global sourcing can give firms more scope to find the best-quality resources at the right prices.

- Global operations allow companies to get closer to their international customers, both before and after sales.
- MNCs are available to a much bigger range of knowledge and scope for innovation.
- MNCs can diversify risk by engaging in a wider range of business activities.

GLOBAL UNCERTAINTY

One of the effects of globalisation is an increase in interdependence (i.e. two or more things relying on each other). This means that a key event in one country can have a serious impact on many other countries. This is because the economies of so many countries are significantly integrated. As a result, the increase in interdependence has raised levels of uncertainty around the globe. Some examples of this are outlined below.

- In 2008, the financial crisis led to a world recession. It started in the USA and was caused by irresponsible lending. This had a particular impact on the whole of the USA and much of Europe. Economic growth in many of these countries was flat or negative for several years after.
- In 2016, the UK voted to leave the EU. The impact of this is not known yet. According to reports, many believe that trade in the region could suffer and that investment will slow down due to huge uncertainty.
- In 2018, the threat of a global trade war emerged. This is discussed in 'Getting started' at the beginning of the chapter.

The events described above (and many others) could have a serious impact on many countries. The level of uncertainty created by such events tends to have a negative impact on international trade. Therefore, it has the potential to reduce job and wealth creation.

EFFECT OF EXCHANGE RATE MOVEMENTS ON BUSINESS

One of the factors which can make international trade uncertain is movements in exchange rates. The exchange rate is the price of one currency in terms of another. Like all prices, they can change. This is because prices are determined by market forces and at any time supply and demand conditions can change. When the exchange rate changes businesses that export or import will be affected.

Appreciation and revaluation: When a nation's currency gets stronger it is said to appreciate. This means that a unit of one currency can buy more of another currency. For example, Figure 2 shows that the value of the pound against the euro appreciated between the beginning and the middle of 2015. It rose from £1 = €1.27 to £1 = €1.41. This is an appreciation of 12.5 per cent.

In a minority of countries, the exchange rate is fixed. This means it does not fluctuate (move up and down) – it stays the same all the time. However, a government might wish to change the exchange rate so that it represents current valuations. If the government raises the exchange rate so that it is stronger the currency is said to have been revalued.

Depreciation and devaluation: When a nation's currency gets weaker it is said to depreciate. This means that a unit of one currency buys less of another. For example, Figure 2 shows that the value of the pound depreciated sharply against the euro after the Brexit vote in June 2016. It fell from £1 = €1.31 to £1 = €1.10 in just a couple of months. This is a depreciation of 16 per cent.

When the exchange rate is fixed, a government might choose to change the exchange rate so that it is weaker. If this happens, the exchange rate will fall and the currency will be devalued.

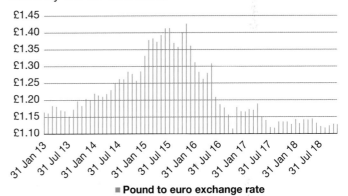

▲ Figure 2 Pound to euro exchange rate, 2013–17

Impact of exchange rate appreciation on businesses: Changes in the exchange rate can have an impact on the demand for exports and imports. This is because when the exchange rate changes, the prices of exports and imports also change. Look at what happens when the exchange rate rises from £1 = US$1.50 to £1 = US$2.

- **Impact on exporters.** If a UK firm *sells* goods worth £2 million to a US customer, the dollar price at the original exchange rate is US$3 million (£2 million × US$1.50). When the exchange rate rises, the dollar price of the goods also rises to US$4 million (£2 million × US$2). This means that demand for UK exports is likely to fall because they are now more expensive.
- **Impact on importers.** If another UK firm *buys* goods worth US$600 000 from a US supplier, the price in pounds at the original exchange rate is £400 000 (US$600 000 ÷ $1.50). When the exchange rate rises, the sterling price to the importer falls to £300 000 (US$600 000 ÷ US$2). This means that demand for imports is likely to rise because they are cheaper.

Impact of exchange rate depreciation on businesses:
A fall in the exchange rate will have the opposite effect on the demand for exports and imports. Look at what happens when the exchange rate falls from £1 = US$1.50 to £1 = US$1.20.

- **Impact on exporters.** If a UK firm *sells* goods worth £2 million to a US customer, the dollar price at the original exchange rate is US$3 million (£2 million × US$1.50). When the exchange rate falls, the dollar price of the goods also falls to US$2.4 million (£2 million × US$1.20). This means that demand for UK exports is likely to rise because they are now cheaper.

- **Impact on importers.** If another UK firm *buys* goods worth US$600 000 from a US supplier, the price in pounds at the original exchange rate is £400 000 (US$600 000 ÷ US$1.50). When the exchange rate falls, the sterling price to the importer rises to £500 000 (US$600 000 ÷ $1.20). This means that demand for imports is likely to fall because they are more expensive.

The effects of movements in the exchange rate on exporters and importers are summarised in Table 1.

Exchange rate	Price of exports	Demand for exports	Price of imports	Demand for imports
Rises (appreciation)	Rises	Falls	Falls	Rises
Falls (depreciation)	Falls	Rises	Rises	Falls

▲ Table 1 Summary of the effects of the movements in exchange rates

ACTIVITY 1　　SKILLS　INTERPRETATION, PROBLEM SOLVING

CASE STUDY: NG MOTOR PARTS

Ng Motor Parts, a Chinese parts manufacturer, exports braking systems to a Japanese car manufacturer. Each system sells for CNY500. Ng also imports steel cable from a Japanese supplier. A regular consignment costs JPY440 000. In 2018 the exchange rate between the Chinese yuan and the Japanese yen was CNY1 = JPY15.

1 Calculate the amount in JPY paid by the Japanese customer for a braking system.
2 Calculate the amount in CNY paid by Ng for the steel cable.

Ng Motor Parts expects the exchange rate to fall in 12 months' time to CNY1 = JPY12

3 Calculate the effect of this change on the prices of exports and imports for Ng Motor Parts.
4 Explain how the price changes in (3) might affect demand?

THE SIGNIFICANCE OF CHANGES IN THE EXCHANGE RATE ON BUSINESS

Elasticity of demand: If there is a depreciation in the value of a currency, the effect it will have on a business and its products depends on price elasticity of demand. For example, if Australian businesses sell goods where demand is price inelastic, then the fall in price would have only a limited impact on the quantity demanded. If demand for exports is price elastic, then there will be a bigger percentage increase in the quantity demanded. The demand for many Australian exports may be price inelastic because many of its exports are important commodities. This is good news for Australian exporters if there is an appreciation of the Australian currency, but bad news if there is a depreciation.

Significance of the cause of the fluctuation in exchange rate: If there is an appreciation in a currency because there have been improvements in efficiency and productivity, then businesses will get used to the stronger currency more easily. However, if a currency rises due to speculation (i.e. the risky practice of buying assets, such as shares, currency or property, in the hope that they will be sold in the future at a higher price) or weaknesses in other countries, then businesses could become uncompetitive. This is because the rise in the currency is not related to either improved competitiveness or productivity.

Fixed contracts: Many businesses use fixed contracts to counter fluctuations in the exchange rate. This means that temporary changes in the exchange rate will have a smaller impact. The price of buying raw materials is often set 12 to 18 months in the future. Exporters may also use special financial instruments to protect themselves from dramatic changes in the exchange rate. It is these fixed contracts that help to reduce the uncertainty around exchange rate fluctuations. It also means that there are delays between changes in exchange rates and the impact on business.

Economic risk: As already discussed, firms trading internationally are almost always exposed to movements in exchange rates. Risks associated with this come in several forms. The most serious is the long-term risk that a strategy of locating in a low-cost production area faces when the currency of the target country's currency appreciates. For example, in the 1990s many firms built factories in China. Here, the costs of production were low and cost savings could be made. These savings depended on the Chinese government's policy of pegging (i.e. maintaining a fixed exchange rate) its currency to the US dollar. Over time, for a variety of political reasons, this peg has relaxed and the yuan has steadily appreciated. This means the low-cost advantages are not as valuable.

The risk described above is known as **economic risk**. It is defined as a risk that future cash flows will change due to unexpected exchange rate fluctuations. This is one of the most serious financial risks facing an international firm because future cash flows form the basis of a business's overall value. Consequently, managing economic risk requires careful analysis of the political, regulatory and cultural environments affecting the currency over time.

For example, the US dollar is the most powerful international currency. Besides having one of the largest economies in the world, the dollar has a role in most international transactions, either directly or indirectly. As a consequence, any movement in the dollar will have an impact on international trade.

At the start of 2015, with the US economy recovering and interest rates likely to rise, the dollar looked set to appreciate against most other currencies. The areas that are most likely to feel the impact of any rise in the dollar are the emerging market economies. This is because companies from the developing world are more likely to take out loans in dollars.

For example, Petrobras, the Brazilian state-owned oil company, raised large amounts of money by issuing bonds measured in dollars. With falling energy prices, Petrobras is not making as much income as it expected when it took on the debt. It is now finding it hard to repay. It will find it harder still if the dollar continues to appreciate against its home currency, the real.

SKILLS SHORTAGES AND THEIR IMPACT ON INTERNATIONAL COMPETITIVENESS

Many industries require highly trained engineers, scientists, technicians or professionals to compete. Companies that have long-term access to skilled and low-cost labour have an advantage over their competitors who do not. If

a firm owns these advantages in its home market, it may be able to produce and export more effectively than its competitors. If it wishes to expand production and chooses to locate abroad, it will hope to improve these competitive advantages, or at least ensure that they are not eroded.

In some countries there are serious **skills shortages**. Governments and businesses define skills shortages slightly differently. A government would like to train and educate the country's workforce in the hope that it would make them more competitive relative to other nations. However, employers are most concerned when they cannot fill specific vacancies or cannot do so at the right skill level. In recent years, businesses in a number of countries around the world have been troubled by skills shortages. These include the USA, Australia, New Zealand, Canada and the UK. One sector which has struggled in particular is manufacturing. Figure 3 shows the rising number of vacancies in manufacturing jobs in the USA.

If businesses are unable to recruit sufficient numbers of skilled workers, their **international competitiveness** can be threatened. The main effects of skills shortages are outlined below.

Higher wages: When there is a shortage of skilled workers in a specific labour market, the price of labour (wages) is increased. This is a reaction to changes in market forces. Wages are forced up because the supply of labour is restricted. The wage increases will also be higher if the demand for that skilled labour is also high

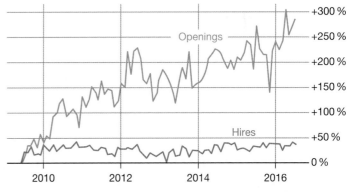

▲ Figure 3 The rising number of job vacancies in US manufacturing 2009–17

and rising. In 2017, a Federal Reserve survey in the USA found that there were labour shortages all over the country. Business had no choice but to pay higher wages to attract and keep skilled workers. In another survey by the Associated General Contractors of America, 73 per cent of businesses were finding it difficult to attract qualified workers. In addition, 55 per cent of businesses surveyed said that worker shortages were a bigger concern than federal regulations and the low infrastructure investment in the country.

Lower quality: If businesses are unable to attract high-quality skilled workers, it is possible that the quality of output will be negatively affected. This is because firms may be forced to recruit workers who are unqualified or lacking in skills and experience. As a result, the quality of output is likely to be poorer. This could threaten the reputation of the business.

Lower productivity: A shortage of skilled labour may result in lower levels of productivity. Lower productivity may be caused by production delays. This is because it takes businesses much longer to recruit skilled labour. In extreme cases, a business may have to stop production altogether if it cannot recruit the required number of skilled workers. Alternatively, businesses may be using workers who do not have the required skill levels. This might result in a slower work rate and more mistakes, which take time to resolve. Either way, the impact on productivity will be negative.

Loss of business: If labour shortages continue for a while, there is a danger that a business will lose customers. This is because customers may be kept waiting for their orders. There is a limit to how long customers are prepared to wait. If it is too long, customers are likely to find alternative suppliers. Once a customer is lost to a rival, it is very difficult to tempt them back. In the long term, this could threaten the survival of a business.

ACTIVITY 2   SKILLS ▶ CRITICAL THINKING, INTERPRETATION

CASE STUDY: SKILLS SHORTAGES IN AUSTRALIA

Figure 4 shows that unemployment in Australia is about 5.5 per cent. However, despite the availability of labour in the country, there are some developing skills shortages. According to a survey by National Australia Bank (NAB), in the last quarter of 2017, more than 50 per cent of businesses said they were having difficulties finding suitable staff. For example, according to the survey:

- 48 per cent of SMEs said there was a skills shortage in their sector
- 62 per cent of SMEs said graduates were not 'job ready'
- around 1 in 3 SMEs said in the future self-motivation, adaptability and services orientation skills will be increasingly important
- 68 per cent of SMEs thought that training in Australia is inadequate.

The skills shortage is hampering economic growth in Australia. This is because SMEs are reluctant to expand due to the labour shortages. To help fill

the skills gaps, 1 in 4 SMEs are recruiting growing numbers of skilled migrants.

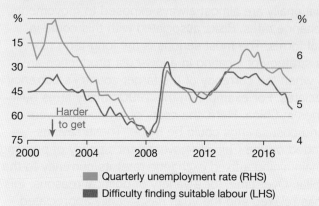

■ Quarterly unemployment rate (RHS)
■ Difficulty finding suitable labour (LHS)

▲ Figure 4 Australia, unemployment rate and recruitment difficulties 2000–18
Based on Reserve Bank of Australia, Underemployment and Labour Market Spare Capacity.

1 Explain two effects of skills shortages in Australia.
2 How might the Australian government help to reduce skills shortages in Australia?

THINKING BIGGER

Muhammad Hazim left Malaysia to come to the UK and become an accountant, but now his home nation wants him back. The fastest growing South East Asian country is looking for thousands like him to return to address a 'brain drain'. Malaysia has tried to prevent the high percentage of skilled workers who leave the country. This is true in India. The cost of Indians studying abroad is as much as $17 billion a year in lost revenue.

The African brain drain is also serious, but the same situation is also affecting European countries. Almost 23 000 German scientists have left the country and in 2015 Chancellor Angela Merkel created programmes to attract them back, and in 2015, over 1.3 million UK university graduates worked overseas. The USA also faces a shortage of IT specialists.

The Malaysian government has run careers fairs in the UK, bringing together UK-based Malaysian students with Malaysian employers. Over 4000 Malaysians attended one fair in London. Their message is, 'you can have an international career in Malaysia'. The government also offers tax breaks for five years if they return.

Therefore, skills shortage is a global problem. One solution is for countries to encourage their own skilled workers to return.

You could use this information in a variety of ways. It can be used when answering questions on skills shortages. It might also be useful when discussing influences on competitive advantage and the impact of a skilled workforce on business.

LINKS

Businesses operating internationally usually began as successful businesses operating in one domestic environment. As such, they understood their market (Student Book 1, Chapters 1–13) and how to operate successfully within it (Student Book 1, Chapters 14–18). They managed their business activities well (Student Book 1, Chapters 26–40) and knew how to assess their competitive environment (Student Book 1, Chapters 41–43). As they grew, they adapted their strategy to suit the evolving business (this book, Chapters 3–8) and planned for where they wanted to be in the future (Chapters 20 and 21). Making the decision to expand internationally involves understanding the competitive advantages held by the firm and evaluating whether these advantages will apply in the international market (Chapters 22–24). Retaining or adapting those advantages requires that a business thoroughly understands the markets in which it is competing (Chapters 22, 26, 28, 29 and 34).

SUBJECT VOCABULARY

appreciation (of a currency) a rise in the value of a country's currency (making exports more expensive and imports cheaper)

competitive advantage the advantage one firm has over its competitors in providing a certain product

depreciation (of a currency) the loss in value of a country's currency (making exports cheaper and imports more expensive)

devaluation (of a currency) the adjustment of the value of a currency in relation to other currencies to make it weaker (usually by a government)

economic risk the risk that future cash flows will change due to unexpected exchange rate changes

international competitiveness the extent to which a business or a geographical area, such as a country, can compete successfully against rivals

revaluation (of a currency) the adjustment of the value of a currency in relation to other currencies to make it stronger (usually by the government)

skills shortages where potential employees do not have the skills demanded by employers

CHECKPOINT

1 What is meant by the appreciation of a currency?

2 What is meant by the depreciation of a currency?

3 Outline the significance for business of changes in the exchange rates.

4 What impact does price elasticity of demand have on businesses facing changes in exchange rates?

5 How can firms reduce the risks of fluctuating exchange rates?

6 What is meant by competitive advantage?

7 How can a business in a global market improve its competitiveness?

8 What impact do skills shortages have on international competitiveness?

EXAM PRACTICE

CASE STUDY: DUBAI INTERNATIONAL AIRPORT

SKILLS CRITICAL THINKING, ANALYSIS, INTERPRETATION, PROBLEM SOLVING, REASONING

Dubai International Airport, in the UAE, is one of the world's busiest airports. The number of passengers passing through the airport has risen dramatically since 2010. Figure 5 shows that passengers using the airport will more than double by 2020. The airport serves more than 90 different airlines flying to more than 240 different destinations across six continents.

The airport complex has experienced significant investment in recent years, which is ongoing. The number of A380 stands at the airport is set to increase by 2018 with more in the future. The next phase of expansion aims to increase the airport's capacity to 118 million passengers per year by 2023.

Dubai International Airport has a huge shopping complex. In 2014, $1.9 billion was spent in the airport. This is a 7 per cent increase on the previous year. Shops are in all three of the terminals but the largest and most modern are found in Terminal 3. All the stores are open 24 hours a day, 7 days a week.

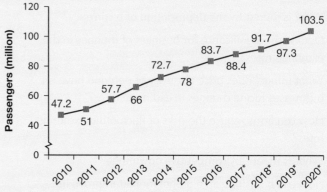

*Estimated

▲ Figure 5 Dubai International airport, passenger traffic 2010–20

The UAE is having problems with skills shortages in some jobs, just like a number of countries around the world. In a survey carried out by recruitment firm Robert Walters, it was found that 72 per cent of people who responded to the survey had been affected by talent shortages across sectors such as financial and business services, technology, media, telecommunications and manufacturing. About a third said they could not find the right people to interview for roles.

Even companies with an effective HR department said they were having staffing problems. Fifty per cent said it was a problem recruiting professionals from both abroad and other talent pools. Even the offer of higher pay was failing to attract sufficient numbers of quality staff. Professional workers were increasingly looking for a better work–life balance, career progression (i.e. moving from one level up to the next) and the opportunity to work abroad.

According to Robert Walters, businesses in the UAE and the wider Middle East needed to speed up the recruitment process. For example, they needed to reduce the amount of time between the job interview and the job offer, especially with overseas candidates, who were often involved in multiple job applications and needed to know quickly if they had got the job.

The UAE government recognises the need to equip young people with vocational skills. It is developing a national technical and vocational education and training (TVET) system. The government is also prioritising building relevant skills to coincide with new and emerging technologies, materials and systems.

One of the challenges in the UAE is that universities and colleges do not always equip students with the range of skills that businesses require. For example, there were insufficient numbers of graduates in science technology, transportation and logistics. Universities were recruiting too many students on business courses. One academic, Mohammed al Ohani, said that universities and colleges needed to meet the needs of society. He said. 'We want to develop a world-class system of a knowledge-based economy by 2025. But for this we need more research centres, more institutions, sustainable funding and educational leadership.'

	2017	*2018
AED1 =	JPY1.6	JPY1.8
AED1 =	CNY1.9	CNY1.6

▲ Table 2 Exchange rate information

Table 2 shows that the predictions for the exchange rate in 2018 are different from the actual exchange rates in 2017.

1 Explain one reason why exchange rates may fluctuate for the UAE dirham (AED). **(4 marks)**
2 In 2017, an airport trader sold goods worth AED250 to a Japanese traveller. Calculate the cost in yen to the Japanese customer. You are advised to show your working. **(4 marks)**
3 An airport trader needs to purchase 10 new tills from a Chinese manufacturer. The cost in yuan would be CNY500 000. Calculate whether the trader should buy the tills now or wait until 2018. You are advised to show your working. **(4 marks)**
4 Construct a supply and demand diagram to show how wages are increased by skills shortages. **(4 marks)**
5 Discuss the possible impact of skills shortages on the international competitiveness of businesses operating in Dubai International Airport. **(8 marks)**
6 Assess the possible impact of changes in the exchange rate (between 2017 and 2018) between the AED and the JPY on future airport trade. **(12 marks)**

EXAM HINT

When considering a question involving international competitiveness, it is useful to think about all the basic definitions and concepts that apply to a small, domestic business. They are often the same for a large multinational firm – it is just that the context is different and the application more complex.

Some students wrongly assume that different rules apply to MNCs and so they need to be evaluated differently. This is rarely the case. For example, the problems (and opportunities) that MNCs face in trading in different currencies mostly come down to familiar concepts: supply and demand, pricing strategies, cash flow and managing risk.

The competitive advantages that they hope to rely upon for growth are more complicated. However, they may come from the same sources as those of domestic firms. The same is often true for the threats that they face: for example, all businesses need suitable employees if their businesses are to succeed and grow.

GLOBAL MARKETING

This section looks at how businesses might adjust their marketing practices when selling goods and services in global markets. For example, it deals with global marketing strategies, global localisation (glocalisation) and different marketing approaches such as ethnocentric, geocentric and polycentric. It explores how the marketing mix might be adapted for global markets and how Ansoff's Matrix and Porter's Strategic Matrix might be applied to global markets. It also covers the cultural differences that exist in some overseas markets and the features of global niche markets. Finally, the section investigates the cultural and social factors that businesses might need to consider when selling in global markets. These might include cultural differences, differences in tastes and preferences, language differences and whether certain brands and promotional methods are appropriate.

32 MARKETING

LEARNING OBJECTIVES

By the end of this chapter you should be able to understand:

- global marketing strategy and global localisation (glocalisation)
- different marketing approaches: domestic/ethnocentric, mixed/geocentric and international/polycentric
- application and adaptation of the marketing mix (4Ps) to global markets
- application of Ansoff's Matrix and Porter's Strategic Matrix to global marketing decisions.

GETTING STARTED

US pizza chain Domino's® is an example of a global marketing success. Global marketing is the ability to deliver a product or service to customers worldwide. Domino's first started trading in 1960 with just one store when Tom Monaghan and his brother, James, purchased 'DomiNick's', a pizza store in Ypsilanti, Michigan. A $900 loan was taken out to fund the purchase. In 1961, James sold his half to his brother Tom for a car.

In 1968, the first Domino's franchise was opened in Ypsilanti, Michigan. By 1978 there were 200 Domino's stores in the USA. In 1983 Domino's opened its first store abroad in Winnipeg, Canada, and by the end of the year there were 1000 Domino's stores. In 1989, Domino's launched its first new product – the Pan Pizza – and by the end of the year there were 5000 Domino's stores. During the 1990s, a wider range of products was introduced and the company launched its own website. Tom retired, with the ownership of the company passing to Bain Capital Inc.

In order to get the Domino's brand accepted worldwide, the company often had to change its menu and recipes to meet the needs of different cultures. For example, in India the dough and toppings are similar to the Indian roti (flat bread) and subji (vegetables). Domino's pizzas also appeal to the Indian market because people like to share plates of food. Indian consumers might also be attracted by the fact that pizzas can be eaten with your hands.

During the 2000s, Domino's introduced more new products and in 2007 started to process online orders. In 2009, it took the risk of getting rid of its 49-year-old pizza recipe and launched a 'new and inspired' pizza with an unusual advertising campaign. In 2012, Domino's changed its logo and launched the 'Pizza Theatre' store design. This was designed to improve the customer experience at Domino's. In 2017, Domino's became the first and only national pizza delivery chain to offer points to its loyalty members.

It opened stores in three new countries – Slovakia, Malta and Austria – and Domino's is now the second-biggest pizza chain in the world, with interests in over 15 000 stores.

Why has Domino's grown so much since opening its first shop? What do you think is meant by a global marketing strategy? Why might Domino's have wanted to expand into countries such as the UK, Japan and India? Why does Domino's sell different types of products in different countries?

GLOBAL MARKETING STRATEGY

Chapter 9 explored marketing strategy as a set of plans that aim to achieve a specific marketing objective. When some businesses operate outside their country of origin, they operate a common **global marketing strategy**. They aim to sell their products beyond their national borders. Global marketing involves the planning, producing, placing and promoting of a business's products in a worldwide market. This process can involve a business having offices in different countries, but the process is also facilitated (i.e. made possible) by the growth of the Internet.

GLOBAL LOCALISATION (GLOCALISATION)

The global localisation approach differs from having a common strategy for all countries. It involves adapting to local expectations in order for a business to succeed in an international market. The phrase, 'think global, act local' is a good summary of what is meant by glocalisation. The phrase suggests that businesses should aim to reach potential customers around the world, but they must consider local tastes, customs and traditions to be successful with those customers. Global businesses should be sensitive to the specific preferences of the different markets in which they want to operate and succeed.

DIFFERENT MARKETING APPROACHES

When considering entering international markets, businesses use a range of different marketing approaches for their products.

Ethnocentric (domestic) approach: Overseas markets are seen as identical or similar to domestic markets. This approach assumes that what is good for the domestic market will be good for global markets. Businesses using this approach make little or no attempt to adapt their product for different markets. For example, Sony's PlayStation 4® is a very popular console worldwide. The console is sold in most countries, but it is the same in every market. Compare this approach with the approach of Domino's in 'Getting started', where different types of products are sold to reflect the different tastes of different markets.

Many businesses use an **ethnocentric** approach, including:

- Pizza Express®, which expanded into China to meet the growing taste for Western food by Chinese customers
- Apple, with products such as the iPhone®, iPad® and MacBook®
- Swatch® watches
- Rolls-Royce cars.

Using an ethnocentric marketing approach has its advantages, such as economies of scale. Because a product is standardised (i.e. made the same) across markets, the scale of production is much larger and so savings can be made on raw materials. In addition, there are no development costs involved in adapting products for different markets. In the case of Domino's, market research and product development had to be carried out to identify and develop products that served local demand. This type of research is costly and leads to further costs in product development. Average

costs can be reduced if this marketing activity is not required. This can lead to lower prices and increased competitiveness.

However, this approach may also have disadvantages. For example, a product may not sell well if is not adapted to the local market. If a marketing mix is not adapted to a local market, a business may be taking a risk about the appeal of the product to a new market.

ACTIVITY 1 | SKILLS | CRITICAL THINKING, ANALYSIS

CASE STUDY: RED BULL®

The Red Bull® energy drink is produced by the Austrian company, Red Bull. Dietrich Mateschitz developed the formula for Red Bull in the 1980s and the drink was first launched in Austria in 1987. The launch was not just a new drink but a whole new product category. In addition to Red Bull, some of the key brands in the energy drinks market include Monster®, Lucozade®, Boost®, Gatorade®, NOS® and Rockstar®.

In 2017, Red Bull was available in over 170 different countries and sold more than 6.3 billion cans. The marketing strategy of Red Bull is to associate the brand with an adventurous lifestyle. The company's marketing slogan implies that the drink gives you so much energy you could fly. Another feature of its marketing strategy is to host extreme sports events all over the world. Examples include:

- Red Bull Indianapolis Grand Prix
- Red Bull Air Race around the world
- Red Bull Cliff Diving in the USA
- Red Bull Soapbox Race in Jordan.

The brand's event marketing strategy helps to promote the brand all over the world.

The company has a clear product differentiation strategy. Red Bull charges a premium price, since the brand is perceived (i.e. how people think about something) to provide consumers with additional benefits. Red Bull claims that consuming the drink will help people to lead a full and active lifestyle and enhance mental and physical performance. It comes from Austria, it is not sold in 12-ounce cans or bottles like Coca-Cola or Pepsi and its packaging has continued to look European since its launch.

1 What is meant by 'ethnocentric marketing', (use Red Bull as an example)?
2 Give one advantage and one disadvantage to Red Bull of adopting an ethnocentric strategy when marketing its soft drink globally.

Polycentric (international) approach: Businesses adapt their product to the local markets in which they plan to sell the product. This involves developing and marketing different products for the demands of local customers in different markets. For example, car manufacturers will adapt cars and model names to meet the expectations of their local markets.

One advantage of this approach is that the product should sell well. By tailoring products to specific customer needs, the product can be targeted precisely within the particular market. This means that it will be a lot easier for a business to gain acceptance in new markets. As a result, it may be possible to reduce advertising and promotion costs since less effort will be required to 'push' the product in new markets. Also, because the **polycentric** approach ensures that products meet the needs of consumers with slightly different tastes and preferences, sales and revenue will be higher.

However, the costs involved are a disadvantage. Developing individual products is expensive, and these costs can be so high that the project itself is risky. For example, in 2007 Tesco launched a new, UK-style supermarket in the USA called Fresh & Easy®. It was tailored to meet American consumers' demands. For example, the stores focused heavily on fresh ready meals to cater for the convenience that American customers expected. They also chose not to use the Tesco name in the American market. However, the project was not as successful as the same approach in the UK market and Tesco sold its Fresh & Easy stores. The project cost Tesco billions of pounds.

Geocentric (mixed) approach: Businesses use a combination of the ethnocentric and polycentric marketing approaches. This **geocentric** 'glocalisation' approach is used by many multinational corporations. The business's strategy is to maintain and promote the global brand name, whilst also tailoring its products to local markets. For example, McDonald's makes sure that its Big Mac® burger tastes the same in every country in which it is sold. This approach is used by various fast-food chains. Some examples of the type of foods they might use to replace what you're used to are shown in Table 1.

Egypt	Japan
Food might include kofta meat, fava beans and different types of bread, like baladi bread.	Food might include teriyaki sauce, noodles or even sushi. Desserts might be different, with sweets called wagashi.
Greece	**India**
Food might include tzatziki sauce, fried cheese (saganaki) or cheese pie (tyropita). Desserts might be more honey-based, like baklava.	Food might include breads like roti or naans and more rice dishes. Drinks might include lassi or masala tea.

▲ Table 1 Types of foods that could be used in 'glocal' meals

Table 2 provides a summary of the advantages and disadvantages of the different marketing approaches.

	Advantages	Disadvantages
Ethnocentric	Lower cost of development and production. Economies of scale.	Product may not sell well. Does not take account of national/cultural differences.
Polycentric	Targeted products for different markets – higher sales.	Higher cost of development. Difficult to compete with established local brands.
Geocentric	Tailoring product to local tastes and needs – higher sales.	Higher cost of product development.

▲ Table 2 Advantages and disadvantages of different marketing approaches

APPLICATION AND ADAPTATION OF THE MARKETING MIX (4PS) TO GLOBAL MARKETS

As mentioned earlier in the chapter, a marketing strategy is the set of plans that a business uses to achieve specific marketing objectives. For example, a local takeaway may aim to become the market leader in the town in which it operates. To achieve this objective, the strategy might be:

- offering locally sourced, organic ingredients (**p**roduct)
- lowering off-peak prices (**p**rice)
- establishing a delivery service (**p**lace)
- a loyalty scheme which offers discounts to regular customers (**p**romotion).

But what about a business that operates on a global scale? What strategies might a business use when operating in mass markets? The marketing mix is used in global markets and must be considered as part of a global marketing strategy.

Price: Decisions around price need to consider local factors such as incomes, taxes, rents and other costs. It is unlikely that a business will charge the same price in all markets. For example, an Apple iPhone might cost less in India than in the USA. Price will also reflect different local factors, such as wage rates and taxes.

Product: To what extent should a business modify or adapt its product for global markets? The section above looked at the different approaches that businesses can take with their products when moving into international markets (ethnocentric, polycentric and geocentric). One example of a business that modifies its products in overseas markets (a polycentric approach) is Domino's, the pizza company. It offers slightly different toppings for its pizzas in different countries, such as in India, where toppings contain more vegetables and spices.

Promotion: When promoting products in global markets, businesses need to be conscious of language differences. Marketers should know the values, beliefs, perceptions, legal and sociocultural aspects of the different foreign environments. So, while trying to create product awareness, generate sales and maximise brand loyalty, marketers have to identify the target customers. They should deliver the message to attract the foreign customers. One common method of promotion is to change the name of products in overseas markets. For example, Mr Clean®, a household cleaning product produced by US company Proctor & Gamble, is called by many different names in different countries. In Mexico it is called Maestro Limpio®, in Spain Don Limpio® in Italy Mastro Lindo® in Germany Meister Proper® and Flash® in Ireland and the UK.

Place: Businesses need to take account of how local consumers buy their products. For example, the Tesco Fresh & Easy stores may not have appealed to how some US consumers shop using larger supermarkets. The development of online selling has helped many retailers, for example, to distribute goods all over the world.

Table 3 provides a summary of some questions to ask raised by businesses when considering the 4Ps.

Product	Price
Should the product be adapted for different markets, or can it stay as it is?	What price should be charged in the global markets? What prices are charged by local competitors?
Promotion	Place
What are the most effective promotion methods in different countries?	How do consumers buy their products in local markets?

▲ Table 3 The marketing mix in global markets: a summary

APPLICATION OF ANSOFF'S MATRIX TO GLOBAL MARKETING DECISIONS

Ansoff's Matrix was discussed in Chapter 2. It is a strategic tool to help a business achieve growth. It can be applied to global markets and help to inform decisions around marketing strategy. It is possible to apply this model to a glocalisation strategy, as used by multinational brands such as Starbucks, Ford and McDonald's.

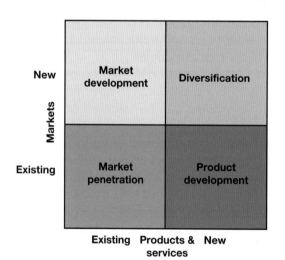

▲ Figure 1 Ansoff's Matrix

As discussed in Chapter 2, Ansoff's Matrix shows four strategies that a business might adopt. Risk can become greater the further a firm extends from its existing products and consumers – for example, the further it extends from the top left-hand corner of the matrix. This can become particularly pronounced when businesses extend into international markets, where expertise of local conditions and tastes might be less secure. When considering global marketing, the focus is on businesses introducing new or existing products into new markets that may have national and cultural differences.

- **Market penetration.** This exists where a business adapts products for markets in which it already operates. For example, McDonald's already operates in Japan. By developing and launching the Teriyaki McBurger® into this (existing) market, the strategy is clearly one of market penetration (i.e. the act of entering a market).

- **Market development.** This involves the marketing of existing products in new markets. It is not always straightforward as customers from different regions of the same country, let alone a different country, may have different tastes and preferences. Chapter 2 showed how a market development strategy relies heavily on understanding local habits, tastes and needs. Even where market development is appropriate and successful, it is often necessary to make slight modifications to suit the new market, for example, in terms of language or labelling.

  Domino's, in 'Getting started', adapted its products in many countries, such an India, to meet local tastes. However, it kept its model of customer service and prompt delivery. This refining of an existing product, to fit into a new – in this case, overseas – market is an example of a market development strategy. This is also an example of glocalisation, where products are modified for local tastes.

- **Product development.** This is where a business promotes new or modified products in existing markets. This approach may be appropriate for a business that markets products with short product life cycles – such as clothes and fashion accessories.

- **Diversification.** This occurs when new products are developed for entirely new markets. This is the riskiest strategy because a business is venturing into markets where it has little or no experience. The Mumbai-based Tata Group is an example of a highly diversified business. It has interests in steel, car making, chemicals, beverages, perfume, financial services, hotels and consultancy services. Diversification is explored further in Chapter 2.

APPLICATION OF PORTER'S STRATEGIC MATRIX TO GLOBAL MARKETING DECISIONS

Chapter 2 explained that Porter's Strategic Matrix can be used by a business to identify the sources of competitive advantage that a business might achieve in a market. Three distinct approaches were identified in the matrix. These were:

- **cost leadership** – where a business attempts to be the lowest-cost supplier in the market
- **differentiation** – where a business successfully distinguishes its product from those of rivals in a mass market

- **focus** – which involves a business targeting a narrow range of customers in one of two ways – either cost focus or differentiation focus. The sale of First Class air tickets might be an example of differentiation focus in the airline industry.

This approach can be used in both domestic markets and global markets. In some circumstances, a business might be able to transfer the competitive advantage it has in the domestic market to a global market. A detailed example of this is highlighted in Activity 2.

ACTIVITY 2   SKILLS   CRITICAL THINKING, REASONING

CASE STUDY: NIKE

Nike has become a global brand by differentiating its products. Nike is known for its innovative (i.e. introducing a new way of doing something) styles and use of new technologies in footwear and other products. For example, in 1979 Nike introduced a pair of trainers with gas-filled plastic membranes (i.e. thin layers) which made running more comfortable. Eventually, rivals introduced their own versions of this technology and caught up with Nike. However, in 1987 Nike launched Air Max®. This shoe contained two independent airbags to absorb the sudden impact from running and jumping. Customers could see the bags through small windows in the heel or toe of the shoe. Nike also customised the product by adjusting the size of bags depending on the pressure exerted by individual users.

After a few years, Nike needed something else to help differentiate its brand from those of rivals. It began to focus on digital gadgets and make further developments with Nike's idea that everyone was an athlete. In 2006, Nike introduced Nike+ iPod Sports Kit® in the US market. This mass-produced gadget was a device to measure the distance and speed of a run or a walk. Since then Nike has continued this connection with technology and introduced:

- Nike+ Sportband Kit®
- Nike+ Sportwatch®
- Nike+ Baseball®
- Nike+ Training®
- Nike+ Fuelband®
- a running app that could be used in the latest iPhones.

All this was based on a small chip which was inserted in Nike footwear.

Nike also made very good use of social media. Today, each Nike+ product has its own Facebook page and, as a result of its success in differentiating its brand, Nike has been able to cut advertising costs substantially below those of rivals. Nike is also able to charge premium prices for many of its products.

1 Which of Porter's strategies has been adopted by Nike in this example?

2 What methods have been used by Nike to distinguish its products from those of rivals?

3 What might be the consequence for a business that fails to adopt one of Porter's strategies when selling in a global market?

LINKS

It might be argued that marketing becomes even more important when selling goods and services in overseas markets. One reason for this is because mistakes can often be very costly, with firms having to stop competing if things go wrong. Many of the marketing issues already discussed in Student Book 1, such as Chapter 9 (Marketing objectives and strategy), Chapter 10 (Product/service design), Chapter 11 (Promotion and branding), Chapter 12 (Pricing strategies) and Chapter 13 (Distribution) can be linked to this chapter. Chapter 2 in this book (Theories of corporate strategy) might also be relevant.

CHECKPOINT

1 What is meant by the term glocalisation?

2 Give three reasons why a business may want to expand into global markets.

3 What is meant by an ethnocentric marketing strategy?

4 What are the advantages to a business of adopting a geocentric marketing approach?

5 State the four strategies outlined by Ansoff's Matrix.

6 According to Porter's Strategic Matrix, what are the three sources of competitive advantage a business might adopt when marketing goods and services?

THINKING BIGGER

What is the best marketing approach for a business planning to expand into international markets? We live in a global economy, full of global brands, and this is largely due to the spread of the Internet. To what extent is this globalisation a positive development for businesses?

The ability to exploit new markets is an obvious advantage. Some of the regions with the highest rates of economic growth – such as China and India – have high population numbers, and consumers in these regions should benefit from having access to a wider range of goods and services. The Internet is also directly impacting on global marketing, effectively reducing the costs involved in operating on a global scale. These regions offer exciting opportunities for Western business. However, there are also risks for businesses wishing to expand internationally. These require careful strategic consideration.

SUBJECT VOCABULARY

ethnocentric approach an approach to global marketing where a business makes little or no attempt to change or modify the product when selling into new foreign markets

geocentric approach an approach to global marketing where a business uses a combination of the ethnocentric and polycentric marketing approaches when marketing a product in new foreign markets

global marketing strategy the process of adjusting a company's marketing strategies to reflect conditions, consumer tastes and demand in other countries

glocalisation a combination of the words 'globalisation' and 'localisation'. It involves the development and sale of products to customers around the world which reflect specific local customs, tastes and traditions

localisation strategies that adjust products to fit with target customers

polycentric approach an approach to global marketing where a business adapts the product to meet the slightly different needs of customers in new foreign markets

EXAM PRACTICE

CASE STUDY: DUNKIN' DONUTS®

SKILLS CRITICAL THINKING, ANALYSIS, INTERPRETATION, REASONING

Like many chains, Dunkin' Donuts® started as a single restaurant set up by Bill Rosenberg in Massachusetts in 1950. He opened a shop serving affordable high-quality coffee and donuts. Dunkin' Donuts has adapted its successful US business model for use in overseas markets. It now has over 12 000 restaurants in over 45 countries.

Dunkin' Donuts has adapted many of its products to satisfy its global customers in each country. For example, Dunkin' Donuts found that their Lebanese customers love chocolate and eat large quantities of fruits like mango. As a result, they created the Mango Chocolate Donut. In Russia, Dunkin' Donuts added Dunclairs. In South Korea, they developed the Grapefruit Coolata. These products were tailored to appeal to foreign consumers. Dunkin' Donuts carried out market research and analysed foreign markets, following up this research with effective product development.

In addition to market research and product development, Dunkin' Donuts has also explored the use of mobile and digital technology. It has introduced loyalty programmes and developed effective one-to-one marketing to help the organisation grow and differentiate itself from other coffee shops and quick service restaurants (QSRs).

Dunkin' Donuts' Senior Vice President of Brand Marketing, Global Consumer Insights and Product Innovation, Chris Fuqua, said that the DD Perks Rewards programme was very important when differentiating its service from that of rivals in the competitive coffee shop market. Dunkin' Donuts now has over 8 million DD Perks Rewards programme members. This is one of the fastest-growing loyalty programs in the QSR industry. Dunkin' Donuts also introduced on-the-go ordering in 2016.

Dunkin' Donuts continues to develop as an innovative business. Some examples of recent innovations are outlined below.

- New beverages such as Cold Brew®, Iced Coffee and Frozen Dunkin' Coffee®, will be pushed harder. There are also plans to extend its premium tea and frozen beverage lines and introduce more espresso products.

- New breakfast sandwiches. Morning sandwiches are being emphasised with both new and returning 'favourites'.

- The Removal of artificial dyes from donuts. In 2017, US stores introduced donuts without artificial dyes. The company wants to stop using artificial dyes from its national US menu by the end of 2018.

- The company launched Dunkin' Deals, a series of value offers. For example, one deal included two Egg and Cheese Wake-up Wrap® sandwiches for $2 to help increase afternoon trade.

- DD Perks® loyalty programme. During 2017, Dunkin' Donuts added more than 2 million members to its DD Perks® loyalty programme. This raised its total membership to about 8 million members.

- There are plans to test 'tender agnostic' payment systems as part of the DD Perks loyalty programme. This means that members will be able to earn points whichever payment method is used, such as DD Card, credit, debit or cash.

- A newly built digital catering platform is being tested and there are plans to expand third-party delivery services. The aim is to create a combined catering/delivery platform in 2019.

- Implementing innovative drive-thru technology. In the future, more than 75 per cent of new restaurants will have a drive-thru lane (where drivers can queue, order and collect their purchases without leaving their vehicles). Restaurants with a drive-thru lane appear to boost sales by around 40 per cent.

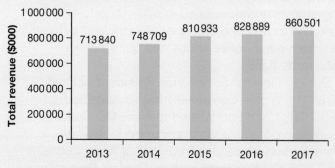

▲ Figure 2 Dunkin' Donuts total revenue, 2013–17

Dunkin brands 2017 Annual Report, http://investor.dunkin brands.com/static-files/797ff4b1-73b5-42ae-8fd1-473b938ad3ed, DD IP Holder LLC

Q

1 Explain one reason why global marketing is important to Dunkin' Donuts. **(4 marks)**

2 Explain one benefit of using Ansoff's Matrix by Dunkin' Donuts. **(4 marks)**

3 Discuss the benefits to Dunkin' Donuts of using a geocentric approach to marketing. **(8 marks)**

4 Assess which of the 4Ps in the marketing mix is being emphasised by Dunkin' Donuts. **(12 marks)**

EXAM HINT

If answering a question on this topic, you should feel prepared enough to use a wide range of knowledge and concepts from the whole course. Any discussion of a business wanting to expand should make you think about economies of scale. One benefit that any business hopes to achieve by expansion – at home or abroad – is the reduction in unit costs that can be achieved by operating on a larger scale. This might be achieved by being able to purchase components or raw materials on a larger scale, or by having one head office serving different markets.

Any discussion of this topic in an exam question should not end at the 4Ps or Ansoff's Matrix. There are many other concepts to consider when analysing global marketing strategy, including:

- markets – supply and demand in local markets
- price and income elasticity of demand – pricing decisions need to take account of demand factors in local markets
- recruitment – the presence or lack of skilled staff in the new market
- ethical considerations
- legislation
- the importance of the Internet in marketing.

33 NICHE MARKETS

LEARNING OBJECTIVES

By the end of this chapter you should understand:
- cultural diversity: recognition that groups of people across the globe have different interests and values
- the features of global niche markets
- the application and adaptation of the marketing mix (4Ps) to suit global niches.

GETTING STARTED

US retailer, Ties.com® is an Internet-based retail company that focuses exclusively on neckties and related products. The business claims to have the most complete selection of neckwear anywhere in the world. According to the company's website, the business has led the market for around 15 years. The company is proud to use traditional labour-intensive methods to communicate with customers and pack boxes by hand.

The talented design team, which is based in Southern California, demonstrates a commitment to high levels of detail when developing new designs for neckties, from skinny ties to bow ties, socks, tie racks and more. The company claims that few can match this level of detail and attention to customers.

The company also claims to offer the best selection of premium neckwear on the Internet. The checkout procedure is fast and secure and Ties.com has an easy return policy with a 100 per cent satisfaction guarantee.

Why do some businesses choose to produce or sell a small range of products? To what extent does Ties.com operate in a niche market? Why might Ties.com not be a popular business in every country? Describe how the Internet has enabled businesses like Ties.com to expand into different countries.

GLOBAL NICHE MARKETS

Global niche markets are similar to the niche markets covered in Student Book 1, Chapter 9. This is because they target a very specific range of people, often referred to as subcultures. These are groups of customers with common interests or hobbies. In global niche markets, the customers live in more than one country and have particular needs that are not met fully by the global mass market. For example, the toy market has millions of different products aimed at all age groups, but the market for interlocking toy bricks is much smaller. The Danish company Lego® operates in this global niche market and has made a very big success of it.

CULTURAL DIVERSITY

Any business that plans to push its sales into global markets needs to understand that groups of people living in different countries may have different cultures. This can impact on their consumption (i.e. buying) patterns. They may have different interests and values. For example, the Chinese use less dairy produce than countries like France, Italy and the Netherlands. Different countries may also have different sporting interests. For example, cricket is very popular on the subcontinent, in countries such as India, Pakistan, Bangladesh and Sri Lanka. However, in other countries like the USA, Spain, Germany, China, Japan and Brazil, there is hardly any interest in the sport. There are many sources of cultural diversity. Some examples are outlined briefly below.

- **Language.** Many countries use different languages. So businesses must ensure that any text used in product instructions, promotional materials and packaging is written in a language that can be clearly understood by people in the target market.
- **Hobbies and interests.** People are likely to have different hobbies and interests in different countries. As stated above, cricket is popular in the subcontinent but in many other countries it is rarely seen. In the USA, American football is one of the more popular sports. However, it has not really popular in any other

country in the world – television broadcasters struggle to export live games around the world since the market is very small outside the USA.

- **Economic development.** Businesses will struggle to sell certain goods and services in some countries because the people that live there do not have enough money to buy them. In developing countries such as Sudan, The Gambia, Bangladesh, Bolivia, Yemen and Burundi, many people cannot afford a holiday abroad. It is also likely that there is no culture of 'recreational shopping' in these countries. Businesses would also have to understand that the poor quality of infrastructure in these countries may hinder the distribution of goods.

- **Religious norms.** Religious beliefs vary around the world. For example, some countries with large Muslim populations such as Bangladesh, Pakistan and many Middle Eastern countries may choose to limit the sale of alcohol because the Muslim faith forbids drinking it. Different religions are also likely to have different holiday periods that are linked to religious events or festivals such as Chinese New Year. In many cases, such events provide opportunities for businesses.

- **Social norms.** Different cultures often have their own informal understandings that govern the behaviour of people. Some of these can have an impact on businesses. For example, it wouldn't be acceptable to invite clients out for business lunches when they might be fasting.

- **Legal systems.** The different legal systems in different countries are likely to have an impact on businesses. In some countries, corruption (i.e. dishonest or illegal behaviour by people with power) is culturally acceptable. For example, paying a bribe to an official to get planning permission for a shop or factory may be common practice in some countries.

- **Weather and climate.** The climate in different countries around the world will influence the demand for different goods and services. For example, there will be little demand for woollen and fur clothing in countries where the climate is hot and humid. During the monsoon season in India, the demand for diesel falls sharply because industrial activity slows down due to the heavy rain.

- **History and traditions.** Consumption patterns in different countries may be influenced by ancient traditions and history. For example, colours may have different meanings in different countries. In Europe, the colour black is associated with mourning but in Cambodia, it is white. Cultural differences mean that businesses have to adjust products and

working practices when selling in niche markets around the world. These differences can also provide opportunities for businesses. For example, although Muslim populations may be relatively small in some European countries, they provide niche markets for certain products such as traditional clothing, halal food and holidays to popular Muslim destinations such as Malaysia and Turkey.

ACTIVITY 1   SKILLS   CRITICAL THINKING, CREATIVITY

CASE STUDY: AIRSTREAM®

Airstream® is a manufacturer of premium caravans based in Jackson, Ohio. The company was founded in 1931 by Wally Byam. He said he wasn't trying to sell a product but a way of life. Airstream caravans are aerodynamic, have an iconic shape and are hand-assembled with thousands of rivets. Airstream, which is now a subsidiary of Thor Industries, also manufactures other brands of recreational vehicles (RVs), including Airstream International®, Classic Limited®, Sport®, Flying Cloud®, Land Yacht® and Eddie Bauer®.

The Airstream caravan is an American icon. In 1987, the Airstream caravan was selected by *Money* magazine as one of '99 things that Americans make best'. The caravans are sold in niche markets in a number of countries. A few years ago, one of them was shipped across to China where it was met by custom officers who were not familiar with them. There are no government regulations in China about RVs, so it was met with confusion. For example, the roof of one caravan was dented when a customs officer climbed on top of the vehicle!

Airstream was keen to capture a share of the growing Chinese middle-class income that is being directed towards the leisure industry. However, there was no culture of using caravans in China. Nevertheless, luxury products like Airstream caravans and Harley-Davidson motorcycles have become very popular. This could be partly because of China's huge investment in the road network which has made travel easier. Sales of RVs in China exceeded those in the USA a couple of years ago. China now has the fastest-growing market for RVs in the world.

Currently, only about 5 per cent of Airstream's sales are overseas. However, they hope to increase that very quickly. In 2014, Airstream began selling vehicles in South Korea and Australia as well as China. According to CEO Bob Wheeler, 'It started with the phone ringing… We got calls from people who wanted to sell them in those countries, and also Russia, Indonesia, Turkey…', but, he claimed, 'China's the interesting one. There's no campgrounds.'

1 Using Airstream as an example, explain what is meant by a global niche market.
2 How might cultural diversity impact on Airstream's attempt to penetrate global niche markets?

FEATURES OF GLOBAL NICHE MARKETS

Some businesses target a specific market segment which is unique. A niche market is often created by identifying the very specific needs and wants of a small customer group. Once these needs have been identified, a business can then develop products which satisfy them in a way that rivals have failed to recognise. However, niche markets do not have to be small. If these small groups of consumers with specialised needs and wants exist in other countries, then global niche marketing becomes possible. Some of the key features of global niche markets are outlined below.

Economies of scale: Businesses that target domestic niches are not likely to be in a position to exploit economies of scale. This is because they could not sell enough output. However, when targeting a *global* niche market, the quantity that needs to be produced will rise quite significantly. As a result, a business might be able to sell enough output to scale up production and lower average costs. However, if it is necessary to adapt products to meet cultural differences, for example, the opportunity to exploit economies of scale is reduced.

Limited competition: Since niche markets are small (or are seen as small) they are often left alone by large multinationals. Therefore, levels of competition in niche markets are often lower. Businesses find this environment suitable because there is less pressure on them to invest in innovation and keep costs under control.

Premium pricing: Businesses selling products in global niche markets can often charge **premium prices**. This may be due to a lack of competition or because consumers are prepared to pay more for products that meet their needs and wants exactly. For example, Rolex®, the luxury watchmaker, can sell some timepieces for quite high prices, and the Patek Philippe® Complications World Time Yellow Gold 5131J-001 was available for AUD186 665 on the Australian website, Chrono24.com.

An emphasis on quality: It is common to find very high-quality products in global niche markets. Consumers in some global niche markets are very wealthy and are prepared to pay high prices for artisanal craftsmanship, high-quality materials and the creation of specialised products. For example, global niche brands such as Ferrari®, Rolex, Prada®, Gucci® and luxury hotel group Soneva®. The quality of customer service is also high in niche markets.

Focus on profit: Businesses serving global niche markets are likely to be more profit-orientated. This is because they produce much smaller quantities than those serving mass markets and are less likely to be concerned about market share. They often charge premium prices and deal with customers on a more individual level.

Brand loyalty: Businesses serving niche markets can often develop stronger brand loyalty than those serving mass markets. This might be because the needs and wants of customers are met more precisely. Therefore, customers usually stay with the brand. It may also be because customer service is more personal. It is possible to build stronger relationships with customers in niche markets because there are fewer customers to accommodate.

APPLICATION AND ADAPTATION OF THE MARKETING MIX TO SUIT GLOBAL NICHES

Businesses that operate in global niche markets need to distinguish themselves from the mainstream or mass market. This can be done through adaptations to the marketing mix (4Ps).

Product: Global niche products often place an emphasis on quality. Examples include luxury cars, watches and perfumes. For example, Montblanc® produces and sells luxury pens, watches and luggage. They are sold around the world and marketed as exclusive (i.e. expensive and high quality, so only some people can afford to buy them) products. For many long-haul airlines such as Virgin®, Emirates® and Etihad®, it is important to differentiate its standard products for economy customers from products that show how they are meeting the needs of its First Class and Business Class customers.

Price: The point of niche marketing is to charge higher prices for products that are not intended for the mass market. For example, the price of an economy ticket between Sydney and Paris on Emirates (departing on 16/06/2018 and returning on 14/07/2018) was AUD2423. However, the First Class price for the same flight was AUD14 905. Businesses can often charge more in niche markets because demand is more price inelastic.

Promotion: Strategies to promote products to global niches are often based around the brand name. They reinforce the exclusivity of the brand and need to be more targeted (i.e. designed to appeal to a particular group of people) than in mass-market promotions. Promotions also have to consider language differences that might exist between countries. Car companies often give different names to the same cars in different countries. One problem with this sensitivity to national and cultural differences is that promotion costs will be higher. This may impact on price and how competitive a product is.

Place: Businesses serving niche markets are often more careful when selecting distribution channels for their product. This is particularly important where exclusive brands are involved. Networks of exclusive dealers are a common method of selling products to global customers. Mercedes-Benz® has exclusive dealerships around the world. Montblanc sells its products through an exclusive network of authorised retailers, jewellers and over 360 Montblanc boutiques worldwide.

With the 4Ps in mind, Table 1 summarises the advantages and disadvantages of niche marketing.

Advantages	Disadvantages
Prices are higher than in mass markets – demand is more price inelastic.	Products sell in low volumes (compared with mass markets), so profit margins need to be high enough to make it worthwhile.
The product is distributed through specialist retailers or directly to the consumer. This has advantages in terms of image. For example, the Billabong® surfer image might be compromised if sold widely in supermarkets.	The niche market must be large enough to support the business and specialist distribution. The small size may prevent economies of scale that allow it to compete with larger competitors.

▲ Table 1 Advantages and disadvantages of niche marketing

Global niches exist where the local market for a product is too small to be profitable, but at a global level the market is very viable. These trends may be present due to international perceptions about certain goods being the same (for example, agreement that a Mercedes is a good car). Firms may exploit these niches as part of a global marketing strategy. Niches are particularly present in high-end goods or high-tech medical or computing goods.

CASE STUDY: MERCEDES-BENZ

Mercedes-Benz is a German car manufacturer which focuses on luxury cars, coaches and trucks. Although it is a German company, Mercedes-Benz makes its vehicles in over 30 countries, from Argentina to Russia to Vietnam.

Mercedes-Benz cars meet the needs of global customers who value the luxury of the product and who have a strong sense of brand loyalty to the business. The business works hard to ensure that its brand is distinguished (i.e. different and admired) from other car manufacturers. This comes from a strong emphasis on quality drawn from expertise in the area of luxury car making.

Mercedes-Benz cars can be more expensive than other cars in the same sector. Customers in this global niche are prepared to pay for the brand name and the luxury this brings. Demand for such luxury products is often price inelastic. This is a real advantage for businesses that serve such niche markets.

1 Give two features of a global niche market using examples from Mercedes-Benz.
2 Why is the demand for Mercedes-Benz cars price inelastic?
3 Give one advantage to Mercedes-Benz of demand for its cars being price inelastic.

THINKING BIGGER

Wider business ideas can be applied to the topic of global market niches. To what extent should a business try to extend a niche product into global markets? The fact that a niche product is successful in one country is no guarantee of success with consumers globally. One of the reasons for the success at home may be because the business has identified a particular need of domestic consumers. Therefore, it meets the need with a bespoke (i.e. made especially for an individual or small group) product. This can be the case with restaurants. A strong reputation for quality using local food may work in a regional setting, but can this be translated to another country? The nature of the restaurant business, with quality being checked by the owner, may be changed through expansion and looking for global niche markets. Gordon Ramsay, a well-known UK chef, successfully opened Maze restaurant in New York after the success of the UK equivalent by the same name in London. Careful marketing, operations and leadership are needed to translate a local niche market into a global niche market.

EXAM HINT

If you are considering global niche markets as an extension of domestic niche markets, you need to consider why a business might want to extend its reach beyond its own national borders. A key benefit of targeting a niche market, rather than a mass market, is the opportunity to charge higher prices than an equivalent, mass-market product. Why, though, are customers in different countries prepared to pay higher prices for such products? Concepts such as price elasticity of demand can be used to explain this appeal. If a product is desirable and has few close substitutes, due to its quality or features, then consumers are likely to be less price sensitive. So, the demand is likely to be price inelastic. For example, with the latest iPhone, it does not matter whether the consumer is in New York, London or Tokyo. The product has such niche appeal that high prices do not significantly affect demand. For a business, having a product with low price elasticity of demand is a very appealing position. But how can this be achieved? One way is by identifying and filling global niches.

When you are answering a question on global niche markets, it is important to consider the appropriate context. You must apply your answer to the case study and the product being considered. Using the mobile phone example, you could contextualise your response by comparing it to competitors (Samsung®, HTC®), or referring to other methods of communication (telephone, email).

CHECKPOINT

1 What is meant by a niche market?

2 Distinguish between a niche market and a mass market.

3 What is a global niche market?

4 Give three examples of products that are targeted at global niche markets.

5 Describe how social media can encourage the growth of a global brand.

6 How does cultural diversity affect global niche markets?

7 How do businesses responsible for luxury products ensure their brand is maintained in different global markets?

SUBJECT VOCABULARY

global niche market a market made up of customers who live in more than one country and have particular needs that are not met fully by the global mass market
premium pricing where a business is able to charge a higher price than normal – possibly because the product is perceived to be of a higher quality
subculture a cultural group within a larger culture, often having slightly different product needs to those of the larger culture

EXAM PRACTICE

CASE STUDY: VINYL RECORDS

SKILLS CRITICAL THINKING, ANALYSIS, INTERPRETATION, PROBLEM SOLVING, REASONING

Listening to music is a popular hobby for people all over the world. According to Figure 1, the average number of hours per week spent listening to music rose from 23.5 hours to 32.1 hours in just three years between 2015 and 2017.

However, unfortunately for musicians, the amount of money made by the music industry has fallen steadily for a number of years. According to Figure 2, the music industry made a total of US$23.8 billion in 1999. However, this fell to US$14.3 billion in 2014. There has been a slight increase since then and in 2016, a total of US$15.7 billion was made by the industry.

One of the main reasons for the decline in revenues is technological. According to Nielsen®, a company that provides information about what people watch, listen

to and buy, on-demand audio streams exceeded 400 billion streams in 2017. This compared to 252 billion in 2016. People all over the world can access music very cheaply, and sometimes for free, from streaming sites such as Spotify®, Deezer®, SoundCloud® and Jango®. Unfortunately, although artists get royalties (i.e. payment each time a song is played) from the music streamed by these sites, the amount they get is much less than from the sales of their albums and singles that they used to get.

Despite the decline in the earnings of the music industry, one niche market that is doing well is the sale of vinyl records (i.e. a thin piece of plastic that music is recorded on). Vinyl grew by 9 per cent to 14.3 million in 2017, up from 13.1 million in 2016. That means vinyl, which has seen 12 straight years of growth, now accounts for 14 per cent of total physical album sales. Figure 3 shows the pattern of global sales for vinyl records. According to Deloitte Global®, vinyl sales, which peaked in the late 1970s, will rise to over US$1 billion in 2017 for the first time this millennium. Deloitte said that new and used records will account for more than 90 per cent of this revenue. Sales of turntables (i.e. record players) and accessories make up the rest. For some musicians, vinyl sales will represent around 10 per cent of total album sales.

Many vinyl record buyers believe that vinyl records have become collectible (i.e. valuable because people want to collect them). The format seems special in a digital world. Many collectors appreciate vinyl records for their cover art, sleeve notes, posters, stickers and other physical content. According to a survey, around half of those who purchased a vinyl record had not even played it – about 7 per cent of buyers didn't even have a turntable on which to play it!

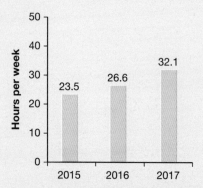

▲ Figure 1 The average number of hours per week spent listening to music (USA)

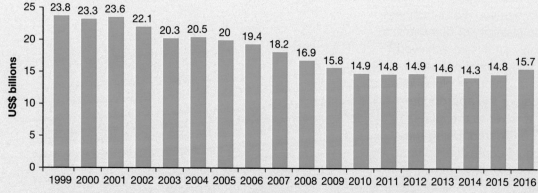

▲ Figure 2 Global recorded music industry revenues 1999–2016

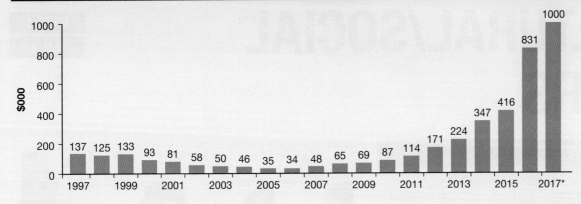

*Estimated

▲ Figure 3 Global sales of vinyl records

Deloitte does not expect the market for vinyl to grow rapidly. However, a small number of music fans will maintain their interest. The market niche is made up of:

- millennials (people who became adults around the year 2000), who like the look and feel of vinyl records
- collectors who purchase new premium releases of albums they already own
- middle-aged consumers who are buying records to replace the ones they threw away years earlier in favour of CDs.

Vinyl records are distributed by fashion retailers, food retailers, department stores and supermarkets. Some of these outlets also sell turntables, which make popular gifts. Digital channels have also helped with distribution. Some music sites sell vinyl records globally online. There is also an increasing amount of information relating to the prices paid for deleted records. This helps buyers and sellers to better understand what prices might be paid for different albums.

Whether the global market for vinyl will continue to grow in the future is uncertain. This may be because:

- the records are expensive to buy – around US$25 per album on average
- the price of a boxed set of vinyl records often exceeds the annual subscription for a streaming service offering millions of tracks
- the production of vinyl records is slow and costly – each record takes 30 seconds to print and they are made from a master pressing that takes hours to produce.

This compares negatively to the short amount of effort needed to produce and deliver digital recordings online. Although it is possible to produce vinyl records using a 3D printer, the quality is not as good and unlikely to match the quality of traditional production methods for 10 to 20 years.

Yet in 2017, music industry giant, Sony Music®, said it would start making vinyl records for the first time since 1989. According to a report, Sony Music has equipped its Tokyo studio with a cutting machine, which is needed in the production process for manufacturing vinyl records. However, Sony Music was struggling to find older engineers with the skills and knowledge needed to make vinyl records.

Q

1 Explain one benefit to Sony Music of identifying a global market niche.   **(4 marks)**
2 Explain one drawback to Sony Music of the pattern of revenues in the music industry as shown by Figure 2.   **(4 marks)**
3 Calculate the percentage contribution made by sales of vinyl records to total revenues generated in the music industry in 2016. You are advised to show your working.   **(4 marks)**
4 Discuss the factors that might have influenced growth in the global market for vinyl records.   **(8 marks)**
5 Evaluate whether or not there is potential for further growth in the global market for vinyl records.   **(20 marks)**

34 CULTURAL/SOCIAL FACTORS

LEARNING OBJECTIVES

By the end of this chapter you should be able to understand the following considerations for businesses:
- cultural differences
- different tastes and preferences
- language and unintended meanings
- inappropriate branding and promotion.

GETTING STARTED

Russia was 35th out of 190 countries in the ease of doing business rankings by the World Bank in 2017. According to the US Commerce Department, doing business in Russia mixes formality (i.e. correct behaviour) with a personal touch. Business people are expected to dress formally and conservatively (i.e. in a respectable way). Russian business people may also consider written material important. They may expect slides, brochures and samples. According to the Australian Trade Commission, such written materials, as well as websites and business cards, should look high quality. Russian business people may also expect agreements and deals to be written and signed.

However, the Russian approach can be relaxed. They might want to chat and get to know potential business partners on a personal level before discussing any details. Once they become more familiar with their potential business partners, they may show more emotion. For example, a positive pat on the shoulder.

Russian business people are reported to expect colleagues to be on time for appointments. However, the International Business Centre advises that the Russians themselves may be late in order to test the patience of their partner. Russian business people may also expect a quick and complete follow-up of the meeting from negotiators (i.e. the people who are trying to reach an agreement through discussion). This is to keep the business deal moving forward.

What might people from other countries think of your own cultural and social factors? Why might being aware of cultural factors help or hinder business?

CULTURAL AND SOCIAL FACTORS AFFECTING GLOBAL MARKETING

Doing business across cultures can be challenging. You must have an understanding of national and corporate cultures and languages, otherwise it is very easy to potentially cause offence. These cultural and social factors and how they affect **global marketing** are examined in this chapter. Cultural and social factors are the beliefs and practices, customs, traditions and behaviours of all those people who belong to a specific culture.

In order to market effectively in other countries, businesses must overcome **ethnocentrism**. People may view their own cultures, ethics and norms as superior to others. For example, people tend to accept the values of the culture around them as ideal values. Since each culture has its own set of values, which are quite different from those values held in other cultures, the concepts of proper and improper, foolish and wise, and even right and wrong can be confusing. In international business, there are questions about what is proper by a culture's values, what is wise by a culture's view of the world, and what is right by whose standards.

CULTURAL DIFFERENCES

When doing business in other countries, cultural sensitivity is crucial. It is very important to understand differences in behaviour and language. Failing to understand things like foreign ways of behaving and communicating can result in embarrassment. At worst, it may cause offence and lose a deal.

Working across differing national cultures can add levels of complexity. You must carefully prepare for and consider each step in carrying out business. This will help with any cultural differences and build trust. Companies need to think about each level of the business relationship in order to understand this: the introductions, the negotiations or discussions and communicating on a day-to-day level.

Meeting someone from a different culture is often awkward. In a business setting, there can be complex formal and informal procedures that have developed over time. If they are not followed, they can cause much offence. For example, in Vietnam, a person is expected to shake hands when first entering a room. People are expected to shake using both hands, upon meeting and when saying goodbye. They must nod the head slightly while doing so as a sign of respect. The two people must then exchange business cards. The behaviour surrounding these is also extremely important. This is discussed in the 'Exam practice' section at the end of the chapter. Every country in every region will have its own norms about introductions. Therefore, it is important to conduct thorough research before the first meeting.

The sources of cultural differences are discussed in Chapter 33. However, some examples are listed briefly below.

- **Language.** Many countries use different languages. Businesses must ensure that any text used in product instructions, promotional materials and packaging is written in a language that can be clearly understood by people in the target market. This is discussed in more detail below.
- **Hobbies and interests.** People are likely to have different hobbies and interests in different countries. For example, ice hockey and polo are games that are not widely popular around the world.
- **Religions and social norms.** Religious beliefs vary around the world. Some countries are dominated by one faith over another, for example in the Middle East the population is predominately Muslim.
- **Legal systems.** The different legal systems in different countries are likely to have an impact on businesses. Practices that are allowed in some countries may be forbidden in others.
- **Weather and climate.** People living in very hot climates may have different customs to those living in milder climates. For example, in parts of southern Europe such as Spain, it is not uncommon for businesses to close down for a few hours in the middle of the day when it is very hot.
- **History and traditions.** Buying patterns in different countries may be influenced by ancient traditions and history. For example, people in Sweden eat pickled herrings on a certain day of the year.

ACTIVITY 1   SKILLS   CRITICAL THINKING, PERSONAL AND SOCIAL RESPONSIBILITY, ETHICS

CASE STUDY: CORDEX®

Cordex®, a British shoemaking firm, decided to expand internationally by acquiring a Vietnamese firm, Vetex®. In planning the takeover, Cordex's senior managers had not thought about how to integrate Vetex after the merger. Once the deal was complete, Cordex selected staff from its London headquarters to relocate in Hanoi. It started to teach Vetex how to do business the 'Cordex way', which was a very expensive process.

After six months, it was clear that the process of integration had not been done well. The remaining members of staff were finding it difficult to understand the business culture. They did not speak Vietnamese or French and so were having trouble communicating effectively. Two key Vetex staff members also quit. Many of the remaining managers found the situation so challenging they were also considering leaving. The CFO of Cordex was deeply concerned at the escalating costs and the CEO was worried that Cordex's international expansion strategy might fail.

1 How was Cordex ethnocentric in its approach to the process of integrating the two firms?
2 Explain the approach that Cordex could have taken.

DIFFERENT TASTES AND PREFERENCES

Depending on the product and the country, there may be the need for more or fewer adaptations. For example, products produced in New Zealand for the Australian market may require fewer adaptations than those for the Chinese market. This is because the **cultural and social differences** between Australia and New Zealand are relatively small.

Some differences are due to local tastes – for example, Coca-Cola has the same base concentrate in every country. However, because it is mixed with the water in local countries it has a slight variation in taste depending on location. This sort of adaptation is not something that a business can control and not something that they would implement themselves.

Other differences can be based on religious beliefs. The use of halal meat is usual in fast-food restaurants in most Middle Eastern countries. In India, many international fast food restaurants will not sell certain meat products due to the religious beliefs of that country. By respecting these beliefs and catering to their market in these countries, businesses ensure that they adapt sufficiently. They are aiming to gain a market share from local businesses who may be better suited to understand the regional specifications.

Product	Adaptation
Cadbury® chocolate	In the USA, Cadbury chocolate tastes markedly different from its Australian and UK chocolate. This is due to the different fat and cocoa content used in order to meet different FDA (Food & Drug Administration) standards in the USA.
McDonald's	There are significant variations in what is sold in different parts of the world. These are often due to religious beliefs, but some are based on the tastes of different countries as well. Japanese branches offer a Chicken Katsu burger and in Finland you can have your burger served on a rye bun. In France, you can have doughnuts for breakfast. In China, you can have pasta soup for breakfast.
Samsung	Samsung have created products that meet specific local demands. For example, in China the number 8 and the colour red are considered lucky. So, some products have been fitted with red covers and TV stands have been shaped into the figure eight. In Korea, a specialised refrigerator has been built to be perfect for kimchi, a local delicacy. The high demand for sparkling water in the USA has been met by installing a specialist dispenser in certain refrigerator models.

▲ Table 1 Product adaptations for different cultures

Some adaptations to products are based upon legal requirements. For example, there are many food products used in the USA that are banned for use within the EU. Brands that want to transfer their products from the USA to the EU will have to adapt them to meet the necessary legal requirements. For example, brands such as Pringles® and Starburst® have had additives removed from their US ingredients list to be able to be sold in the EU. Some further examples are summarised in Table 1.

LANGUAGE AND UNINTENDED MEANINGS

Although much international business is conducted in the English language, understanding other languages makes communication much easier and helps to build relationships. Relying too much on one language is risky. This is because it may lead to miscommunication and less sensitivity towards other cultures.

However, communication is much more than just language. For example, there are differences in the nature of communication between **high-context** and **low-context** cultures. Low-context cultures, such as those of the USA and Europe, tend to say what they mean. For example, in discussions what is said can usually be taken at face value (i.e. as it appears to be). Firms do business and then leave socialising until after the deal is done. Agendas, letters, contracts and other formal documentation are essential. They are relied upon during negotiations, as well as after they are completed.

However, in high-context cultures, 'yes' often does not mean 'yes'. For example, 'Yes, I agree' might mean, 'I hear you' rather than 'I agree with you'. Communication in Asian countries, for example, tends to be high context and can have an impact on business. For example, after making a pitch for business in Japan, the Japanese negotiator might close the long meeting saying, 'We are going to study your proposal and get back to you'. In a high-context culture such as Japan, this language may mean 'no', rather than providing a positive response in a few days or weeks, which is the norm in a low-context culture. However, the Japanese never use the word 'no' in negotiations. Initial meetings are there to build trust. Socialising is used to create relationships for the next stage of negotiations. This is very different from what might take place between, for example, a Swedish firm negotiating with a Danish one.

Verbal communication has many pitfalls (i.e. difficulties that are not obvious at first), but so does physical communication. Gestures that are common in one region may have different meanings in other regions and cultures. Table 2 illustrates some examples from around the world.

Gesture	Examples of countries or regions where gesture might be considered offensive
Thumbs-up gesture, meaning 'well done' (e.g. USA, Canada, Russia).	Australia, Greece, Middle East.
The 'OK' sign, made with forefinger and thumb (e.g. USA, Australia, UK).	Brazil, Uruguay, Germany, Russia.
Pointing with the index finger.	China, Japan, Indonesia, Latin America, Africa, parts of Europe.
Curling the index finger with the palm facing up, to indicate 'come here' (e.g. USA, Australia, UK).	Greece, Pakistan, parts of Africa and Asia.
Use of left hand to give or receive items or to eat.	India, Nepal, Middle East.
Clicking fingers (moving your thumb and finger together to make a short sharp sound).	Latin America.

▲ Table 2 Some examples of gestures that can cause offence in cross-cultural business settings

Also, **barriers to communication** may be more of a problem when communicating across borders. For example, businesses need to:

- avoid using unclear communication resulting from poorly written or poorly expressed messages
- ensure that technological communication methods, such as websites, are working properly
- provide adequate communication training to staff
- avoid the use of jargon
- use the most appropriate medium when communicating
- eliminate sources of distraction, such as background noise, when communicating
- ensure that the chain of command is not too long.

INAPPROPRIATE BRANDING AND PROMOTION

There are many examples of mistakes involving language, mistranslations and unintended meanings when businesses operate abroad.

A well-known incident that caused embarrassment was when General Motors® sold its branded Nova® car in Latin America, where its name in Spanish means 'No go!'. This is not a very good name for a car! It is very important to check with native speakers of the language that translations are correct.

One example of transferring a brand without considering the new market was when Gerber®, a Nestlé-owned baby food company, copied the packaging on their products in Africa. The packaging displayed an image of a smiling baby. However, due to high levels of illiteracy (i.e. not being able to read) in the country, most African product packaging includes an image of what is found *inside* the product …

Promotions must also be versioned (i.e. different versions of the same product are made) across different international markets. Many brands want to create a global image and become an internationally recognised brand. This does not mean that the same marketing campaign that worked well in the USA will work as successfully in an entirely different market.

The audience is key when creating marketing campaigns. If you do not consider the cultural norms of your audience, then your expansion into that region will not be successful. For example, a Proctor and Gamble television advert was originally made for the US market. It featured a husband and wife in a bathroom and intended to show how soap could make the woman more attractive. However, when the advert was transferred to Japan, it was considered inappropriate. Some people found it was unfair to women.

Failing to consider your new market will be costly to businesses. Advertising campaigns and packaging costs are expensive, but also there can be a greater cost to the business if sales of the product are badly affected in that country for the whole time it is available. Table 3 shows some examples of inappropriate branding.

Product	Issue
Pee Cola®, a soft drink.	A popular soft drink in Ghana, this product would not be suitable for sale in the USA.
Barf®, a detergent powder.	An Iranian product, where its name means 'snow'. It means something far less suitable in English-speaking countries.

▲ Table 3 Examples of inappropriate brand naming

ACTIVITY 2   **SKILLS**   CRITICAL THINKING, CREATIVITY, PERSONAL AND SOCIAL RESPONSIBILITY

CASE STUDY: TRANSLATION ERRORS IN INTERNATIONAL MARKETING

Translation errors in marketing are not uncommon. Even large and well-resourced companies make mistakes, especially when launching new products in new overseas markets. Errors often happen when translating marketing slogans. Some examples are given below.

- The American Motors Corporation® named one of its new models The Matador. This was to suggest that the product was associated with energy and enthusiasm. However, when the car was exported to Puerto Rico it was not very well received. This was because the word 'matador' means 'killer' in Spanish.

- Drinks company Schweppes® launched Schweppes Tonic Water in Italy. But a direct translation of the brand into Italian was 'Schweppes Toilet Water'.
- HSBC® bank used an advertising campaign in the USA which used the tag line 'Assume nothing'. However, when using the same campaign in Europe, in some countries the tag line was understood to say 'Do nothing'. As a result, HSBC had to spend $10 million modifying the campaign.

1 How might language differences impact on a business that markets its products in a range of different countries?

2 What might be the consequences for a business of the errors described above?

THINKING BIGGER

In business, international companies must 'think global, act local'. This suggests that they should respect local norms, values and expectations in the global marketplace, or face the consequences. The same has applied to the management practices of top employers. International branches might have the same logo above the door, but cultural factors in the workplace, from pay and benefits to leadership styles and attitude toward diversity, can vary widely from country to country.

However, organisations such as international bank Santander® are not using such localised approaches. Instead, they are joining up their global operations. In 2014, Santander had banking operations in more than 40 countries with 182 000 employees, in Europe, the USA and South America. They are moving towards having more corporate policies and ensuring that customers have the same experience in all places. The idea is that a Santander manager can step into a branch in Argentina and feel a culture similar to that of the US or Portuguese offices.

LINKS

Chapter 14 explores how corporate culture affects business operations, while the focus of this chapter is making sense of culture in the context of international businesses. This builds on your understanding of how culture affects marketing and people (Student Book 1, Unit 1) and impacts directly upon business decisions and strategy (this book, Unit 3). You will need a thorough grasp of the relevant cultural and social factors when you focus on global business (this book, Unit 4), as this will inform your understanding of a market or location (this book, Chapters 28, 29, 32 and 33), helping you to assess the impact of MNCs and how to control them (this book, Chapters 35 and 37) and to evaluate the ethical issues that may be involved (Chapter 36).

CHECKPOINT

1 Give two examples of ethnocentrism.

2 How might cultural differences impact on a business?

3 Why is relying too much on one language risky?

4 What are the pitfalls of unintended meanings?

5 How do differing tastes and preferences impact on marketing?

6 Why must care be taken in transferring brand names?

7 Give an example of an inappropriate brand name.

8 How might the use of an inappropriate brand name impact on a business?

SUBJECT VOCABULARY

barriers to communication obstacles that prevent effective communication between the sender and receiver
cultural and social differences the differences in beliefs and practices, customs, traditions and behaviours of people from different cultures
ethnocentrism the way some people view their own cultures, ethics and norms as superior to those from different cultures
global marketing involves the planning, producing, placing and promoting of a business's products in a worldwide market
high-context cultures cultures, including much of the Middle East, Asia, Africa, and South America, that are relational, collectivist, intuitive and contemplative. This means that people in these cultures emphasise interpersonal relationships. Developing trust is an important first step to any business transaction
low-context cultures cultures, such as those of North America and much of Europe, that tend to say what they mean. A communication style that relies heavily on explicit and direct language

EXAM PRACTICE

CASE STUDY: SUNBEAM HOLIDAYS

SKILLS CRITICAL THINKING, REASONING

The number of Japanese tourists visiting the USA has varied little in the last 15 years or so. It has gone up and down slightly between 3 million and 3.8 million per year. In 2022, around 3.76 million tourists are expected from Japan. One US travel company based in Florida, Sunbeam Travel, has decided to try and attract more Japanese tourists by marketing holidays that are tailor-made for Japanese visitors. The company has done some initial market research. They think that Japanese holidaymakers might enjoy a two-week tour of the USA, visiting popular attractions such as the Grand Canyon, Manhattan, Disneyland, the Everglades, Yellowstone National Park and Las Vegas.

Sunbeam Holidays carried out online research to find out what Japanese tourists thought about their visit to the USA. Sunbeam discovered that the Japanese were:

- unfamiliar with the US custom of tipping waiters, porters, drivers and other staff
- worried about the lack of public toilets
- surprised that there were no toothbrushes in US hotels
- disappointed with the conduct and friendliness of US taxi drivers
- frustrated by waiting in queues at checkouts while customers chatted with cashiers
- shocked at the high price of cigarettes
- uncomfortable with the lighting in many rooms – they were often too dark.

Sunbeam Holidays planned to invest in an advertising campaign in Japan. However, they thought it would be better if the campaign was designed by a Japanese marketing agency. Sunbeam sent a group of four representatives to Japan to plan and discuss the terms of the campaign. Before the group left, they were briefed on Japanese business customs. The following issues were addressed at the briefing.

- **Level of directness.** In the USA, people are direct in their communication and say what they are thinking. A lack of directness might suggest that a person is disorganised or unprepared. However, in Japan people are more indirect. Communication that is too direct might be considered rude. They may use more non-verbal communication and assume

that they have been understood. Also, the 'hard-sell' approach (i.e. the use of aggressive selling or advertising) does not work in Japan.
- **Privacy.** In Japan, privacy is valued. Therefore, it is important to avoid asking too many questions at the beginning of a relationship. Although questioning might be a genuine attempt to start a new business relationship, it may be considered rude in Japan.
- **Facts and emotions.** The use of facts and opinions in communication is common in the USA. Although this is also acceptable in Japan, the Japanese will tend to avoid disagreements. Disagreements are more likely to be discussed indirectly and it is rare that a Japanese businessperson would speak out against the group's consensus. This helps to create a sense of unity in the group.
- **Speed versus consistency.** In the USA, decision making is likely to be quick, as this is believed to save time and money. However, in Japan the process of decision making is much slower. For example, there is likely to be more discussion, more documentation and a greater number of meetings. This is to avoid errors and ensure that the right decision is reached.
- **Gifts.** When doing business in Japan, it is common practice to exchange inexpensive gifts and lunches. However, gifts might be refused in the initial stages of a business relationship in case they create an unwanted sense of debt. There is also the danger that gifts represent a bribe. Many companies have clear codes of conduct which cover the exchange of gifts in negotiations.
- **Business cards.** In Japan, business cards are considered an extension of the person. They should be received with both hands and held with respect. The card should be briefly read and then placed in a business card holder. If given a card whilst seated, it should be placed on the table for the duration of the meeting. At the end of the meeting, it should be transferred into a business card holder. A business card should not be placed into a back pocket or wallet.
- **Dress code.** The Japanese have a conservative dress code for business meetings. For example, business suits are worn by everyone, colours tend to be simple and dark (such as black or grey) and not much jewellery or perfume is worn.

EXAM HINT

Working across differing national cultures adds a new dimension to any assessment or evaluation. You must be able to define what you mean by culture in particular contexts, and you also need a balanced understanding of how a variety of cultures and societies might differ from your own. Businesses will try to reduce the costs involved in behaving like other cultures with different social attitudes when marketing products across borders. However, they often face a dilemma because such costs could reduce profit margins. This could be an issue for evaluation when answering an exam question. Independent reading and thinking will help you to provide evidence in support of your judgements.

Q

1 Explain one difference in tastes and preferences between the US and the Japanese consumer.

(4 marks)

2 Discuss the benefits to Sunbeam Holidays of taking into account the cultural differences that may exist between Japan and the USA when doing business.

(8 marks)

3 Assess the benefits to Sunbeam Travel of employing a Japanese marketing agency to produce an advertising campaign.

(12 marks)

GLOBAL INDUSTRIES AND COMPANIES

Multinational corporations (MNCs) play a big role in international business. This section addresses the impact MNCs might make on local economies across borders, such as the impact on wages, working conditions, job creation, local businesses, the local community and the environment. It also looks at their impact on economic growth, FDI flows, the balance of payments, technology, consumers, business culture and tax revenues in national economies. The section also deals with international business ethics by focusing on stakeholder conflicts, environmental considerations such as emissions, waste and sustainability; supply chain considerations such as pay and labour exploitation; and marketing considerations such as product labelling and inappropriate marketing activities. Finally, the control of MNCs is discussed. Factors considered here include the power of MNCs, political influence, legal control, consumer and pressure groups, social media and self-regulation.

35 THE IMPACT OF MNCs

LEARNING OBJECTIVES

By the end of this chapter you should be able to understand:

■ the impact of MNCs on the local economy: local labour, wages, working conditions and job creation, local businesses and the local community and environment

■ the impact of MNCs on the national economy: economic growth, FDI flows, balance of payments, technology and skills transfer, consumers, business culture and tax revenues.

GETTING STARTED

MNC Nestlé is the largest food and beverages business organisation in the world. It has operations in 189 different countries and employs around 330 000 people. It markets over 2000 brands, including Nescafé®, Milo®, KitKat and Nesquik® (a brand name for some Nestlé products such as milk, breakfast cereals, syrups and confectionery bars).

In 2017, Nestlé started to build a new factory in the Mariel Special Development Zone in Cuba. This is a state-run business development area. It is specifically designed to attract foreign direct investment and business expertise to Cuba. In partnership with the Cuban food producer Corporación Alimentaria, the factory will produce:

- Nescafé
- Serrano, the local Cuban coffee brand
- Nestlé Fitness® cereal snacks
- Nesquik products
- Maggi® products.

Nestlé is planning to invest CHF54 million in the project. About 260 new jobs will be created. Nestlé will also sponsor a permanent education facility in Palacio de los Pioneros Ernesto Guevara in Havana. The project will target school children and focus on healthy food habits.

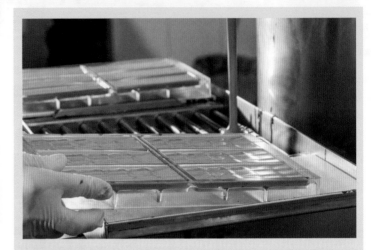

What are the possible benefits to the local Cuban community of the new factory? How might the Cuban national economy benefit from the development? What might be the possible disadvantages to the new factory?

IMPACT OF MNCs ON THE LOCAL ECONOMY

The arrival of MNCs in local communities is generally welcomed. This is because a new factory is likely to create employment, provide work for businesses in the supply chain, give a boost to the local economy and provide an opportunity for people to learn new skills.

Local labour and job creation: One of the main impacts of MNCs on local economies is the creation of jobs. For many people, the opportunity to work in a full-time job with the possibility of training, a regular income, financial security and the opportunity to build a career is very appealing. For example, in 2014 Tenneco-Walker® (part of Tenneco Inc., a global US-headquartered company) opened a new factory in south Wales, UK. The new plant makes exhausts for a range of car manufacturers, including Jaguar Land Rover. It was expected to create 220 local jobs, providing a boost for the area where unemployment is high. For example, in 2018 it was 7.3 per cent – well above the national average of around 4.1 per cent.

Wages and working conditions: Wages in the locality may rise if a large business opens. This is because the demand for workers in the local economy is likely to drive up rates. If unemployment is low, and if other employment opportunities already exist in the area, wages are more likely to go up. It is also possible that the jobs created will have favourable working conditions. This is because MNCs often have a modern approach to business development. Their facilities are likely to be new and have the latest technologies. Their working practices are likely to be modern and efficient. Most MNCs are also likely to adopt internationally recognised standards of health and safety and employee welfare. In 2017, Foxconn®, an electronics MNC based in Taiwan, opened a new factory in Wisconsin, USA. Foxconn said that the wages would be good. Workers at the plant are projected to have an average annual salary of $53 875 plus benefits. Such high wages were offered to attract workers both locally and from across the whole nation.

THINKING BIGGER

Some MNCs are criticised for creating low-value jobs. For example, sometimes the majority of jobs in a new factory may be unskilled, requiring little training or expertise. If there is a need for highly skilled personnel, some MNCs transfer or recruit staff from their home countries. As a result, there are often limited opportunities for local workers to develop high-level skills.

In the past, some MNCs have also been criticised for exploiting people in local economies. For example, in 2016 it was reported that in countries like India and Bangladesh, some workers employed in supplier factories for MNCs such as Gap® and H&M® were exploited. The Asia Floor Wage Alliance released a series of reports on the working conditions across the companies' supplier factories. One report said that workers reported the rules of international labour standards were broken in the following ways:

- being paid wages that were too low for their skill level
- not being paid the legal overtime rates
- having deductions made without permission
- payments being made late
- workers not receiving payment for their work.

Some workers in India were also made to work on Sundays and national holidays in very hot conditions, without breaks and without access to clean drinking water. However, in these countries, and others, the opportunity to earn money in factories can be better than working in the primary sector where many people often live in severe poverty.

Local businesses: MNCs can have a positive impact on local businesses when they arrive. Initially, local businesses may be involved in the construction of the new plant. For example, there may be jobs for builders, carpenters, plumbers, electricians and welders. Once a new facility opens, there may be a need for local businesses to supply materials, components, commercial services and utilities. As a result, businesses in the area may benefit from an increase in trade, higher revenues and more profit. They may also need to recruit more workers of their own to meet demand. There will be other benefits to local businesses. People who take up jobs created by the MNC will have income to spend. This spending will provide more demand for local businesses in general. For example, retailers, restaurants, service providers and the entertainments industry in the area are likely to enjoy a boost in trade.

However, when MNCs develop operations overseas, there may also be a negative effect on local businesses. This is most likely to happen if MNCs attract workers from other businesses by offering better conditions or higher wages, or supply products that compete directly with those produced by local businesses. For example, in 2018 the US supermarket chain, Walmart, said it plans to open 50 new stores in India in the next four to five years. Although these new developments will create employment in those locations, they are likely to also take trade away from local rivals, who may struggle to compete and be forced out of business. This means that some people may lose their jobs. However, the competition from MNCs might put pressure on local businesses to make improvements. This might provide some longer-term benefits, such as more efficient and more innovative local enterprises.

The local community and environment: The people living in local communities are likely to welcome the location of MNCs in their area, but this is only if the benefits outweigh the drawbacks. In addition to employment opportunities and a boost to the local economy, MNCs might also provide the following benefits:

- **Improvements in infrastructure.** MNCs might invest some of their own money to help develop roads, electricity, water and gas supplies, schools, hospitals and other public amenities. They might do this to help build trust with the community. Also, a better infrastructure is likely to improve the quality of human capital in the area. Better roads and improved transport links would also benefit the MNCs.

- **Contributions to local government taxes.** In some countries, businesses have to pay local taxes to local authorities. Similar payments are likely to be paid by MNCs when they operate in other countries. This money can be used by local governments to help fund spending in the area.
- **Help in local communities.** Some MNCs make an effort to build strong links with the local community. They might participate in local cultural or sporting events. They may give money to local charities, organise fundraising events or give locals access to the company's facilities. For example, Scotiabank®, the Canada-based global financial services provider, has a 175-year history of making contributions to local communities around the world.

Some MNCs may have a negative impact on the local community and environment when operating overseas. As a result of environmental damage, communities may be left struggling to survive in areas where farming is made almost impossible. Mining industries can have an impact if there are oil spills that lead to environmental harm from oil pollution. This can have a significant impact on the health and activities of local people, especially farming and fishing.

ACTIVITY 1   SKILLS ▶ CRITICAL THINKING

CASE STUDY: PANASONIC®

The MNC Panasonic® is one of Japan's largest producers of electronic goods. A few years ago, it opened a new factory in the Binh Duong province of Vietnam, making wiring devices and circuit breakers. It said it expected the initial operating output to double after four years.

The factory is large, with nearly 9000m^2 and employing 670 people. It has an environmentally friendly design, adopting Panasonic's energy-saving and energy-creating products. This includes solar power generation systems, LED lighting products, and motion sensor lighting control systems. It also uses fast and flexible Japanese processes and technologies. Panasonic planned to use the factory as a showroom to allow visitors to experience high-quality manufacturing. Panasonic is committed to the principle of using local production for local use. This involves using factory products to meet the increasing demand for electrical construction materials and equipment in Vietnam.

1 What might the possible impact be on the local community of the new Panasonic factory in Binh Duong province, Vietnam?

IMPACT OF MNCS ON THE NATIONAL ECONOMY

The overwhelming majority of governments around the world are in favour of MNCs setting up operations in their countries. This is because they are likely to generate income, employment, wealth and prosperity.

Economic growth: One of the main benefits to a country when a large MNC sets up an operation is the boost provided to national income. One of the main benefits of foreign direct investment (FDI) is the employment created when MNCs arrive and establish factories, warehouses, shops and other business facilities. When multinationals set up operations overseas, income in those countries rises. Local suppliers are also likely to get work when a multinational arrives. The extra output and employment made by multinationals will increase economic growth. It will also raise living standards for people in these countries. From the worker's perspective, jobs created by FDI are often good because they pay higher wages. For example, evidence from Hungary and Brazil suggests that wages offered by foreign businesses are between 4.5 and 6 per cent higher than those offered by domestic employers.

FDI flows: When an overseas business locates a new facility in a foreign country, the amount of money spent on establishing that facility is classified as FDI. For example, it was widely reported that in 2014 Honda, the Japanese vehicle producer, opened a factory in Guanajuato, Mexico, costing Honda around around $800 million. The factory employed 3200 workers and produced around 200 000 cars per annum. This flow of money from an overseas business into a country, such as from Honda to Mexico, is likely to be welcomed by the host country (i.e. the country receiving the FDI). This is because the national economy will benefit. Examples of specific benefits to the economy include the following.

- **Increase in income.** Generally, flows of FDI should result in higher levels of GDP for the host nation. The extra output and employment resulting from new FDI will increase economic growth and should help to raise the living standards for people in the host country.
- **Increase in tax revenue.** The profits made by MNCs are taxed by the host nation. This increases tax revenue for the government. This money can be spent on improving government services, such as healthcare, education, housing and transport networks.
- **Increase in employment.** The flow of FDI creates new jobs in the host nation. For example, the single investment by Honda in Mexico created 3200 jobs in the Guanajuato region. This helps to reduce unemployment and save money that

would otherwise be paid out in benefits to the unemployed (in some countries, the government provides financial benefits to the unemployed). Businesses in the host country may also get a boost when an MNC invests in a project because a range of local suppliers will be needed. For example, the Honda factory is likely to need supplies of raw materials, car components, utilities, telephone services, commercial services, distribution services, maintenance crews and cleaning contractors. These demands will help to sustain and expand other businesses in Mexico. Therefore, it will create even more jobs in the national economy.

- **Reduce national debt.** Some of the money received by the government from FDI might be used to reduce national debt. This has a positive impact on a country's finances. If a country can reduce its debt, it tells the world that it is more financially stable. As a result, interest payments might be reduced. The country should also find it easier to borrow in the future.

Balance of payments: Investment by MNCs will have a positive impact on the host nation's balance of payments. There will be a double impact. Initially, the flow of FDI when a project is being established will improve the balance of payments. This is because money will flow into the host nation's account. For example, the $800 million spent by Honda when building the new car plant in Guanajuato will improve the balance of payments for Mexico.

Once a facility is open, there may be a further boost to the balance of payments. This is because if any of the output from a new factory is sold abroad, there will be a further flow of money into the balance of payments account of the host nation. For example, if some of the cars produced in Guanajuato are sold to the USA, the value of those sales represents a flow of money into Mexico's account (even though the company has a Japanese owner). This boost in the balance of payments will help a host nation when trading internationally.

For some less-developed countries, the impact on the balance of payments from MNC investment may be even more significant. This is because they often find it difficult to get established in global markets. FDI allows them to boost their sales of goods overseas.

If MNCs buy resources from overseas, such as machinery, tools and equipment, this will have a negative effect on the balance of payments of the host country. This is because there will be a flow of money out of the

country. There will also be a negative impact if profits are repatriated (i.e. returned to the country of origin) to the MNC's base. **Repatriated profits** represent a flow of money away from the host country.

Technology and skills transfer: MNC investment in foreign countries often means that new technologies and modern working practices are introduced into the host nation. This might result in the transfer of technologies and knowledge to local businesses. This transfer may be horizontal or vertical.

- **Horizontal transfers** are when knowledge is transferred across the same industry. For example, new technologies and working practices used by Japanese car manufacturers, such as Nissan and Toyota. As these companies became established globally, they were copied by other car producers. Just-in-time manufacturing and kaizen are examples of production techniques that have been copied from Japanese corporations.
- **Vertical transfers** may be forward or backward. For example, MNCs often provide technical assistance, training and other information to their suppliers located in the host country. Many MNCs also help local suppliers to buy resources and modernise production facilities. These are examples of backward vertical transfers. Forward vertical transfers are likely to occur when businesses in the host nation buy goods and services from the MNCs. For example, a domestic business making washing machines using components made by an MNC may adopt and adapt the technologies, working practices and managerial methods used by the MNC.

The transfer of technology and skills from an MNC to businesses in the host nation will improve efficiency and productivity. This will help to make domestic producers more competitive. It will generate sales both at home and abroad if the improvements are significant. In some cases, the copying of technologies, products and working practices can lead to the development of domestic producers. This poses a real threat to MNCs in their markets. Through a process called **reverse engineering**, some businesses analyse a rival's product very closely. They take apart the product to see how it has been made. Then, they identify the features of the product that they think are worth copying. For example, reverse engineering is used quite commonly in the development of computer hardware and software.

ACTIVITY 2 — SKILLS: CRITICAL THINKING, REASONING

CASE STUDY: EMPRESS CONSTRUCTION®

Empress Construction® is a leading US manufacturer of construction machinery and equipment. In 2017, it opened a new factory in Malaysia to add to the one it already operated in the country. The new plant cost $25 million to construct.

The investment by Empress Construction is expected to generate around 500 new jobs and the company's chairman commented that he could never have imagined that the family business would employ 2000 people in Malaysia making its products, with thousands more employed elsewhere in the supply chain. The new factories mean that the firm's contribution to the Malaysian economy will grow. The chairman said he is grateful to the Penang government for their support in helping Empress Construction make their investment ambitions a reality.

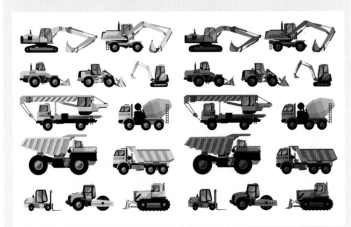

1 Explain the benefits to Malaysia of FDI, such as the investment made by Empress Construction.
2 Assess the possible impact on the Malaysian balance of payments of the investment by Empress Construction.

Consumers: Consumers are likely to benefit from the arrival of MNCs in their countries. This is because they will be free to buy some of the goods that they produce. Specific benefits to consumers include the following.

- **More choice.** The products supplied by MNCs will add to the choice already available in the host country. For example, MNCs like Coca-Cola, Starbucks and McDonald's have set up in many countries around the world to sell their products. However, not all MNCs produce consumer goods. Some make components or provide services for other businesses.
- **Lower prices.** The arrival of MNCs is likely to increase competition in the host country. The products made by MNCs may be cheaper because they use modern and efficient production techniques. Since their costs will be lower, they can offer products at lower prices. This competitive pressure may also force domestic producers to lower their prices.
- **Improved quality.** If MNCs use new technologies, modern materials and more efficient working practices, such as total quality management, the quality of products might also be improved. For example, they may be better designed, higher quality, more efficient and more attractive.
- **Better living standards.** In general, it is possible that many people in the host nation will enjoy better living standards if MNCs set up operations. They may benefit from employment opportunities and enjoy higher incomes. They may have more choice and enjoy access to cheaper and better-quality products. If products are cheaper then they will have more income left over to fund other expenditure.

Some MNCs are very powerful. In some cases, the annual revenue of a multinational can be greater than the GDP of an entire country. This can give them a strong presence. However, if too many domestic producers leave the market due to intense competition, this could result in less choice for consumers in the long term. Also, if MNCs are left with little or no competition, they may dominate the market and exploit consumers.

Business culture: There is some evidence to suggest that MNCs can have an impact on the business culture in the countries where they set up operations. In some cases, people who are employed by MNCs may eventually leave their jobs and start their own businesses. This might happen because:

- individuals may have saved some money from employment, which can be used for start-up capital
- workers may have developed skills that they think could be put to better use working for themselves
- multinationals may encourage workers to set up businesses and become suppliers. If quality standards can be maintained, it provides MNCs with more flexibility.

As more MNCs develop enterprises around the world and globalisation accelerates, it will become more culturally acceptable for people to set up their own businesses. MNCs may help to create a culture of enterprise. This will encourage entrepreneurs to set up new businesses.

It is also possible that business cultures in the host country will be influenced by the cultures in MNCs. For example, Japanese MNCs used modern production methods as they started to build factories globally. They developed different corporate cultures, and, over time, many businesses started to match the production techniques and working practices of the Japanese. This eventually led to a change in corporate cultures, for example, they became more open and less likely to have disagreements.

Tax revenues: Multinationals pay taxes to national economies. Taxes can pay for government spending in areas such as health and education. However, MNCs are often accused of paying as little tax as possible, seeking locations where taxes are low. A common technique to avoid tax on profits is **transfer pricing**. Assume an MNC has to make a product in country A, a country which charges high taxes on profits. MNCs can often reduce their tax burdens by recording certain business transactions in other countries where tax rates are lower.

Inevitably, because MNCs are profit-seeking companies, they will seek to minimise their tax liabilities. If Slovakia offers lower taxes than Spain, this will be one factor which a US multinational will take into account when deciding where to put a new plant in Europe. Therefore, governments need to assess the benefits of attracting investment by offering low taxes against loss of tax revenues. They also need to be tough with multinationals to ensure that they pay their fair share of taxes.

EXAM HINT

The impact of MNCs is often very positive for a country. However, it is important to remember when discussing the impact of MNCs that they can have negative effects. For example, some MNCs might damage the environment, exploit local workers and have a negative impact on local businesses which may force them to close. You can practise this when answering question (3) in the 'Exam practice' section below.

Remember that to demonstrate evaluation skills you need to make a judgement. This judgement must be effectively supported with clearly explained reasons. Also, remember that it may not matter if your judgement is different from that of other candidates. In business, there are many ways of achieving the same objective. It is not impossible for the ideas of different decision makers to be in complete contrast.

LINKS

There may be a number of opportunities for you to demonstrate your synoptic skills when discussing MNCs. For example, there is a very strong link between the impact of MNCs and their control (Chapter 37). Information in this chapter might also be linked with Distribution (Student Book 1, Chapter 13), Legislation (Student Book 1, Chapter 42), along with in this book, Theories of corporate strategy (Chapter 2), Growth (Chapter 5), Corporate culture (Chapter 14), Business ethics (Chapter 16), Contingency planning (Chapter 21) and many of the chapters in Unit 4.

CHECKPOINT

1 What might be the main advantage to a local economy when an MNC arrives?

2 How might wage rates rise as a result of MNC operations in a local economy?

3 How might local workers be affected by the arrival of an MNC?

4 How might local businesses be adversely affected by the arrival of an MNC?

5 State two impacts an MNC might have on the local community.

6 How might the arrival of an MNC impact on the local environment?

7 How does an MNC influence the flow of FDI into a country?

8 How might the location of an MNC improve the balance of payments for a nation?

9 How might consumers be affected by the arrival of an MNC?

10 Suggest how technologies and skills might be transferred from an MNC to a country.

SUBJECT VOCABULARY

horizontal transfer the transfer of knowledge across the same industry
repatriated profit the return of the profit made by an MNC to the country where the MNC is based
reverse engineering a method of analysing a product's design by taking it apart
transfer pricing a system operated by MNCs. It is an attempt to avoid relatively high tax rates through the prices which one subsidiary charges to another for components and finished goods
vertical transfer the transfer of knowledge, backwards or forwards, along the chain of production in the same industry

EXAM PRACTICE

CASE STUDY: FDI AND MNCs IN NIGERIA

SKILLS CRITICAL THINKING, REASONING

Falling FDI in Nigeria: In recent years, Nigeria has been the most popular destination for FDI in Africa. However, recently the flows of investment coming into the country have started to fall. One of the main reasons for this was the fall in the price of oil. A significant proportion of FDI arriving in Nigeria is channelled into oil production. Oil accounts for 90 per cent of Nigeria's exports.

However, the low oil price is not the only problem. Nigeria's infrastructure has often held back economic development in the country. The value of Nigeria's stock of infrastructure is about 25 per cent of its GDP. Comparable middle-income countries the size of Nigeria have a GDP of about 70 per cent. Inside Nigeria's main port at Apapa, boats queue for days waiting to enter the port. Then, once the cargo is unloaded, the trucks leaving the port are held up for hours in crowded streets. It can be time-consuming and expensive.

It has been estimated that about $3 trillion will be needed over the next 30 years to improve Nigeria's infrastructure. The government, however, has begun to make a move. A plan has been devised which identifies the key investment requirements. They include:

- energy
- transport
- agriculture
- water and mining
- housing and regional development
- information and communication technology
- social infrastructure
- security.

Energy and transport are currently a priority. In 2016, US MNC, General Electric® (GE) announced that it would be investing $150 million in Nigeria's railway system. GE said that it was the beginning of a long-term $2 billion investment project in Nigeria's infrastructure.

MNC environmental damage in Nigeria: Sometimes, FDI results in damage to the environment. This happened in Nigeria between 2008 and 2009 when two significant oil spills damaged the environment in the Niger Delta. The spills caused very serious damage to thousands of hectares of mangrove (swamps found in tropical and subtropical tidal areas). This polluted water supplies, crops and was detrimental to the livelihoods of thousands of farmers.

Following the spills, which were caused by the MNC Shell®, there was a legal battle between communities and the company. Shell did not take responsibility for the damage. However, in 2015 the case was settled. Court documents showed that Shell knew that their pipes and equipment could fail. Shell admitted it had underestimated the amount of oil spilled. The court forced Shell to pay out $84 million in compensation. The 15 600 farmers and fishermen affected by the spills were to receive about $2000 each. However, the money will not reverse the damage done to the environment, which the community relies on for water, food and their livelihoods.

▲ Figure 1 Oil price 2013–18

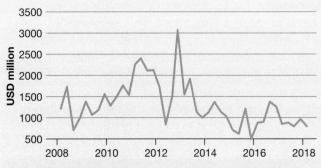

▲ Figure 2 Nigeria FDI 2008–18

1 Explain one reason why General Electric can help to foster a business culture in the countries where they locate operations. **(4 marks)**
2 Discuss reasons for the pattern of FDI in Nigeria between 2008 and 2018. **(8 marks)**
3 Evaluate whether MNCs such as Shell have had a positive impact on the local and national Nigerian economy. **(20 marks)**

36 INTERNATIONAL BUSINESS ETHICS

LEARNING OBJECTIVES

By the end of this chapter you should be able to understand:

- stakeholder conflicts
- environmental considerations: emissions, waste disposal and sustainability
- supply chain considerations: pay and working conditions, the exploitation of labour and child labour
- marketing considerations: misleading product labelling and inappropriate marketing activities.

GETTING STARTED

Corruption means using public power for personal benefit. In some countries, corruption is common and culturally accepted. However, in others it is illegal and may carry severe penalties. When setting up operations abroad, businesses need to be aware of corruption. In Canada, businesses are given advice about what sort of practices might be expected in countries with corruption. For example:

- There may be corruption during the procurement process (i.e. the process of obtaining something) where a business is bidding for a contract. For example, contracts may be awarded to businesses that have contacts with government officials.
- It may be necessary to bribe an official or someone in authority to get something done. For example, goods may not be unloaded from a container ship until a bribe is paid.
- Dealers, agents or distributors working for a foreign company may be engaged in bribery without their knowledge.
- Internal fraud (i.e. cheating somebody to obtain money illegally) or **embezzlement** may occur. For example, in some countries it is possible to buy fake receipts. They can be used by employees to obtain money from businesses even though there has been no expenditure.

Explain why corruption may be an ethical issue. How might a business be affected by corruption? How might a business deal with corruption when setting up operations in a country that is known to be corrupt? Should businesses avoid doing business in countries that are known to be corrupt?

ETHICS

Ethics refers to the principles and acceptable norms that govern behaviour. Business ethics at the company level were introduced in Chapter 16, which looked at the trade-off between profit and ethics. It looked at how ethics might affect pay and rewards, as well as what is meant by corporate social responsibility. At the international level, ethics may or may not be expressed in a country's laws and regulations. If a firm establishes itself in a country, it will have to work within the **institutional framework** of both the home and the host country. This means a firm may be acting within the law of its home country but could be seen to be acting unethically in the other. Equally, although a business may be matching the ethical norms abroad, its activities could breach the ethics of its home base.

Generally, ethics involves respecting human rights and local traditions, but avoiding corruption. Bribery is the most common example of a corrupt practice. However, it can be hard to define what a bribe is. For example, gift giving between business colleagues is very common in some countries, but considered wrong or even illegal in the USA and Europe. In fact, if you work for an EU business, you could face prosecution for offering or accepting a bribe. Many international businesses have written **codes of conduct** that set out policies to guide employees' decision making.

STAKEHOLDER CONFLICTS

Many people have a stake in the decisions that firms make. This means they have an interest in it or a right associated with it. As explored in Chapter 15, a stakeholder in a firm is an individual or a group that is affected by – and can affect – an organisation. The types of stakeholders in an international firm are listed in Figure 1.

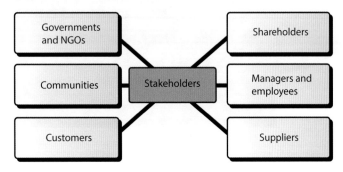

▲ Figure 1 Types of stakeholders in an international firm

Stakeholder issues can arise in any area of a business, including the following.

Consumers:
- conflicts of interest (i.e. when one person or organisation has two roles and is unable to treat them both fairly at the same time), such as where an energy firm manipulates the markets. This results in consumers paying more than they would have if the situation was different. They do this by using a different measure to report on their profit margins to the public. It means that an increase in household bills could be made to seem acceptable
- product safety, such as involving rotten meat that reaches consumers in the supply chain
- misleading advertising.

Employees:
- employee safety, ensuring healthy and safe conditions, and avoiding failings that might lead to injury or death. For example, at refineries and oil rigs, including the Deep Water Horizon oil spill in the Gulf of Mexico in 2010

- employee redundancies. A company may need to reduce staff numbers to regain profitability or they may choose to outsource some work for cheaper returns
- pay and conditions.

Shareholders:
- conflicts of interest between the management and the shareholders
- short-term versus long-term returns on shares. Shareholders invest for a variety of reasons, but one of the major factors is seeking a return on their investment through dividends. The business will make a decision on how much profit it will retain each year for investment and how much to return in dividends to the owners – the shareholders. The business will take a long-term view in that it needs to invest in new equipment or expand its branches. Reinvesting profit can finance future growth. Using retained profits is the cheapest way to reinvest. It needs to persuade shareholders that investing to earn profits in the future is in their long-term interests, rather than paying out more in dividends in the short term.

Countries or communities:
- safety, where people's wellbeing is compromised. For example, the reported pesticide chemical leak at the Union Carbide® plant in Bhopal, India, that poisoned over 300 000 people and caused 5200 deaths
- environmental concerns, where the activities of the business pollute or damage the environment. For example, the mining of tar sands impacts on the local wildlife and air and water quality
- resource depletion (i.e. using so much of something that there is very little left), where a company's extraction objectives are not good for the future for that country. For example, if resources are depleted before they are able to be replaced or are exploited in a way that damages the country's environment. An example of this is the pollution associated with the extraction of rare earths, such as yttrium and lanthanum. There is a high demand for these elements for electrical components and other hi-tech applications, but they are only found in certain countries.

ACTIVITY 1   SKILLS ▶ ETHICS, PERSONAL AND SOCIAL RESPONSIBILITY

CASE STUDY: SUGAR CONTENT IN PRODUCTS

In recent years, a wide range of health groups have argued that eating and drinking too much sugar is unhealthy and potentially dangerous. High levels of sugar consumption can cause weight gain. It can also increase the risk of heart disease, diabetes, cancer, depression and cellular aging. Too much sugar has also been linked to acne, a fatty liver, low energy and the skin aging process. As a result, in a minority of countries, governments have passed legislation to limit the use of sugar in products. However, in most countries there are no such limits.

Businesses use sugar in food processing for a number of reasons. The main reason might be because it improves the taste of products that might not be tasty or popular without it. Sugar can enhance the flavour of ingredients. It is also used as a preservative and a colouring. Sugar can also help to give a pleasant texture and a satisfying taste when eaten.

Many businesses have tried to hide the amount of sugar they add to food products as a response to its health risks rather than reduce it. They can do this by:

- calling sugar by a different name, such as glucose, fructose and sucrose
- using many different types of sugar – there are around 59 different types to choose from
- adding sugar to foods that you wouldn't expect, such as breakfast cereals and yoghurt
- using 'healthy' sugars instead of sucrose
- combining added sugars with natural sugars, such as those contained in fruit and vegetables

- adding a health claim to products such as those labelled as 'healthy', 'low fat', 'diet' or 'light'.

It could be argued that businesses that use more sugar in their products will attract more consumers. This will increase their sales levels, resulting in more revenue, higher profits and increased dividends for shareholders. It is an incentive for businesses to continue using high levels of sugar in food products, despite the health warnings.

1 What is the disagreement that appears to exist between consumers and shareholders in relation to sugar content in products?
2 Do you think that businesses should be free to choose the sugar content in food products?

ENVIRONMENTAL CONSIDERATIONS

Companies are becoming increasingly concerned about the impact their activities have on the environment. They are under pressure from many stakeholders to stop or minimise any damage that their activities might inflict on the environment. For example, some businesses set environmental targets and publish their performance in a social responsibility report at the end of the financial year.

HSBC is a multinational bank and is active in a Climate Partnership with the World Wide Fund for Nature (WWF) which helps to take care of forests. Yet it's reported that HSBC also funds unsustainable logging in Malaysia that has removed more than 90 per cent of the old growth forests on the island of Sarawak. Global Witness, an international human rights and environmental protection

pressure group, suggests that, over three decades, loans and financial services to logging interests have generated close to $120 million in revenue for the bank.

Emissions: Emissions of carbon rose by 1.6 per cent in 2017 after stabilising in the previous three years. Figure 2 shows the annual growth in global carbon emissions between 2007 and 2017.

There is strict legislation in many countries governing the environmental output of a business. This includes climate change legislation that requires companies to report on their greenhouse gas emissions. However, this legislation does not always exist in developing nations where many MNCs base their manufacturing industry. As they are creating employment within the developing country, environmental protection may not be a key priority.

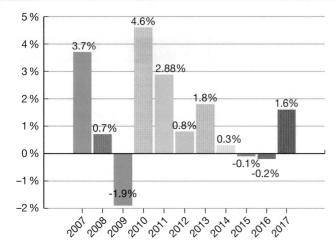

▲ Figure 2 Annual growth in carbon emissions between 2007–17

The highly urbanised areas that develop around industry in developing countries can suffer from bad air pollution and waste disposal issues. For example, the Bhopal chemical leak in India affected a lot of people living in slum towns near the plant.

Waste disposal: Many governments enforce legislation regarding how companies dispose of waste, as they do with air emissions. This legislation is often missing or not enforced in LEDCs (less economically developed countries). There are many barriers to effective waste disposal in LEDCs, such as the lack of a proper infrastructure to allow for efficient waste removal. For example, poor roads can mean that lorries are not able to remove waste effectively. There are huge environmental considerations when looking at the ways companies dispose of waste. The UN's Step Initiative estimated that by 2017 there will be enough 'e-waste' (discarded electrical products) to fill a 24 000 km line of 40-tonne lorries. This waste contains toxic elements that deteriorate over time. They are being dumped illegally in LEDCs, causing a huge environmental concern.

Sustainability: In business and economics, the term 'sustainability' has a specific meaning. A sustainable business is one that operates without negatively affecting the ability of future generations to meet their needs. This means that businesses should implement policies that preserve the environment so that it can support human life in the future. For example, businesses should use resources effectively so that there are enough for future generations. For business development to be sustainable, it must address issues such as economic efficiency, social equity and environmental accountability. This might mean that businesses should adopt production methods that:

- avoid the use of large quantities of non-renewable resources
- make more use of recycled materials

- reduce or eliminate waste and pollution
- have a positive impact on the environment, such as encouraging employees to cycle to work instead of driving.

Environmental sustainability forces businesses to look beyond making short-term gains. They need to look at the long-term impact they are having on the environment. Businesses need to emphasise their '**green credentials**' and be more sustainable.

ACTIVITY 2 **SKILLS** ETHICS, PERSONAL AND SOCIAL RESPONSIBILITY, CRITICAL THINKING

CASE STUDY: NISSAN'S SUSTAINABILITY REPORT

Many companies include sustainability reports in their annual reports and accounts to emphasise their green credentials. Most reports are based on a framework produced by the Global Reporting Initiative (GRI) in 2000. A sustainability report addresses the economic, environmental and social impacts of a company's daily business activities. The report helps to provide evidence of transparency (i.e. a situation where the truth can be seen easily) and accountability (i.e. responsibility for your decisions and being able to explain them when asked to), improves internal processes and engages stakeholders. A sustainability report should help to make a business more sustainable. This is because it usually publishes quantitative data which shows whether specific environmental targets have been met.

Nissan is just one example of a large business organisation that produces sustainability reports. According to Hitoshi Kawaguchi, Nissan's Chief Sustainability Officer, the company is committed to a zero-emission and zero fatality society in its new sustainability strategy – Nissan Sustainability 2022 - published in 2018. Below is an extract from a message written in the sustainability report by Hitoshi Kawaguchi.

'Environmental is the centerpiece of Nissan's "zero emissions" commitment. Our first midterm environmental action plan, the Nissan Green Program (NGP), was introduced in fiscal 2001. In 2006, we set specific long-term goals for 2050, including:

- Reduce CO_2 emissions from new vehicles by 90% compared to fiscal 2000
- Reduce CO_2 emissions from corporate activities by 80% compared to fiscal 2005
- Reduce use of new natural resources to 30% compared to 80% per vehicle in 2010

Under the fourth-generation Nissan Green Program 2022, launched in fiscal 2017, we will focus our efforts on addressing four key environmental issues as we look toward 2050: climate change, resource dependency, air quality and water scarcity'.

A copy of the full report can be accessed on the Nissan website.

1　What is the purpose of a sustainability report?
2　Why is sustainability an ethical issue?
3　To what extent can a car manufacturer like Nissan reduce environmental damage?

SUPPLY CHAIN CONSIDERATIONS

Global businesses have global supply chains. There are many ethical issues involved in global sourcing and logistics as it becomes more complex. For example, if you have a mobile phone, it is very likely that some of the components within it have been sourced from war zones. Many of the world's rarest and most valuable minerals come from the Democratic Republic of the Congo (DRC). It is reported that human rights abuses take place in some of the DRC mines. However, many of the firms buying these minerals may not want to look more closely at their supply chains because of the costs of doing so. To try and address the issue, the Organisation for Economic Co-operation and Development (OECD) has drawn up guidelines designed to minimise the use of these 'conflict minerals'. Some of the key supply chain issues are outlined below.

Pay and working conditions: A major problem for business ethics involves the complexities of global supply chains and the working conditions of employees in other countries. Many countries have laws that cover pay and working conditions of local suppliers, employees and managers. So, all employees have certain rights at work relating to their pay, conditions, holiday entitlement, sickness and time off work, health and safety, discrimination (i.e. treating somebody less fairly) and bullying. There are also detailed procedures and protections for dismissing an employee. However, such clear guidance does not always exist in many countries.

As a result of globalisation, many MNCs have their manufacturing operations in other countries. The business rationale for this is often the availability of cheap labour in developing economies. Some of these countries do not have the same level of legislation to protect employees compared to countries in the EU, for example. This means that the standard of working conditions is low, and workers may not be paid a living wage because there is no legal requirement to do so. These factories are sometimes referred to as 'sweatshops'. They can be dangerous, with limited access to fresh air, little space and even dangerous chemicals. The buildings can also be poorly built, as evidenced by the collapse of a factory in Dhaka, Bangladesh, in 2013 that killed over 1000 people. These working conditions may not occur in countries with tight controls on the environment in which people work.

As MNCs can locate anywhere in the world, the market for their business is very competitive. This is why the practice of offering below the living wage can continue. The lower the wage, the less money the MNC needs to invest in that manufacturing area. It can then increase its profit. However, this practice has become less prevalent due to the international protest over whether it is ethical to pay workers in developing economies a lower wage than their equivalent (such as the USA). For example, clothing manufacturers may outsource the manufacturing of their products to overseas factories in order to increase their profits. However, if the factories in developing countries do not pay a decent wage, this may attract criticism. Some companies try to reduce the negative attention by publishing lists of the factories that they use. It will often include an audit of these factories' ethical practices. This is an example of disagreeing interests, not only between the larger business and their employees, but also between the business and its customers. This is due to consumers being unhappy with its practices.

There are a number of initiatives and organisations that are working to ensure fair working practices for all. Some are concerned with the employment practices of multinationals and may address the following issues:
- employment is freely chosen
- freedom of association and collective bargaining is freely chosen
- working conditions are safe and hygienic
- **child labour** is not used
- living wages are paid
- working hours are not excessive
- no discrimination is practised
- regular employment is provided
- no harsh or inhumane treatment is allowed.

Pay can also be an issue between different structural levels within companies. Managers are responsible for trying to balance the interests of stakeholders (in this case, their employees). However, they are also stakeholders, and this can lead to disagreements. If a manager is in a position of power, the balance between interests is an important consideration, especially in relationship to, for example, executive pay.

Exploitation of labour: From the number of cases that appear in national courts and are documented by the International Labour Organisation, it appears that exploitation of labour is common throughout the world. The ILO, part of the United Nations, estimated that in 2016 there were around 24.9 million people being exploited by their employers.

A life as a 'modern slave' often begins when an individual seeking work contacts a recruiter. The recruiter charges the employee fees to find them a job. Once a position is found, the employing firm will repay the recruiter, but ask the new employee to pay them back. This is called 'bonded labour'. It forces the worker to stay with the employer until the debt, plus interest, is repaid. For example, according to the Freedom Fund, an NGO, most of the workers in the seafood industry in Thailand are bonded labourers.

Businesses are starting to try and keep products free from exploited labour. In some countries, governments or other relevant organisations publish guidelines for business' and members' supply chains that ban bonded labour and set minimum working conditions.

Child labour: Many businesses who outsource production overseas rely on local suppliers who follow local traditions and norms, which don't always comply to the standard practice or regulations in the businesses' country of origin. Child labour is one of the most difficult ethical dilemmas. In most cases, child labour has nothing to do with MNCs, but may be commonplace in local area businesses and on farms. This is because very young children are put to work as soon as they are able.

Implementing new sanctions around child labour have to be managed carefully to include further protection for young workers. For instance, when Bangladesh was forced to stop employing children in some of its factories or face trade sanctions, the reported result was that up to 7000 young girls went from being factory workers to taking work in more exploitative situations.

The issue of child labour in the supply chain is not as clear-cut as it may first appear. In 1973, Convention 138, approved by 135 countries, banned all forms of child labour. However, in 1999, Convention 182 changed this to cover only the worst examples of labour. Some suggest that stopping child labour in developing countries can be damaging to families. For example, if the child's earnings are a key source of income for the family, the loss of

that income can be devastating. Also, there may not be a formal education system that the child can join, which may force them into worse situations.

However, MNCs do not have to accept child labour in local area businesses. They can choose to locate elsewhere, in places where child labour is not acceptable. Alternatively, they can copy the Swedish furniture manufacturer IKEA. It is helping to support families by offering workers a good wage and providing their children with an education while they work.

ACTIVITY 3
SKILLS | ETHICS, PERSONAL AND SOCIAL RESPONSIBILITY, CREATIVITY

CASE STUDY: STARBUCKS

The American coffee retailer, Starbucks emphasises the role of ethics in its operations. It has a Corporate Social Responsibility Department and works with NGOs to ensure its coffee is sourced fairly. However, several years ago, an NGO named Global Exchange suggested that it was not providing a living wage for its coffee producers. Global Exchange argued that Starbucks should pay the living wage of US$1.26 per pound (the market price at the time was 64 cents per pound). They planned a protest at Starbucks' stores if the firm did not agree. Starbucks was already paying $1.20 per pound, so the wage increase was not substantial and the impact to the quality assurance of the business could be significant. Its customers expect only the best coffee from Starbucks. Any change in perceptions of how the business operates might have affected its brand.

This example shows the difficulties of ensuring that the expectations of stakeholders are met. Starbucks' stakeholders include its suppliers, especially the people who grow its coffee. But it also includes social organisations, such as Global Exchange, who have an impact not only upon the treatment of the supplier-stakeholders, but also upon operations and future strategy.

Managers must try and balance the interests of stakeholders. This is difficult and can lead to balancing different viewpoints. For example, with Starbucks, many of its suppliers and the NGOs supporting them wanted higher payments for coffee beans. This was a different point of view than some of its consumers. They wanted to pay less while also ensuring the consistent quality of their coffee.

It is often the role of managers to help the business grow and survive even if there are disagreements. Starbucks tried to help by increasing its purchases of Fairtrade coffee, which meets an international standard for pay and conditions of suppliers. It also created guidelines for the purchase of the most ethically sourced coffee that it could. They made this process fully transparent in its annual Corporate Social Responsibility Report.

1 Which might be more important for an upmarket coffee retailer: providing a high-quality brew or paying more for coffee beans?
2 To what extent do you agree with this statement? – 'You can never keep all stakeholders happy.'

MARKETING CONSIDERATIONS

There are a number of issues that companies must consider when they are looking to market their products. They will depend on the type of business and product as well as the specific market. Some things will need to change in order to be suitable for the market. Cultural and social factors that could affect this are considered in Chapter 34.

Misleading product labelling: Businesses should ensure that the labels on their products are not misleading. This is so that consumers can make a fully informed choice as to whether to buy their products and how to use them once bought. In many countries, legislation exists that states exactly what businesses should include in their labelling. Labels must be accurate and avoid using false information on price, quantity or size, materials, what it can do, or who might have endorsed it. They must also explain if there is any aspect of the product that could be hazardous.

When exporting goods, businesses have to be aware of local legislation and ensure that they comply with the laws that apply. What does a firm do when there is no law on product labelling? This is an ethical question. Should it keep the highest standards of all of the countries that it operates in, the minimum ones, or none at all?

The United Nations Economic and Social Council has published guidance on this in relation to food labelling. False labelling is not permitted, but it may be difficult for a consumer to distinguish between labels that are 'truthful and non-misleading' or 'truthful but misleading'. Also, one culture may find a label to be misleading while another might not.

An example of a misleading statement might be, 'Contains only 1 gram of sodium'. This suggests that the product is low in salt (sodium chloride), when it is actually very high in salt.

Inappropriate marketing activities: Product and business marketing can cover a broad range of different activities, such as advertising, publicity and direct marketing. These can be considered inappropriate if they are actually illegal or are offensive. In 2013, the Chinese government suggested that GlaxoSmithKline (GSK), a British pharmaceutical firm, was involved in 'illegal marketing activities' in order to increase drug sales. These activities supposedly included generous entertainment, including all-expenses-paid conferences for doctors, gift giving and cash payments.

Promotional activities in China can follow the Chinese cultural tradition of guanxi. This involves the use of personal connections in business activity that can include gift giving, doing favours and socialising. But in the UK, for example, these practices might be seen as unethical and may be illegal. However, many businesses acknowledge that these cultural aspects are part of their business context when operating in a global environment with China and many other countries.

LINKS

Ethical considerations run through almost every aspect of international business, including: what motivates people (Student Book 1, Chapter 17), what areas governments choose to legislate (Student Book 1, Chapters 37 and 42); how corporate and national cultures impact upon operations (this book, Chapters 14, 34 and 37), and what might drive change or choices of markets (this book, Chapters 28 and 29).

THINKING BIGGER

The corporate world has many examples of where ethics within business are key considerations. For example, when two children tragically died from carbon monoxide poisoning from a faulty boiler at a hotel on a Thomas Cook® holiday, the UK travel company could have been more sympathetic. The group was not directly responsible for the deaths, but the media reported that their 'heartless' corporate manner was not acceptable. It was reported that the management said only what the legal brief allowed them to and executives were silent at the children's inquest. It took 10 years to offer an apology and Thomas Cook reportedly received £3 million in compensation, nearly ten times the amount received by the parents of the children who died. The group was criticised for the approach taken. Yet some reports also said that by the standards of most modern corporations, Thomas Cook did little out of the ordinary. The board was reported as acting in a way to protect its investors' interests. However, the shareholders' near-term interest was in direct disagreement with the company's wider commercial one. It was reported that management had not appreciated how the company's behaviour would be viewed. They should have shown compassion and not only paid attention to its lawyers. However, consumers (also stakeholders) have their own logic and they will judge the company. In this incident, it should have balanced the needs of *all* its stakeholders.

You could use this information in a variety of ways. Obviously, it can be used when answering questions on business ethics, but it might also be useful when discussing corporate governance and the influence of stakeholders.

CHECKPOINT

1 How might a business be operating within the law but still be acting unethically?

2 How might stakeholder disagreements arise?

3 How might disagreements be avoided?

4 Why are MNCs criticised for their activities in developing countries?

5 What incentives exist to ensure fair working practices for all?

6 Why does the existence of global supply chains create ethical issues?

SUBJECT VOCABULARY

child labour the illegal employment of young children by a business
code of conduct a set of rules outlining the proper practices of an organisation that contribute to the welfare of key stakeholders and respect the rights of all affected by its operations
embezzlement the theft of money or other belongings from a business by an employee who has control over such resources
green credentials commitment to practices that do not damage the environment
institutional framework the system of formal laws, regulations and procedures, and informal conventions customs and norms that shape activity and behaviour

EXAM PRACTICE

CASE STUDY: KHROMA TEXTILES

SKILLS ETHICS, PERSONAL AND SOCIAL RESPONSIBILITY, REASONING

Khroma Textiles is a German company that produces clothing for customers around the world. It is well known for its unusual print designs and styles. About five years ago, Khroma was questioned about the ethical treatment of its workers in their overseas factories.

Khroma had outsourced its production to factories in developing countries to reduce manufacturing costs and gain economies of scale. However, it was alleged by some critics that Khroma would manufacture in a particular country until local workers demanded higher wages and safer working practices. Then, the company would move production out of that country and into another location where their costs would be lower.

Khroma said it couldn't be held responsible for the treatment of the workers at the factories that it used. As it had outsourced the work to a third party, it had no control over the working conditions in the factories. However, German journalists and non-governmental organisations campaigned to influence Khroma's attitude towards working practices.

News coverage of Khroma at this time was almost all negative. Journalists focused on the issue and did undercover investigations of conditions in the factories run by Khroma's suppliers. Some reports showed that child labour was used in some of them. Pressure groups used social media to inform the public and encourage people to boycott the company's products.

Khroma could not deny that their suppliers were treating their workers very badly. There was a lot of evidence to show that workers were not paid fairly, or not paid at all for doing overtime. The factories were using child labour and, in some cases, forced labour. Health and safety standards in the factories were very low. Kimmich said that other clothing companies used factories with similar working conditions.

In response to these issues, Khroma created a **code of conduct** for its suppliers. The company now will not work with suppliers who refuse to sign up to and implement the standards. Khroma also started to report annually on ethical issues in its supply chain. It appointed independent factory inspectors to audit working standards with no warning.

In the last nine months, Khroma also announced that it wants to set up a training programme for young people in the countries where their suppliers' factories are located. This programme will train them how to become skilled sewing machinists. This training ensures that they will earn a higher wage in the future.

In 2018, a number of reports emerged in Germany that some clothes marketed by Khroma were incorrectly labelled. The washing instructions were not clear and the dye had run out of some clothes, changing the colour of all the clothes inside the washing machine. Khroma issued an apology. It would investigate operations further down the supply chain. The company also offered to help customers by giving them €50 gift vouchers if they returned the clothes.

EXAM HINT

When you see the command word 'assess', you know that you must give a balanced answer, often employing competing arguments. Therefore, when looking at ethics in the context of international business, you should be aware of the differing corporate and national cultures that may affect business and employee behaviour. You should read widely about different countries and their cultures. This will help you to draw on examples in support of your points.

Q

1 Explain one way misleading product labelling could be an ethical issue. **(4 marks)**
2 Discuss the possible impact of the publicity surrounding child labour on Khroma Textiles. **(8 marks)**
3 Assess the influence of pressure groups on changing the behaviours of businesses such as Khroma. **(12 marks)**

37 CONTROLLING MNCs

LEARNING OBJECTIVES

By the end of this chapter you should be able to understand the factors to consider relating to the control of MNCs, such as:

- the power of MNCs
- political influence
- legal control
- consumer pressure
- pressure groups
- social media
- self-regulation.

GETTING STARTED

Multinational companies (MNCs) can have a powerful influence when they locate operations in a particular country. For example, in Ireland around 1 in 5 people in the private sector are employed by international companies. According to the Industrial Development Agency (IDA) in Ireland, in 2017 almost 200 000 people were employed by international companies. This is the highest on record. In 2017, 19 000 new jobs were created by MNCs and job losses at MNCs have been the lowest since 1997.

The USA is a very important investor in Ireland. It is believed that US MNCs contributed about €11 billion to the Irish economy in 2015. Figure 1 shows how this money was spent. There are also other financial benefits such as VAT, other taxes and indirect spending on services such as security, logistics, catering and cleaning. Thousands of agency workers are used by these companies.

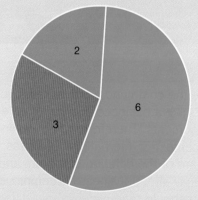

■ Wages   ■ Capital investment   ■ Corporation tax

▲ Figure 1 The financial contribution made by US MNCs in Ireland ((€ bn, 2015) 2015)

MNCs also create more employment by outsourcing manufacturing, quality control and research activities. They also spend more on professional services such as legal, accountancy and tax specialists. It is difficult to evaluate the exact amount generated by MNCs. Figures show that companies supported by IDA Ireland spend about €4 billion a year on Irish goods and services.

There is also a **multiplier effect** when employees and suppliers of multinationals, along with the government, spend this money. Across all revenue sources, it is likely that the Irish government collects over €5 billion a year from US MNCs alone.

One of the main attractions of Ireland to MNCs is the very low level of corporation tax. It is one of the lowest in the world at 12.5 per cent. However, a number of giant corporations such as Google, Apple and Starbucks have been accused of avoiding tax by moving to Ireland. For example, Apple has its European, Middle East and African HQ in Cork, Ireland. In 2017, Apple was ordered to repay a huge €13 billion in tax (covering a period from 2003–14) following a court order from the EU. After the court hearing, Apple provisionally (i.e. in a way that might change one day) agreed to pay €13 billion back to Ireland. The EU called this illegal state aid. During the stated period, Apple only paid Ireland 0.005 per cent in corporation tax. This was lower than the country's normal 12.5 per cent rate. The EU claimed that Apple had a deal with Ireland called a **tax ruling**.

How does Ireland benefit from MNC operations? What evidence is there in this case to suggest that MNCs are powerful? How does this case highlight the need for controlling MNCs? Suggest three ways in which MNCs might be controlled.

THE POWER OF MNCs

MNCs are powerful organisations. Altogether, they contribute significantly to wealth and job creation all over the world. They often provide inward investment for developing nations and help to build their foreign currency reserves. Because they are so large, they can exploit economies of scale and produce goods and services more cheaply. This can benefit consumers and make more effective use of the world's resources. Some of the profits made by MNCs can be invested in useful research and development.

However, MNCs are often criticised because they are too powerful and may exploit a range of stakeholders. They sometimes operate as monopolists and exploit consumers by charging high prices. They can dominate markets and make it very difficult for smaller firms to survive. In developing countries, smaller rivals cannot compete with powerful MNCs, so they are forced to close.

MNCs aim to maximise profits and so might be prepared to use working practices that pollute the environment or consume large quantities of non-renewable resources. Some MNCs control flows of revenues and profits through countries where tax rates are really low, such as Ireland, Luxembourg and Bermuda. As a result, they avoid huge tax payments. Figure 2 shows the revenues generated by each of the Top 10 MNCs in 2017.

Many MNCs are so well resourced that they can afford to defend themselves in court battles. For example, in 2018 it was reported that Apple had $285.1 billion in cash reserves. This is more money than the entire national incomes of many countries in the world, for example, according to 2017 estimates, the GDP of Bolivia ($83.5 billion), Chad ($29.64 billion), Burundi ($7.98 billion) and The Gambia ($3.58 billion).

There is a need to control MNC activity to try and prevent them from exploiting stakeholders. However, today, with interconnected international markets and globalised businesses, controlling MNCs is very challenging and complex. Many modern global companies have huge economic power. They can relocate their headquarters easily, giving national governments less direct control over their behaviour. These MNCs can threaten to relocate out of a country – and take their FDI, tax revenues and employment with them.

This raises very big questions about who is in control of the actions of a company. The shareholders? The managers? The home or host governments? Additionally, how is control enforced? This chapter looks at some of the ways in which MNCs might be controlled to prevent the exploitation of stakeholders.

POLITICAL INFLUENCE

In some countries, large MNCs are owned by the state. For example, in Figure 2, three of the biggest MNCs in the world are state-owned enterprises (SOEs). In China, over 120 companies are owned or controlled directly by the state, involving most sectors, including manufacturing, banks, telecommunications, transport, agriculture and basic commodities. State ownership is a very effective method of control. Political power can be exercised to create, manage and end a business. Therefore, political influence over these organisations is extensive. This can lead to numerous commercial and ethical issues.

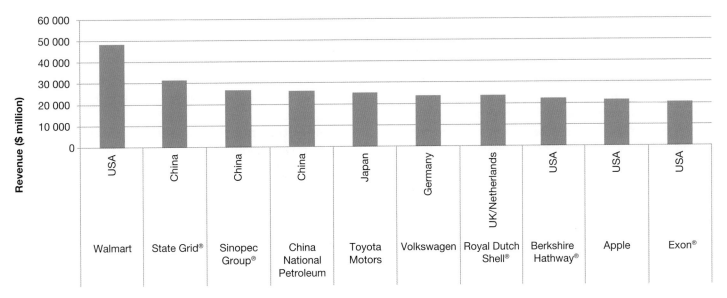

▲ Figure 2 The Top 10 MNCs in 2017 by revenue

However, state ownership or control is not very efficient, and so the drawbacks often outweigh the benefits.

- Corruption can be a problem as SOEs might be favoured by powerful politicians. For example, a few years ago it was reported that there was a political scandal with the state oil company of Brazil, Petrobras. A former president, the speakers of both chambers of congress and 54 others were accused of taking illicit payments from the company. This was in return for providing favourable outcomes to the company. Petrobras lost much of its market value when the story became public.
- State-owned operations may take the capital that other firms might better employ. This is because politicians or regulators, rather than the market, decide where funding should go. This means inefficient businesses may be given more money than they need while also not being subjected to the competitive forces that would otherwise reduce prices and improve efficiency.
- Shareholders' and other investors' rights may be reduced or ignored because they are not the true beneficiaries of the business. The actual beneficiaries (as may be the case with Petrobras) may be the politicians themselves. However, some state enterprises benefit the population as a whole. For example, the international oil company Statoil®, mostly owned by the Norwegian government, puts a percentage of proceeds into its government pension fund known as the 'Oil Fund'. The remainder of the shares in Statoil are publicly traded.
- Investment expenditure, especially on research and development, may be ignored. There is likely to be less competitive pressure from other firms with state ownership. This means there will be less incentive to undertake expensive research to create new or better products or services.

Even where a firm is not owned or controlled by the state, political influence may still be important. There could be national strategic priorities, such as energy independence or the development and preservation of key industries. Governments may want to boost employment or regulate financial institutions.

Privately owned businesses can be controlled using a number of political initiatives.

- Tariffs, quotas, regulations and local content requirements can be used to protect domestic businesses from international competitors. For example, Nigeria has a law that states the 'minimum amount' (by value) of 'Nigerian content' that must exist in equipment used for the extraction of oil and gas in the country.

- Many countries even place direct or indirect ownership restrictions on businesses that they consider to be critical. Therefore, political opposition prevented the Chinese state oil company, CNOOC, from taking over Unocal®, a private US firm.
- Countries can also support domestic industries through subsidies or tax breaks. Subsidies can be designed to help create factories to produce and distribute goods. They can also help consumers to buy products and assist domestic firms in exporting their goods and services.

There are many other forms of political influence that can serve to direct the behaviour of businesses, including the following.

- Lobbying by politicians to influence the decisions of businesses. For example, a politician may wish to prevent the foreign direct investment of a competitor, as this could threaten jobs in his or her electorate.
- Politicians 'retiring' to seats on the boards of plcs. It is not clear whether having former politicians on a board adds value because of their knowledge, or their influence and connections. However, many businesses hire politicians as soon as they leave office.

Some benefits and drawbacks of using political influence to control MNCs are shown in Table 1

Benefits	Drawbacks
Can create, manage and end a business.	Helps to facilitate corruption.
Helps elected officials to challenge the power of private business and to address issues of concern (e.g. ethics and the environment).	Can add to inefficiencies, such as the misallocation of capital and lack of research and development.

▲ Table 1 Benefits and drawbacks of using political influence to control MNCs

LEGAL CONTROL

One of the best ways of controlling large international businesses is through regulation, competition laws and taxation policies.

Competition policy: Competition policy exists to promote competition and ensure that markets operate as efficiently as possible. In many countries, there are specialised agencies set up by the government to protect producers and consumers from unfair or anti-competitive practices. For example, the EU Competition Commission takes on this role across Europe. Such institutions ensure that firms do not abuse (i.e. use unfairly) their market power, do not attempt to fix prices or use pricing strategies to drive out competition, and do not work together illegally against other producers or the consumer.

In 2017, Google's **parent company** Alphabet® was fined €2.4 billion by the EU because it abused its dominance in the search engine market. Google manipulated the search engine as it developed its own online shopping site. The EU said that consumers were being exploited by Google. This was because Google was artificially promoting its own price comparison site when searches were made by online shoppers. This denied shoppers a genuine choice in the market and prevented rivals from competing effectively.

Taxation policy: Governments use taxation policies to raise the revenue to run their countries. However, these policies can also be employed to help control the activities of MNCs. For example, Ireland maintains a policy of low corporate taxation. This is to attract huge amounts of foreign direct investment. The policy can upset politicians in other countries, who see it as an unfair practice that allows businesses to avoid paying their fair share of tax. So, Ireland's corporation tax in 2018 was 12.5 per cent compared to the USA's 21 per cent (it was 35 per cent up until January 2018).

There are concerns that many big companies can use countries' differing systems to avoid tax. **Tax avoidance** involves using legal methods to reduce the amount of tax that a company pays. This differs from **tax evasion**, which is the illegal avoidance of tax. Tax avoidance is an issue of ethics that can bring bad publicity. In 'Getting started' on page 306, Apple was forced to repay €13 billion to the Irish government as a result of tax irregularities.

Legislation: One of the roles of the government is to provide a legal framework in which businesses can operate. This includes a system of incentives and penalties to ensure that at-risk groups are protected. However, it is important for the government to find the 'right balance'. Too much intervention will discourage enterprise and deter foreign investment. This might prevent growth in national income, reduce job creation, decrease tax revenues and reduce consumer choice. Too little, and some stakeholders' best interests might not be given enough attention. Many countries have introduced a wide range of legislation to penalise companies that damage the environment, exploit employees, engage in anti-competitive practices, bully suppliers and exploit consumers. Even countries that do not regulate businesses very much have started to use legislation to control the activities of businesses. For example, in China, the State Administration for Industry and Commerce (SAIC) is responsible for developing and enforcing legislation relating to the administration of industry and commerce in the country. It has many divisions, one of which is the Anti-monopoly and Anti-unfair Competition Enforcement Bureau. In 2016, SAIC found that Tetra Pak®, the Swiss packaging firm, had broken anti-monopoly regulations. It was discovered abusing its monopoly status by forcing customers to purchase packaging materials. Tetra Pak had also prevented other suppliers from providing materials to its rivals. Tetra Pak was fined $97 million.

Table 2 shows a summary of the benefits and drawbacks of using laws to control MNCs. Many countries around the world use political or regulatory institutions that help to monitor and control the activities of businesses that operate internationally.

Benefits	Drawbacks
Can be used to improve competition in the domestic market.	It is difficult to achieve consistent legal practice between countries, so businesses have an incentive to find the friendliest legal environment, where the laws and tax policies are the best for them.
Helps to check corporate power.	It is easy for big international firms to move to friendly environments and avoid treatment that they consider to be unfavourable to their business.
Facilitates consumer protection.	Even where there is agreement over laws, policies and standards, they are often not easy to enforce.

▲ Table 2 Benefits and drawbacks of using laws to control MNCs

ACTIVITY 1   **SKILLS**   CRITICAL THINKING

CASE STUDY: THE NATIONAL COMMISSION OF MARKETS AND COMPETITION (SPAIN)

In Spain, the National Commission of Markets and Competition (CNMC) is responsible for monitoring industry and ensuring that markets are sufficiently competitive. The CNMC has a number of legal duties. These include:

- supervising and monitoring economic sectors in Spain. For example, electricity and gas, electronic communications and audio visual, railway and airport, postal markets
- enforcing competition law that addresses anti-competitive behaviour, merger control and state aid
- resolving trade disputes between organisations
- promoting competition.

A few years ago, the CNMC fined 21 car manufacturers and two consultancy firms €171 million for anti-competitive practices. The two MNCs, General Motors (GM) and Ford, were hit the hardest with fines of €22.8 million (GM) and €20.2 million (Ford).

Three French firms, Renault, Peugeot® and Citroen® were each fined €18.2 million, €15.7 million and €14.8 million respectively. The Spanish competition authorities said that they exchanged information relating to car sales, repairs, maintenance activities and car parts to avoid competition. For example, some of the information included details of price incentives to avoid a price war for new car sales. Volkswagen and its subsidiaries, including its Spanish brand, Seat®, avoided a penalty because they co-operated fully with the CNMC.

1 Using this case as an example, what is meant by an anti-competitive practice?
2 What is the role of the CNMC in Spain?
3 How might consumers benefit from the action taken by CNMC?

CONSUMER PRESSURE

If a giant MNC damages or goes against consumers' interests, many consumers may not think they have the power to fight the MNC. However, this is not always the case. In some cases, MNCs have changed their behaviour due to consumer pressure. Consumers can apply pressure by campaigning against an MNC or by avoiding their products. For example, in 2016, luxury perfumes and cosmetics brand Lancôme® (owned by L'Oréal®, the French cosmetics group) cancelled a marketing event in Hong Kong, China. The event was due to feature a Cantonese pop star. However, Chinese consumers were angry because of the singer's political views, which were disagreeable to China. The event was cancelled because China is L'Oréal's second-biggest market. According to Shaun Rein, managing director of China Market Research, Chinese consumers and the government have the power to influence the behaviour of companies. Companies are being forced to consider a wide range of social, political and historical sensitivities when marketing products in ethnically and culturally diverse regions such as Asia.

In other examples, changes in consumer buying patterns forced Nestlé to remove artificial colours and flavourings from Nestlé Crunch® and Butterfinger® confectionery bars in the USA. Consumers in the US market wanted more 'natural' and organic products. Mars® were also thinking about phasing out the use of artificial food dyes from one of its high-profile brands M&Ms®. Finally, McDonald's gave in to consumer pressure and promised to stop using chickens that had been raised using antibiotics. It was thought that these antibiotics had resulted in the spread of 'superbugs,' which are resistant to certain drugs used on humans.

Another development that has given consumers more power is the use of review systems. These allow consumers to write freely about their experiences when consuming certain products. Reviews can be positive or negative and can be written by anyone. For example, the online travel site TripAdvisor® uses a review system so that consumers can rate their holiday experiences. The influence of consumer reviews is difficult to evaluate, but people might be influenced by lots of bad reviews, for example.

| **ACTIVITY 2** | SKILLS | CRITICAL THINKING, ANALYSIS |

CASE STUDY: ONLINE CUSTOMER REVIEWS

Online review sites such as TripAdvisor, Yelp®, Google and Facebook allow people to share their experiences with both businesses and other consumers. The power of these sites is difficult to evaluate, but there have been a number of surveys carried out to find out how often customers use such sites and whether or not they are influential. The reasons why consumers write reviews is shown in Figure 3.

One survey, published in 2017 by Podium, gathered the following information about consumers and their use of online reviews:

- 60 per cent looked at online reviews at least once a week
- 93 per cent said that online reviews influenced their purchasing decisions
- 68 per cent would pay up to 15 per cent more for a product if it had favourable reviews
- a star rating of 3.3 is the minimum for consumers to engage with a business
- 82 per cent paid very careful attention to the content of reviews
- 77 per cent were willing to leave reviews if asked
- 80 per cent found reviews for local businesses as useful as those for MNCs
- 66 per cent would not trust unfamiliar review sites

▲ Figure 3 Reasons why people write reviews

1 Explain two ways in which consumers can influence MNCs.
2 How might MNCs use online reviews?

PRESSURE GROUPS

Companies' behaviour may violate what many people consider to be acceptable standards. But, these behaviours may not break any laws. Pressure groups act as another control on MNCs. They can publicise bad behaviour and threaten to damage the image of the firm. Pressure groups are often voluntary organisations that operate at all levels of society. This includes on international levels, and they aim to change either political or commercial decision making. For example, organisations like Corporate Watch investigate such areas of concern as tax avoidance and payday lending. They attempt to provide information on the unethical practices of corporations.

Pressure groups have several methods that they can use to control MNCs.

- **Boycotting.** Business ethics can be promoted through boycotting. This involves withdrawing from commercial or social relations as a form of protest. For example, several years ago, the Swiss food company Nestlé was accused of aggressively marketing its baby milk formula in developing countries. Pressure groups highlighted research that indicated that breast milk is not only better for babies, but it is also safer because formula has to be made with water that is potentially unsafe. Also, breast milk is free. A variety of pressure groups started a boycott of Nestlé's products, and they continue to monitor the company's international sales of baby milk formula.

- **Media criticism.** Starbucks, Google and Amazon have also been criticised in the media for their alleged (i.e. stated as a fact, but without proof) complex tax avoidance schemes, in which they paid less than what some considered to be their 'fair share' of taxes. In the past, the mining firm DeBeers® was criticised in film and print media for contributing to the problem of 'conflict diamonds'. It was argued the diamonds were being used to finance civil wars in parts of Africa. Famously, there was criticism of firms that continued to trade in South Africa when the official Apartheid policy was still in place. Apartheid was a government-supported system of racial segregation (i.e. separating people based on race) that existed between 1948 and 1994. The system led to many worldwide protest movements against firms, such as Coca-Cola, that continued to trade with or in South Africa.

- **Direct action.** Direct action is the use of demonstrations, protests, strikes or even sabotage to achieve a political or social goal. Environmental protection can receive a boost from pressure groups such as Greenpeace, which uses direct action. Interventions have included using its ships to interfere with whaling or to delay drilling in the Arctic. Direct action can be controversial. This is the case with Greenpeace's active opposition to so-called 'golden rice', strains that have been genetically modified or enhanced to contain additional nutrients. Greenpeace opposes any genetically modified food entering the food chain. However, many non-governmental organisations and health organisations believe that golden rice could help save millions of undernourished (i.e. not healthy because there is not enough food) children in the developing world.

- **Lobbying.** This is the taking of issues directly to government in an effort to influence change. Organisations such as Amnesty International and the World Development Movement often lobby governments on human rights and development issues. They also publish their own research and make detailed suggestions for addressing the issues of concern.

Benefits	Drawbacks
It enlists committed people, including volunteers.	Campaigns may be ill-informed or misguided.
Particularly where social media is involved, activists can be enlisted incredibly quickly to engage in information gathering or protest.	Information going viral (i.e. when an image, video or link spreads rapidly through a population by people sharing it electronically with friends and colleagues) may mean it is impossible for a pressure group to influence the message that is ultimately communicated.
It raises issues that may otherwise not become public knowledge.	Direct action can lead to violence or miscarriages of justice.
It alerts politicians and authorities to issues of concern to the public.	Direct action can be very disruptive which may be counterproductive.

▲ Table 3 Benefits and drawbacks of using pressure groups and social media to control MNCs

SOCIAL MEDIA

Social media can be defined as an interaction between electronic and mobile devices, applications and people, that allows users to create content. Such media include online magazines, weblogs, social blogs (e.g. Twitter®), podcasts and wikis (e.g. YouTube®, Wikipedia®), and social networking (e.g. Facebook, Instagram®).

As well as being a tool for the promotion of a business's objectives, social media can act as a means of controlling its behaviour, by:

- making the collection of information from a variety of sources easier
- increasing social awareness through communication
- ensuring greater transparency
- bringing together people in order to create a kind of social authority to challenge the power of large companies.

For example, Greenpeace has used social media a lot in its 'Save the Arctic' campaign. This included efforts to stop Lego's partnership with the oil company Shell. The campaign began with an animated film using Lego and showing the Arctic being flooded with oil. The film was watched by millions of viewers. In 2014, Lego confirmed that they would not renew their partnership with Shell due to sustained pressure from the campaign. Greenpeace also had success in its campaign to stop Nestlé's use of palm oil from producers linked to deforestation. Nestlé promised to remove all potentially offending companies from its supply chain.

As noted in Table 3, the benefits and drawbacks of using social media to control MNCs are similar to those for pressure groups, but the speed with which something can now go 'viral' means that it is increasingly hard to control the message that the pressure group may want to tell the public.

SELF-REGULATION

In some industries, businesses are self-regulated. This means that a group of firms in the same industry (or perhaps the entire industry) agree to follow a set of rules and guidelines to ensure 'proper conduct'. The rules and guidelines are specific to that industry. They are designed to ensure that companies maintain common standards in their operations. The regulations are likely to address issues such as health and safety, ethical behaviour, responsibility to employees and consumers and environmental practices. Such a list of rules might be called a code of practice.

Self-regulation also involves **self-policing**. This means that the businesses who are signed up to an agreement monitor their own activities. They might do this by measuring emissions, recording consumer complaints and listening to employees' issues. It is likely that firms will be required to set performance targets. If these are not achieved, a business might have to explain its failure and how improvements will be made. Some of the advantages of self-regulation are outlined below.

- Government regulation might be avoided. This is likely to be more rigorous and expensive. Compliance costs can be a burden when the government imposes rules and regulations.
- The needs of business stakeholders might be better served. This is because members signed up to an agreement will be more aware of the practices in a particular industry than an outside agency.
- The reputation and image of businesses might be improved if consumers and employees see a genuine attempt to safeguard their interests.
- It may be easier for businesses to encourage its employees to adopt ethical behaviour and principles. This is because the rules are based on social norms and accepted practices. They are not forced upon them from above.

- Self-regulation can also benefit the taxpayer. The cost of setting up government agencies to make rules, monitor business activity and enforce rules can be very expensive.

However, there is a clear disadvantage of self-regulation. There could easily be a conflict of interests. Businesses may find it very difficult to comply with an industry code of practice if its financial performance is seriously threatened.

There are many examples where a lack of regulation has caused unpleasant outcomes. For example, the financial crisis in 2008 partly resulted from a lack of regulation in the financial sector. This led to a global recession and hardship for millions of people all over the world. The Internet is almost entirely self-regulated. As a result, it has been alleged that democratic elections have been weakened, personal data has been taken without the permission of individuals, and the safety of children has been put at risk. These outcomes, and others, have meant that Facebook and other Internet companies, have come under increasing pressure to provide more safeguards for Internet users.

THINKING BIGGER

Who won the 2014 World Cup? For footballers, the answer is a matter of record; Germany beat Argentina in the final. For the companies involved in the World Cup, the success of brands is not so clear-cut. Adidas®, the German brand, has been a long-time sponsor of the World Cup. Nike, the US-based sportswear brand, was not a sponsor, yet sponsored ten of the World Cup teams. However, local brands in South America – who also were not sponsors – are fighting back against multinational brands. One example is Peru's Inca Kola®, which has now overtaken Coca-Cola with a 30 per cent market share against 20 per cent for the American giant. It now exports to Asia. Falabella®, the Chilean retailer, is now expanding across the continent and South American brands are now selling widely in Europe.

South Americans are switching away from multinational brands to local cheaper ones as South American companies develop their brand access across the region. More local icons will appear in the Top 50 South American brands. If so, that is good news for local brand enthusiasts but not for the multinationals. Perhaps encouraging local brand buying is the best control of multinational behaviour.

You could use this information in a variety of ways. Obviously, it can be used when answering questions on the influence of multinationals, but it might also be useful when discussing factors influencing globalisation and global competitiveness, and the impact of multinationals.

LINKS

To demonstrate your synoptic skills, you could use information from other chapters to help support your answers. For example, you might use the information about the impact that tariffs and quotas, protectionism and trading blocs (Chapters 25 and 26) can have on the countries in which MNCs operate to assess the types and extent of control. Further, you might consider to what extent MNCs take into account ethical practices and how these might affect controls of MNCs (Chapter 16 and 36). Chapter 35, which focuses on the impact of MNCs, could also be used to support arguments for controlling their activities.

CHECKPOINT

1   State two ways in which an MNC can exert its power.

2   Why are there legal controls on the activities of multinationals?

3   What are the benefits of multinationals in the global market place?

4   How are multinationals' global activities controlled?

5   What political influences do multinationals have?

6   How can taxation policies influence the activities of multinationals?

7   How might consumers apply pressure on MNCs?

8   What role can social media have in controlling multinationals' behaviour?

9   Describe the role of a code of practice in self-regulation.

SUBJECT VOCABULARY

boycotting withdrawing from commercial or social relations as a form of protest

competition policy government policy that exists to promote competition and ensure that firms don't abuse their market power, do not attempt to fix prices or use pricing strategies to drive out competition, and do not work together illegally against other producers or the consumer

direct action the use of demonstrations, protests, strikes or even sabotage to achieve a political or social goal

multiplier effect where an increase in spending, such as government expenditure, generates a much greater level of total spending in the economy

parent company a company that has control over another company

payday lending short-term lending where the loan may or may not be repaid when the borrower gets paid from work

self-policing where businesses monitor their own activities without reference to an external authority

tax avoidance using legal methods to reduce the amount of tax that a company pays

tax evasion using illegal means to avoid paying taxes that are owed

tax haven a country where taxes are relatively low

tax ruling an advance arrangement between the tax authorities and a taxpayer, such as an MNC, to clarify the tax implications of a transaction

EXAM PRACTICE

CASE STUDY: WALMART

SKILLS ⟩ CRITICAL THINKING, REASONING, ETHICS

Walmart® is a US retail corporation that operates a chain of hypermarkets, department stores and grocery stores, with nearly 12 000 in countries all over the world. In 2017, it generated revenues of US$485 873 million. The business started in 1950 and was set up by Sam Walton. His main aim was to offer customers low prices. He kept costs low and accepted lower profit margins than his rivals, hoping he would sell a lot more in order to make more money. As the business grew, Walton continued to save money and established a culture of spending only as much as necessary in the organisation, which still exists today.

It has encouraged manufacturers to be more efficient and changed the way that even large companies manage their operations. It has even influenced some suppliers to relocate overseas.

Walmart sells a wide range of goods, including clothes, shoes, toys, home appliances, electronic products, sporting goods, bicycles, groceries and food. Therefore, it has had an influence in a number of industries including encouraging some manufacturers to improve their efficiency in order to lower costs. For example, as reported on the LA Times and other publications, in the 1990s, Walmart asked one supplier to lower the price of a fan from US$20 to US$10. The manufacturer, Lakewood Engineering & Manufacturing Co., automated production and laid off workers. Eventually, it moved production to China where, in 2003, workers were earning just 25 cents an hour. Walmart has also increased the amount of produce it imports from around 6 per cent in 1995 to over 60 per cent a decade later. Although Walmart offers its customers goods and services at very low prices, the giant MNC has often had criticism for the way it operates.

- It has been criticised in the past for tax avoidance. It has been alleged that Walmart takes capital from the countries where it was earned and channels it through subsidiary companies in **tax havens** around the world. In 2017, Americans for Tax Fairness (a campaign group) estimated that around US$76 billion was stored in tax havens around the world.
- Walmart has often been criticised for paying low wages. There have been many reports in the media over many years about how Walmart's employees are poorly paid. Wages are reportedly so low that the employees have to seek government assistance,

costing the US state 6.2 billion in public assistance according to a 2015 report by Americans for Tax Fairness. Walmart had at times opposed trade unions e.g. closing a brand-new store in Canada when workers organised a union in 2005. Ten years later, a Canadian court ordered Walmart to pay the workers.

- It has been accused of using overseas suppliers that sometimes place employees in unsafe conditions. For example, in 2012, a factory belonging to a Walmart supplier in Bangladesh caught fire, killing 111 people. Another factory fire in 1990 killed 32. Two reports, as reported on The Guardian in 2016 list threats of termination, forced overtime and denial of sick leave; workers in Cambodian factories reported working 10 to 14 hour days, they also reported working in heat, without breaks or access to water. Walmart has also been accused of buying goods from suppliers that employ child labour and in 2005 agreed to pay fines to settle federal charges because of violation of child labour laws in three U.S states as reported on the New York Times.
- Walmart has also been challenged for demonstrating discrimination (i.e. treating particular people less fairly than others). There have also been reports of pregnant women being overworked and placed in potentially dangerous positions (like being denied restrictions on heavy lifting and additional breaks) by Walmart. Some of these cases have gone to court including the notable Dukes v. Walmart, the largest class action gender discrimination lawsuit in the U.S.. With regard to disabled workers, in 2001, Walmart paid US$6 million to disabled workers following 13 court cases. Also, in 2014, Walmart paid US$363 419 to settle a lawsuit filed by the Equal Employment Opportunity Commission on behalf of a Walmart worker.
- There are many reported examples that suggest Walmart has used its power to control and influence operations that might be considered controversial. However the number of complaints made may be in complete proportion to the size of the corporation (although this might be difficult to measure accurately). In recent years Walmart has appeared to respond to the criticism that it pays low wages. For example, in 2018 the corporation announced that it would raise its minimum wage to US$11 per hour and pay a US$1000 one-time bonus to 'eligible associates'. It has also added a paid family leave

plan. This announcement came after it was revealed that Walmart would be a significant beneficiary of new tax legislation in the USA.

Walmart is not the only supermarket which has been accused of exerting its power. For example, in 2018 Australian supermarkets, Coles and Woolworths, were accused of asking for sensitive commercial information from their suppliers. They wanted some key suppliers to give them detailed business information, including invoices, to prove that any price increase reflected higher costs in their own ingredients. A former Australian Competition and Consumer Commission chairman said the process was not leading to the best outcomes for suppliers or consumers.

EXAM HINT

You could consider the extent and impact of methods used to control MNCs from different areas. For example, is political and legal control or consumer pressure coming from the country of origin of the MNC or from other countries in which the MNC is operating? Are these controls consistent or are there conflicting objectives? You could also consider the effect that the controls can have on the country of origin, the country in which the MNC has its headquarters, and other countries in which it operates. Evaluate to what extent these effects may differ and whether there is any conflict.

Q

1 Explain one way that pressure groups might help to control MNCs. **(4 marks)**
2 Discuss whether governments should change taxation policy so that businesses cannot avoid paying their 'fair share' of tax in the future. **(8 marks)**
3 Assess whether MNCs such as Walmart have become too powerful. **(12 marks)**
4 Evaluate whether or not governments should encourage more self-regulation in businesses such as Walmart. **(20 marks)**

INDEX